American Political Parties

HUGH L. LeBLANC

American Political Parties

St. Martin's Press • New York

Library of Congress Catalog Card Number: 81-51852
Copyright © 1982 by St. Martin's Press, Inc.
All Rights Reserved.
Manufactured in the United States of America.
65432
fedcba
For information, write St. Martin's Press, Inc.,
175 Fifth Avenue, New York, N.Y. 10010

cover design: Claire Nelson

typography: Bernard Klein

maps and charts: Rino Dussi

ISBN: 0-312-02891-1

Acknowledgments

Table 2-1. From Jerome M. Clubb, "Party Coalitions in the Early Twentieth Century," in Seymour Martin Lipset (ed.), *Party Coalitions in the 1980s* (© 1981, Institute for Contemporary Studies). Reprinted with permission.

Tables 2-1, 2-2, and 2-3. Derived from *Transformations of the American Party System*, Second Edition, by Everett Carll Ladd, Jr., with Charles D. Hadley, by permission of W. W. Norton & Company, Inc. Copyright © 1978, 1975 by W. W. Norton and Company, Inc.

Figure 2-1. From *Leadership and Change: The New Politics and the American Electorate* by Warren E. Miller and Teresa E. Levitin. Copyright © 1976. Reprinted by permission of Winthrop Publishers, Inc., Cambridge, Massachusetts.

Table 3-1. Derived from Malcolm E. Jewell and David M. Olson, *American State Political Parties and Elections*, by permission of The Dorsey Press. Copyright © 1978 by The Dorsey Press.

Table 3-2. Derived from Willis D. Hawley, *Nonpartisan Elections and the Case for Party Politics*, by permission of John Wiley & Sons, Inc.

Tables 4-1 and 4-2. From Lewis Bowman and G. R. Boynton, "Activities of Grassroots Party Officials," *Journal of Politics* 28 (February 1966). Reprinted with permission.

Table 5-1. From Lewis Bowman and G. R. Boynton, "Recruitment Patterns Among Local Party Officials," *American Political Science Review* 60 (September 1966). Reprinted with permission of the American Political Science Association.

Table 5-2. From Lewis Bowman, Dennis Ippolito, and William Donaldson, "Incentives for the Maintenance of Grassroots Political Activism," *Midwest Journal of Political Science* 13 (February 1969). Reprinted with permission of the University of Texas Press.

Acknowledgments and copyrights continue at the back of the book on page 427, which constitutes an extension of the copyright page.

Contents

Preface

Although American political parties do not play as prominent a role in the political life of the nation as they once did, they are neither dead nor dying. They continue to perform functions that are essential to American democracy as we know it. This book attempts to explain what parties do that makes them valuable contributors to the electoral and governing processes of the nation. In brief, parties serve to structure electorates and organize governments, thereby linking leaders and led. That they do so imperfectly, however, will be amply demonstrated, for my objective is to provide a realistic assessment of their strengths and weaknesses. Instructors whose view of American parties is less positive than my own will find a good deal of evidence here with which to argue their case.

My experience over the past twenty-five years with many different textbooks has impressed upon me that the inherent excitement of politics is all too easily concealed by turgid prose and arid abstractons. I have written this book with undergraduate students in mind and have tried to make it as readable and as engaging as possible. I have tried to write simply and clearly, avoiding professional jargon whenever I could and taking care to explain key terms and concepts as I went along. Further, I have taken every opportunity to bring principles and issues to life for the reader with concrete examples from contemporary politics. A special instance of this is the inclusion at the end of each chapter of a section entitled "The Contemporary Parties," which evaluates our parties in terms of the particular thesis developed in that chapter. Each chapter is also enlivened by one or more cartoons which, while amusing, make serious and relevant points. Chapter summaries are provided to help students confirm their understanding as they progress through the text and to facilitate their review later on.

The book is organized around a central theme: the role of parties in linking citizens to their government. Chapter 1 describes the ways that linkage is accomplished and discusses conflicting views about what kind of party system is most appropriate for Americans. Chapter 2 provides a historical background, illustrated by three electoral maps, of the coalitions that have been associated with the two major parties from the New Deal to the present and delves into the issues that have shaped their development. A detailed recent history has been chosen over a broader review of past party systems to provide students with an understanding of the forces that produced the contemporary parties. Chapter 3 examines the party role in states and cities in order to assess party performance in a setting that allows a comparison between two-party and one-party states and partisan and nonpartisan cities.

Beginning with Chapter 4, a closer look is taken at party organizations. The older patronage-style party is shown to be giving way to organizations more suited to the needs of modern campaigning. In Chapter 5, the activists who staff party organizations are distinguished from the identifiers who provide the party with electoral support.

The next two chapters examine nominating politics: Chapter 6 treats nominations within the states, and Chapter 7 describes the presidential nominating process. The emphasis is upon the increasing democratization of the nominating process and the loss of power by organizational leaders.

Chapters 8 and 9 are concerned with political campaigning. The influence of money and the regulations that control its use are discussed in detail. Linked to this is the new style of campaigning that exploits costly technological innovations in winning office.

Chapter 10 carries over the discussion of political campaigns to electoral decisions. An explanation of why some citizens turn out to vote and others do not is followed by an examination of why voters make the choices they do. Although it is often neglected in parties texts, I believe that voting behavior is a key element in understanding why the parties are losing their grip on the American electorate.

The parties as organizers of government are examined in the next two chapters. In Chapter 11, reforms that have curbed the power of committee chairmen and potentially strengthened the hands of congressional party leaders are contrasted with the growing diffusion of legislative power. Chapter 12 studies the president's central role in conditioning long-term partisan loyalties.

The several threads of the book's analysis are intertwined in Chapter 13. Whether the parties are undergoing realignment or dealignment is discussed along with prospects for their further reform. A final assessment is made of the contemporary parties and their likely future.

I have been assisted in writing this book by a number of my colleagues who were generous with their time. Stephen J. Wayne read the entire manuscript and gave me the benefit of his considerable knowledge of American politics. Susan J. Carroll, Christopher J. Deering, and Steven S. Smith each read individual chapters and made helpful suggestions on style and substance. I turned to my neighbor, Jack Hurt, a practicing politician, to ensure that the manuscript had an air of reality to it. An able graduate student, John Hearty, performed yeoman's service on the computer to provide me with up-to-date election data. The people at St. Martin's Press, particularly Robert Woodbury and Carol Ewig, have given me encouragement and professional assistance. Finally, I owe a debt to my family for their love and devotion, which endured the preparation of this manuscript.

Hugh L. LeBlanc

1

The Parties and Their Role in American Political Life

Political parties are unlikely to win a popularity contest among American institutions. Although it was the American experience that gave birth to the modern political party,[1] Americans today show little affection for their progeny. Many citizens believe that parties confuse rather than clarify issues, create conflict where none existed, and do little to make government responsive to public demands. Public confidence in political parties may be at an all-time low.[2]

The irony is that more Americans take part in party processes today than ever before. Virtually every citizen can now participate in the nomination of party candidates. National party platforms are drafted after public hearings and adopted by delegates elected to the national conventions. The days when party bosses could meet in smoke-filled rooms to pick a president, slate a ticket, or close a deal with other power brokers are past. Instead, party affairs are conducted in the glare of publicity. But somewhere along the way to democratization, the parties began losing their partisans. Republicans and Democrats are less attached to their parties and more likely to cast their ballots for the opposition party's candidates than they once were. Independent affiliation and split-ticket voting are also on the rise.

An eroding electoral base is only one sign of diminished party strength. As the rank-and-file voter has become more active in party affairs, the power of party leaders has been diluted. They are no longer able to hand the nomination to the candidates of their choice, nor do they control the resources that candidates need to win office.

For all these reasons, it is said that the parties are losing their separate identities. Descriptions of the contemporary parties—"decaying," "decomposing," and "disaggregating" are favorite terms—imply imminent demise. Yet the two major parties have managed to survive through most of the twentieth century, their officeholders continue to occupy center stage in American political life, and a majority of voters are still willing to declare a party affiliation. It may be premature to conclude that the parties have fallen into a state of disrepair from which they cannot recover.

What Is a Political Party?

The term *political party* conveys different meanings to different people that are reflected in the variety of definitions offered by scholars. Some writers emphasize the principal activities that parties undertake. One of them, Leon Epstein, defined a party as ". . . any group, however loosely organized, seeking to elect government officeholders under a given label."[3] Other scholars single out the programmatic or ideological goals of parties. To the eighteenth-century English conservative Edmund Burke, for example, a party was " . . . a body of men united, for promoting by their joint endeavors the national interest, upon some particular principle in which they are all agreed."[4] Still others focus upon the nature of the organizations that the parties maintain. "A party is a community with a particular structure," said French political scientist Maurice Duverger. "Modern parties are characterized by their anatomy."[5] Taken together, these various aspects of a political party can help us to create our own definition, and thus bring us closer to understanding the American party system.

Throughout most of our political history, partisan conflict has been channeled through two major parties. Since the middle of the nineteenth century, when the Republican party replaced the Whigs, these parties have been the Democrats and the Republicans. If, as Epstein writes, a party's principal reason for being is to elect officeholders, then the two major American parties have been highly successful. Since the 1860 presidential election, only Democrats and Republicans have held the nation's highest office. But are political parties only electoral machines to contest elections? Are their members also united by commonly shared political values, principles, or issue stands? These questions lead us to Burke's definition of a party. And although few analysts would apply his rather idealistic portrayal to the American party system, the notion that election contests are fought over meaningless issues is not satisfactory either. The 1980 presidential election which placed a Republican in the White House, for example, produced sharp partisan exchanges over the government policies that Ronald Reagan pursued. Many Democrats charged that his program of slashing budgets and cutting taxes benefited the rich at the expense of the poor, just as many Republicans defended his efforts as a way to nourish an economy that had become stagnant under Democratic management. These are not unimportant differences. Finally, seeking to elect the president is not the only preoccupation of the major parties. Democrats compete against Republicans for most of the major elective offices in the nation, reflecting a collective undertaking that would not be possible without some organizational basis. Thus as Duverger rightly observes, the nature of a party's organization will influence both its ability to contest elections and to unite its members.

What is clear from this analysis is that not only can a political party be many things to many people, but it can successfully be viewed through many different perspectives. Only by examining its role in the governing process—the aim of this book—can a party be fully understood.

With this cautionary note in mind, we offer our own working definition. *A political party is an organized effort to win elective office in order to gain political power and control the policies of government.* Each aspect of party included in the definition—its organizational status, its contesting of elections, and its control of public policy—will be developed in later chapters.

The essential nature of a political party is revealed in how it goes about its tasks. Political parties nominate candidates for public office. Other political groups display an interest in who wins elective office or what public policies are proclaimed, but only the party gives its label to its candidates.[6] By doing so, the party accepts responsibility for the actions of those who are its standard bearers.

But while knowing that a party nominates candidates helps to distinguish political parties from political interest groups, it does not tell us much about the "organized effort" that such nominations entail. American parties are not organized with the definitiveness of a trade union. There is no ambiguity over who the leaders of the AFL-CIO are, who its members are, or how its business is conducted. The structure of a political party is more amorphous. Indeed, it is commonly suggested that the political party is composed of three separate but interacting groups:[7]

1. A formal party organization.
2. A party in the electorate.
3. A party in the government.

Figure 1.1 shows the interrelationships of these individual units.

Figure 1-1
THE TRIPARTITE AMERICAN POLITICAL PARTY

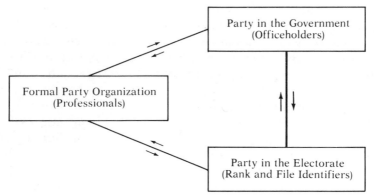

THE FORMAL PARTY ORGANIZATION

The formal party organization consists of the men and women who are responsible for conducting party business outside of government. Included as part of the formal party organization would be the national committees and their chairpersons, as well as committees organized around electoral subdivisions of the country such as states, cities, and counties. The members of this group are the political professionals and activists, for whom politics is either a vocation or a strong avocation. Their primary responsibilities are twofold:

1. To see to it that party traditions are carried forward by those who receive the party's nomination.
2. To ensure that the party has the resources to make its candidates electorally competitive.

The influence the professionals wield over party affairs is considered an important gauge of the strength of the political party.

THE PARTY IN THE ELECTORATE

Those who identify with a political party constitute the party in the electorate. They provide the popular base that candidates use in building electoral coalitions. Membership in such a group is indistinct because it rests upon psychological attachment rather than formal enrollment. The relationship of the rank and file to the party professionals and to the officeholders (see "The Party in the Government," below) also is revealing of party strength. If the party professionals command a loyal electorate who vote their party allegiance, the party is judged strong. On the other hand, if the voters' loyalty is to the candidate, not the party, the party is judged weak. Since the heyday of urban political machines earlier in this century, political professionals have not been able to deliver a vote. Aided by new campaign techniques, many candidates have acquired followings among voters that are in part unrelated to party attachments.

THE PARTY IN THE GOVERNMENT

The party in the government consists of those public officials who owe their office to their party affiliation. Thus presidents, governors, congressmen, state legislators, mayors, city councilmen, and county supervisors are all members of the party in the government. The officeholders have the ultimate responsibility for formulating the public policies by which the parties are known, and their relationships to the party professionals are a key factor in the organizational presence the parties project. The freer the officeholders are of obligations to the political professionals outside the government, the weaker the party is judged. Since political professionals today can neither control nominations nor command the resources in general elections to make their candidates dependent on their services, American parties are characteristically described as weak.

THE IMPORTANCE OF THE PARTY LABEL

Despite the apparent thinness of their ties, the three party groups are so linked by repetitive institutional practices that together they merit the phrase "organized group." The key to understanding this collective effort is the near monopoly that the major parties have on who will hold public office. Such control is aided by state laws that give the major parties an advantage in obtaining ballot space, but legal provisions alone do not explain the electoral victories of Democrats and Republicans. Independents and minor party candidates have frequently met statutory requirements to contest offices at national and state levels, but have not had notable successes on election day.

What enable the political parties to function as effective institutions are the sets of interests, policies, and principles that are perceived as distinguishing one party from the other by: (1) those who decide to run under a party label; and (2) voters whose loyalty to a party can survive unpopular candidates and the policies they extol. The traditional policy positions associated with a party, or the interests and groups it has championed, encourage a self-selection process among those who would run as its candidates. The political attitudes of would-be officeholders dictate which party label fit them more comfortably. Although the amorphous nature of the American political party system at times produces strange bedfellows, most Democratic officeholders do differ from most Republican officeholders in political attitudes. Once the parties have awarded their nominations, voter support generally flows to the candidates according to partisan loyalties. Whether an act of faith or reason, voters ordinarily express more confidence in their own party's candidates than in the opposition's. It is the party label, and what is has come to mean to those who wear it and those who support it, that has allowed the parties to survive as collective undertakings.

What the Parties Do

Political parties link citizens to their government. They do this in straightforward fashion by mobilizing voters behind their banners and in behalf of the candidates who have received their nominations. The party that is electorally victorious then has the task of organizing and managing the government in a fashion that will curry popular favor. As this process is repeated over time, certain things become expected of one party but not of the other, and each is perceived as having a characteristic way of solving governmental problems. These expectations and perceived characteristics allow voters to rely on the party label, rather than on the individual candidate, in making their electoral choices. It is important to note that if the linkages between the professionals, the office-holders, and the rank and file are weakened, the party as a collective undertaking also is weakened (see Table 1.1).

MOBILIZING THE ELECTORATE

The initial step in the linkage function performed by parties is organizing the electorate. Despite the widely proclaimed weakening of parties today, the tasks they accomplish in channeling the vote are little short of remarkable. Reflect for a moment on the physical size of the nation, the number of states or regions with peculiar histories and political cultures, the richness of our racial and ethnic strains, the number and diversity of occupational groups and classes, and the variety of religious sects and denominations. And then consider that the Republican and Democratic parties meet in delegate conventions, make their presidential nominations, and thereby effectively limit the choice of the American voter. To channel the vote toward the nominees of the two major parties is an organizational task of herculean proportions, and the striking fact is that it is accomplished without elaborate organizational structures. The power of the parties to mobilize the American electorate is based in large part on the commitment most voters maintain to one or the other of the parties. Indeed, so effective is the parties' hold on some voters that a substantial proportion of the electorate knows how it will cast its vote in presidential elections even before the candidates are announced.[8]

The two major parties serve as a funnel through which successful candidates must pass on their way to political office. This is so not only in presidential and congressional races but in most gubernatorial and state legislative contests, and many city and county elections as well. If the parties did not have the capacity to structure the vote, candidates would not bother to earn the party label before competing for office.

ORGANIZING THE GOVERNMENT

The victorious party has the opportunity and the responsibility to organize the government. If party professionals had their way, the same party would organize both the executive and the legislative branches. Although over the years, at both the national and the state level, such unified control has been more common than not, it has not been habitual. Republican presidents, for example, have confronted at least one hostile (that is, Democratic) house of Congress in all but two of the post–World War II years they have held office.

Regardless of whether there is unitary or divided control, the government is organized along partisan lines. The party with a congressional majority provides the chairs of legislative committees and subcommittees, as well as a majority of each committee's membership. The successful presidential candidate becomes his party's leader and makes several hundred executive appointments from among his closest preelection advisers, spokespersons for prominent elements of the coalition that lifted him to power, and leaders who reflect the traditional sources of party support. This practice guarantees a partisan cast to government. Only rarely do opposition party members find their way into high political office.

Hewing to the party line in passing out legislative committee assignments or making executive appointments would be a meaningless exercise unless Republicans did things differently from Democrats once in power. The political meaning attached to a party label must ultimately come from what each party does when it is in power. In 1968, George Wallace said that there wasn't a dime's worth of difference between the Democratic and Republican parties. Was he right? Do Republican officeholders take essentially the same policy stances as Democratic officeholders? Hardly. Despite popular impressions, scholarly evidence clearly reveals important policy differences between party leaders.

The work of John L. Sullivan and Robert E. O'Connor is illustrative.[9] These two political scientists surveyed contestants in the 1966 House races to determine their attitudes in three broad issue domains—domestic policy, civil rights, and foreign policy. Having determined the attitudes of the candidates, they were then able to create "hypothetical" Congresses. For example, what if the voters followed the adage of "throwing the rascals out"? Sullivan and O'Connor created a Congress in which the losers replaced the winners wherever a congressional seat was actually contested. Did the exchange bring in a Congress with materially different views from those of the actual Congress? No, they said. Probably little change in the actual outcome of roll call votes would have occurred.

If throwing the rascals out would prove fruitless, do the voters have a choice? Indeed they do. Not only were there differences in the aggregate attitudes of Democrats and Republicans, but the parties' candidates tended to differ as contestants in individual battles within congressional districts. Moreover, the differences reflected the distinctions between present-day liberals and conservatives.[10] A hypothetical Congress composed only of Democratic officeseekers was quite similar to a Congress created by designating the more liberal contestant in a race as the winner. And a hypothetical Republican Congress was not unlike a Congress of conservative winners.

What this tells us is that the voter does have a choice. Not surprisingly, that choice is greatest in designating the desired direction in domestic economic and social welfare policies— vintage New Deal-style issues. But if the voters are to realize their choice, they must be selective—not indiscriminate—in throwing out the rascals. The party label is still an effective guide for voters who want to signal their judgment that public policies are in need of change.

PROVIDING COLLECTIVE RESPONSIBILITY

As the process of holding election contests is repeated, with the winners gaining the right to organize and manage the government, the party takes on meaning as a collective enterprise. The candidates do not run on their own, but have institutional backing; standing behind each candidate is a party that offers not only a tradition but also, based on that tradition, a promise of what its future policy directions will be like. That knowledge of the party as an ongoing institution is valuable both to those who wear the party label as officeholders and to the parties' mass following.

For the officeholders, the notion of the institutional party often influences their choice of banner to run under. The label sorts out the two sets of party leaders, with the political center-of-balance of most Democrats to the left and of most Republicans to the right. The apportionment is not perfect, but neither is it meaningless. It is, after all, similarity in outlook that enables party members to cooperate as well as they do in their legislative endeavors. Their cooperation is further spurred by a felt need to carve out a legislative record that will not place their party at an electoral disadvantage.

The collective responsibility that parties accept for the candidates who wear their label is no less important to the voter, who can reward or punish collective sets of leaders. If the party label is devalued, all who wear it can be affected.

Consider the impact of the Watergate scandals on the fortunes of the Republican party in the 1974 elections. Republican ranks were hit hard in both congressional and state races. No matter that the candidates running were unassociated with the White House staff or the Committee to Reelect the President, where the scandals arose, the repercussions of perfidy were visited on wicked and virtuous alike because they shared the same label. The consequences may be unfair, but they suggest that officeholders cannot always avoid the responsibilities they accepted when they agreed to carry the party's standard.

Parties and Ideology

What has been conveyed so far is that political parties, when in office, do differ in the way they go about solving governmental problems. Does this mean, then, that American parties are "ideological"? The answer is too complex for a simple yes or no response. Much depends upon what is meant by ideological, and which party group is being addressed.

THE LIMITS OF DISAGREEMENT

The question of whether American political parties are ideological must be more clearly specified before it can be answered accurately. Do the American parties offer the voters a choice between competing ideologies? Are the ideological choices comparable to the alternatives available in European party systems? In other words, by our definition, do the major American parties provide a choice between fundamentally different ways of organizing and interpreting social, economic, and political experiences? Phrasing the question as we have makes the answer self-evident. Of course they do not, because American parties lack a socialist or left party with a mass base.

But we still have not answered the question of whether American parties are ideological. If the American parties do not provide full-blown ideological choices, may it be said that they hold no preferences as to the role of government in society? Again, the answer is self-evident. Both major parties subscribe to a democratic-capitalist order. They are clearly ideological, but their commitment is to the same ideology.

Knowing that both American parties subscribe to the same fundamental ideology is a political datum of some significance, for it suggests the limits of political orthodoxy in the United States and what is or is not an appropriate subject of political debate. Anyone who has listened to Fourth of July oratory or campaign rhetoric knows that our politicians all pay homage to the same symbols and rituals of American democracy. The only candidate who can afford to make a frontal attack on the American system is the one who represents a noncompetitive party—that is, a candidate whose chances of electoral success are unrealistic. The effects of such orthodoxy extend beyond minor party candidates of the radical left or right to those major party candidates who are perceived, correctly or not, to be outside the political mainstream. Both Barry Goldwater in 1964 and George McGovern in 1972 were perceived as outlying candidates by the public and each suffered an electoral disaster. The American party system appears firmly anchored in the middle of a left right political continuum.

Why have socialist or left parties arisen in Europe but not in the United States? At least two conditions are necessary to the rise of a left-leaning mass party:[11]

1. A sizable industrial work force.
2. A felt need to organize politically, as well as industrially, to advance working-class interests.

The United States has long had a large industrial work force, so the first condition is satisfied. But our trade unionists have shown few inclinations to organize a workers' party. Most of the sizable minor parties of economic protest of the late nineteenth and early twentieth century had more of an agrarian than a labor base. The reasons why American labor has not organized its own party revolve about its failure to develop a class consciousness. That failure, in turn, has several causes:[12]

1. Unlike the European continent, the United States has no feudal past that emphasized class distinctions. When industrialization spread throughout Europe, industrial workers became a new class in a society already firmly organized along class lines.
2. Industrialization came to Europe before workers had the right to vote. In the United States, universal white male suffrage was the rule before industrialization was widespread, suggesting a more egalitarian society in which workers felt less of a need to band together politically.

3. The American trade union movement was first organized heavily along craft, rather than industrial, lines. Crafts were the more skilled occupational groups and the better paying. Thus, unlike the industrial worker, the craft worker was economically secure.

4. Ethnic rivalry had the effect of impeding the development of class solidarity. In some communities, the party an ethnic group belonged to was dictated by which groups were dominant in the opposition. In New Haven, resentful of the prescriptive right of the Democratic-leaning Irish to city jobs, Italians responded favorably to ethnic appeals by the Republican party.[13]

5. Finally, the abundance that has always characterized the United States must be considered. As long as the horn of plenty was sufficiently bountiful that all who came to draw from it were rewarded, those of low estate would not believe their condition was permanent.[14] To Americans, the concept of equality has long meant equality of opportunity. To Europeans, it has signified a need for redistribution of wealth so that all might share more equally. The phrase "income redistribution" is only now entering the American political vocabulary. Class differences are recognized in American politics, but they are not sharply etched on the consciousness of the labor force.

"LIBERALS" VERSUS "CONSERVATIVES"

That a party of the left has failed to gain mass support in American politics does not mean that elections are contested over meaningless issues. Within the broad commitment to democratic capitalism, the major American parties have disagreed over policies the government should enact, and the most commonly employed terms to distinguish the central thrust of each party's policy positions are "liberal" and "conservative." Even though the meanings of the labels are not precise, their widespread use in political analysis makes them unavoidable. They may be thought of as ideologies, but less fundamental than those, for example, that distinguish Christian Democrats from Communists in European party systems.

Distinctions between liberals and conservatives tend to focus on the use of governmental power to effect social and economic change. During the 1930s, the Democratic party embarked on programs aimed at regulating industry and promoting economic security, clearly marking it as the liberal party. On the other hand, by opposing the intrusion of government into the private sector the Republican party earned a reputation for conservatism. Although neither party's leadership was entirely cohesive, most analysts agree that the labels were fairly placed and that most voters perceived this distinction between the parties.

As the Depression became a faded memory and the second major war of the century was successfully concluded, liberal and conservative distinctions became less sharply drawn. Democrats muted the rhetoric of class conflict, and Republicans conceded an enlarged role for government. The nation enjoyed relative prosperity and Democrats and Republicans alike used government power to ensure its continuance. Nevertheless, two caveats must be entered here. The Republican party's acquiescence in a new role for government in such areas as business regulation and social welfare policies did not mean that its leadership wished to see an expansion of these policies. By comparison, Democrats were more likely to see the need for an extension of measures to curb business power and to benefit the underprivileged. The second caveat is that although the expansion of government power continued as an issue between Democrats and Republicans, it was selectively argued. Postwar Republicans were less hesitant to use government power to restrict credit, raise tariffs, or to regulate trade unions.[15]

As early as 1948, the simple formula of distinguishing Democrats and Republicans along lines of economic cleavage was shattered when the Dixiecrats revolted against a relatively mild (by today's standards) civil rights plank adopted by the Democratic convention. This conflict was a harbinger of things to come. In the 1960s, what has been called the "social issue" added a new dimension to the liberal-conservative conflict that cut across the bread-and-butter issues of the New Deal. Rising crime rates, civil riots in the cities, and the sometimes bloody confrontations between antiwar demonstrators and police and national guardsmen suggested alternative roles for government: treating their causes or cracking down on their outbreaks. The military venture in Vietnam also seriously undermined the faith of many liberals that governmental power would be used only for benevolent purposes.

Different perspectives on the 1960s led to different attitudes on the proper role of government. Some who were

troubled by the breakdown of public authority blamed an un-
just society and called for a renewed government effort to ensure social justice, if necessary by the establishment of quotas
based on race, sex, and ethnicity. At the same time, those who
saw the Vietnam war as immoral and imperialistic moved to
curb the power of intelligence agencies, cut defense spending,
and adopt a more accommodationist foreign policy. Disagree-
ment over these controversial new issues weakened the internal cohesion of the parties and gave rise to a variety of new
labels applied to party factions. Within Republican party
ranks, "moderate conservatives" are less adamant than "orthodox conservatives" in resisting the growth of the service
state. Democrats are separated into "old-fashioned liberals"
and "new liberals," the former more worried over the perceived threat of Soviet expansionism and bothered by the mission of government to improve the quality of life in society.[16]
Such factional differences have often emerged in presidential

"*The old labels just don't seem to mean much anymore.*"

Drawing by Whitney Darrow, Jr.
© 1980 The New Yorker Magazine, Inc.

nominating contests and have contributed to the governing problems of the presidential party, but they show no signs yet of permanently fracturing either party.

Today's party leaders do not engage in broad public debates on liberal and conservative principles that would guide individual acts of state and make them ethically plausible to the voting public. Rather, they take stands on specific issues that are not necessarily linked in a cogently argued public philosophy. Democrats are judged liberal and Republicans are judged conservative, in large measure, because of the social groups and organized interests that tend to support each.[17] The national Democratic party has built a broad coalition from lower socioeconomic groups, racial, ethnic, and religious minorities and their middle-class sympathizers. The Republican party has been supported by business interests and the electorates of rural, small-town, and suburban America, disproportionately Protestant, Anglo-Saxon, and middle and upper class. Though each party supports policies with an eye toward its constituency base, the issue stands they take are not always clearly differentiated, because each is seeking majoritarian support in a pluralist society committed to a market economy. Nor do all officeholders of a party agree on what its policy positions should be, given their personal convictions and the diversity of their constituency support. Nevertheless, the parties can still be distinguished by their central tendencies.

More Democrats than Republicans believe that only government can deal adequately with the social and economic problems confronting the nation. Democrats are more willing to spend money for health, welfare, education, housing, urban transportation, environmental controls, and other problems they see as constituting the social agenda. Republicans are more inclined to believe that government is not the most appropriate or efficient instrument for solving the ills of society. Freeing the private sector from excessive regulation and burdensome taxes, they argue, will produce the prosperity that will ultimately eliminate the problems of concern to Democrats. Certainly not all modern Democratic administrations have actively pursued a program of broadening the service state, nor until Reagan's election did a Republican administration make massive cuts in Democratic programs to aid the poor and the needy. Yet those sympathetic to allocating more government resources to improving the quality of life or aiding the disadvantaged would scarcely turn to the Republican party to accomplish their objectives. Nor would those who fear the growth of the public sector turn to Democratic party leaders to stem the tide of government spending or restrict the application of regulatory policies. Despite internal party rifts, the images the parties carry remain important in distinguishing the two leadership groups.

DIFFERING ISSUE PERSPECTIVES

To speak of issue differences between the parties, although correct, may also be misleading. We referred earlier to the political party as encompassing three distinct groups: officeholders, political professionals, and rank-and-file supporters. It is useful to examine the broad issue perspectives of each of these groups because each has its influence on what stand the party eventually adopts.[18]

The officeholders and the political professionals are more sophisticated in their ideological references than the party's electoral following.[19] Their time is more heavily committed to political affairs, and their interest is greater. The rank and file as a group are less keenly interested in politics and spend less time in its pursuit. Their issue positions are not as well thought out. When one compares the attitudes on issues of Democratic professionals and officeholders with those of their Republican counterparts, one finds them disagreeing on more issues than their respective sets of followers. Moreover, the extent of the differences between the two groups of leaders is likely to be greater than among the followers.

The point that must be conveyed, in view of criticisms of the parties by the public, is that the leadership is not ignoring either a hidden conservative or liberal vote. In the two post–World War II presidential elections offering the broadest issue choices, 1964 and 1972, the candidates perceived as holding extreme positions, Goldwater and McGovern, were soundly beaten. Indeed, it is an axiom of American political analysis that because so many voters are resolutely middle-of-the-road, candidates cannot wander too far from the political mainstream and still win majority support.

It is not being suggested here that voters do not feel strongly about certain issues. Considerable evidence suggests they do. But they do not always see the solutions to the problems that elicit their concern. Many citizens are concerned about inflation without knowing how to hold down prices. Others feel equally strongly about the size of their tax bill, but cannot agree on how or where to cut government spending. It is the officeholders who must provide specific solutions to the problems that arouse the public. The complexity of the problems may be beyond the grasp of the mass public, but there is no gainsaying that those left unsolved by incumbents—widespread unemployment, unpopular wars, highly publicized scandals, runaway inflation—have exacted their political toll.

The ideological perspective of the officeholders is not necessarily the same as that of the party professionals, although both may share the goal of victory and may cooperate toward that end. Sometimes the more ideologically pure among the professionals only reluctantly support a candidate whose centrist views give him a better chance of winning a general election. Beginning with the nomination of Wendell Willkie in 1940, Republican professionals avoided their more conservative candidates out of electoral necessity until, in 1964, they voted their hearts and proved the wisdom of their earlier strategem. In 1980, although Ronald Reagan had come to national prominence and won the Republican nomination by championing conservative causes, he successfully moderated his image in the general election compaign to ensure victory.

The Democratic party pattern in presidential contests has been somewhat different. In 1972, following rules changes in delegate selection procedures, the convention nominated a candidate whose policy views were less accommodationist than probably a majority of professionals would have preferred. In 1976, however, the selection of Jimmy Carter left the more liberal professionals dissatisfied, a dissatisfaction that grew during his term of office and led to Edward Kennedy's 1980 primary challenge.

Characterizing a party's policy positions with any precision, then, is made difficult because the political party does not speak with a single voice. Its organizational structure does not provide the mechanisms for resolving internal differences and evolving an official party line. The best gauge of what a party stands for is what its officeholders do when they hold power. Even this measure, however, provides an ambiguous guide. Individual party officeholders do not always agree on the appropriate course of policy to follow. Still, Democrats do not trade positions with Republicans from election to election. Over time, the central thrust of a party's approach to solving governmental problems does emerge and, however imprecise, suggests the differences that might be expected if one party rather than the other is responsible for governing.

Two Opposing Views of American Parties

The equivocal commitment of the parties to well-defined programs has been criticized by some political analysts and defended by others. The debate centers on the type of party system that is most desirable for American society. The arguments put forward by each side contribute to an understanding of what our parties do and do not do.

RESPONSIBLE PARTY GOVERNMENT

Some who find American parties defective base their criticisms on four major grounds:[20]

1. The parties rarely provide the electorate with a choice between fundamentally different programs.
2. They do not have the discipline to carry out the platforms they have enacted.
3. They are held together less by principle than by sectional, ethnic, and interest group ties.
4. They do not reflect the opinions and attitudes of the electorate.

What the United States needs, these critics have argued, is responsible party government.[21]

The case for responsible party government rests upon two major assumptions concerning the nature of democracy. First, in a large nation, democracy must consist of popular *control* over government and not popular *participation* in day-to-day decision making. Popular control can be achieved if the electorate determines who is to run the government. Second, popular control of government can best be established if voters are offered a choice between unified and disciplined, or responsible, political parties. The victorious party would then have the power to enact its program and could stand accountable for its record at the next election.[22]

Responsible political parties, its proponents argue, would perform indispensable functions in a democratic society. They would focus political debate on general principles concerning the directions for government to take. They would stimulate public discussion and involve the electorate in the issues confronting the nation. Finally, they would make the government as a whole responsible to the people. They would do this by replacing individual accountability of officeholders to their constituencies with collective party responsibility.[23]

How are the parties to be made disciplined and programmatic? The most detailed blueprint is contained in the 1950 report of the American Political Science Association's Committee on Political Parties entitled *Toward a More Responsible Two-Party System*.[24] In it, the committee called for parties that were "democratic, responsible, and effective."

The committee proposed that democratically run parties would be the best method of achieving unity of purpose among their supporters. If the rank and file had a say in adopting the party program, it was argued, they would be more likely to support it. Greater cohesion among congressional members was to be achieved by centralizing the party leadership in each house and requiring individual members to vote with the position determined by a majority of their partisan colleagues.

The committee's most novel recommendation was the creation of fifty-member party councils composed of party leaders and major officeholders. Each council would "screen" potential presidential candidates; make recommendations concerning the qualifications of congressional candidates; provide a preliminary draft of the party platform for consideration by its national convention; and make recommendations to its national convention, national committee, or other appropriate body when state or local party organizations conspicuously departed from general party decisions. In addition to these sweeping powers, the committee suggested that a smaller group of the council might serve in an advisory capacity to the president when its party controlled that office.

One would be hard pressed to defend the recommendations of the committee as realistic proposals for party reform. The most sweeping suggestion, and the most critical to the success of the proposals, was the creation of a party council to centralize party affairs. Confronted by a system of separated powers and a two- or three-tiered governmental structure, with interests vested in or surrounding each tier, a council operating as the committee envisioned stretches credulity.

The committee's proposals also appear to be running at cross purposes. At the same time that it recommended a party council as the mechanism to achieve the desired goal of party unity, the committee report stressed the need for broad participation by the rank and file in party affairs. As committee chairman E. E. Schattschneider argued elsewhere, it is difficult to see how such a broadly based intraparty democracy could be consistent with the development of a coherent party program.[25] Too many voices would be raised by participants whose interests in the well-being of the party as a corporate entity were remote. Far from promoting party unity, popular participation runs the risk of exposing and exacerbating clashing views. Certainly rank-and-file participation in selecting delegates to recent national conventions has not produced the party harmony the report envisaged.

In fairness to the committee report, its authors were describing a model party system as a standard against which to judge the existing parties. Nevertheless, they did believe their model should serve as a goal toward which the parties should strive. Indeed, committee members were apparently convinced that if the report were properly explained, the electorate would grasp the significance and the advantages of disciplined and programmatic parties.

DEFENSE OF THE STATUS QUO

Not all analysts were convinced by the arguments put forward by the advocates of responsible party government. Quite apart from the likelihood of achieving programmatic parties, some political observers thought they were undesirable. Parties built on principled stands, it was said, would intensify political conflict. Rather than two parties competing to govern, many parties would arise to represent particular ideological or issue positions, and party leaders would be unwilling to compromise for fear of alienating their committed followers. In an atmosphere of rigid and doctrinaire parties, governing the nation would become measurably more difficult.

Defenders of the American party system did not rest their case on an attack of the responsible party model, but argued that there was much to admire in the existing party system.[26] Above all, American parties brought stability and continuity to the nation's political system. Election contests that replace one party with another are not disruptive, because the parties have no sharply differentiated principled stands. Because they are compelled to seek majoritarian support, the parties put together coalitions of diverse groups and interests in a bargaining process that moderates political conflict. Voters are still provided with a choice, but one that avoids extreme positions on policy.

"The great virtue of the two-party system," wrote the late V. O. Key, is "not that there are two groups with conflicting policy tendencies from which the voters can choose, but that there are two groups of politicans."[27] Key arrived at that conclusion after studying the one-party factionalism in the South of the forties. The fluidity of factions was such that no stable groups of "outs" were available to challenge the "ins" on whatever issues were conveniently at hand. Key recognized that politicians, even in two-party systems, have a tendency to ignore, suppress, or postpone taking clear issue stands because they produce conflict and possibly an early end to a political career. But that tendency is magnified, he believed, in a one party or nonparty system without a cohesive opposition eager for office.

Although Key was too much the realist to be attracted by the prospect of parties with clearly formulated programs, he did not approve of an issueless politics. Indeed, he felt that party competition encouraged conflict over issues. At the same time, the value of parties was that each represented a continuing *and* cohesive group. In other words, Key felt that the mutual desire for victory by parties in a two-party system would lead them to cohere around certain issue positions as a route to that goal. And once in power, parties could achieve their legislative goals more easily than factions.

The Decline of Parties

The debate over what type of party system is most suitable for Americans was at its height more than two decades ago. Since then, the system that responsible party advocates examined and found wanting has deteriorated further. Those who defended the stability and moderation of the older system now complain that parties are less able to build stable coalitions for electoral and governing purposes. No matter what side they took on the controversy, scholars see today's growth of special-interest lobbies and single-issue groups as endangering timely and coherent policymaking.[28] Some commentators believe that the parties have lost their capacity to resolve the differences and mediate the disputes that divide the nation.

After the 1978 off-year elections, a leading weekly magazine solemnly proclaimed the death of the parties with few disclaimers.[29] The interesting facet of this type of analysis is that it assumes party malaise is of relatively recent origin. The changes that have occurred, these analysts believe, go to the core of the system that historically facilitated political conflict between two more or less cohesive sets of "ins" and "outs." In the remainder of this chapter, we will introduce recent antiparty developments; more detailed analyses are provided in the chapters that follow.

THE FORMAL PARTY ORGANIZATION

As we observed earlier, the structure of American parties is rather amorphous. One of the elements of a party is the core of activists who are referred to in the popular press and political science literature as *political professionals*. Although loosely defined, these are the men and women who staff and sustain the party organization outside of government. Their role is to see to it that the candidates who receive the party label have some commonality of purpose, and then to work to elect those who have been chosen. It is said that the influence of political professionals has been steadily declining because of changes in the nominating and electoral processes. The developments that have eroded the power of professionals are of two sorts:

1. Those that have involved the rank-and-file supporter more fully in the selection of party candidates.
2. Those that have weakened the influence of the professionals in managing political campaigns.

Professionals have had to share nominating power with the party following since the turn of the century when the direct primary was introduced. The professionals managed to accommodate themselves to the direct primary as long as they retained sufficient resources to control the outcome of primary elections. However, that ability to command resources has been seriously strained by contemporary innovations.

The candidate of today depends less on party resources than candidates in the past did. Professional campaign consultants, acquainted with the uses of the private poll and expert at building favorable media images, are available for hire. Advances in the art of direct-mail solicitation of funds and restrictions on party financial contributions in federal elections have further freed the candidate from dependence on the party and its professionals. Indeed, the whole style of campaigning has changed. No longer does the candidate rely heavily upon a structured vote turned out by a party and its allied interest groups. Today, candidates for major offices make mass appeals (targeted, to be sure) in thirty-, sixty-, and ninety-second television and radio ads. What all this means is that the candidate owes less to the party for his or her electoral success.

The erosion of the power of professionals in presidential politics is a more recent phenomenon. Although the first presidential primaries were introduced at approximately the same time as the direct (state) primary, their spread was neither so fast nor so wide. Unlike the direct primary, which results in the nomination of a candidate, the presidential primaries have neither displaced the national convention as the ultimate nominating authority nor, until very recently, seriously threatened the professionals' domination of convention proceedings. Spurred by the reforms of the Democratic party that took effect in 1972, presidential primaries have proliferated, and the professionals have lost the control they once held over the nominating process.

The professionals have not simply lost power in selecting the head of the party ticket. Their services are no longer considered essential to the conduct of the general election campaign. Supplied with public funds, presidential candidates now build their own organizations and devise their own strategies to win votes. In this way, their political fortunes are becoming ever more independent of the fortunes of those who share the same party label.

The limited role that party professionals now play in the presidential selection process has had major consequences for the party system. National parties, as we know them, were created as mechanisms for winning the presidency. National coalitions were formed to select a nominee and to provide him with electoral support. When state and local leaders were more heavily involved in the process, the political party had a greater organizational presence. The presidential contender relied on his party contacts to gain the nomination, to win office, and, once in power, to govern successfully.

The question that is sometimes overlooked, perhaps out of nostalgia for a romanticized version of the political past, is just how often traditional political professionals used their resources to seek national goals and objectives. They did try to pick winners and, in the process, pursued an accommodationist politics in order to piece together a successful electoral coalition. But where their power was strongest—in the machine cities of the past—political professionals were more interested in their own survival than in the great issues of the day. As E. E. Schattschneider caustically observed, they "read no books, have vague ideas on public business, and are indifferent to conflicts of policy as far as personal prejudice is concerned."[30] That is why reformers long advocated more democratically run parties.

The traditional political machine has disappeared, except in isolated wards of some midwestern and northeastern cities. With the decline of patronage as an incentive for party work, the door has opened to party activists motivated by ideology or issues. But the party system these activists encounter has been weakened by contemporary developments. Although the Republican party at the national level—and both parties in some states—has moved to strengthen the campaign-related services it offers to candidates, many activists choose to channel their efforts through political-interest groups or devote their energies to specific candidates. The parties must compete for this corps of activists to staff their organizations.

THE PARTY IN THE ELECTORATE

Although few are enrolled, dues-paying members, most citizens do identify with a party. Party identification is important because most voters still vote in accordance with it. The stronger the attachment voters feel to a party, the greater the chances they will support that party's candidates. The recent decline in the strength of party identification and the concomitant growth of Independents within the electorate provide convincing evidence that the parties' hold on their followings has weakened.

The estrangement of voters from the parties has multiple and complex causes. Part of the explanation lies with the growth of television's role in political communication. Television is the means by which most Americans become acquainted with candidates for federal office. Because more and more candidates make direct video appeals to the voters, television has supplanted the party as the intermediary. In addition, office seekers tend to project video images and cultivate video styles that obscure the distinctiveness of the parties whose labels they wear.

It is not simply the candidates' heavier reliance on tele-vised advertisements that has undercut the voters' dependence on party cues. The central importance of television as a news source and the nature of political reporting have taken their toll as well. Both broadcast and print media have an interest in exposing and highlighting the controversies that surround the attempts of government to grapple with seemingly intractable problems. They regard themselves as the government's adver-sary. At the same time, there has been a dramatic change in the educational level of voters since the close of World War II. Almost one of three adults today has received some college training, and these citizens constitute a formidable group. They have learned the importance of ideas, and their constant exposure to political controversies has caused them to be wary of partisan pronouncements. Party tutelage that was readily accepted in the past is now disdained.

Still another development has caused voters to question their party attachment. The post–World War II years have seen steady advancement in workers' income: the impoverished are a shrinking minority of today's population. With relative abundance has come a change in the political agenda. The New Deal–style issues of industrial regulation and economic secur-ity now share the stage with such newer social and cultural issues as abortion, the environment, and the rights of women and minorities. These newer issues crosscut older political divisions built around religion, region, and ethnicity. Party positions on the new political agenda are not clearly perceived, yet they are issues that arouse intense feelings.[31] The failure of the parties to respond unambiguously to these issues has un-doubtedly caused many voters to withhold their loyalty.

THE PARTY IN THE GOVERNMENT

The party in the government is represented by the party's officeholders. If they are to be held collectively accountable for their performance, they should display a spirit of cooperation in their policymaking duties. To the extent that party cohesion in Congress has waned in recent years, the causes can not be at-tributed to a deliberate attempt at weakening the legislative parties. To the contrary, reforms undertaken in the seventies have potentially strengthened the party role in the Congress. On the House side, the ability of the Speaker to lead his party has been enhanced by newly gained power over committee assignments and the scheduling of bills for floor debate; and both the House and the Senate have adopted procedures to make committee chairmen more accountable to the membership of the majority party. If the legislative parties today are less able to agree on a course of action, the explanations are to be sought in the changes that have occurred elsewhere in the party, and in the nature of decision making in contemporary America.

As we have seen, congressmen are no longer assured of support by a loyal party following. Neither do they feel obligated to party professionals for the label they wear or the office they hold. With over half of its members elected for the first time since 1974, the Congress is increasingly composed of politicians who gained office through the new campaign style. Thus their willingness to cooperate with their partisan colleagues in government is largely discretionary. Still, as we shall see, the disintegration of the legislative parties is not as advanced as we have been led to believe.

There is another phenomenon that partly explains the difficulty the party in the government has in legislating. Federal regulation of the private sector and federal aid to achieve social goals have increased remarkably since 1960. Consequently, a multitude of institutions and organized groups, including state and local governments, now maintain permanent staffs in Washington to protect their interests and promote their policy goals. Law firms whose sole business is to represent their clients' stake in public policy issues have proliferated. Indeed, decision making has become the province of networks of issue experts and is incredibly complex and technical. Under these conditions, party officeholders cannot be neatly arranged on the opposing sides of policy controversies that are easily intelligible to the voting public. As Hugh Heclo has observed, "systems for knowledgeable policy making tend to make democratic politics more difficult."[32]

The Contemporary Parties: A Preliminary Assessment

The changes that have weakened the party have affected the influence of the professionals, the allegiance of the party following, and the cohesion of the officeholders. It is difficult

to measure systematically the loss of power by the professionals, but the hold the party has on its following and the
cohesion of the legislative parties can be examined in summary
fashion.

Over the last two decades, the loyalty of partisan identifiers has unquestionably weakened. The trend that is most
damaging to the achievement of party government has been the
rise in split-ticket voting. In 1960, 78 percent of all partisans
voted a straight ticket in federal elections, but that proportion
had fallen to 55 percent in the 1980 presidential race when Independent John B. Anderson drew votes from both Democrats
and Republicans.[33] Rather than rewarding or punishing a
party, a substantial proportion of voters are evaluating the individual merits of candidates.

The different electoral dynamics operating in House,
Senate, and presidential contests contribute to split-ticket
voting. Presidential candidates are more visible than congressional candidates, which gives voters a better chance to assess
their personal strengths. The choice of a president is also affected by issue controversies that are national in scope. By contrast, House races are more insulated from national political
forces and voters are often attracted to House incumbents of
either party because of their district service. In Senate elections, the incumbency advantage is less marked, and Senate incumbents are more vulnerable to national moods.[34] All of these
separatist tendencies strain the electorate's partisan commitments.

At the same time, the decline of partisanship must be kept
in perspective. Party ties have not become so loose that candidates now have no base upon which to build their electoral
coalitions. Almost 90 percent of those who vote in presidential
elections are either party identifiers or Independents who admit they feel closer to one of the parties. These attachments are
not meaningless. Since 1960, the loyalty of all partisans has not
dipped below 76 percent in House and Senate elections, nor
below 73 percent in presidential races. Aggregate figures, of
course, tell an incomplete story since partisan defections ordinarily injure one party more than the other. It can also be
argued that a more rigid loyalty would endanger the responsiveness of the political system. Nevertheless, partisan affiliations are not freely cast aside. Democrats hold a partisan edge
in the electorate, and when a national tide favors them, have an
easier time winning the presidency and organizing the Congress. With a weaker electoral base, Republicans have a more

difficult time in capturing both branches. These patterns would be reversed only if the Republicans became the majority party.

Partisanship also structures conflict within Congress. A president's legislative tasks are made easier when his own party controls Congress, just as his leadership is subject to challenge when the opposition party has a majority in one or both houses of Congress. Prior to Ronald Reagan, Democratic presidents of the past two decades enjoyed greater congressional backing than Republican presidents, largely because they started with more partisan support. Although the early success of Ronald Reagan has been spectacular, party lines have not been obliterated. Both his budget and tax proposals were challenged by the House leadership where the Democrats held a majority. In the fight over the tax bill, for example, only one Republican member deserted his party. The defection of 48 Democrats (mostly from southern or border states) gave Reagan his victory.

Not all legislation is contested along partisan lines. Seeking a middle ground for electoral purposes, the parties often find themselves on the same side of political controversies. Still, since 1960, anywhere from one-third to three-fifths of all recorded votes in any one session of Congress have found party majorities on opposing sides. Congressional partisanship appears to be a function of the trend and tempo of new legislative ventures. The "New Frontier" and "Great Society" measures of the early 1960s commonly produced party battles. Partisanship was weaker in the late 1960s and early 1970s when the nation was preoccupied with the Vietnam war and the internal dissension it sowed. One may speculate that partisanship will intensify if Reagan's budget and fiscal policies do not produce the economic recovery promised.

That party lines are drawn on a substantial number of legislative votes suggests that the parties differ in their central tendencies. At the same time, party ranks are not perfectly mobilized. Northern Democrats and southern Republicans are the most likely to vote with a majority of their partisan colleagues; southern Democrats and northern Republicans are the most likely to defect or to abstain. In the last year of the beleaguered Carter administration, for example, the average House Democrat voted with his party 69 percent of the time, compared to 71 percent for the average Republican. Comparable figures in the Senate were 64 percent for Democrats and 66 percent for Republicans.[35]

ENDURANCE OF THE PARTIES

What may we make of the data? A preliminary analysis suggests the political parties retain a vitality in American political life that is understated by all the evidence that we live in an antiparty age. The party system that exists scarcely conforms to the responsible party government model, yet the system does provide the collective sets of leaders competing for power that contributes to responsive government. What has sustained the party system is not an elaborate extra-governmental organization that controls votes and applies an ideological litmus test to candidates who seek the party label. The parties have endured because most voters remain committed to one or the other of the parties, and because candidates who seek public office do not randomly select a party label to run under.

SUMMARY

Political parties have been defined as organized attempts to win elective office in order to gain political power and control the policies of government. Their overarching role is to link citizens to their government, and they do this by nominating candidates for office and mobilizing support for them in the general election. The victorious party then organizes the government and formulates public policies that give meaning to the party label. As this process is repeated, the parties are distinguished by the manner in which they try to solve the nation's problems when they hold power. Voters often take their cues from party labels when they are not well acquainted with either the candidates or the issues.

Both the Democrats and the Republicans subscribe to the ideology of democratic capitalism. Although this commitment limits the range of ideology in American politics, the two parties have taken opposing stands on economic and social welfare policies. Over time, their differences have been sharp enough to distinguish the Democrats as the more progressive or liberal party and the Republicans as the more moderate or conservative.

Some students of American politics would like to see more highly programmatic and cohesive parties capable of delivering on their electoral promises. But the difficulty with such an objective, their critics point out, is that the parties would become too rigid and doctrinaire to command majority status in our pluralistic society. The present system lends both continuity and stability to American politics without making election contests issueless.

Political parties are composed of three separate but interacting groups: political professionals who staff the party organizations outside of government; officeholders who owe their positions to their partisan affiliation; and voters who identify with a party and commonly support its candidates. A party is judged strong when a well-organized cadre of political professionals controls party nominations and delivers a vote in general election contests. The ability of professionals to perform either task has been seriously eroded, and candidates today must often rely on their own resources in seeking the nomination and campaigning for office.

The leaders of our major parties are unquestionably their officeholders. Except in the machine cities of the past—and then only to sustain their base of power—political professionals never really had the interest, much less the power, to dictate policy positions to officeholders. Officeholders do welcome the electoral support the professionals can turn out because it frees them to devote their energies to policymaking. Without that support, officeholders are obliged to rely on their own resources and to cater to whatever temporary moods or passions sway the electorate. So the weakened power of the professionals has had an effect on officeholders, although this sometimes has been exaggerated.

The officeholders of each party are bound together by little more than respect for the past stand or future possibilities of the party they represent. It could scarcely be otherwise, because the parties have few mechanisms for resolving internal disputes. Neither party's officeholders are perfectly matched in their political attitudes, and the more the individual officeholder is left to his own devices in mobilizing electoral support, the less likely he will feel secure enough to compromise differences with his partisan colleagues. Yet virtually every study that has examined the question has concluded that Democratic officeholders differ from their Republican counterparts on many issues of public policy.

The most damaging development to the parties has been the rise in split-ticket voting. Different forces act on the vote in presidential, House, and Senate elections, and these separatist tendencies strain the partisan attachments of the voters. Yet party affiliations remain important in structuring the popular vote. Because of the partisan advantage they enjoy within the electorate, Democrats are more likely than Republicans to control both branches of government when a national tide favors them.

Without doubt, contemporary developments have weakened the parties, but they are far from fatally wounded. The parties still provide the cover allowing two more or less continuing and cohesive groups to compete for power.

Notes

[1]Maurice Duverger, *Political Parties* (New York: Wiley, 1954), p. xxiii.

[2]See, for example, Jack Dennis, "Trends in Public Support for the American Party System," in *Parties and Elections in an Anti-Party Age*, ed. Jeff Fischel (Bloomington: Indiana University Press, 1978).

[3]Leon D. Epstein, *Political Parties in Western Democracies* (New York: Praeger, 1967), p. 9.

[4]Edmund Burke, "Thoughts on the Cause of the Present Discontents," in *Works* (Boston: Little, Brown, 1971), vol. 1, p. 151.

[5]Duverger, *Political Parties*, p. xv.

[6]See the discussion in Epstein, *Political Parties*, pp. 9–12.

[7]Frank Sorauf was one of the earliest writers to describe the tripartite structure of American parties. See his *Political Parties in the American System* (Boston: Little, Brown, 1964), pp. 68–71.

[8]In the 1980 presidential election, for example, 45 percent of all voters reported that they "knew all along" how they would cast their ballot. *Public Opinion*, December/January 1981, p. 26.

[9]John L. Sullivan and Robert E. O'Connor, "Electoral Choice and Popular Control of Public Policy," *American Political Science Review* 66 (December 1972), pp. 1256–1268. The findings of Sullivan and O'Connor are all the more convincing because they focused on the attitudes and behavior of congressional candidates during a period of political turbulence in which voters' allegiances were in a state of disarray. On the latter point, see Richard E. Dawson, *Public Opinion and Contemporary Disarray* (New York: Harper and Row, 1973), esp. pp. 9–12.

[10]See below, pp. 12–16.

[11]Epstein, *Political Parties*, p. 132.

[12]See the useful discussion in ibid., pp. 138–145.

[13]Robert A. Dahl, *Who Governs?* (New Haven, Conn.: Yale University Press, 1961), pp. 44–51.

[14]For an exploration of this thesis, see David Potter, *People of Plenty* (Chicago: University of Chicago Press, 1957).

[15]Herbert McCloskey, Paul J. Hoffman, and Rosemary O'Hara, "Issue Con-

flict and Consensus among Party Leaders and Followers," *American Political Science Review* 54 (June 1960), esp. pp. 410–418.

[16]Everett Ladd, Jr., "The New Lines Are Drawn: Class and Ideology, Part II," *Public Opinion*, September/October 1978, pp. 14–20.

[17]Theodore Lowi, "The Public Philosophy: Interest Group Liberalism," *American Political Science Review* 61 (March 1967), esp. pp. 12–13.

[18]For a discussion of the "ideological trichotomy," see Sorauf, *Political Parties in the American System*, pp. 68–71.

[19]McCloskey, Hoffman, and O'Hara, "Issue Conflict and Consensus"; and Jeanne Kirkpatrick, "Representation in the American National Conventions: The Case of 1972," *British Journal of Political Science* 5 (July 1975), pp. 313–322.

[20]Edward C. Banfield, "In Defense of the American Party System," in *Political Parties in the Eighties*, ed. Robert A. Goldwin (Washington, D.C., and Gambier, Ohio: American Enterprise Institute and Kenyon College, 1980), pp. 133–149. The essay was originally published in Robert A. Goldwin, ed., *Political Parties, U.S.A.* (Chicago: Rand McNally, 1961).

[21]The best discussion of the responsible party doctrine is Austin Ranney, *The Doctrine of Responsible Party Government* (Urbana: University of Illinois Press, 1962).

[22]Ibid., pp. 10–12.

[23]Ibid., pp. 12–14.

[24]The report appeared as a supplement to the September 1950 issue of the *American Political Science Review*.

[25]E. E. Schattschneider, *Party Government* (New York: Holt, Rinehart and Winston, 1960), pp. 50–61.

[26]See, for example, Arthur N. Nolcombe, *Our More Perfect Union* (Cambridge, Mass.: Harvard University Press, 1950); Pendleton Herring, *The Politics of Democracy* (New York: Norton, 1940); and Herbert Agar, *The Price of Union* (Boston: Houghton Mifflin, 1950).

[27]V. O. Key, *Southern Politics* (New York: Vintage, 1949), pp. 309–310. The following discussion is taken from chap. 14.

[28]The concern has been recently voiced in the *Report of the President's Commission for a National Agenda for the Eighties* (Washington, D.C.: Government Printing Office, 1981), pp. 91–94.

[29]*Time*, November 20, 1978, p. 42.

[30]Schattschneider, *Party Government*, p. 137.

[31]Dawson, *Public Opinion and Contemporary Disarray*, pp. 185–186.

[32]Hugh Heclo, "Issue Networks and the Executive Establishment," in *The New American Political System*, ed. Anthony King (Washington, D.C.: American Enterprise Institute, 1978), p. 119.

[33]On straight-ticket voting, see Hugh L. LeBlanc and Mary Beth Merrin, "Independents, Issue Partisanship, and the Decline of Party," *American Politics Quarterly* 7 (April 1979), pp. 244–245.

[34]Congressional voting is discussed in Thomas E. Mann and Raymond E. Wolfinger, "Candidates and Parties in Congressional Elections," and Alan I. Abramowitz, "A Comparison of Voting for U.S. Senator and Representative in 1978," *American Political Science Review* 74 (September 1980), pp. 617–640.

[35]*Congressional Quarterly Weekly Report*, January 19, 1980, p. 79.

2

National Party Coalitions: The New Deal and Beyond

Speculation abounds over the direction that the American party system is taking. Is it in the process of being fundamentally transformed? If so, what is the nature of the transformation and how will it differ from the party system it is displacing? The answers to these questions rest with the development of the New Deal party system and the changes that have occurred in the party coalitions since the decade of the thirties.

Classifying Presidential Elections

A useful starting point for our analysis is the classification of presidential elections developed by Angus Campbell and his associates, because it is built upon partisan attachments.[1] The Campbell group identified three types of elections: (1) maintaining, (2) deviating, and (3) realigning.

In a *maintaining election*, the basic partisan commitments that prevailed in the preceding election continue and determine the outcome of the contest. Democratic victories from 1932 through 1948 were so classified.

Partisan identifications remain undisturbed in a *deviating election*, but short-term forces on the vote bring about the defeat of the majority party's candidate. The post–World War II victories of Dwight Eisenhower and Richard Nixon would fall into this category. Democrats bolted their party because they either were dissatisfied with their own candidates, were attracted to the opposition's candidates, or were influenced by issues or conditions at the time of the elections. The large

number of Democratic defections was only a temporary setback for the party and did not signal an enduring change in
voter loyalties.

The most complex of the three election types is the realigning election or, more accurately, a realigning era. *Realignment*
signifies a shift in the balance of partisan loyalties that en-
dures beyond a single election or two.[2] Some realignment undoubtedly takes place in every election. Major realignments,
however, tend to occur during great national crises when
popular feelings about politics are especially intense. The most
dramatic realignment of this century occurred during the
Great Depression of the 1930s. Yet had not Franklin Roosevelt
and his New Deal programs won the confidence of a majority
of citizens, party lines might have reverted to patterns that existed before the Democratic victory in 1932.[3]

Two caveats must be offered in regard to realigning elections. First, not all changes in the relative strengths of the
parties involve partisan conversions. The composition of the
electorate changes as new groups are enfranchised (women,
southern blacks, eighteen-year-olds), a new generation of
voters replaces the old, or former nonparticipants cast their
first ballots. As the electorate changes, one party may be the
beneficiary. The entry into the active electorate of first- and
second-generation immigrants added significantly to the Democratic following in the New Deal realignment.[4]

Second, realignment need not be sharp and sudden but can
proceed over a period of time so that it gradually alters the partisan commitments of voting groups. The more sudden shifts
have been labeled critical realignments, while the long-term
changes have been called secular realignments.[5] James L.
Sundquist believes that the latter are merely a delayed reaction to the forces that created the former.[6] What both kinds of
realignment have in common is their durability. It is this that
distinguishes them from the temporary deviations that occur
from election to election.

Because of the requirement of durability, it is premature to
classify the 1980 presidential election as a realignment. Republicans captured the White House and took control of the
Senate—an impressive victory for a party that has been in the
minority for so long. Yet the Democrats held on to the House
and a majority of state governorships and legislative houses. If
the American people judge that Ronald Reagan is successful in
meeting the problems that beset the nation, he may be able to

turn around the fortunes of the Republican party as Roosevelt did those of his party in 1932. Only future elections will determine whether 1980 was a deviating or a realigning election.

In the pages that follow, the last major realignment of the parties will be discussed and the coalitions formed then will be traced to the present. Some realignment has taken place since the 1930s, but not enough to indicate a new party majority. Deviating presidential elections have been common enough to suggest diminished party strength. Some see in the voting patterns prospects for a new realignment, while others view them as an opportunity to revitalize the New Deal party system. Whichever analysis proves correct, contemporary politics cannot be understood without a look backward.

The Pre–New Deal Setting

The party system prevailing on the eve of the so-called Roosevelt Revolution can best be described in sectional terms (see Table 2-1). After the victories of Woodrow Wilson and his New Freedom brand of Progressivism, the Democratic party had retired to its stronghold in the South and the southern border states. The only states that gave their overwhelming support to the Democratic party were the eleven that had seceded to form the Confederacy. The border states of

Table 2-1
REPUBLICAN PARTY ADVANTAGE 1896–1930

| Region | Percentage Republican Control | | |
	Electoral College	U.S. House	Governorships
New England	82.4	83.0	89.2
Middle Atlantic	88.1	68.7	71.9
East-North-Central	84.2	73.0	80.6
West-North-Central	71.6	68.8	75.2
Solid South	5.1	2.8	1.2
Border States	43.3	35.5	37.1
Mountain States	57.9	60.3	43.5
Pacific States	74.6	79.9	74.5
Nation	60.2	53.4	52.9

SOURCE: Derived from Jerome M. Clubb, "Party Coalitions in the Early Twentieth Century," in Seymour Martin Lipset (ed.), *Party Coalitions in the 1980s* (San Francisco: Institute for Contemporary Studies, 1981).

Maryland, West Virginia, Kentucky, Oklahoma, and Missouri leaned toward the Democratic party but were much less secure. Elsewhere across the nation the Republican party dominated. There were rumblings of agrarian discontent in the West after the prolonged agricultural depression of the twenties; and in the Northeast, Democrats held pockets of power in such cities as Boston and New York where the urban political machines successfully organized the immigrant vote. But the distribution of partisan strength decisively favored the Republican party.

In the absence of survey research data, identification of the specific population groups that supported each of the parties is difficult. Unquestionably, white southerners provided the core of Democratic party support, and the Irish and the "new" immigrants from southern and eastern Europe who entered the nation in the decades surrounding the turn of the century constituted a second, if not altogether compatible, element of Democratic strength. Democrats also received spotty support from farmers after the McNary-Haugen agricultural bill was twice vetoed by President Calvin Coolidge. The nomination in 1928 of the Irish Catholic and city-bred Alfred E. Smith, however, was scarcely the choice to capitalize on long-simmering agrarian discontent.

Republican party support could be characterized, with only slight exaggeration, as a "coalition of substantial, stable, middle class, Protestant, and native-stock Americans."[7] Farmers outside the South generally remained within the Republican party, partly because Republican farm-belt congressmen at least attempted to address their grievances while the Democrats were too divided to capitalize on their dissatisfactions. William McKinley's promise of a "full dinner pail" and his courting of the Catholic vote were successful in garnering the support of industrial labor early in the twentieth century. By the decade of the 1920s, however, the Catholic immigrant labor contingent was lost to the Republicans.[8] The larger the proportion of foreign stock in the nation's cities, the less successful was the Republican party. Increasingly nativist in outlook, the Republican party carried the image of respectability, privilege, and Protestantism.

The distribution of partisan strength tells only part of the story during the 1920s. Voting participation was high in the latter part of the nineteenth century, with over 90 percent of the electorate casting ballots in several northern states in the 1896 election. Thereafter, the rate of participation dropped until fewer than 45 percent of eligible voters went to the polls in 1920 and 1924. Several factors contributed to this decline.[9] The heavy wave of immigration in the early decades of the twentieth century introduced into the electorate groups that had neither a firm knowledge of contemporary American politics nor past ties to either party. Their children, who came of age during the twenties, had no inherited partisan affiliation. The enfranchisement of women created another group who were politically inexperienced, doubly so if they were of foreign stock. And although their number is difficult to estimate, some people stayed away from the polls because the two major parties did not address their needs. Whatever the cause, a large pool of uncommitted voters became available for mobilization in the late 1920s.

PARTY IDEOLOGY

The representation of early ideological differences between the Republican majority party and the Democratic minority party can be clearly seen in the presidential election of 1900 (see map, The Presidential Election of 1900). The power

The Presidential Election of 1900

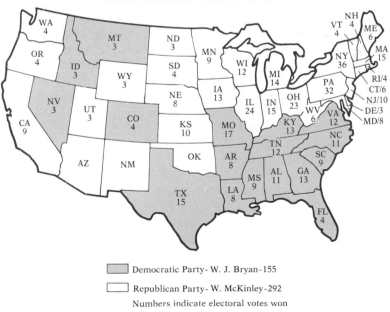

Democratic Party- W. J. Bryan-155

Republican Party- W. McKinley-292

Numbers indicate electoral votes won

of the Republicans stretched from Northeast to West; the strength of the Democrats was concentrated in the South and, to a lesser extent, in the border states, though Democrats did have influence in some Northeastern cities where the political machine flourished. But the reasons for these differences in partisan support need some explanation.

The Republican party championed the cause of private business. Under its sponsorship of private industrial development unfettered by government controls, the United States had changed from an agricultural society into an urbanized and industrialized nation. In the sense that its industrial nation building met the expectations of important segments of the public and was accorded popular approval, the Republican party was the progressive party during its reign from the close of the Civil War through 1928.[10] At the core of its philosophy was the belief that government should not interfere with the workings of private market mechanisms. Thus on December 19, 1930, Herbert Hoover told the Congress:

> Economic depression cannot be cured by legislative action or executive pronouncement. Economic wounds must be healed by the action of the cells of the economic body—the producers and consumers themselves.[11]

The Democratic party was too divided during the twenties to serve as a viable party of protest. The convention contest of 1924 is illustrative. Northeast, urban, Catholic, and wet (anti-Prohibition) elements of the party rallied behind Al Smith. The southern wing of the party—rural, Protestant, and dry—threw its support to William McAdoo. After 102 ballots failed to nominate a candidate, the convention compromised on John W. Davis, a counsel to J. P. Morgan. Davis's association with the business and financial world scarcely qualified him as a serious reform candidate.

The division within Democratic party ranks continued through 1928, when Smith was successful in his bid for the nomination. Reared in the East Side tenements of New York, Smith might have been more credible than Davis as the leader of a reform-minded party, but he had some serious limitations. With an accent that announced his New York origins, he had difficulty in convincing the farm belt that he understood the plight of the farmer. A Catholic who repudiated his party's dry platform plank, he was doubly damned in the rural Protestant areas of the South and Midwest. And he took pains to reassure business and financial interests that he embraced none of the "radical" proposals of the 1924 Progressive party candidate, Robert M. LaFollette. Only in the cities—and there because the issues were Catholicism and Prohibition—did Smith make dramatic gains.[12] Democratic candidates for lesser offices did not enjoy similar success.

Through 1928, then, the Republican party maintained its majority status. The times were generally prosperous. Only the farmers had been hard hit financially by the prolonged agricultural depression. Protest was there, but it was weakly articulated in the alternative programs championed by the major parties.

The Roosevelt Realignment

Hoover had scarcely settled into office when a stock market crash precipitated a depression of unprecedented magnitude. Great numbers of investors had purchased stocks on credit that they did not have the cash to cover. With the first drop in prices, speculators began to unload their holdings, a panic ensued, and a few days after "Black Thursday" the value of stocks listed on the New York Exchange had fallen by one-third. Some optimists reasoned that the collapse of the market had little relation to the underlying soundness of the American business structure. Hoover requested the nation's business leaders to maintain production and employment. But as prices dropped, plants curtailed production and laid off workers. Prices dropped lower, the economic slide continued, and seven million workers were idled in 1931. By 1932, the number of unemployed had risen to twelve million. A full-scale economic disaster was in progress.

Given the enormity of the crisis and Hoover's limited recovery program amid demands for government action, nothing save a divided opposition could have continued the Republicans in power. That the Democratic party was the appropriate vehicle for reform was questioned by liberal intellectuals. Paul H. Douglas (later a prominent Democratic senator from Illinois) favored the creation of a new party because the Democratic party was "basically controlled by conservative Southerners and the corrupt political machines of the North."[13]

If a new party had challenged the Democrats as the party of protest, the division among opposition forces might have allowed Hoover to survive. But a third-party movement along the lines of the LaFollette Progressives of 1924 failed to develop. No obvious leader emerged to head such a challenge, and more importantly, Franklin Roosevelt headed the list of potential Democratic nominees and his progressive record as governor of New York held forth the promise of a reinvigorated Democratic party. Roosevelt had won the 1928 election when Al Smith failed to carry his home state. In 1930, Roosevelt was reelected with an even more impressive plurality. After some bitter wrangling at its convention, the Democratic party nominated Roosevelt.

All classes had suffered under the Depression—poor and rich, farmers, laborers, and factory owners—and thus all were receptive to change. Roosevelt did not have a clear idea of what was needed to lift the Depression—at the beginning, he was rather orthodox in his economic thinking and agreed with Hoover that relief was a responsibility of state and local governments—but he did promise to work out a "new deal" for all groups. On election day, his popular-vote margin was 57.4 percent and he carried every state but Connecticut, Delaware, Maine, Pennsylvania, and Vermont (see map, The Presidential Election of 1932). The Democrats won a 193-seat plurality in the House and enjoyed a 24-seat plurality in the Senate.

The Presidential Election of 1932

Democratic Party–F. D. Roosevelt–472

Republican Party–H. C. Hoover–59

Numbers indicate electoral votes won

The forces of change had captured the Democratic party at the same time as it had gained majority status. By personality and temperament, Roosevelt was an activist, but he did not act alone. His Congress was not a rubber stamp, but the originator of important legislation of its own. Together their pace was feverish. The period of unbridled capitalism was over, and in its place the era of government intervention in the economy to provide economic security was inaugurated. A new political agenda, managed by the Democratic party, emerged.

CONTINUITIES WITH THE PAST

Clearly the severity of the economic crisis determined the outcome of the 1932 elections—what party could withstand an unemployment rate of 25 percent during its last years in office? but a single election is not adequate evidence that a realignment is in the making. For that, as we explained earlier in this chapter, voting patterns must persist into subsequent elections. The Roosevelt coalition did endure and influenced the character of political conflict for decades. But the new alignment did not signal a complete break with past voting patterns. There were continuities as well as changes.[14]

The White South. Since the end of Reconstruction, the South had been a bastion of Democratic party strength. The loyalty of southerners to the Democratic party had only been strained when they were called upon to support Al Smith. To vote for a Catholic and a wet was more than many could swallow in a region dominated by nativist stock and fundamentalist religions. Even so, Smith carried six of the eleven states of the old Confederacy.

The southern electorate in the 1930s was white (too few blacks were enfranchised to constitute a significant electoral force), and white southerners were not at all uncomfortable with Roosevelt and his New Deal programs. Predominantly an agricultural society, the South had little in common with the party of Lincoln and its promotion of business interests. Like other regions of the country, the South had been hit hard by the postwar agricultural depression. The Rooseveltian farm program of price supports for cotton, rice, and tobacco provided direct aid to southern farmers and federal relief programs aided the economically dislocated. So Dixie provided solid support for Roosevelt, and it would be some years before its allegiance to the Democrats would become ambiguous.

Catholics and Protestants. In a nation built on successive waves of immigration, the influence of ethnic rivalries on partisan alignments should not be unexpected. Often partisan attachments were less based on the great issues of the day than on such ethno-cultural issues as Sunday observance and Prohibition.[15] Although the election of 1932 did not rest on whether one could buy a legal glass of beer, long-term loyalties have a way of persisting and coloring people's perceptions of the political world. If it is understood that the terms convey general ethno-cultural rather than specifically religious values, the terms Protestant and Catholic can be usefully employed to portray a general pattern of ethnic rivalry.[16] Viewed in this fashion, the attachment of Catholics to the Democratic party can be traced to the nineteenth century when Democratic opponents, first the Whigs and later the Republicans, drew disproportionate support from Protestants.

The pattern of immigration in the first three decades of the twentieth century decidedly favored the Democratic party. Between 1900 and 1914, thirteen million immigrants poured into the country to settle mainly in the cities of the East and Midwest.[17] These immigrants were not the by then familiar English, Irish, Germans, and Scandinavians of northern European stock, but the peasantry of southern and eastern Europe. Most of them were Catholic, but a substantial number were Russian and eastern European Jews. If they needed an impetus to drive their partisan loyalties toward the Democratic party, it came in the form of a series of immigration acts passed under Republican administrations in the 1920s. These acts first set quotas which discriminated against nationals from southern and eastern Europe, and then limited the absolute numbers arriving from all of Europe to 150,000. Nativist fears that the country could not assimilate such a polyglot group caused a revival of the Ku Klux Klan, an organization dedicated to the preservation of the racial and ideological purity of Anglo-Saxon Protestant America. Its wrath was turned principally on Catholics, Jews, and blacks. Even the conservative Democratic nominee Davis had denounced the Klan in 1924, and Al Smith's opposition to it was well known. If the most recent wave of immigrants were ignorant of nineteenth-century immigration squabbles with their undercurrent of anti-Catholicism, they could scarcely have been unaware of the developments of the twenties.

It was not simply the new immigrants' numbers which were important to the politics of the 1930s, it was also their birth rates. Immigrant couples had, on the average, larger families than the more nativist stock. Two and a half times as many unskilled workers as businessmen had a family size greater than five; miners and laborers had twice the number of children as bankers.[18] The children of the immigrants who came earlier in the century were reaching voting age at about the time the Depression hit. Their memories of a deprived childhood were sharpened and they, too, were ready for a "new deal."

The ethno-cultural factor was often associated with class divisions. Many of the newer immigrants worked at low-paying unskilled or semiskilled jobs, while northern European Protestants dominated business and finance. But it would be a mistake to underestimate the potency of ethno-cultural factors alone. Upper-status white Protestants, outside the South, voted for Republican candidates more frequently than upper-status Catholics. Catholic blue-collar workers were more Democratic than their Protestant counterparts.

Northeast Republicans. Through the 1928 elections, the Republican party had maintained its dominance in all regions of the country excluding the South and the border states. After the 1932 election, the Republican party enjoyed no regional hegemony comparable to that of the Democratic party in the South during the period 1896–1928. Six states of the Northeast did stay with Herbert Hoover in 1932, but only Maine and Vermont cast their electoral votes for Alfred M. Landon in 1936. Yet middle- and upper-class white Protestants continued to favor the Republican party throughout the thirties. It was these voters that sustained the GOP, and their allegiance in the Northeast was more reliable than in other regions of traditional Republican support.

That northeastern Protestants were the main supporters of the Republican party during the early years of the New Deal is not surprising. Industrialization had begun in the Northeast and its leaders were Protestant businessmen. The region had prospered under their leadership and the rule of the Republican party, and many people had got into the habit of looking to the Republicans for economic progress. At the same time, the Democratic party had gained a toehold in the immigrant wards organized by the urban political machines. Under these conditions, ethnic rivalry was sharply etched, and it reinforced partisan affiliations.

NEW VOTING PATTERNS

If voting patterns had remained unchanged, the Democratic party would not have emerged with majority status during the 1930s. The changes that took place were of two sorts. Some who had not participated in electoral politics now joined the fray, disproportionately on the side of the Democrats because they followed the partisan loyalties of their co-ethnics. The largest pool of new voters was the immigrant population: those who were recently naturalized, women who were newly enfranchised, and children coming to voting age. These new voters contributed importantly to the Democratic victory.

But it was not simply the mobilization of former non-participants that produced a political realignment. Hoover's popular vote declined from 21.4 million in 1928 to 15.8 million in 1932, at the same time that the number of voters increased by 3 million. Obviously, voters who had formerly supported the Republican party had changed their allegiance. The three principal groups of switchers were blacks, Jews, and the working class.

Blacks. From the conclusion of the Civil War until World War I, the black population was heavily concentrated in the South. Although blacks had the opportunity to vote during Reconstruction and for a short time thereafter, the passage of discriminatory laws in the 1890s left all but a handful of them disenfranchised. The southern black vote, then, was a negligible factor in the formation of the New Deal Democratic coalition.

Beginning with World War I and continuing through the twenties, blacks migrated northward in search of economic opportunities. The exodus was momentarily halted during the Depression, but was renewed during and after World War II. Although a small minority, blacks in northern industrial cities had an opportunity for significant political participation. Their loyalty was to the party of Lincoln,[19] and although their privations during the early years of the Depression must have been great, they continued their allegiance to the Republican party through 1932. Beginning in 1936, blacks began their exodus from the Republican party. But this conversion was not the result of any concerted effort by the Roosevelt administration to attack racially discriminatory practices. Rather, blacks were attracted to the party by its policies of relief to the jobless and the hungry. Their affiliation with the Democratic party was to become increasingly important in the post–World War II years.

Jews. Close to two million Jews were included among the influx of immigrants from eastern Europe in the first two decades of the twentieth century. Most settled in the cities of the Northeast, many in the tenements of New York. Although they never constituted more than a small percentage of the total population, Jews were so regionally concentrated that in states like New York their electoral power was significant. More than the other ethnic groups with whom they arrived, Jews were able to attain social and economic success that, in later years, enhanced their political influence. Today they are important contributors to Democratic party strength.

Available evidence suggests that most Jews voted for the Republican party before the New Deal.[20] Although a majority may have supported Wilson in 1912 and 1916, analyses of wards with heavy Jewish concentrations reveal substantial support for Republican presidential candidates in the 1920s. Sometime in the 1930s, the Jewish vote switched dramatically to the Democratic party, where it has stayed.

A number of theories have been offered to explain why the Jewish vote became predominantly Democratic.[21] Certainly part of the explanation rests with the immediate benefits they enjoyed from Roosevelt's recovery and relief programs. Roosevelt's early condemnation of Nazi Germany was also a contributing factor. At the core of Jewish support for the Democrats, however, might be their own history of repression, engendering in them a sympathy for the economically downtrodden and socially dispossessed. That the Democratic party was clearly the party of reform in the 1930s supports such a contention.

The Working Class. Neither the blacks' nor the Jews' switch in party allegiance alone can explain the precipitous fall from power of the Republican party. The explanation for the new majority status of the Democratic party in the 1930s has to be sought in the cities. Outside of the loyal South, Democratic candidates before 1932 polled heavily in urban places but usually lost the countryside to their Republican opponents.[22] The urban strength of Democrats was clearly shown by Al Smith in the 1928 election. Still, it is questionable whether the votes he garnered would have remained with the Democratic party had it not been for the Depression, particularly if Democratic candidates with less appeal to urban immigrants and their children had been nominated.

If it was in the cities that the Democrats gained their edge, the vanguard of that surge was the urban working class. Unquestionably the Depression magnified the advantage the Democrats already enjoyed among Catholic working populations: some Catholic workers switched their allegiance from the Republicans to Roosevelt, and others, particularly among the immigrant populations, entered the ranks of voters for the first time. But working-class Protestants also turned their support to the Democratic party. Ethno-cultural rivalry had not been obliterated, but it had been submerged. "Put crudely," political analyst Samuel Lubell writes, "the hatred of bankers among the native American workers had become greater than their hatred of the Pope or even of a Negro."[23] So the Depression fostered a degree of working-class consciousness that partially overcame racial and religious antagonisms. The formation of the CIO and its organization of the mass-production industries was tangible proof that native stock and immigrant elements could be forged into an effective alliance.

The New Deal party system organized voters along class lines on the basis of a new role for government. Disadvantaged classes favored the use of government power to alleviate economic hardship and to regulate the economic system, while business and other advantaged classes opposed such a heavy intrusion into the private economic sector. Class lines had not been so clearly drawn since 1896.[24] But though class polarization accounted for much of these voting shifts, and thus aptly characterizes the realigning era, the extent of class conflict

Table 2-2
DEMOCRATIC PRESIDENTIAL VOTE OUTSIDE THE SOUTH BY SOCIOECONOMIC STATUS AND RELIGION, 1936–1940

| | 1936 | | 1940 | |
	White Protestants	White Catholics	White Protestants	White Catholics
High SES	35%	69%	20%	42%
Middle SES	48	81	32	58
Low SES	60	83	49	74

SOURCE: Derived from Everett Carll Ladd, Jr., with Charles D. Hadley, *Transformations of the American Party System*, 2nd ed. (New York: Norton, 1978), p. 69.

must not be overdrawn (see Table 2-2). Low-status white Protestants outside the South, for example, gave a slim edge to Republican Wendell Willkie in the 1940 presidential race.

The Persistence of the New Deal Coalition

Entry into World War II temporarily halted domestic social reform as the nation became preoccupied with the war effort. The style of conflict generated by the New Deal party system, however, was to linger until the 1960s, when under the pressure of new political issues that cut across traditional loyalties, the old party coalitions began to disintegrate. In the intervening years, however, the New Deal party system persisted and was extended.

Although the legacy of New Deal politics was to establish the Democratic party as the party of governmental activism, the sharpness which in the past had distinguished the parties was gradually blunted. The landslide defeat of Alfred M. Landon in 1936 demonstrated to the Republicans that they could not stubbornly continue to resist all New Deal programs. Shunning their more conservative candidates, they nominated Wendell Willkie in 1940, turned to Thomas E. Dewey in 1944 and 1948, and finally achieved the presidency with the popular Dwight D. Eisenhower in 1952 and 1956. At the same time, the nation had recovered from the throes of the Depression and was enjoying prosperity. Many who had existed on the edge of poverty during the 1930s had become middle class, so in a sense, the very success of the Democratic party appeared to threaten its electoral base. In response, Democratic candidates softened their class rhetoric and also began moving toward the center during this period.

Although the memory of the Depression had grown dim and the program differences between the parties was tempered, the underlying social group composition of each party was reflective of, if not identical with, the patterns set in the 1930s. Blacks and Jews, who had converted to the Democratic side, continued to provide healthy majorities to Democratic party candidates. Catholics voted disproportionately Democratic, particularly in congressional races, although many found the candidacy of Eisenhower attractive. When a co-religionist, John F. Kennedy, was nominated in 1960, Catholics gave him overwhelming support.

Class conflict within the electorate, ameliorated somewhat during the war years, was revived by Harry Truman in 1948, declined during the Eisenhower years, and increased marginal-

Table 2-3
DEMOCRATIC VOTING OUTSIDE THE SOUTH BY
SOCIOECONOMIC STATUS AND RELIGION, 1948–1960

	1948		1952		1956		1960	
	Pres.	*Cong.*	*Pres.*	*Cong*	*Pres.*	*Cong.*	*Pres.*	*Cong.*
White								
Protestant								
High SES	21%	22%	19%	21%	22%	30%	18%	16%
Middle SES	33	35	32	39	31	39	36	41
Low SES	57	53	39	51	42	54	52	52
White								
Catholic								
High SES	36	35	30	36	35	56	62	58
Middle SES	58	56	53	61	49	66	76	75
Low SES	74	74	61	70	51	74	85	80

SOURCE: Derived from Everett Carll Ladd, Jr., with Charles D. Hadley, *Transformations of the American Party System*, 2nd ed. (New York: Norton, 1978), p. 123.

ly in the 1960 contest.[25] Part of the difficulty in assessing class conflict in election contests is its entanglement with the religious factor in voting choices. In 1948, when Truman won on the basis of a "bloody shirt" revival of class animosities of the previous decade,[26] class was more salient than religion. The reverse was true in 1960, when Kennedy's religion influenced the choice of many voters. The combination of the two factors in differentiating the vote is impressive, as Table 2-3 attests. Outside the South, high-status white Protestants supported Republican presidential and congressional candidates at a level that did not dip below 70 percent. The support of Democratic party candidates by low-status northern Catholics, excluding the Eisenhower presidential contests, was equally high.

The New Deal coalition began to crack in the late 1940s. What became the most enduring change occurred in the South, precipitated by a racial controversy. The nation's first goal, Truman proclaimed in his State of the Union message to Congress in January of 1948, was "to secure fully the essential human rights of our citizens."[27] He followed his pronouncement with a series of civil rights proposals that included fair employment, antilynching, and voting rights measures. Later that year at the Democratic convention, a relatively mild civil rights plank endorsed by the White House was strengthened on the floor by northern liberals led by Hubert Humphrey. The entire Mississippi delegation and half of the Alabama delegation walked out.

After assembling in Birmingham in July, disaffected Democrats—called Dixiecrats—nominated Governors J. Strom Thurmond of South Carolina and Fielding Wright of Mississippi as their presidential and vice presidential candidates. Their strategy was to capture state party machinery and place the Thurmond-Wright ticket on the ballot as the Democratic choice. Where the strategem was successful—in South Carolina, Alabama, Mississippi, and Louisiana—the Dixiecrats also captured the electoral votes. Where Democratic loyalists retained control of the party, Truman won.

The revolt of the Dixiecrats began a long-term dissolution of southern white allegiance to the Democratic party in presidential elections. Southern Democratic support eroded further when high-income city and suburban areas supported the candidacies of Eisenhower and then Nixon. But the regional loyalty of the South to the Democratic party did not crumble immediately. Through 1960, Democratic presidential candidates captured the electoral votes in a majority of the states of the Confederacy. It was only after the 1960 elections that Republicans captured more than seven congressional seats in the South. To this day, a substantial proportion of southern whites continue to claim Democratic party identification.

The restiveness of the South was not the only indication that Democratic party support had frayed about the edges. Eisenhower won impressively in most regions of the country in 1952 and 1956. Still, his victories did not signal the end of New Deal politics. For one thing, the general was a man of immense popular appeal. For another, he had no prior political experience, which also meant that he had not alienated any sizable voting group. Indeed, his political views were so vague that some Democrats had hoped he might be induced to replace Harry Truman as the Democratic nominee in 1948. And the fact that Eisenhower battled conservative Senator Robert A. Taft for the Republican nomination indicated that the general's sympathies were with the more moderate wing of the Republican party.

The Democratic party was not without its problems in the first Eisenhower contest. Wracked by scandals, charged with softness on communism, and confronted by an increasingly unpopular war in Korea, the party could not produce a candidate with the personal magnetism to overcome these deficits. The urbane and witty Adlai Stevenson was ill-equipped to campaign in the hot-tempered fashion of a Harry Truman, but he made no less of an appeal to partisan loyalties. His call went unanswered, however, and the Democrats lost the presidency for the first time since 1928.

Eisenhower made inroads into the normal Democratic vote in all regions of the country: Northeast, Midwest, South, and West. Yet the distribution of the vote, as we observed earlier, followed the religious and class lines of the 1930s. Thus more than any other factor, Eisenhower's victory was a personal triumph, a deviating rather than a realigning election. Basic partisan attachments remained unchanged, and in 1960, the Democratic party was "reinstated" to power.[28]

Disorder Within the System

The strategies of a majority party necessarily differ from those of a minority party. As the majority party since 1932, the Democratic party had every reason to continue to exploit the issues that brought it to power and to straddle those that divided its adherents. Republican strategy was to make the most of issues that crosscut traditional loyalties.[29] The Vietnam war and the social turbulence of the 1960s offered opportunities to the Republicans, but only if they could adopt the popular side in both of these controversies and link the Democrats to the unpopular side.

In the eight-year period from 1964 to 1972, the political fortunes of the Democratic party swung dramatically from the landslide victory of Lyndon Johnson to the humiliating defeat of George McGovern. Republicans captured the White House in 1968 and 1972, but unlike Eisenhower in 1952, Richard Nixon was unable to carry a Republican Congress in with him. Even with the devasting loss by McGovern in 1972, the Democrats managed to dominate contests below the presidential level. The old Democratic coalition had fallen into disarray, but the Republicans were unable to capitalize on it. By 1976, the Democrats had been temporarily restored to power.

THE RISE OF THE SOCIAL ISSUE

At some point in the sixties, a new set of national concerns emerged to displace—temporarily at least—the primacy of economic concerns in the minds of voters. Labeled the "social issue," this new voter interest was compounded from several developing controversies[30] and its potential for precipitating partisan realignment was great.

Part of the social issue involved the perennial American question of race, only it took on a new cast. Even in the South, attitudes toward school integration had softened and a majority of southern parents reported by 1970 that they would not object to sending their children to a school where half the students were black.[31] The image of neatly dressed black schoolchildren being escorted to class by federal marshals while national guard troops protected them from jeering crowds elicited sympathy from all but the most hardened racists. But the picture of frenzied black looters ransacking stores while policemen stood idly by and a city was consumed in flames was an altogether different matter. Neither image was an accurate portrayal of race relations in America, but both were seen by millions on their television screens and the image of the urban riots was the more recent and impressive.

"Crime in the streets" and "lawlessness" were additional components of the social issue. Murder, rape, robbery, and aggravated assault rose sharply during the 1960s and many people found it easy to link the crime issue to that of race because blacks committed a disproportionate share of violent crimes. The riots by blacks in Los Angeles, Chicago, Detroit, Newark, Washington, and elsewhere further alarmed and angered the white middle classes. As Sundquist observed, "law and order was a *separable* issue from race, but it was not always a *separated* issue."[32]

Even Vietnam could be linked to the social issue. It was not the Vietnam war per se that intertwined with race and crime to form a new set of voting issues, but, rather, the domestic violence, demonstrations, and dissension the war caused. It was the spectacle of the American flag being burned, universities being disrupted, and the "trashing" of property that followed some demonstrations.

The America that many people knew and believed in was changing as traditional moral values gave way to new life styles. Hair got longer as skirts grew shorter, drug use became commonplace, and pornography enjoyed legal protections. Above all else, the 1960s were a time of social change, and those changes were profoundly disturbing to many who cherished the America of their childhoods. The social issue would only work to Republican advantage if the Democrats could be blamed for the turbulence it created. Of course, Democratic candidates would not willingly accept such a responsibility. Although it undoubtedly cost them votes, the damages to the Democratic party were not lasting.

Barry Goldwater attempted to capture the social issue when he told the 1964 Republican convention:

> ... Tonight there is violence in our streets, corruption in our high offices, aimlessness among our youth, anxiety among our elderly, and there's a virtual despair among the many who look beyond material success toward the inner meaning of their lives. ....[33]

Then he proceeded to throw the social issue away by intemperate campaigning: striking out against Social Security, proposing the sale of the Tennessee Valley Authority, and suggesting that the decision to use nuclear weapons be given to field commanders in Vietnam. Goldwater placed himself so far outside the political mainstream that his election chances were slim from the outset.

Goldwater's appeal also came too early. The social issue was only gathering momentum in 1964. Beginning in 1965, crime and race relations shared top billing with Vietnam among the problems that most concerned Americans, a pattern that was to continue into 1970.[34] At the same time, protests against the war escalated. Ultimately, Lyndon Johnson found himself beset by problems he could no longer master, narrowly avoiding defeat by challenger Eugene McCarthy in the New Hampshire primary. Johnson announced early in 1968 his decision to withdraw from the nominating race.

The Democratic party's difficulties did not end with Johnson's decision to retire. The convention held in Chicago in 1968 was marked by unruly demonstrations against the war that were forcefully contained by the police. Amid chants of "the whole world is watching," demonstrators were clubbed and tear-gassed into submission. The action *outside* the convention halls was followed by the television audience as closely as the proceedings within and the majority sympathized with the Chicago police, not the youthful demonstrators.

Reactions to the antiwar protestors must be distinguished from attitudes toward the war itself. As late as 1968, sentiment for pulling out of Vietnam immediately was a minority position. However, in that same year, a clear majority for the first time believed that entering the war had been a mistake.[35] Johnson was opposed not only by those with moral objections to

American intervention but also by those who felt he had failed to use our full military power to secure an early victory.

Democratic candidate Hubert Humphrey was saddled not only with the unpopular Johnson war policies but the social issue as well. The Kerner Commission appointed by Johnson to investigate the causes of urban riots reported in 1968 that "white racism is essentially responsible for the explosive mixture which has been accumulating in our cities."[36] If Humphrey believed that urban crime and lawlessness had sociological roots—and it was clear that he did—he also knew that to advance such an explanation to a campaign audience would only strengthen Republican charges that the Democratic party was "soft" on law and order. So in speaking to the American Legion National Convention, Humphrey told the legionnaires that "rioting, burning, sniping, mugging, traffic in narcotics and disregard for the law are the advance guard of anarchy. They must—and they will—be stopped."[37]

Further, the Republican party could not reap all the benefits of the social issue in the 1968 election because there was a third-party candidate. Supporters of George Wallace, who ran under the American Independent party label, were clearly the most disturbed over such issues as protest marches, the speed of school integration, and the protections afforded those accused of crime. Nixon was perceived as the centrist candidate on the same issues, with Humphrey seen as more to the left.[38] Wallace's support peaked in September 1968, when 21 percent of a national sample preferred him over either Nixon or Humphrey. Thereafter, his popular support waned, but he still received ten million votes, 13.5 percent of the total cast. Pollster Louis Harris chronicled the decline of Wallace support:

> By the last week in October, the number who thought Wallace could handle law and order shrunk from 53 to 43 to 33 to 24 to 21% in consecutive polls. The number who viewed him solely as a regional candidate had grown from 34 to 39 to 44 to 49 to 57%. By the same token, the percentage who viewed him as a "racist" jumped from 40 to 51 to 59 to 67%, and those who looked upon him as an "extremist" rose from 51 to 56 to 62 to 69%. Conversely, his vote began to drop precipitously from 21 to 18 to 16 to 13%.[39]

If a three-way presidential race robbed the Republicans of the advantages of the social issue, the 1970 off-year congressional races posed no similar handicap. In a well-orchestrated attack on Democratic "permissiveness" led by Vice President Spiro Agnew, the Republican party attempted to rid the country of "radical liberals" whose voting records had contributed to the breakdown of social order. The efforts of the Republican party could only be judged a failure. Democrats made a net gain of eleven governorships and twelve House seats. In a year when most contested Senate seats were held by Democrats, the Republicans gained but two seats. Still, it was questionable whether the social issue played to either party's advantage.[40]

The social issue, together with the war policies side of Vietnam, continued as a dominant concern in the Nixon-McGovern contest of 1972. Although analysts differ over the specific role issues played in voting choices, the outcome was decisive. Democrats defected in great numbers to vote for Nixon, McGovern losing votes even among those who seemingly preferred his issue positions.[41] The outcome apparently hinged more on negative feelings about the personal qualities of McGovern as a leader than on the ability of the Republican party to stand on the popular side of the social issue, and Democratic successes throughout the nation contradicted the stunning Republican presidential victory.

The social issue as a dominant political force soon gave way to the drama of the Watergate scandals that saw first the vice president and then the president resign in ignominy. The Democratic party rode the wave of scandal to score heavily at all governmental levels in the 1974 off-year elections. In 1976, "normalcy" was restored. Economic issues once again dominated, partisanship was revived, and the Democratic party captured the presidency and continued its control of both houses of Congress. The social issue had been blunted as a tactic for realignment, and the public appeared more willing to tolerate, if not enthusiastically embrace, the changing mores and morals of society.

SHIFTING COALITIONS

To say that in the 1960s and 1970s the social issue failed to alter the balance of partisan forces is not to say that party coalitions remained unchanged. The Democratic party lost the once-dependable support of white southerners in presidential elections. Prompted by the civil rights stands of the party, white southern Democrats defected to third-party and Republican presidential candidates. Even Jimmy Carter, a native

Georgian, failed to secure a majority of their vote both in 1976 and 1980. Although the underlying racial appeal of the social issue may explain the voting behavior of many white southerners, such an explanation alone is inadequate. White southerners were becoming differentiated along class lines.[42] As the South became economically modernized, new managerial and technical classes provided Republican votes. The turn to Republicanism was not evident simply in presidential races; the monopoly the Democrats enjoyed in congressional, state, and local offices was also eroding. The Democratic party remained dominant below the presidential level, but the South's politics did not deviate so markedly from that of the nation.[43]

Status polarization within the electorate also displayed a secular decline in the post–World War II years. The erosion of class-based politics occurred less because the Democrats lost their hold on lower socioeconomic groups (although the social issue cut into their presidential majorities in 1968 and 1972) than because they gained support among upper-class groups, particularly in the Northeast. Had it been otherwise, the Democratic party would have ceased to be the majority party, for structural changes in the economy had precipitated a growth among white-collar groups and a decline among blue-collar workers. Table 2-4 shows the relationship between socioeconomic status and voting in congressional and presidential elections.

Table 2-4
DEMOCRATIC PROPORTION OF WHITE VOTERS BY SOCIOECONOMIC STATUS, SELECTED YEARS

	1948	1960	1968	1972	1976
Presidential Elections					
High SES	30	38	36	32	41
Middle SES	43	53	39	26	49
Low SES	57	61	38	32	53
Congressional Elections					
High SES	33	46	42	48	55
Middle SES	49	60	51	49	58
Low SES	63	66	55	54	68

SOURCE: Derived from Carll Ladd, Jr., with Charles D. Hadley, *Transformations of the American Party System*, 2nd ed. (New York: Norton, 1978), pp. 287 and 289.

The decline of status polarization in election contests was paralleled by a decline in the extent to which occupational class determines political attitudes.[44] Until the 1960s, low-status occupational groups were distinctly more receptive to government regulation of business and welfare spending than high-status groups. Different attitudes toward government intervention did not disappear in the 1960s, but they no longer followed occupational and income lines so clearly. While skilled workers and, to a greater extent, unskilled laborers continued to support the traditional economic and welfare policies of the New Deal, there was a growing acceptance of New Deal liberalism among the professional and business classes. Their willingness to tolerate industrial regulation and welfare state policies explains the upward expansion of the Democratic party's electoral base.

Attitudes on components of the social issue also did not follow occupational lines very clearly.[45] Skilled workers voiced the strongest opposition to school integration, and next to farmers were the least tolerant of urban riots and political demonstrations. Professional and technical groups, on the other hand, were among the most liberal in their attitudes toward these issues. That attitudes on the social issue crosscut those on more traditional New Deal policies contributed to the disarray within the electorate in the late 1960s and early 1970s.

If there was a lessening of the class basis of politics, the New Deal coalitions built along religious, racial, and ethnic lines still were not obliterated. Blacks, Jews, and Catholics remained disproportionately within the Democratic party. Blacks were the most pro-Democratic, particularly when it came to support of presidential candidates and northern congressmen. Jews also provided solid support for Democratic party candidates, and although their Democratic party identification had declined, the Republican party was not the beneficiary. Instead, the slight erosion of Jewish ties to the Democratic party was explained by a rise among Jewish Independents. In the case of both Jews and blacks, their partisan preferences were matched by their liberal attitudes on both economic and social issues.

The support of Catholics for the Democratic party was more complex. Although their loyalty was not so strong as that of blacks and Jews, they were still more Democratic than the electorate as a whole. But whereas Jewish and black Democratic party preferences could be explained on issue grounds,

"*How would you like me to answer that question? As a member of my ethnic group, educational class, income group, or religious category?*"

Drawing by Dana Fradon
© 1969 The New Yorker Magazine

Catholic support was seen as ripe for picking.[46] Nevertheless, in their attitudes on economic, welfare, and racial issues, Catholics were as comfortable with Democratic party affiliation as were Protestant Democrats. Both lagged behind the liberalism of blacks and Jews. On issues of sex, pornography, and abortion, however, Catholics were out of step with their fellow partisans. But as Andrew M. Greeley has shown, they would have been no more content as Republican party adherents.[47]

The Democrats' success in holding on to their traditional sources of party strength while broadening their electoral base meant that the cause of the Republican party had been hurt. Alterations in the social composition of the parties benefited the Republican party only in the South, where middle- and upper-income whites were abandoning the Democratic party and moving toward the Republicans. Northern white Protestants continued to give Republican candidates more support then the population at large. However, the decisive advantage the Republican party once enjoyed among middle- and upper-class white Protestants was gone. The tale was told most vividly by voting patterns in subpresidential contests: although individual Republican candidates were successful, the hegemony of the Democratic party in congressional and state races held firm.

A WEAKENED PARTY SYSTEM

The anomaly calling for explanation amid the general weakening of the Republican party was the strength it displayed in post–World War II presidential contests. Through 1976, Republicans won four postwar presidential contests and narrowly lost two others. Why were presidential elections but not congressional elections vulnerable to the issues and candidates of the moment? Phrased differently, why was partisan loyalty stronger in congressional than in presidential elections?

Much of the answer rests with the greater visibility of presidential candidates. Presidential campaigns are eminently newsworthy so the news media give them daily coverage. Although the depth of journalistic analysis may be questioned, the fact of candidate exposure is not. Moreover, television is an incomparable instrument for conveying personal traits and mannerisms. The voter who sees a candidate in action does not have to rely on partisan tutelage to make up his or her mind. Congressional elections do not receive comparable news coverage so voters are more likely to use partisan cues in evaluating the candidates.

Simultaneous Republican successes in presidential elections and Democratic victories in congressional races do not indicate a complete breakdown in partisan influences. The "normal vote" graphed in Figure 2-1 may be thought of as the vote cast solely on the basis of partisan identification. If party identification alone determined an election outcome, Democrats would have organized each Congress and won every presidential election since 1952. But this did not happen. Though the actual vote for House members did not deviate markedly from a normal or expected party vote, the presidential vote often did. Divergence from the normal vote was greatest when

Figure 2-1
DEVIATIONS OF THE REPUBLICAN VOTE FOR PRESIDENT AND CONGRESS FROM NORMAL VOTE EXPECTATIONS, 1952–1976

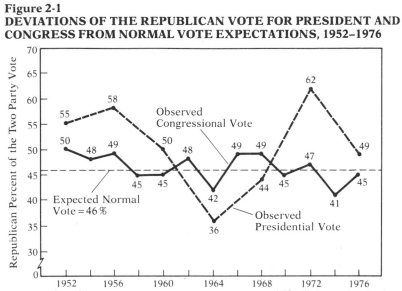

SOURCE: Warren E. Miller and Teresa E. Levitin, *Leadership and Change: The New Politics and the American Electorate* (Cambridge, Mass.: Winthrop Publishers, 1976), p. 41.

the presidential candidates were perceived as most distinctive. The Nixon-McGovern contest in 1972 is a case in point. However, voters did not move freely between the two parties in that election. Many Democratic party supporters rejected the McGovern candidacy, but 93 percent of Republican identifiers gave their vote to Nixon.

The pattern of a *two-tiered system* in which somewhat different popular majorities elect the Congress and the president is evidence of a weakened party system.[48] The outcome of a presidential election could be determined by a transfer of a relatively small proportion of the vote from one partisan column to the other. If the Democrats can "normally" expect 54 percent of the two-party vote, a defection rate of 10 percent among their ranks (5 percent of all voters) would theoretically give an election to the Republicans. Particularly in presidential races, enough voters feel capable of evaluating the candidates without the mediation of party to make a Democratic victory uncertain. At the same time, the electoral dynamics of congressional elections have worked in favor of the Democrats. Except for the 80th Congress under Harry Truman, Democrats have provided their presidents with congressional majorities since 1932.

The Contemporary Parties: Republican Ascendancy?

The disarray that characterized the electorate in the 1968 and 1972 presidential races gave way to more partisan voting in 1976. An economic recession accompanied by high unemployment and inflation turned the nation's attention from social and cultural issues, thus benefiting the Democratic party. The lingering effects of the Watergate scandals, symbolized in the public's mind by Gerald Ford's pardon of Richard Nixon, also worked to the detriment of the Republican candidate. Although Jimmy Carter lagged behind his congressional running mates, the Democrats were once again reinstated in the White House.

But whatever hopes the Democrats held for extending their reign as the majority party were dashed by the 1980 elections. The size of the Republican party victory came as a surprise to most political analysts—the Reagan-Bush ticket carried forty-four states, received 50 percent of the popular vote in a three-way contest, and amassed 489 electoral votes (see map, The Presidential Election of 1980). Republicans won majority control of the Senate for the first time in a quarter of a century, turning out such liberal Democratic stalwarts as George McGovern, Frank Church, Birch Bayh, and John Culver in the process. Further, with a net gain of thirty-three seats, Republicans were able to cut significantly into the Democratic House majority.

As in 1976, economic issues were once again the major concern of the public in 1980; however, this time they worked to the advantage of the Republicans. Reagan continually reminded the nation that worsening inflation, widespread unemployment, and high interest rates were the legacy of the Carter administration and the Democratic majority in Congress. Carter's failure to secure the release of American hostages held by Iranian revolutionaries also damaged the Democratic party's cause, and issues such as school prayer, busing, abortion, and women's rights determined how some people cast their votes. Still, it was the state of the economy that was the decisive issue of 1980.

Clearly voters had greater confidence in Reagan's ability to manage the economy than in Carter's. But what else did 1980 signify? Are the Republicans on the verge of becoming the majority party?

The Presidential Election of 1980

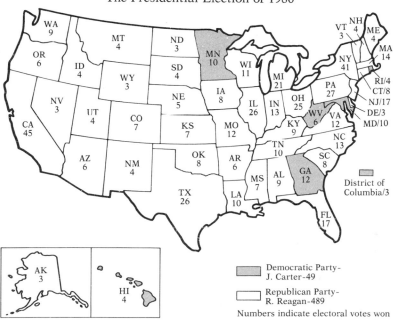

As we have seen, in 1952 Dwight Eisenhower led his party to national power, but Republican ascendancy proved short-lived: the partisan edge Democrats held within the electorate enabled them to regain control of the Congress in the first off-year elections. At the same time, Eisenhower made few attempts to roll back Democratic programs. A growing economy and modest inflation rates during most of the 1950s did not call for major Republican surgery. An immensely popular figure, Eisenhower won reelection in 1956 without enunciating a clear philosophical alternative to Democratic rule.

Economic conditions today have created a political climate that is quite different from the relatively prosperous and quiescent 1950s. One does not have to agree with Republican charges that the nation confronted an "economic Dunkirk" in 1980 to recognize that economic issues were uppermost in the minds of voters. Unlike Eisenhower, Reagan embarked upon a widely publicized program of cutting taxes and reducing government expenditures to turn the economy around. If the electorate judges him successful in his efforts, Reagan should be able to expand the Republican base of power.

Voters moved in a partisan direction in 1980—they vented their accumulated grievances *against* Carter and the Democratic party, not just against incumbents indiscriminately. All the same, the lasting effects of 1980 are uncertain. Democrats may have defected to Reagan and helped to defeat several incumbent Democratic senators, but they have not yet shed all their partisan habits. The 1980 election left Democrats with a majority in the U.S. House, twenty-seven of the nation's governors, and over three-fifths of the members of state legislatures. The Democratic party is waiting to reclaim its former position of power if the Reagan programs fail to satisfy the expectations of the public.

Ideological continuity with the past is found in the debate over the uses of federal power and resources. During the early New Deal, power at the national level was called upon to regulate the economy and to provide aid to the economically displaced. In later years, this same power was aimed at improving the quality of life by offering entitlements to women and to racial and ethnic minorities, increasing aid to the socially disadvantaged, and protecting people and their environment from the accumulated hazards of technological developments. In the minds of many of its supporters, the Democratic party has spearheaded the drive for necessary economic and social reforms. Its detractors see in the same efforts a regulatory stifling of free enterprise, an unwarranted curtailment of personal freedoms, a fueling of the fires of inflation, and an increasingly burdensome tax rate. The battle lines have been drawn, and they are not too far removed from their New Deal origins.

That the present-day coalitions of the parties reflect both continuities with the past and secular changes in their makeup is not remarkable. The nation has undergone a transformation since the decade of the 1930s. Amid increasing prosperity, the number of have-nots has been sharply reduced; the proportion of professional and technical classes has doubled since 1950, while the proportion of white-collar clerical and sales personnel has shown a less dramatic but still substantial increase. As the nation has prospered, the class rhetoric spawned by the New Deal has softened and new social, cultural, and environmental issues have gained the political agenda.

Yet the unparalleled growth in prosperity shows signs of stagnation, and herein lie both opportunity and danger for the

Republican party. An activist role for the federal government has survived the New Deal era and is widely accepted as appropriate in general, if not in specific, applications. Declaring federal activism excessive, the Reagan administration speedily moved to slim down the size of the federal government by imposing a hiring freeze and slashing departmental budgets. An alternative to Democratic rule has been articulated, and ultimately it will be the voters who will determine its success.

SUMMARY

The American party system is undergoing a transformation and the changes that are occurring can only be understood by a look backward into the nation's political history. A starting point for such a retrospective view is the classification of presidential elections. In a maintaining election, the basic partisan attachments that prevailed in the preceding election continue to determine the public's voting behavior. A deviating election occurs when short-term forces cause the defeat of the majority party's candidate, but voters still retain their traditional partisan identification. Finally, a realigning election signifies an enduring shift in partisan loyalties that, if widespread, can create a new party majority. Debate now centers on whether 1980 was a deviating or a realigning election.

From 1896 to 1932, a rigid sectional politics dominated the nation's political landscape. The Republican party enjoyed majority status and its power stretched from Northeast to West; the Democratic party's strength was concentrated in the South and, to a lesser extent, in the border states, although urban political machines gave it a toehold in some of the cities of the Northeast. The Republican party was preeminently the party of white Protestant middle- and upper-class America, whose commitment to industrial development had produced growth and prosperity. The Democratic party was too internally divided to constitute an effective alternative for disaffected groups.

The stock market crash of 1929 and the economic depression that followed brought down the Republican party.

Franklin Roosevelt led the Democratic party to power in 1932 and, with the aid of an activist-minded Congress, secured its continued success. In ideological terms, an era of private business operating without government restraints had ended. In political terms, a class-based politics had developed, tempered by ethnocultural and regional loyalties.

Although the Roosevelt victories realigned American politics, there were continuities with the past. White southerners continued to support the Democratic party, as they had since Reconstruction, and Catholics, whose Democratic party preference can be traced to the nineteenth century, also remained loyal. On the Republican side, white Protestants, particularly in the Northeast, continued to support their historical leaders.

On the other hand, there were many breaks with the past as well. Blacks deserted the party of Lincoln as they increasingly benefited from Rooseveltian welfare measures. Jews, too, shifted their support to the Democratic party, partly out of sympathy for Roosevelt's progressive policies, partly because of his early stand against the Nazis. Neither group was electorally significant in the formation of the New Deal coalition, but each was to become important to the party in later years.

It was the forging of a broadly constituted lower-class coalition that turned the tide for the Democratic party. Protestant workers joined Catholics and blacks in the newly created CIO, thus beginning labor's long association with the Democratic party. And the ranks of Democratic voters were swelled by the increased participation of immigrants from southern and eastern Europe who were drawn into Democratic party politics by the candidacy of the urban Irish Al Smith in 1928.

The essential elements of New Deal politics dominated the nation until the 1960s. Although reform came to a halt during World War II, the 1948 campaign of Harry Truman replayed the class rhetoric of the 1930s. Thereafter, class antagonism became muted, as the poverty-stricken people of the Depression advanced to middle-class status. The popular Eisenhower twice won the presidency for the Republican party and made inroads into the Democratic party's stronghold in the South, but his successes were not duplicated elsewhere for the Republicans. Kennedy restored the Democratic party to power in 1960, and his support reflected its New Deal flavor. Class lines were not as sharply etched as in the 1930s, but they had not disappeared—Catholics, Jews, blacks, and blue-collar workers accorded the Democratic candidate handsome support.

It was in the politically turbulent 1960s that New Deal alignments fell into disarray. Blacks rioted in the cities and left them in flames; antiwar demonstrators sometimes engaged in violent confrontations with police; law-and-order (which some said were code words for racism) became a popular issue; and a counterculture developed that directly challenged traditional moral values. The breakdown in public authority, with its underlying tone of racism, was labeled the "social issue," and it challenged more traditional economic issues for the attention of the voting public.

Saddled with the social issue and Johnson's war policies, the Democratic party again saw the presidency slip from its grasp. Nixon won a tight three-way race in 1968 and trounced McGovern in 1972. Republicans' efforts at rebuilding their party, however, were negated by the Watergate scandals and the recession of the mid-seventies. The Democratic party won the presidency in 1976, which added to its already secure control of Congress, state legislatures, and state governorships.

Although the Democratic party regained majority status, the political coalitions built in the 1930s did not survive intact. The class basis of politics diminished as Democrats extended their base upward to include substantial portions of the middle and upper classes. Republicans made inroads into Dixie, capturing a majority of white southerners in presidential races and becoming increasing competitive there in gubernatorial and congressional races.

But continuities abounded. Blacks, Jews, and Catholics continued to support the Democratic party in proportions greater than the electorate as a whole. So too did blue-collar workers. If anything, it was the Republican party that saw its core support dwindle. It no longer could count on middle- and upper-class white Protestants.

The Democrats' hopes of extending their reign were dashed by the 1980 elections. The full implications of 1980 are not clear because, while the Republicans gained the presidency and captured the Senate, the Democrats retained control of the House and held on to a majority of state offices. A realignment is a serious possibility, however, because Americans are aroused by economic stagnation and high inflation, unemployment, and interest rates. The widely publicized Reagan prescription for turning the economy around offers a clear alternative to the years of Democratic rule, yet the social and economic reforms spearheaded by the Democratic party retain their appeal among much of the electorate. It will be some time before we know whether the Reagan election signifies a realignment.

Notes

[1]Angus Campbell et al., *The American Voter* (New York: Wiley 1960), pp. 531–538.

[2]For a more restricted definition of realignment, see James L. Sundquist, *Dynamics of the American Party System* (Washington, D.C., The Brookings Institute, 1973), pp. 5–10.

[3]Campbell et al., *The American Voter*, p. 535.

[4]Norman H. Nie, Sidney Verba, and John C. Petrocik, *The Changing American Voter* (Cambridge, Mass.: Harvard University Press, 1976), p. 75.

[5]See V. O. Key, Jr., "A Theory of Critical Elections," *Journal of Politics* 17 (February 1955), pp. 3–18; and "Secular Realignment and the Party System," *Journal of Politics* 21 (May 1959), pp. 198–210.

[6]Sundquist, *Dynamics of the American Party System*, p. 8.

[7]Jerome M. Clubb, "Party Coalitions in the Early Twentieth Century," in *Emerging Coalitions in American Politics*, ed. Seymour Martin Lipset (San Francisco: Institute for Contemporary Studies, 1978), p. 70.

[8]See Sundquist, *Dynamics of the American Party System*, pp. 147–153.

[9]See Nie, Verba, and Petrocik, *The Changing American Voter*, pp. 76–77.

[10]Everett Carll Ladd, Jr., with Charles D. Hadley, *Transformations of the American Party System*, 2nd ed. (New York: Norton, 1978), p. 41.

[11]Quoted in Sundquist, *Dynamics of the American Party System*, p. 185.

[12]Ibid., pp. 111–112.

[13]Quoted in ibid., p. 190.

[14]The best single source of the continuities and changes in the party coalitions is Ladd with Hadley, *Transformations of the American Party System*. The author has borrowed generously from their analyses of survey data.

[15]Samuel P. Hayes, "Political Parties and the Community-Society Continuum," in *The American Party System*, ed. William Nisbet Chambers and Walter Dean Burnham (New York: Oxford University Press, 1975), p. 158.

[16]Ladd with Hadley, *Transformations of the American Party System*, pp. 46–47.

[17]Samuel Lubell, *The Future of American Politics*, 2nd ed. (New York: Anchor, 1956), p. 29.

[18]Ibid., p. 31

[19]Oscar Glantz, "The Negro Vote in Northern Industrial Cities," *Western Political Quarterly* 13 (December 1960), p. 999.

[20]Lawrence Fuchs, *The Political Behavior of American Jews* (Glencoe, Ill.: Free Press, 1956), chap. IV.

[21]See ibid., chap. XI.

[22]Sundquist, *Dynamics of the American Party System*, p. 200.

[23]*The Future of American Politics*, p. 49.

[24]Sundquist, *Dynamics of the American Party System*, p. 202.

[25]See Paul R. Abramson, "Class Voting in the 1976 Presidential Election," *Journal of Politics* 40 (1978), pp. 1067–1069.

[26]Sundquist, *Dynamics of the American Party System*, p. 216.

[27]Quoted in ibid., p. 248.

[28]Philip E. Converse et al., "Stability and Change in 1960: A Reinstating Election," *The American Political Science Review* 55 (June 1961), pp. 368–377.

[29]Sundquist, *Dynamics of The American Party System*, p. 309.

[30]Richard M. Scammon and Ben J. Wattenberg, *The Real Majority* (New York: Coward-McCann, 1970), chap. 3.

[31]Richard E. Dawson, *Public Opinion and Contemporary Disarray* (New York: Harper, 1973), p. 115.

[32]Sundquist, *Dynamics of the American Party System*, p. 323.

[33]Quoted in Scammon and Wattenberg, *The Real Majority*, p. 37.

[34]Ibid., pp. 37–39.

[35]Dawson, *Public Opinion and Contemporary Disarray*, pp. 34–37.

[36]Quoted in Sundquist, *Dynamics of the American Party System*, p. 326.

[37]Quoted in ibid., p. 327.

[38]Dawson, *Public Opinion and Contemporary Disarray*, p. 177.

[39]Quoted in Scammon and Wattenberg, *The Real Majority*, pp. 191–192.

[40]Sundquist, *Dynamics of the American Party System*, pp. 328–331.

[41]Warren E. Miller and Teresa E. Levitin, *Leadership and Change* (Cambridge, Mass.: Winthrop, 1976), p. 146.

[42]Nie, Verba, and Petrocik, *The Changing American Voter*, pp. 221–223.

[43]Sundquist, *Dynamics of the American Party System*, chap. 12.

[44]Dawson, *Public Opinion and Contemporary Disarray*, pp. 90–93.

[45]Ibid., pp. 95–99.

[46]Kevin P. Phillips, *The Emerging Republican Majority* (New Rochelle, N.Y.: Arlington House, 1970), p. 464.

[47]Andrew M. Greeley, "Catholics and Coalition: Where Should They Go," in *Emerging Coalitions in American Politics*, ed. Lipset, pp. 271–295.

[48]See Ladd with Hadley, *Transformations of the American Party System*, pp. 262–269.

3

The Party Role in States and Cities

The common tendency in describing American party politics is to focus on national struggles. Political analysts study the social composition of each party's electoral base to discover the nature of political divisions, to discuss new issues as harbingers of political realignments, and to dissect presidential initiatives and congressional responses for what they reveal about the tendencies of each party's leadership. This emphasis on national politics is not misplaced, for what the president and the Congress do is of great importance to the future of the nation.

But political parties are organized at state and local, as well as national, levels. Party organizations in the states have dual roles to perform. First, as subordinate units of a national system, they send representatives to the national conventions every four years to prepare party platforms and nominate presidential candidates. They also nominate members of Congress and campaign for their election, as well as for the national party ticket. In these ways, state and local officials are intimately involved in national party affairs.

In addition, the same party leaders often are concerned with both state and local governments. They recruit candidates, mobilize the electorate, and organize governments on the state and local levels. Sometimes they receive campaign related assistance from the national party, but the management of party affairs is largely in their hands.

Because of this, state and local parties have a life of their own, and their activities are the focus of this chapter. To determine the extent of state and local party importance, the central question to be explored is this: do the parties link citizens to their government in the way that Chapter 1 claimed they should? Although the variations that occur across the nation are too rich for detailed descriptions, comparative analyses are useful in isolating the effects of parties and understanding their role in governance.

Party Patterns in State Politics

National party alignments influence the electoral patterns found in state politics. Political analyst James Sundquist called the changes that occurred in the balance of party strength in the decades following Roosevelt's ascension to power in 1932 the "product of aftershocks to the political earthquake of the 1930s."[1] The changes to which he referred were the pro-Democratic trends in the North and the inroads the Republicans made into the Democratic stronghold of the South. This realignment took place in two stages, noticeable first in presidential voting, then later in registration figures and voting in subpresidential elections. The second stage of realignment in the North is virtually complete, but the process has not yet run its course in the South.

The aftershocks of 1932 tended to nationalize politics. Roosevelt's presidency created a new Democratic party that was "issue-oriented, working-class-based, even more urban-centered than before, activist, radical and wholly devoted to Rooseveltian leadership."[2] This transformation of the Democratic party did not appear suddenly in all political contests across the country. Conservative Senate holdovers in the East and Midwest, for example, were less supportive of Roosevelt than their southern Senate colleagues.[3] Support for Roosevelt in traditionally Republican areas of the North was not always accompanied by a Democratic vote for lesser offices. In fact, the second stage of New Deal realignment in the North was not completed until a new leadership of liberal activists took command of the state Democratic parties in the post–World War II years.

Political realignment in the South has been complicated by racial politics. Many southern voters have been attracted to the candidate whose racial views are compatible with their own.

This voting pattern was evident in white southern support for the third party candidacies of Strom Thurmond in 1948 and George Wallace in 1968. Nevertheless, class-based voting has been developing. Dwight Eisenhower's successes in the South were not due simply to his war hero fame. The higher income areas of city and suburb supported him, while working-class districts voted for Adlai Stevenson. This so-called metropolitan Republicanism has proved stable, but it has not reached the smaller cities and the countryside.

The realignment in the South, in Sundquist's terms, is far from complete. For this to happen, the divisions that have appeared in presidential politics must be carried over into state and local races. Southern Democratic leaders would have to moderate their conservative habits, conceding to the Republicans those voters who found the change unacceptable. As racial antagonisms recede, the potential for Sundquist's second-stage realignment appears ever more realistic. Nevertheless, Republican state organizations are not yet in a position to challenge Democratic party dominance of state offices in the South.

Even though there is a broadly conceived nationalizing trend in American politics, it would be a mistake to assume that national battles are fought out on a smaller scale at the state level. The assignment of constitutional responsibilities alone would make for differences. State governments have only limited influence over issues of transcendent national importance—the conduct of diplomacy, the size and nature of defense forces, and the management of the economy. Those responsibilities the states do have—in education, health, welfare, public utility regulation, and highway construction, for example—do not always produce political controversies that are synchronized with national party divisions. To some extent at least, the struggles to control state governments are fought over different issues.

A second and more important reason why party systems at the state level are not simply miniatures of the national party system is that variation rather than conformity characterizes state parties. It could scarcely be otherwise because, although they share a common national heritage, the states have been molded by their own distinct histories and political cultures. States differ in size and economic diversity, in the mix of rich and poor, black and white, and in the number and kinds of ethnic strains. The variations provide the ingredients out of which partisan politics are fashioned.

For these reasons, the party politics of states must be considered on their own merits. To make the task manageable, the performances of state parties will be measured against those of an idealized model of two-party competition. According to such a model, the party labels are a useful guide to voters in rewarding or punishing incumbent officeholders when four conditions are met:

1. The two parties would contest elections autonomously on the basis of issues that are within the power of state governments to control.
2. The two parties would compete on more or less even terms so there is the possibility of an alternation of power between the two sets of party leaders.
3. Each party would show some semblance of cohesion when it holds power.
4. The same party would organize both houses of the legislature and control the office of governor.

How frequently these conditions occur will be discussed in the pages that follow.

CAN STATE PARTIES OPERATE AUTONOMOUSLY?

Can a full-blown party politics, independent of outside forces, develop at the state level in a federal system? Ideally, the selection of a state's leadership should be free of external distractions. The isolation of state politics is impossible, however, because the American states are not autonomous political units but integral parts of a national political system.

One reason a state's party system cannot operate autonomously is that voting in state elections is influenced by national tides. Sometimes candidates at the state level are swept into office on the coattails of popular presidential candidates; other times they see their election hopes dashed by unpopular candidates at the head of the national ticket. The timing of state elections is thus an important component of electoral strategy. Only fourteen states today hold gubernatorial elections in a presidential election year. However, an additional thirty-one states elect governors at the same time as members of the U.S. House of Representatives. Although split-ticket voting is increasing, the available evidence suggests that the surge for the winning party nationally still benefits the state candidates sharing its label.[4]

Sometimes national issues are interjected into state contests. Republican candidates who sought state office in 1974 were saddled with the Watergate scandal; therefore, their losses were greater than would have been expected if each contest had been decided on the merits of the contenders. From time to time, presidents accept invitations to campaign for governors in off-year elections and the outcomes are seen as tests of presidential stewardship. Other evidence suggests that the popularity of a president may influence the gubernatorial choice of some voters.[5] In each instance of external influence cited, the connecting link is the party labels that national and state candidates share.

By its very nature, a federal system affects the character of state party systems. When issues of fundamental importance to a state or region can be decided only at the national level, they may inspire a solidarity that restricts the normal divisions occurring in state politics. The states of the old Confederacy have provided the most clear-cut illustration of this phenomenon. To protect the southern position on race relations, political contests in the South were long fought out within the Democratic party primary. V. O. Key, Jr. has written, "The party that functions as the sectional instrument becomes overwhelmingly dominant in state matters. The hopeless minority, although it may have a good cause locally, remains handicapped by the fact that it bears the name of the party that is the sectional enemy nationally."[6]

Though state party systems are clearly influenced by external forces, they have a vitality of their own. A number of related trends bode well for the significance of state party competition. Paradoxically, they have to do with the nationalization of politics. To the extent that state leaders frame political issues roughly as their national partisan colleagues do, a swing toward one party could be equally meaningful to national and state party politics.

The most obvious nationalizing trend has been the gradual decline of the sectional politics that arose in the aftermath of the Civil War. Sectionalism was destroyed first in the Northeast and the Midwest, and is currently weakening in the South. The urbanization and industrialization of formerly agricultural regions provides a base for organizing politics along the lines of national party divisions. Partly as a result of these changes in the structure of the economy, the nation's population has become increasingly mobile. Population movements have tended to erode peculiar state and regional political cultures. The national media also encourage a less provincial outlook. And as these forces are at work, what Sundquist called the aftershocks of the New Deal political alignment are being felt in state party politics.

The nationalization of politics is far from complete, and the variations that remain affect the nature and the performance of state party systems. It is to these differences that we now turn.

THE EXTENT OF TWO-PARTY COMPETITION

Discussions that stress the importance of the party role in democratic politics assume that the parties compete on more or less even terms. Less than twenty years ago, however, the foremost student of state politics surmised that reasonably competitive parties existed in only a third of the states.[7] Nationalizing trends since then favored the development of two-party competition, and today a good half of the states are reasonably competitive. As we shall see, the competition is keener in gubernatorial races than for legislative seats.

In attempting to assess the degree of party competitiveness, several factors must be kept in mind. A state may be competitive in presidential elections yet be dominated by a single party in its state elections. The measures of competitiveness, then, must be restricted to state offices since our interest is in state politics *qua* state politics.

A second consideration is the time span selected for measurement. Too short a period may distort the analysis by catching a party that is temporarily enjoying electoral success or suffering defeat as a result of transient forces. On the other hand, too lengthy a period may misrepresent competitiveness because certain conditions may no longer be applicable. States like Massachusetts and Rhode Island were controlled by the Republican party in the pre–New Deal period, but then became competitive during the heyday of the New Deal. More recently, the Democratic party has emerged dominant in those states, at least as measured by its control of the state legislatures.

In Table 3-1, the states are grouped by their partisan tendencies in gubernatorial and state legislative elections. Overall, the Democratic party holds the clear edge in state politics, an advantage that stems from the partisan edge the party still enjoys within the electorate. It is also readily apparent from the table that gubernatorial elections have become more competitive than state legislative contests. The

Table 3-1
STATE PARTY COMPETITION

| | Years of Party Control, 1961–1978† | | | | | |
| | Governor | | Senate | | House | |
State*	Dem.	Rep.	Dem.	Rep.	Dem.	Rep.
Dem. dominant						
La.	18	0	18	0	18	0
Ala.	18	0	18	0	18	0
Miss.	18	0	18	0	18	0
S.C.	14	4	18	0	18	0
Tex.	18	0	18	0	18	0
Ga.	18	0	18	0	18	0
Ark.	14	4	18	0	18	0
Dem. majority						
N.C.	14	4	18	0	18	0
Md.	16	2	18	0	18	0
Va.	9	8	18	0	18	0
Tenn.	14	4	18	0	18	0
Fla.	14	4	18	0	18	0
Haw.	16	2	16	2	18	0
Okla.	10	8	18	0	18	0
N.M.	12	6	18	0	18	0
Mo.	14	4	18	0	18	0
Ky.	14	4	18	0	18	0
W. Va.	10	8	18	0	18	0
R.I.	12	6	18	0	18	0
Competitive **two-party**						
Mass.	6	12	18	0	18	0
Nev.	14	4	12	4	14	4
Calif.	10	8	16	0	16	2
Alaska	10	8	10	6	14	2
Conn.	14	4	16	2	10	8
Mont.	10	8	16	0	8	10
N.J.	13	4	6	12	12	6
Wash.	6	12	18	0	12	6
Neb.	14	4	nonpartisan			
Oreg.	4	14	18	0	10	8
Minn.	12	6	nonpartisan			
Del.	12	6	10	6	10	8
Mich.	2	16	6	8	12	4
Pa.	10	8	8	8	12	6
Utah	14	4	8	10	8	10
Ariz.	6	12	10	8	8	10
Ill.	12	6	4	12	6	12
Wisc.	12	6	4	14	10	8
Ind.	8	10	8	10	4	14
Iowa	6	12	8	10	6	12

Table 3-1
STATE PARTY COMPETITION (continued)

| State* | Years of Party Control, 1961–1978† | | | | | |
| | Governor | | Senate | | House | |
	Dem.	Rep.	Dem.	Rep.	Dem.	Rep.
Competitive two-party						
N.Y.	4	14	2	16	8	10
Maine	8	6	2	16	6	12
Ohio	6	12	4	12	6	12
N.H.	6	12	0	14	0	18
N.D.	18	0	0	18	4	14
Rep. majority						
Ida.	8	10	0	18	0	18
Colo.	6	12	2	16	6	12
Kas.	10	8	0	18	2	16
S.D.	8	10	4	14	0	16
Vt.	8	10	0	18	2	16
Wyo.	6	12	0	16	2	16

*The states are listed according to the Ranney index of party competition (1962–1973), which gives equal weight to four factors: the average Democratic percentage of the gubernatorial votes; the average Democratic share of seats in the state senate; the average Democratic share of seats in the state house; and the percentage of terms the Democrats controlled the governorship and each legislative branch.

†Years of Democratic and Republican control do not total 18 when a legislative chamber had an equal number of Democrats and Republicans.

source: Derived from Malcolm E. Jewell and David M. Olson, *American State Political Parties and Elections* (Homewood, Ill.: Dorsey, 1978), pp. 34–35.

organizational requirements to contest a single statewide office are considerably less stringent than those necessary to field a slate of legislative candidates competitive enough to win a majority of seats. At the same time, gubernatorial candidates, being more visible, can trade on the new campaign style to overcome entrenched partisan attitudes. Not only is the office of governor more accessible to minority party challenge, it is the single most important state office to acquire. The power of the governor in shaping state policies is not the only consideration. The patronage that many states accord their governor provides a useful base for building a party organization.

With a few exceptions, the states that tend to be dominated by a single party reflect the vestiges of the pre–New Deal sectional alignment. The states of the Confederacy are a case in point. Most of the states that fought on the Union side (or were settled by Union loyalists) have succumbed to two-party competition. Why has the Democratic party monopoly in Dixie persisted longer than Republican party dominance north of the Mason-Dixon line? The best answer is that the states less affected by national forces of change are the most likely to retain traditional party loyalties.

The South lay outside mainstream America for three major reasons:

1. The immigrants who came to the nation in the first decades of the twentieth century and provided such a leveling influence on American society largely bypassed the South. The southern states were dominated by a planter class whose agrarian philosophy was antithetical to industrialization, and thus the region had no need for a cheap source of industrial labor. Blacks provided cheap labor for southern agriculture.
2. Partly as a consequence of its agrarian commitment, the South lagged behind the nation in both industrialization and urbanization. The nation became urban by census classification in 1920, the South as a region only in 1960.
3. A key to southern politics has always been the peculiar importance of race. Early attempts by southern Populists such as Tom Watson to portray economic issues as more important than racial divisions were unsuccessful. The South remained racially polarized because whites were willing to overlook differences among themselves and accept a planter-merchant-banker-lawyer ruling class.

Southern politics have undergone dramatic changes in the past decade or two, but the effects of heritage linger in the primacy of the Democratic party in state politics.

Northern Republican sectionalism, on the other hand, did break up under the onslaught of New Deal-style politics. Sectional solidarity gave way to issues based broadly on class-status lines. The heavy migration of people from southern and eastern Europe, urbanization and industrialization, and the deprivations of the Depression provided the stimulus for reordering traditional political loyalties. States that retain Republican tendencies are more likely to have nativist populations and to be less advanced industrially than the two-party states.

STATE VARIATIONS IN LEGISLATIVE COHESION

The fact that a state is classified as electorally competitive does not guarantee that its citizens can rely on a party label to locate the general policy positions of those who wear it. Even where parties contest elections on fairly even terms, the party label may provide few clues as to how legislators will line up with their partisan colleagues in support of legislative measures.

Partisanship in contesting legislative roll calls is associated with the more industrialized and urbanized states of the Northeast and Midwest, which are characterized by a heavy concentration of citizens of Irish and southern and eastern European extraction. The core of Democratic party strength comes from urban constituencies of industrial workers, Catholics, Jews, and blacks. Republican party support is centered in suburbia, rural areas, and small towns, and among the more nativist and Protestant groups of the population. By representing their constituencies, the parties have developed policy positions reasonably dissimilar and modeled along the lines of national party politics.

The two-party states of the mountain and western regions of the country exhibit less legislative partisanship than states such as Ohio, Pennsylvania, and Connecticut. One obvious difference between East and West is the greater number of industrial states east of the Mississippi. A more interesting phenomenon that may help to explain the differing levels of legislative partisanship is the salience of ethno-cultural factors. The immigrants who settled in the cities of the East and Midwest at the turn of the century contributed to a distinctive brand of politics based on the urban political machine. In contrast, the egalitarian influence of the frontier and its more sparse settlement fostered an individualism that eschewed partisanship in politics. The effects of these political styles still influence legislative partisanship today.

Some of the industrialized states of the Northeast and Midwest come closer than others to satisfying the tenets of party government. Although the contrasts are possibly exaggerated, John Fenton distinguishes between "job-oriented" states, in which the parties are mainly interested in the patronage and perquisites of officeholding, and "issue-oriented"

states, where the parties are concerned with contemporary
issues.[8] Fenton classified Illinois, Ohio, and Indiana as essentially job-oriented, and Wisconsin, Michigan, and Minnesota as
issue-oriented.

What is particularly interesting about Fenton's classification is that it is based on the motiviations for officeholding
rather than on the strength of party organizations. Party organizations are stronger in Illinois than in Wisconsin, for example,
but party voting is greater in the Wisconsin legislature.[9] Presumably, then, the issue-oriented states realize the beneficial
aspects of party government more than the job-oriented states.

THE FREQUENCY OF DIVIDED PARTY CONTROL

If party government is to prevail, the same party must control the governor's office and both houses of the legislature.
Otherwise, the majority party could be frustrated in its
legislative efforts. The surprising matter is the frequency of
divided party control. From the close of World War II until today, only four states—all in the Deep South—have escaped the
vicissitudes of sharing governmental responsibilities between
the two parties. Among the two-party states, a single party has
controlled both executive and legislative branches only about
half the time.

The election of a governor of one party and a house or senate of another is obviously the consequence of split-ticket
voting. But why do voters split their tickets? One explanation
is that some combination of the absence of the governor's coattails, lower voter turnout, and dislike of the gubernatorial program accounts for a shift in partisan control of one or both
legislative houses in a nongubernatorial election year. After
all, a midterm loss of congressional seats by the party controlling the presidency is common. The logic of this theory fades
when we realize that divided control between the governor and
the lower house is twice as likely to occur in a gubernatorial
election year as at midterm.[10]

There is a more valid explanation of split-ticket voting in
gubernatorial election years, and it is one we have already
touched upon: the party of minority status has a greater
chance of winning the office of the governor than of controlling
either house of the legislature. The gubernatorial success of
the minority party in formerly one-party areas, then, is likely

to result in divided party control. As northern Republican sectionalism broke up, Democratic governors were more likely than Republican governors to face opposition legislatures. The reverse is true in the South, where Republican governors have faced Democratic legislatures.

There is another explanation for the incidence of divided control. Before the court-mandated changes in apportionment in the 1960s, rural areas were overrepresented in the state legislatures and urban areas were underrepresented. This pattern of representation was a handicap to the Democratic party because, outside the South, its strength was usually concentrated in the cities while Republicans held power in the countryside. The number of Democratic voters sufficient to win the office of governor was often inadequate to gain control of the legislature. The opposite was true of the Republicans. A Republican gubernatorial victory commonly meant control of the legislature as well.

Court decisions on malapportionment have not eliminated all partisan tampering with the representative system. Two analytically distinct processes are commonly involved in reapportioning a state legislature: the carving out of district boundaries (more properly called redistricting); and the apportionment of representatives among the newly created districts (under court doctrine, in accordance with population). Unless designed to dilute the black vote, redistricting is left untouched by court decisions. In other words, the gerrymander is still legal as long as the standard of one-person, one-vote is met.

The gerrymander is a partisan device for carving out legislative districts in such a manner as to enhance a party's majority in the legislature. One technique is to create districts that concentrate the strength of the opposition party and cause it to waste votes in a kind of electoral overkill. An alternative is to spread the opposition party strength thinly across district boundaries in order to limit the number of seats it can gain. One New York legislator was heard to remark that he could carve out districts that were as compact as a cigar, would meet court tests, and still would improve his party's legislative chances.

A final explanation for split-ticket voting is the diminished importance of partisan voting. Today many voters evaluate the individual qualities of the candidates instead of automatically voting their partisan affiliation. Limited evidence suggests that these partisan defections are more common in gubernatorial elections than in state legislative races.[11] Such a finding is not surprising, since gubernatorial campaigns attract more public attention. However, two caveats are in order here: (1) split-ticket voting is more common where one party has been the dominant party historically; (2) and it takes only a limited amount of ticket-splitting to produce divided party government in competitive states.

The State Party Role: An Assessment

The evidence examined so far suggests that the role played by political parties at the state level varies from state to state. In some states, party competition is keen and vigorous; in others, one party consistently wins a majority of state offices. The legislative parties of some states are cohesive in support of party measures, while in other states, legislators cross party lines at will. Some states experience divided party control of government more than others. The question that begs asking is: Does this make any difference?

Proponents of responsible political parties assuredly would answer in the affirmative. The idea of a political party strong enough to write a legislative program and then stand accountable for it is appealing. Even though all state parties fall short of the ideal of responsible parties, some come closer to its realization than others. But is there empirical evidence to support the assumptions underlying the responsible party doctrine? In this section, we explore some of the answers to this question.

THE VALUE OF PARTY COMPETITION

The starting point of any assessment of party performance is a comparison of one-party states and competitive-party states. The single most important study of one-party states is the monumental effort of the late V. O. Key, Jr., *Southern Politics*.[12] Key focused on the states of the Confederacy in the late 1940s, but his study is valuable because it tells us much about the nature of state political parties in general. In Key's South, and to only a slightly lesser extent today,[13] factions, not parties, competed for power. A central question Key addressed was whether these factions were the equivalent of political parties elsewhere.[14]

The distinguishing characteristic of southern factions was their fluidity from election to election. The factions not only lacked a name or label, but they often displayed little or no leadership continuity. Under such circumstances, voters were bewildered. Constantly confronted by new faces arguing new programs, they had no better guide in making a voting choice than campaign promises.

Key further found that there was no contest between collective sets of leaders, no battles between the "ins" and the "outs." Unless an incumbent governor decided to run for reelection on his record, there was little focus to political debates. Legislative candidates, except in the Louisana ticket system, remained aloof from gubernational contests. Under these conditions, protest voting was frustrated because there was no firm target to praise or blame.

The absence of identifiable and continuing groups competing for power had other profound consequences. The recruitment of leaders suffered under an individualistic and disorganized politics. There were no party professionals to sift out those candidates whose extravagant tastes for the spectacular would harm the party's image. Campaigners concentrated on the immediate election without regard for the future of any collective undertaking. It was no accident, Key believed, that the South has had more than its share of demagogues.

The discontinuity of factional contests made government peculiarly susceptible to favoritism and the pressures of specialized interests. Unstable coalitions were held together by whatever means were within easy reach. "This contract goes to that contractor, this distributor is dealt with by the state liquor board, that group of attorneys have an 'in' at the statehouse, this bond house is favored."[15] It was not so much that these practices did not occur in two-party states, but there an organized party system was better equipped to deal with them simply because it was concerned for its existence beyond the immediate set of officeholders in power.

Loosely organized factions were in no position to organize the government toward any sustained program of action. Where every candidate ran an individual race, there were few common bonds between a governor and his legislature. The outcomes of public policy, however, did not fall randomly. If politics comes down to a battle between those who have and those who have less, as Key argued, then it is the have-less who suffer in a politics of disorganization. Because those leaders who promised reform did not have the political muscle to achieve it, the status quo was not easily affected in the South. And the preservation of the status quo benefited those who had already claimed their stake from society.

Key's findings were supported by Duane Lockard's study of New England state politics.[16] Key examined only the one-party South and drew upon his considerable knowledge of state politics to contrast factionalism with two-party politics. Lockard's analysis included both one-party and two-party states. In New England during the late 1950s, a single party dominated Maine, Vermont, and New Hampshire, while the parties were competitive in Connecticut, Massachusetts, and Rhode Island.

Lockard found that the politics and policies of the one-party state differed from those in the two-party states in precisely the ways that Key had described. The two-party states were more generous in their welfare policies. Their tax systems, although not models of fairness, were less regressive than those of the one-party states. And the effects of malapportionment were more often mitigated in the two-party states than in the one-party states. The explanation for this last finding turns on the collective nature of political parties. According to Lockard, Republican legislators from small towns in Rhode Island and Connecticut, and to a lesser extent in Massachusetts, had little to fear in their reelection bids. But if they hoped to reap the benefits stemming from control of the governor's office, they had to cooperate with their urban and suburban colleagues in supporting public policies that had statewide appeal. The state leadership was generally able to dissuade small-town legislators from embarrassing their party in statewide races.

Neither Key nor Lockard claimed that competitive parties were unsullied by political favoritism, corruption, or dishonesty. Nor did they believe that parties were always sensitive to popular pressures brought by disadvantaged classes. What they did argue was that responsive, accountable government is more likely to occur under conditions that favor two-party competition.

THE BENEFITS OF LEGISLATIVE COHESION

Although reasonably balanced two-party competition exists in only about half the states, there are but a handful of states where the majority party maintains such consistent electoral strength that it can afford to disregard an organized opposition. As we explained earlier, however, electoral competition per se does not advance the cause of party government. Voters who rely on party cues are misled if the legislative candidates they support do not back the governor when he is of the same party, or do not vote with their fellow partisans in the legislative assembly. The absence of discipline in the legislative parties defeats the basic concept of party as a cooperative endeavor and destroys the corporate accountability that is its goal.

Of course it can be said that voters are responsible for evaluating the individual candidates who run for state offices. Would it not be sensible for them to support legislative candidates who represent their interests? And would it not be equally rational for legislators to represent their constituencies rather than acceding to the demands of state leaders for conformity? Such an argument is not only theoretically appealing; it oftentimes explains the voting behavior of legislators. Still, the party leadership is not unmindful of its electoral support, and caters to it. Under which pattern are constituent interests better represented?

The present author examined the roll call votes of twenty-three nonsouthern state senates to see how well they reflected characteristics of the constituencies the legislators represented.[17] Included among the constituency variables were measures of income, race, ethnicity, education, occupation, and voting patterns. The roll calls studied were those in which a majority of one party opposed a majority of the other party. The result was this: the votes of legislators in states that exhibited the greatest amount of party cohesion were more closely tied to their constituencies than the votes of senators in states with less disciplined parties. In other words, constituency interests are not smothered by a system in which legislators are more or less faithful to their parties—they are enhanced.

There is an additional benefit accrued to states with disciplined parties, and it is in the management of governing processes. As at the national level, the chief executive is the keystone of a state's political processes. Governors cannot govern effectively if they are confronted by a shifting kaleidoscope of factions. If gubernatorial leadership is rejected, it matters little to the governor whether the opposition comes from his own or the other party. But if the governor's party can produce the legislative votes he needs to enact a program, the success of his administration can be judged on the quality of that program.

THE FRUSTRATIONS OF DIVIDED CONTROL

Even states with reasonably disciplined and competitive parties do not always provide the setting for party government. An additional requisite is that the same party control the office of governor and both houses of the legislature. As we have seen, the incidence of divided party control is more widespread than popularly suspected. In such a setting, disciplined party members could be more troublesome to the governor than free-spirited legislators.

Evidence supports the contention that divided party control frustrates state policy processes. Wayne Francis asked the legislators of the fifty states to list the most important problems they faced in a legislative session. He then asked them whether legislation intended to solve the problems had been passed. On the basis of the responses, a crude index of policy success (a passage-defeat ratio) was constructed. States with the highest index of policy success were those with unified party control, but in which the majority party's legislative plurality was small. States with the next highest policy success were also characterized by unified control, but the minority party held only token seats in the legislature. As expected, policy success was lowest for those states in which the governor faced opposition party control of one or both houses of the legislature.[18]

THE EFFECTS OF THE POLITICAL ENVIRONMENT

Our analysis has pursued the traditional line that state policymaking is enhanced when the parties compete on more or less even terms, the legislative parties are reasonably disciplined, and a single party organizes the legislative and executive branches. This view of parties has been challenged by a new group of scholars who argue that the social and economic environment of a state conditions the type of public policies it enacts.

Socioeconomic Factors. Thomas R. Dye, for instance, has argued that the level of economic development in a state, not its political characteristics, is the most important determinant of policies. Although states with a high level of expenditures for health, welfare, and education are generally competitive-party states, Dye argued that such expenditures resulted more from the socioeconomic system than from the level of party competition. When he controlled for economic development, party competition (as well as other political variables) had little explanatory power.[19]

The resources that a state has at its command, the occupational classes it includes, and its demographic makeup certainly influence the type of public policies that states enact, and Dye and others are to be commended for emphasizing this fact. Still, these studies tend to minimize the role of political parties and other political variables, primarily because these are difficult to measure. For example, the party effort has been typically measured by the degree of electoral competition. As we observed earlier, electoral competition does not necessarily lead to cohesive parties. If a party's officeholders do not cohere around certain policy goals, their party's contribution to the governing process will be slight. On the other hand, a party that displays a semblance of cohesion when in power is an important resource in policymaking.

The social and economic needs of a state are not automatically translated into public policies. Leadership is required, and that typically comes from the governor. In turn, his power is strengthened when he can count on the support of his fellow partisans in securing the votes he needs to pass his legislative proposals. To lose sight of the distinctions among party systems is to overlook the role that some parties have played in the governing processes of their states.

The Changed Character of City Politics

Whether political parties have an appropriate role to play in city politics has been hotly debated since the municipal reform movement of the late nineteenth century. The goals of the reformers were to curb the power of political machines, eliminate graft and corruption, and promote efficiency and economy in local government operations. They hoped to achieve their objectives through electoral and structural reforms in municipal government that would undercut the power of the political boss and his party machine. The effects of the reform movement are widely felt in municipal government today and call into question the efficacy of partisan activities. In this section, we will briefly describe the political machine and its fall from power, trace the spread of the reform ideal, and weigh the consequences to the party role in municipal government.

THE CLASSICAL POLITICAL MACHINE

The political machine in its classical form once ran most large cities of the northeast quadrant of the nation. Today only fragments of the earlier organizations exist, and they cannot deliver a vote with the regularity that once sustained their power. After the death of Richard Daley, for example, the fabled Cook County Democratic machine could not secure the renomination of its incumbent mayor. A political organization that cannot control its primary elections is a toothless tiger.

A characteristic of a political machine is that those who lead it and those who work for it are motivated by material incentives and have only a secondary interest in issues or ideological causes.[20] The machine is therefore apolitical. It is "a business organization in a particular field of business—getting votes and winning elections."[21] Like any business organization, it pays its employees so it can closely supervise their performance.

The classical machine that flourished from the close of the Civil War until the New Deal era could count on electoral support, not because it bought votes, but because it offered friendship to its supporters. Certainly those who placed their votes at the machine's disposal were the beneficiaries of traditional favors—hods of coal in the winter, Christmas and Thanksgiving turkeys, jobs when they were unemployed—but these material benefits were viewed as expressions of friendship. The loyalty built on friendship was not only more lasting, it was eminently more economical than purchasing votes.[22]

The success of the classical machine was based on a triangular relationship between the business community, the immigrant populations, and those who shared in machine rewards.[23] The forms of government that evolved in the nineteenth century were unsuited to the tasks of supplying the needs of urban masses. Compounded out of Jacksonian direct democracy and Madisonian checks and balances, urban governments were too weak and splintered to govern effectively. At the same time, the tasks of providing for the needs, licit and illicit, of an urban population attracted the interest of entrepreneurs. They wanted to pave the city's streets, operate its street railways, and construct its buildings. The political bosses stepped into the governmental void to make it possible

Thomas Nast's 1871 cartoon portrayed New York City's "Boss" Tweed and his cronies as "a group of vultures"—"Let us *prey.*"

for business to do these things. They charged a price for their aid and, in exchange, overlooked building codes, protected gambling, prostitution, and other illegal activities, and awarded contracts, franchises, and licenses. But to serve as brokers for business, the machine politicians needed a firm electoral base so they could control the office of government.

The working class, especially the immigrants, was the electoral mainstay of the classical machine. The life of the average worker in the nineteenth century was harsh, and doubly so if that worker was confronted by an alien culture and language. "The plight of the newcomers was so pitiful, their needs so elemental, and their prospects of achieving security and independence so problematical in the foreseeable future [that] they must have appeared like a windfall to the machine proprietors."[24]

The machine politician fulfilled three kinds of needs for the immigrant groups. The most basic was simply to provide for their physical existence—jobs, rent money, loans to tide them over difficult times. Since the American governmental system posed problems to the new immigrants, ward heelers and precinct captains helped them to obtain peddler's licenses, interceded with police, and persuaded health officials to license meat markets and delicatessens. And finally, immigrants needed friendship and sympathy in their strange surroundings. Machine politicians rejoiced with their neighbors on felicitous occasions, mourned with them on sad occasions. In an era when charitable functions commanded very limited resources, the political machine performed valuable services for the immigrant populations.[25]

There are a number of reasons for the disintegration of the old-style machine. The tide of immigration was brought to a halt by restrictive immigration laws. As older groups became assimilated into the American cultural system and advanced in its class structure, the machine's hold on its clientele weakened. The advent of the New Deal brought with it government-sponsored welfare programs, and professionalized social services supplanted the more sporadic handouts of the ward heeler. When local captains of industry gave way to national and international corporations whose mobile managerial class had no proprietary interest in city affairs, an important source of the "gravy" or "boodle" that sustained the machine operations was lost. Finally, the municipal reform movement changed the form and structure of urban governments.

MUNICIPAL REFORM

From its earliest beginnings, the political machine was opposed by municipal reformers. Their efforts at reform earned them the epithet of "goo-goos" in derision of their espousal of "good government." They were ridiculed as "morning glories" because of their inability to displace the machine politicians except in the short run. But as external forces sapped the strength of the political machines, reformers gradually were able to effect the transformation of municipal governments.

The conflict between machine politicians and municipal reformers was not merely a contest between alternative forms for governing the city. It reflected a clash of cultures as well. The Catholic lower-class immigrant origins of the machine politician contrasted sharply with the Yankee Protestant middle-class background of the reformer. According to the historian Richard Hofstadter, the tradition of each gave rise to particular conceptions of political ethics.[26] The immigrant tradition emphasized personal and family needs and loyalties; it was unmoved by such abstract concepts as honesty, impartiality, and efficiency. The Anglo-Saxon Protestant middle-class tradition believed in the superiority of general laws and codes of conduct over personal needs.

These two contrasting political ethics were developed by political scientists Edward C. Banfield and James Q. Wilson into a general theory explaining conflict in city politics.[27] Banfield and Wilson have argued that the reform tradition is widely held by the middle class and is reflected in a conception of the public interest that is "public-regarding," that is, it emphasizes the good of the community as a whole rather than the particularistic interests of the groups that compose it. The immigrant tradition is represented by a "private-regarding" conception of the public interest, and is the view of those who identify with ward or neighborhood and look to politicians for favors and help. Considerable debate exists over the origins of these two political ethics and their prevalence today.[28] What is unarguable, however, is that the municipal reform movement spawned political structures that stand in marked contrast to the old-time machines.

Reformers attempted to break the power of the machine boss, or at least render him less effective. They proceeded along a number of lines. Some reformers became active in the movement to check the flow of immigration that supplied the machine with its electoral following, while others pushed for civil service reform, both to cut back on machine patronage and to professionalize government operations.

Other reforms were aimed at the electoral system. The direct primary was designed to wrest control of the nominating process from machine leaders by involving the populace in the naming of party candidates. To weaken the party grip on who held office, the reformers introduced the nonpartisan election. And to focus attention on the city as a whole and destroy the neighborhood base of machine power, they advocated at-large elections. Reformers proposed the short ballot to draw attention to the heads of a ticket and not overtax the abilities of voters to inform themselves on competing candidates.

Still other reforms were directed at the form of government. Plans to strengthen the office of the mayor were proposed on the theory that dispersed governmental power was an open invitation to the boss to run the city. The apotheosis of structural changes was city manager government with its complement of professional civil servants.

The reform movement has had a sweeping effect on party systems at the municipal level. The direct primary is almost universally used to nominate candidates in cities with partisan elections, and the city manager plan, which uses professional managers who are not subject to electoral competition, is widespread. Over 60 percent of cities with a population of over five thousand hold nonpartisan elections. Patronage has been cut back to the point where it is no longer very useful in building partisan strength. In short, in the cities where it has taken hold, reformism has seriously eroded traditional party functions.

What consequences has diminished party strength had for urban politics? There is a whole literature on the distinguishing characteristics of reformed and unreformed cities, but it is not our intent to analyze the effects of reformism in general. Our objective is more limited. We propose to assess the impact of nonpartisan elections on municipal politics, recognizing that the effects of nonpartisanship are difficult to disentangle from the effects of reformism more generally.

The Nonpartisan Election: Does It Matter?

A nonpartisan election is one in which the candidates are not identified on the ballot by partisan affiliation. The use of a nonpartisan ballot does not prevent partisan activity in an election, but it does make it more difficult. Cities that have adopted nonpartisan elections have been grouped into the following categories according to the role that parties or other organizations play in structuring the electorate:[29]

1. Those in which the political parties remain dominant in determining the election outcome. Elections for aldermen in Chicago are nonpartisan only to the extent that names of the parties are not printed on the ballot. No one other than a major party candidate is likely to sit on the Chicago City Council.
2. Those in which the political parties are not assured of controlling the election outcome, either because they must work covertly or compete against slates of candidates put forward by civic organizations or interest groups. Denver, Seattle, Cincinnati, and some California cities have been categorized in this fashion.
3. Those in which parties are not active but other local organizations engage in slate making. Party affiliations of candidates, either because they are considered irrelevant or are unknown, have little effect on voters' choices. Dallas, Forth Worth, and many California and Michigan cities have this type of nonpartisan election.
4. Those in which neither the major parties nor local slate-making organizations have an active role in election contests. This is the typical pattern of nonpartisanship in the smaller cities. Los Angeles would fall closest to this type among the larger cities.

Categories 3 and 4 are by far the most common, and most of the generalizations in the literature concerning the effects of nonpartisanship pertain to these two types of city. However, because it is so difficult to collect information on a city-by-city basis, the more quantitative studies have not distinguished between *types* of nonpartisan elections. We will now describe the *effects* of nonpartisanship.

THE RATE AND BIAS OF TURNOUT

The reformers' theory—that citizens would turn out to vote in larger numbers if election contests were not manipulated by political bosses—has proved to be unfounded. In fact, voting participation in cities that use a nonpartisan ballot is lower than in cities with partisan elections.[30] The distinction holds even when controls are entered for governmental form, regional location, or demographic characteristics. For those who believe that popular participation in public affairs is not simply a means to an end but is valuable in itself, a low turnout rate is a cause for concern. On the evidence, partisan elections may be one way to counteract the growing alienation of many citizens from their community.

More important than the lower voter participation rate in nonpartisan cities is the bias of the electorate. Conventional wisdom holds that poorly educated and low-income groups need to be organized to turn out. Since political parties are designed to mobilize electoral support, the lower classes should be most affected by the absence of active parties. Some empirical evidence supports such an argument. A study of Des Moines concluded that nonpartisanship reduced the turnout of lower-class groups there.[31] If this is generally the case, the Democratic party should be the loser since it has disproportionate strength among low-income groups. This supposition was supported by separate studies of selected Michigan[32] and California[33] cities that use the nonpartisan ballot.

The most systematic investigation into the biases of nonpartisanship was undertaken by political scientist Willis D. Hawley.[34] Hawley compared how eighty-eight nonpartisan cities in the San Francisco Bay area voted in partisan state and congressional elections with how many registered Democrats or Republicans were elected to the nonpartisan city councils. He found that the bias was in the expected direction—that is, more registered Republicans than Democrats were able to overcome the partisan trend of their communities.[35] However, the advantages Republican candidates enjoyed were greatest in the bigger cities. The larger the number of voters in a city, the more the candidates depend on organizational resources in their election bids. "The politics of acquaintance" that elects candidates in small communities is inadequate in mobilizing the big-city vote. Democratic candidates have traditionally relied on party resources and the party label to secure their vote. Republican candidates, drawing their support from middle- and upper-income voters who are more likely to be attentive to public affairs, are not so dependent upon party activities. The backing of civic organizations and friendly treatment by the local press serves them well. Because Democratic candidates felt the loss of party in getting out the vote in their lower-class constituencies, Republican candidates did much better than expected in the sixteen cities of over fifty thousand population that Hawley studied.[36]

DEMOCRATS AND REPUBLICANS IN NONPARTISAN CITIES

A question that must be asked here is whether councilmen's partisan affiliations are an accurate guide to their
policy views in a nonpartisan city. Might it not be that registered Democrats who win election in nonpartisan cities without active party support are indistinguishable from their Re-
publican-affiliated counterparts? This could be the case if
their likelihood of election depended upon backing by the local
press and the financial and organizational resources of prestigious business and civic groups. Alternatively, Democrats
might act no differently from Republicans because, as the
reformers argued, there is no Democratic or Republican way
to run a city.

The direct evidence of roll call voting in city councils has
seldom been used to analyze council decision making. However, some political analysts have studied the attitudes of state
and local officials on policy questions, and their findings can
serve as an approximation of what officials do when they are
empowered to govern.

Hawley used this stratagem.[37] He asked city councilmen
and party leaders what priorities they would assign to eighteen
problems previously identified by a panel of knowledgeable
people as important to their communities. Table 3-2 shows
clear differences between the councilmen according to their
partisan affiliation, though these were not as sharp as the differences between Republican and Democratic party leaders.

Hawley concluded from the data that partisan elections
would sharpen conflict and change the solutions proposed for
municipal problems. Particularly in the larger cities, partisan
elections would mean that a Democratic point of view would
be more aggressively argued.

THE QUESTION OF LINKAGE

The final issue we will consider here is the effect of nonpartisan elections on the representative character of city
government. The class and partisan biases we have already
described create a presumption of representational bias, but
there is evidence of a more direct sort. In a study based on
sixty-four communities of under sixty thousand population,

Table 3-2
PRIORITIES ASSIGNED TO SOCIAL PROBLEMS BY SAN FRANCISCO BAY AREA LEADERS

	Percent Indicating First Priority*			
	Rep. Party		*Dem. Party*	
Problems	*Leaders*	*Councilmen*	*Leaders*	*Councilmen*
Low-income housing	7.1	6.1	14.3	14.0
Social welfare services	0	0	0	0
Open housing in suburbs	15.7	6.1	26.2	19.0
Urban redevelopment	0	.8	4.8	2.0
Employment opportunities	1.4	0	2.4	1.0
Total	24.2	13.0	47.7	36.0

*The percentages reported are those who assigned first priority to specific class-related problems from a list of 18 community problems.
SOURCE: Derived from Willis D. Hawley, *Nonpartisan Elections and the Case for Party Politics* (New York: Wiley, 1973), pp. 116–117.

Susan Blackall Hansen found that citizens were more likely to agree with their community leaders, both elected and non-elected, on what problems confronted their cities when there were partisan elections, active political parties, and competitive elections.[38] This concurrence did not depend on community leaders educating an apathetic public. Leaders who saw their citizens as active and involved were more likely to agree with them about priorities. And the voice of lower-class groups registered the loudest in partisan cities with active competition.

Robert L. Lineberry and Edmund P. Fowler considered the entire question of political reformism in their study of the taxing and spending policies in two hundred cities with a population of fifty thousand or more.[39] Their central conclusion was that reformed cities (cities with manager governments, at-large constituencies, and nonpartisan elections) were less responsive to the socioeconomic cleavages in their constituencies than unreformed cities (cities with mayor–council governments, ward constituencies, and partisan elections). They also found that the effects of reformism were cumulative; the more reforms a city had adopted, the less responsive it was. Finally, they concluded that the presence or absence of partisan elections affected the representative character of a municipality.

"YOU SHOULD HAVE BEEN HERE IN THE OLD DAYS, BEFORE THE BUDGET CUTBACKS,,,, THERE WERE COPS AND FIRE ENGINES AND PLANES BUZZING AROUND,,,, "

Mike Peters for The Dayton Daily News, Dayton, Ohio, U.S.A., 1980.

The Contemporary Parties: Lessons from States and Cities

No one would claim that the presence of political parties solves all problems of representation in either states or cities. Nor can it be reasonably argued that state and local parties always channel political conflict toward workable compromises on issues of public policy. In particular, too little is known about the diffuse effects of partisanship in city governments to support such sweeping conclusions. Nevertheless, the gross patterns that emerge from comparative studies support the contention that political parties make important contributions to democratic government.

What political life would be like in the absence of political parties can be discerned from an examination of one-party states and nonpartisan cities. In the former, the dominance of a single party deprives a state of the benefits of competition between two organized groups seeking political power. In the latter, because the local parties are likely to atrophy, the effects are much the same. Political conflict is not structured by party organizations trying to place their candidates in office. In both cases, a more fluid politics results in which the already powerful in society hold a political advantage.

Despite all their well-known inadequacies, political parties do try to build majorities. In a competitive setting, they must appeal for the support of the voting masses. As they do, they encourage the participation of the poorer, less educated, and less sophisticated groups within the electorate—those who are powerless unless they are organized to utilize the strength of their numbers. The political party historically has provided the mechanisms by which these groups acquired political power.

Two-party states and partisan cities are scarcely models of responsible party government. Yet to argue their case one does not have to make extravagant claims on behalf of parties. Despite all limitations of parties as instruments of popular government, no alternative structures of collective power have worked as well. To belittle the contributions of American parties is to overlook the elemental findings that have emerged from comparative studies. Political parties provide a continuity to political competition that enables a mass electorate to influence the decisions of government.

SUMMARY

Parties at state and local levels have dual roles: they function as part of the national party system and they carry on partisan activities directed at their respective state and municipal governments. This chapter has focused on the latter role.

National political alignments affect the divisions which occur in state politics and contribute to a nationalization of politics. Franklin Roosevelt's ascension to power in 1932 created a new image of the Democratic party as activist minded and working class-based. This new Democratic image spread in the states of the North as liberal activists took command of the state parties, but was resisted by southern state leaders concerned with racial politics. Class-based voting is appearing in the South, but its progress has been slow.

Although a broad nationalizing trend is evident, state party systems are not simply miniature versions of the national party system. State and national governments do not address the same problems, and among themselves states vary in their political cultures, levels of industrial development, and demographic characteristics so that state elections are unique. Therefore, state party systems must be assessed independently. The easiest way to do this is to start with an idealized model of a two-party system against which to evaluate particular state systems.

The model says that state parties should be organized around state issues and not be influenced by external forces, and that parties perform their functions best when they are competitive, with each set of officeholders acting cohesively in the pursuit of party goals. A final specification of the model is that the same party should organize both executive and legislative branches. Under these conditions, the voter's choice would be both clear and simple.

State party systems scarcely meet the rigorous tests of the model. A purely autonomous state politics is impossible under a federal system because national tides influence state races and national issues are often interjected into state contests. Although clearly influenced by external forces, state politics retain a vitality of their own. Even when national party struggles are reflected in state politics, no great harm may be done to the independence of a state political system. A congruence of voting between nation and state may signify nothing more than that voters are consistently signaling the directions they wish governments to take at all levels.

The number of two-party competitive states has increased in the past twenty years, but about half the states do not satisfy the requirements of electoral competition specified by the model. In one-party states, factions—rather than parties—compete for power. Most factional alliances lack the durability and cohesiveness necessary to assist voters in their candidate selections and to implement programs when in power. In such a politics of disorganization, constituents who have less suffer the most.

The mere fact of electoral competition does not suffice for party government, because the party label has little significance if the legislative members of a party do not vote together to support their governor. Although it has been assumed by many that legislators represent their constituencies best when they refuse to accept party discipline, the evidence suggests otherwise.

Even with competitive and cohesive parties, party government can be frustrated if one party holds the office of governor and the other organizes one or both houses of the legislature. There are several reasons for divided party control besides the loose grip the parties have on their followings. Malapportioned legislatures have given an electoral advantage to one party in legislative races that was not duplicated in gubernatorial contests. Malapportionment has been judically prohibited, but the gerrymander is still used in carving out legislative districts. In states moving toward two-party competition, the party of minority status needs fewer resources to compete for the office of governor than it does to back a full complement of legislative candidates with a chance of victory. Whatever the causes of divided government, it hampers the ability of the governor to lead his state.

Whether parties should have a role at the city level is disputed. Some reformers have argued that there is no Republican or Democratic way to pave a street and have attempted to "depoliticize" the city through electoral and structural reforms that would professionalize government operations. The city reform movement arose in reaction to the corruption, fraud, and waste that accompanied the old-time political machine that existed from the late nineteenth century until after World War II in many large cities in the East and Midwest.

Reformers sponsored both electoral and structural changes in city government, but the reform modification that most directly affected the role of parties was the introduction of the nonpartisan election in which candidates are not identified on the ballot by partisan affiliation. Used in more than 60 percent of all cities with a population of over five thousand, the nonpartisan election has had the effect the reformers intended, but it has also reduced the representative character of municipal government. A comparison of partisan and nonpartisan cities reveals that nonpartisanship reduces voter turnout, especially among low-income and poorly educated classes.

Nonpartisan elections actually have a partisan bias, as seen in the ability of candidates with a Republican party affiliation to win in cities that normally vote Democratic. Moreover, in nonpartisan cities, councilmen's partisan affiliations are not meaningless, for Democratic councilmen differ from Republican councilmen in assigning priorities to municipal problems.

Although no one would argue that competitive parties are a panacea for all the ills of either state or city government, they unquestionably enhance the linkage between citizens and their government. So political parties accomplish at least some of the objectives that their proponents claim for them.

Notes

[1]James L. Sundquist, *Dynamics of the Party System* (Washington, D.C.: The Brookings Institution, 1973), p. 308.

[2]Ibid., p. 212.

[3]Ibid., p. 211.

[4]Malcolm E. Jewell and David M. Olson, *American State Political Parties and Elections* (Homewood, Ill.: Dorsey, 1978), pp. 242–244.

[5]Ibid., p. 238.

[6]V. O. Key, Jr., *American State Politics* (New York: Knopf, 1956), p. 24.

[7]V. O. Key, Jr., *Politics, Parties, and Pressure Groups*, 5th ed. (New York: Crowell, 1964), p. 289.

[8]John H. Fenton, *Midwest Politics* (New York: Holt, Rinehart and Winston, 1966), p. 1 and in passim.

[9]Richard C. Elling, "State Party Platforms and State Legislative Performance: A Comparative Analysis," *American Journal of Political Science* 23 (May 1979), p. 385. Elling concluded that the parties of both Wisconsin and Illinois performed reasonably well in enacting their platform pledges, with the Wisconsin parties displaying the better record.

[10]Jewell and Olson, *American State Political Parties and Elections*, pp. 253–254.

[11]Ibid., pp. 261–262.

[12]V. O. Key, Jr., *Southern Politics* (New York, Vintage, 1949).

[13]Jewell and Olson, *American State Political Parties and Elections*, p. 167.

[14]The consequences of factionalism are described in Key, *Southern Politics*, chap. 14.

[15]Ibid., p. 305.

[16]Duane Lockard, *New England State Politics* (Princeton, N.J.: Princeton University Press, 1959). Lockard's findings are summarized in chap. 12.

[17]Hugh L. LeBlanc, "Voting in State Senates: Party and Constituency Influences," *Midwest Journal of Political Science* 13 (February 1969), pp. 33–57.

[18]Wayne L. Francis, *Legislative Issues in the Fifty States* (Chicago: Rand McNally, 1967), pp. 54–58.

[19]Thomas R. Dye, *Politics, Economics, and the Public* (Chicago: Rand McNally, 1965).

[20]Edward C. Banfield and James Q. Wilson, *City Politics* (New York: Vintage, 1963), p. 115. Scholars disagree over whether a machine necessarily centralizes power in a city. Fred I. Greenstein argues that it does in "The Changing Pattern of Urban Party Politics," *The Annals of the American Academy of Political and Social Sciences* 353 (May 1964), pp. 1–13. Raymond E. Wolfinger disagrees in "Why Political Machines Have Not Withered Away and Other Revisionist Thoughts," *The Journal of Politics* 34 (May 1972), pp. 365–368.

[21]Banfield and Wilson, *City Politics*, p. 115.

[22]Ibid., p. 117.

²³See Greenstein, "The Changing Pattern of Urban Party Politics," pp. 4–5; and Elmer E. Cornwell, Jr., "Bosses, Machines, and Ethnic Groups," *The Annals of the American Academy of Political and Social Sciences* 353 (May 1964), p. 28.

²⁴Cornwell, "Bosses, Machines, and Ethnic Groups," p. 30.

²⁵Ibid.

²⁶Richard Hofstadter, *The Age of Reform* (New York: Knopf, 1955), p. 9.

²⁷Banfield and Wilson, *City Politics*, p. 46.

²⁸See, for example, Raymond E. Wolfinger and John Osgood Field, "Political Ethos and the Structure of City Government," *The American Political Science Review* 60 (June 1966), pp. 306–326; and Robert L. Lineberry and Edmund P. Fowler, "Reformism and Public Policies in American Cities," *The American Political Science Review* 61 (September 1967), pp. 701–716.

²⁹Charles R. Adrian, "A Typology for Nonpartisan Elections," *Western Political Quarterly* 12 (June 1959), pp. 449–458; and *Governing Urban America* (New York: McGraw-Hill, 1977), p. 111.

³⁰Robert R. Alford and Eugene C. Lee, "Voting Turnout in American Cities," *The American Political Science Review* 62 (September 1968), pp. 796–814.

³¹Robert H. Salisbury and Gordon Black, "Class and Party in Partisan and Nonpartisan Elections: The Case of Des Moines," *The American Political Science Review* 57 (September 1963), pp. 584–592.

³²Oliver P. Williams and Charles R. Adrian, "The Insulation of Local Politics under the Nonpartisan Ballot," *The American Political Science Review* 53 (December 1959), pp. 1052–1063.

³³Eugene C. Lee, *The Politics of Nonpartisanship* (Berkeley: The University of California Press, 1960), pp. 139–140.

³⁴Willis D. Hawley, *Nonpartisan Elections and the Case for Party Politics* (New York: Wiley, 1973).

³⁵Ibid., pp. 31–33.

³⁶Ibid., pp. 77–84.

³⁷Ibid., chap. 6.

³⁸Susan Blackall Hansen, "Participation, Political Structure, and Concurrence," *The American Political Science Review* 69 (December 1975), pp. 1181–1199.

³⁹Lineberry and Fowler, "Reformism and Public Policies in American Cities."

4

The Formal Party Organization

If we define a political party as an organized attempt to gain political power by contesting elections, we should be able to specify the structural elements of its organization. In the broadest sense, the structure of American parties encompasses the relationships among their component units—the professionals, the officeholders, and the rank and file. More commonly construed, party organizations are the official bodies the parties maintain outside of government to provide the cover for contesting elections. It is through the latter meaning that this chapter discusses party organizations.

The committees and other offices that exist at each governmental level are responsible for managing the day-to-day operations of the parties. In some cases, their tasks are prescribed by state laws; in other cases, they are empowered to act by their membership or its representatives. The men and women who staff party posts help keep alive a party's symbols and traditions and provide important electioneering and campaign services to their candidates. Without formally constituted party organizations, election contests would be fought out between individual political entrepreneurs whose electoral successes would provide few common bonds for governing.

Two important trends are noticeable in the role played by party organizations. The first is that the power of organizational regulars has diminished because they have lost most of their ability to control nominations for major offices and some of their ability to structure the popular vote.[1] The opposite trend is the rise in the level of organizational activity. Over the past two decades, state parties have increased the size and budgets of their headquarters staffs.[2] Since the mid-1970s, the Republican National Committee has developed a large and well-financed professional staff, and if the Democrats follow the Republican lead, as many of their leaders hope they will, both parties will control substantial electoral facilities. Improving a party's campaign-related services is an important antidote to a further individualization of politics because candidates who win offices with organizational aid are often under a stronger compulsion to cooperate with their fellow partisans.

The American Party Structure in Context

Party organizations in the United States are weak compared to many European parties, and this weakness derives from their limited influence on the life of the party.[3] This fact must be acknowledged as a first step to understanding how our parties operate. The antiparty developments described in Chapter 1 were, in the main, no more than a weakening of the already proscribed role played by the party organizations outside of government.

The most important theoretical study of the structure of political parties was undertaken by French political scientist Maurice Duverger.[4] Since he studied the parties of both Europe and the United States, he provides a useful general context for evaluating American parties. At the risk of some oversimplification, two aspects of Duverger's work can be singled out. One concerns the effects of a party's origin on the type of organizations it creates. The other focuses on the organizational differences between middle-class and socialist parties, differences that are linked, at least partly, to the conditions of their creation.

PARLIAMENTARY VS. EXTERNAL ORIGIN

Some political parties were formed from the electoral committees that legislators created to aid in their election.[5] The local electoral committees were at first only indirectly linked by the informal cooperation of members within the parliamentary assembly. It was when these informal relations

PEANUTS ®   By Charles M. Schulz

© 1958 United Feature Syndicate, Inc.

became institutionalized that the political party was born. The formation of electoral committees among unorganized constituencies was next attempted, followed by the creation of a party structure distinct from the organization within the parliament. This pattern was typical of the older middle-class European parties and was true of American parties as well.[6]

Other political parties were established by preexisting organizations that did not have parliamentary ties. Most of these parties were founded later than the parties of parliamentary origin, many of them by trade-union or working-class movements to serve their electoral and parliamentary goals. The British Labour party, for example, was created by a vote of the Trades Union Congress in 1899. Differences between parliamentary-founded parties and externally-created parties conform to certain general tendencies.

Parties created by groups outside the parliamentary system are likely to be more centralized than those founded within the system. Because externally created parties started from a preexisting center, the center could impose such restrictions as it wished upon the party. Parliamentary-founded parties, on the other hand, had to build upon and coordinate local constituency committees to form their central committees. They were thus forced to grant a great deal of local autonomy. As one might expect of a party created out of the parliamentary system, its officeholders do not relinquish their power to any extra-parliamentary organization. The opposite tends to be true of externally-created parties. The extra-parliamentary party often distrusts its officeholders and tries to subject them to its will.

The final difference between the two party types concerns the importance of election contests. Winning seats is the essence of the life of the party with parliamentary beginnings. A major reason for the party's creation in the first place was to ensure members' return to the parliament. To be sure, election contests are also important for the parties of extra-parliamentary origin, but since they were created to pursue certain political ends, doctrine plays a relatively greater role for them.

Not all the differences between parties can be attributed to their origins, and Duverger does not claim that they can. But the reasons for creating a party are of consequence, and Duverger's description of the party of parliamentary origin fits American parties quite well. American party organizations are decentralized, their officeholders are their most influential figures, and they are more electorally than doctrinally oriented. Furthermore, their pattern of organization is set and will not yield easily to fundamental alterations.

CADRE VS. MASS PARTIES

Duverger makes a more general classification of parties by sociological types.[7] We will concentrate on the two most prevalent democratic forms he described: the cadre and mass parties.

The cadre organization had a parliamentary origin and is a common form of the middle-class parties founded when the franchise was first extended.[8] The mass party is of more recent origin and is typical of socialist parties established by working-class movements. To grasp the distinction between the two, one must understand Duverger's concept of membership. A party member is someone who is formally enrolled, pays dues, *and* is an active participant in party affairs. Voters who psychologically identify with one party but do little besides vote for its candidates would be considered party supporters, not party members. Rather than attempting to expand the number of party activists among the voters, the cadre party is restrictive. Its major goal is to contest elections, and its leadership circle is composed of those who can aid candidates in winning elective office—financial contributors, campaign experts, and people who, because of social or economic position, ethnic kinship, or organizational ties, are able to influence votes. Since cadre parties eschew strong doctrinal commitment, they tend to preserve the status quo. They are not geared to reform politics.

The mass parties, of which the socialist parties of Europe are the purest examples, are quite different. Their goal—to challenge the existing economic order—dictates that they organize the classes whose interests they advocate. They therefore attempt to organize as large a proportion of the masses as possible and to involve them in party affairs. Dues are an important source of party finances, and activity is year round, since the party is doctrinally as well as electorally oriented and political education is important. But the real distinctiveness of the mass party is the role its membership plays in selecting leaders, assuming leadership posts, and deciding questions of doctrine. Unlike the cadre party, the mass party is more than an electoral machine. It is reformist minded, especially in its socialist guise, and exercises a greater control over its parliamentary candidates.

American parties are not mass-membership organizations by Duverger's definition. They are middle-class cadre or skeletal organizations. But this characterization of American parties must be qualified. His terminology of middle-class and socialist parties applies more accurately to the European spectrum of politics. American parties are parties of the status quo in his terms, comfortable in the center of the left-right continuum. Yet the status quo is modified in the United States, generally in incremental steps, and the accretion of changes has transformed the character of the nation's social and economic policies over the years. Furthermore, the American system does have a unique feature—the widespread use of the direct primary—that tempers the power of the political professionals in the selection of party candidates. The power over nominations Duverger attributes to organizational leaders might surprise American commentators, although Duverger would respond that the weakening of party ties has had little effect on either the types of candidates who win elections or the policies they pursue.[9]

Even though Duverger underestimated the reformist potential of American parties and misread the role played by the primary electorate, much of what he says about cadre parties is applicable to the American party system. American party organizations are skeletal in structure and seasonal in nature, fleshing out their staff around election time. The party is run by activists, and the party's supporters do not play a central role in party affairs other than in nominating politics. Winning elections is the primary if not the exclusive goal of American party organizations. And the officeholders are free, exclusive of constituent pressures, to say what the policy postures of the party are. These characteristics of American parties must be kept in mind in the discussion that follows.

Party Structure at the National Level

The structure of American parties inevitably is influenced by the fact that they operate under a federal governmental form. Formally organized political parties exist at national, state, and local governmental levels. In many respects, the national party structure is the most tenuous because it must rely on state and local parties as its field units. And as we discussed in Chapter 3, since the state and local parties have a life of their own, the several units are poorly integrated under a central leadership. Although the cliche that there is no single Democratic or Republican party but fifty separate versions of each is an exaggeration, it does convey the difficulty the national party often experiences in coordinating party tasks.

THE NATIONAL CONVENTIONS

The national convention is the primary institution of the party as a national political force. The primacy of the convention stems from its several roles. In the first place, it has the formal authority to pass such rules to govern party affairs as it deems appropriate. The national convention may prescribe how its own delegates are selected, and the Supreme Court has upheld this authority even when it conflicts with state laws. In *Cousins v. Wigoda*,[10] arising out of the successful challenge of delegates elected from Cook County at the 1972 Democratic convention, the Court observed:

> If the qualifications and eligibility of delegates to the National Political Party Conventions were left to state law . . . each of the

> 50 states could establish the qualifications of its delegates to the various party conventions without regard to party policy, an obviously intolerable result.

Although this decision may provide a legal basis for nationalizing the parties, too much must not be made of it. Most of the party rules prescribed by national conventions have concerned the presidential selection process. Very little has been achieved by way of enunciating party doctrine to which party officeholders, at all levels, are committed. Even in the limited area of delegate selection, only the Democratic party has fashioned machinery to police the state parties. The Republican party, believing more in the principle of decentralization, has merely established guidelines and left their enforcement up to the state parties.

Legal support of their authority to govern party affairs is not the principal reason the national conventions are at the apex of American party organizations. The national conventions are the culmination of processes that end in the adoption of party platforms and the selection of candidates to head the national tickets.[11] The two processes are related, for candidates with the delegate votes necessary for nomination can usually write the platforms they wish. In this sense, the national convention *is* the national party. No activity, other than the performance of its officeholders, conveys so readily what a party stands for as the selection of a presidential nominee.

Although the conventions are in session for only a few days during the summer of a presidential election year, candidates begin competing for delegates as early as the January Iowa caucuses and work on the party platforms starts months before the delegates convene. The candidates who are ultimately chosen by the conventions, and the winning coalitions that are put together, inevitably affect voter perceptions of the two parties. The platforms adopted also add meaning to the party labels. If appropriate compromises are made with losing contenders and the interests and groups they represent, a truly national party coalition may emerge from a convention. However, if contending factions remain bitter after the nominating contest is over, party unity will suffer. So the convention process is still the most useful vehicle for brokering diverse interests within the national party.

The national conventions have little to say or do about the more prosaic but important day-to-day tasks of maintaining effective party organizations. They do not set fund-raising goals, nor do they adopt a party budget. Other than the composition of the national committees, they mandate no specific organizational structures. Responsibility for electioneering and party-maintenance activities is in the hands of party committees and party chairmen who operate party headquarters at each governmental level.

THE NATIONAL COMMITTEES

The national committees are the central executive committees of the two major political parties. The terminology may be more misleading than descriptive, since the national committees do not command their extra-governmental parties, formulate party programs, select party candidates, or exercise disciplinary power over officeholders who wear the party label. In truth, they have little power over the national chairmen whom they formally select. They might be dismissed with only passing mention were it not for the fact that they hold formal powers that can be appealed to when customary practices no longer serve to govern party relations. Thus the Democratic National Committee became the forum in which to challenge the delegate apportionment formula mandated by a commission authorized by the party's 1968 national convention. The allotment of delegates to the smaller states was increased at the expense of the larger states, a reflection of the former's influence within the national committee at that time.[12]

The national committees were created in the middle of the nineteenth century by their respective national conventions. Originally, the committees were composed of one representative from each state, territory, and the District of Columbia; a national committeewoman was added after women were enfranchised. The practice of equal representation among the states overlooked both the size of a state and its patterns of partisan voting. The effect of this practice in both parties was to overrepresent more conservative elements.

Republicans have done little to modify committee representation. Although they did extend membership in 1952 to the state chairmen in states that elected major party officeholders, the idea was not so much to redress any ideological imbalance as to accord a voice to state party leaders at the latter's insistence. In 1966, all Republican state chairmen were placed on the national committee.

Democrats have gone further than Republicans in building a representative national committee. After considerable intraparty wrangling as part of a more general reform effort, important changes were made and incorporated into the 1974 Democratic charter. Unlike Republicans, who accord equal representation to the states, Democrats apportion committee members according to a formula that reflects both population size and popular votes cast for Democratic presidential candidates. The present makeup of the Democratic National Committee is:

200 Apportioned to the states on the same basis as delegates to the national convention (size of the electoral college vote and average popular vote cast for Democratic presidential candidates in the three preceding elections).

104 Highest-ranking opposite-sex pairs in the party organizations of the fifty states, the District of Columbia, and Puerto Rico.

13 Three governors, three mayors, four congressional leaders, and three representatives of the Young Democrats of America.

0–25 Additional members to represent other territories and Americans abroad.

Members of the national committees, who serve four-year terms running from one convention to the next, are selected by the state parties. The most common methods employed are:

1. Selection by state conventions.
2. Selection by delegates to the national conventions.
3. Selection by state central committees.
4. Election in state primaries.

Even though committee members, especially the state chairmen, are influential in their state parties, they have had little effect on national party policies. Scheduled meetings of the national committee are infrequent, and national chairmen seldom involve their committees in planning election strategy or developing party resources. The national committee asserts itself only when, in out-party status, it is called upon to mediate among contending party factions and future presidential aspirants in the selection of a national chairman. It has been no accident that state party leaders' demands for a greater voice in national party affairs have been loudest when their party has lost the presidency.

CONGRESSIONAL AND SENATORIAL CAMPAIGN COMMITTEES

The national committees are not the only national party groups concerned with federal elections. Each party maintains congressional and senatorial campaign committees to assist in the election of its members. The independently organized congressional committee originated out of the strained relations that existed between President Andrew Johnson and the Republican majority in Congress after the Civil War. Fearing that he would use the Republican National Committee to further his own interests, House Republicans created their own campaign organization. Democratic House members followed suit shortly thereafter. Senatorial campaign committees were not organized until after the passage of the Seventeenth Amendment, providing for the direct election of senators, in 1912.

Although the congressional committees (the House campaign organizations) are formally composed of one representative from each state party delegation, they typically work through smaller executive committees. The senatorial committees are selected from senators who are not up for reelection. With the exception of the Republican congressional group, the committees are principally fund-raising operations. They raise and distribute money, mainly to incumbents, and assist campaigners by providing speakers for their fund-raising dinners.

The Republican Congressional Campaign Committee is the more elaborate and innovative of these party groups. Located in a wing of the new Eisenhower building that houses Republican party headquarters, the committee employs a professional staff that is a miniature replica of the national committee's staff. The congressional staff engages in election research, conducts party schools, and provides technical guidance in campaign management. Such campaign-related activities emphasize the party's responsibility for electing Republican officeholders. The committee also contributes money to Republican campaigners. After raising large sums through a direct-mail solicitation of funds, the Republican committee outspent its Democratic rival in 1980 by almost six to one.[13] Moreover, reflecting overall Republican strategy, it gave much more money to challengers than its Democratic counterpart did.

The continued existence of separately organized congressional campaign committees reflects the congressional view that the national committees and their staffs are primarily oriented to presidential politics. Particularly for the party occupying the White House, such a view is justified. Congressional Democrats complained bitterly that their national committee, preoccupied with the reelection bid of Jimmy Carter, gave them no financial aid and little technical assistance in 1980. Recent efforts of the Republican National Committee (RNC) stand in sharp contrast to Democratic party practices. Not only did the RNC help finance a $9.4 million advertising campaign on behalf of all Republican candidates, but it also made direct cash outlays and offered valuable campaign services to its congressional candidates. Because it has a solid financial base, the RNC is likely to continue to support the congressional wing of its party and reverse the pattern of neglect associated with the presidential party.

THE NATIONAL CHAIRMEN AND PARTY HEADQUARTERS

The national chairmen are the kingpins of the official party organizations. They are formally appointed by the national party committees, but this masks the reality, for when a national convention nominates a presidential candidate, a chairman who does not have the confidence of the nominee resigns his office. The national committee then accepts the presidential nominee's choice as chairman. Although there have been exceptions, custom also requires the resignation of the chairman who presided over a party's losing presidential effort. Then, after consultation with party leaders, the national committee is free to exercise its authority in naming a replacement.

In-Party Chairmen. The role of chairman in the party that controls the presidency has traditionally been limited because when a party assumes responsibility for governing, its formal organization is generally neglected.[14] The chairman of the in-party is the personal choice of the president, who wants someone loyal to him and his policies, not someone who engages in party-building tasks. Upon accepting appointment as Republican chairman in 1971, Senator Robert J. Dole reflected his subservience to the White House when he told the national committee that "loyalty to the president will be my primary concern."[15] The allegiance of Democratic Chairman John C. White to Jimmy Carter extended to his endorsement and active support of Carter's renomination bid, which enraged the supporters of Carter's chief challenger, Edward Kennedy. Under White, the national headquarters made little effort to devise a party strategy in the critical months before the general election.

The strength of the Republican party's national organization suggests that party affairs will not suffer under the Reagan White House. Although urged by some of his supporters to replace William Brock after the Republican convention in 1980, Ronald Reagan retained the popular chairman through the election and then rewarded him with the post of special trade representative with ambassadorial rank. Brock's successor, former Utah state chairman Richard Richards, took over a well-financed organization of more than 260 staffers. Given the strides they made in the 1980 elections, the Republicans are likely to continue the party-building activities that have proved so successful. However, Richards drew an angry response from some congressional Republicans when he stated that it was more important to pass Reagan's economic package than to win Republican control of the House in 1982.[16]

Out-Party Chairmen. The chairman of the out party does not have to contend with White House strategists more concerned with the personal fortunes of their leader than with the long-term interests of their party. Having lost its bid for the presidency, the party must regroup its forces to contest future elections. For this it needs a party chairman who is more professionally than ideologically oriented, one who can heal party wounds—particularly if the party was defeated decisively. Thus, following the defeat of Barry Goldwater in 1964, Republican Chairman Dean Burch, who did not volunteer his resignation, was removed by the Republican National Committee and replaced with the successful Ohio state party chairman, Ray Bliss. The Democrats replaced George McGovern's choice as chairman, Jean Westwood, with the affable and respected Robert Strauss. And following their substantial 1980 election losses, Democrats turned to Charles Manatt, who had formerly served as California state chairman and as finance chairman of the Democratic National Committee.

Republican Headquarters' Recent Growth. The national chairman presides over party headquarters' staff. Because the Republicans are more financially solvent than the Democrats, their staff is currently the larger and more professionally organized. Republicans employ a successful direct-mail solicitation of funds that has produced almost three-quarters of party funding in recent years ($33 million in 1980, after deducting fund-raising costs). With these kinds of financial resources, Republican party headquarters can afford the type of services that build a party from the grass roots. This was the objective of ex-Senator William Brock when he took over the chairmanship after the defeat of Gerald Ford in 1976.

At the heart of the Republicans' efforts to build their base of power is the Political Affairs Department, which provides campaign services to candidates at all levels. In 1978, the Local Elections Division of the department consisted of eastern and western directors, fifteen professional field coordinators, a research staff, and other personnel who conducted seminars and party schools on campaign tactics. After collecting data on literally thousands of state legislative districts around the country, the staff targeted certain districts where they would concentrate their resources. Virtually all direct cash contributions of over $1 million went to open-seat contests or to challenges of Democratic incumbents. Some seventy-five party seminars held for candidates and their campaign staffs throughout the country drew representatives from 95 percent of the targeted races. In some cases, the field staff assisted in the conduct of opinion polls undertaken by volunteers and run through the computer at the headquarters' office. For their efforts, the Republicans made a net gain of 317 seats and organized an additional seven legislative houses—no mean accomplishment, especially since the congressional reapportionment dictated by the 1980 census, generally considered to be favorable to the Republicans, had not yet taken place. The Republican successes on the state level widened their recruiting base for congressional contests (approximately two-thirds of the members of Congress have had prior state legislative experience).

State legislative races were not the only concern of Republican headquarters. It made cash contributions totaling several million dollars to gubernatorial, senatorial, and congressional candidates in 1978 and 1980. It also conducted a thirteen-week campaign-management "college" for managers and professional staffers who would be involved in the 1978 congressional races. Nor did it neglect the building of state and local organizations. There was a paid professional executive manager for each Republican state headquarters in 1977, but this style of organization was abandoned the following year in all but a few states in preference for the activities of a field staff. In addition, plans have been set up to make a sophisticated computer facility available to state party headquarters through computer terminals. All these steps suggest the directions that an efficiently run party headquarters might take.

Democratic Headquarters' Lagging Operation. The Democratic party is not similarly developed. Burdened by past debts in conducting its presidential campaign, it has been forced to operate on a meager budget. Federal funding of presidential campaigns has not materially improved its financial status. At the Democratic party headquarters, professional staff numbered about forty in 1979 and was characterized by a heavy turnover. Internal organization was fluid. In late 1979, the staff concentrated on organizing the 1980 convention and spent little time or effort on the upcoming congressional races. The party had no computer facilities and its research library was small. Only a handful of field personnel were maintained during the Carter presidency, and they primarily were occupied with planning the visits of high-level administration spokesmen.

The Democratic national headquarters has not been actively involved in state legislative and other local races beyond maintaining a list of political consultants to recommend to Democrats seeking office and distributing political handbooks on how to undertake campaign operations. The Democratic National Committee has seldom had money enough to make direct cash outlays for races other than the presidential campaign; it has not contributed significantly to congressional races since 1966. In a presidential election year, the staff at party headquarters undergoes sizable expansion, but most of its effort is directed at electing the president. Although registration and get-out-the-vote drives typically benefit all Democratic candidates, Democratic leaders complained after the 1980 elections that their national party was little more than a Carter reelection effort.

Further, the Democratic national headquarters was not under pressure to develop additional services because the party was successful in state and congressional races for so long. Although the massive defeat suffered in the 1972 presidential race evoked considerable soul-searching on the future direction of the party, Chairman Strauss concentrated on healing the wounds opened by the McGovern candidacy and on the new presidential delegate selection procedures. He did not assign a high priority to building a grassroots political organization.

There is a further reason why Democrats have not matched the Republicans in party-building efforts. The more professional national party headquarters the Republicans maintain is offset to some extent by the support Democrats receive from labor organizations. The registration drives and get-out-the-vote campaigns conducted by labor unions are an enormous asset to Democratic candidates. Moreover, labor's organizational work is considered "nonpolitical" or "educational," so the costs involved are not restricted by federal limitations on campaign contributions. Particularly in the industrial states, labor manpower provides the Democrats with a formidable grass-roots organizational capability.

The unexpected size of their losses in 1980 brought demands from Democratic leaders to strengthen the party's national headquarters. Believing they had been "outcomputered" by the Republicans, Democrats sought a chairman who would put their party on a sound financial basis and offer their candidates the same services the Republicans provide for theirs. Their man, Charles Manatt, promised to do just that. In his first address to his committee, Manatt described his "deep commitment to the principle that the Democratic National Committee exists to elect candidates at every level, from city council to the United States Senate. . . . It is not dedicated solely to the pursuit of the presidency. . . ."[17] As an initial step toward his promise, Manatt appointed former Arkansas governor William Clinton to head a newly created Local Elections Division. If Manatt is successful in rebuilding the Democratic party, the two parties will be an imposing presence at the national level.

Party Structure at the State Level

National efforts at aiding and coordinating the work of state and local party personnel are fruitless if there are no organizations worthy of assistance in the first place. There are signs today of revitalized state party systems. More states have become two-party competitive over the past twenty years, and with the increased competition has come a degree of professionalization of state party headquarters. The creation of associations of state chairmen has facilitated the exchange of ideas and techniques of party building and electioneering. Not all the states have shown equal progress in their development, but a widespread change in the state party role is apparent.

The organizational form of state parties differs little from that at the national level; the party apparatus is controlled by a state chairman who is appointed by and, nominally at least, is responsible to the state committee. But unlike the national party committees, which are an extra-legal creation, most state party organizations are governed by state law. They were brought under state supervision primarily because of their role in election administration. State party officials otherwise operate according to their own bylaws and customs and traditions developed over the years.

STATE COMMITTEES

At the top of the formally constituted state party sits the state committee. Committee size varies from a few dozen to over several hundred members. Representation is typically based on electoral subdivisions of the state, reflecting the view of state legislatures that the chief function of parties is to contest elections. The county is the most frequently represented lower unit, although congressional districts, state legislative districts, and cities are not uncommonly allotted membership. The method of selecting committee members also varies. Selection at a local party caucus, election at party primaries, and selection by state convention delegates are the most common methods.

It is the rare state committee that undertakes an active role in state party affairs. Most—and in this they resemble their national counterparts—meet only once or twice a year and give free rein to their chairmen. Still, their formal authority, sometimes buttressed by state law, is clear enough that they cannot always be ignored. Particularly in the case of the out party, state chairmen may find it expedient to work with their committees because they need their support to build up their own positions within the party. In most cases, however, it is the willingness of chairmen to involve state committees that determines their activities.

STATE CHAIRMEN

Without question, the success of the state party organization depends on the abilities of the state party chairmen. In contrast to national practice, in-party/out-party status is not the sole determinant of the role of state chairmen. In the most complete study of the office, Robert J. Huckshorn has identified three types of state party leaders:[18]

1. The political agent.
2. The in-party independent.
3. The out-party independent.

The three leadership types were almost equally represented among the hundred state chairmen in the early 1970s.

Sometimes the state chairman serves as the political agent of the governor or, more rarely, of some other elected official. The typical governor does not take office with a smoothly functioning state organization ready and willing to assist him in seeing his legislative proposals through the state assembly. He must fashion the party to serve his own programmatic goals and secure his political future. Because his own energies are directed at managing the state government, the governor typically appoints a trusted colleague to serve as party chairman and run the party for him. The political agent consults with the governor on patronage appointments, advises him on legislative strategies, seeks out the support of local party officials, and serves as the governor's spokesman upon request. Although some political agents are permitted little discretion, others insist that they work *with* the governor and not *for* him.

Some chairmen have sufficient political support of their own to be elected to office without the active backing of a governor or to defeat the governor's choice. These chairmen are the in-party independents, and their term of office not uncommonly antedates that of the governor. Their role differs from that of the political agent. Although they are expected to support gubernatorial programs, their tenure does not depend on the pleasure of the governor. They are more party than candidate oriented. Since they are concerned with the long-term success of the party, they devote their time to organizational matters, candidate recruitment, and nominating and electoral politics. Their tie to the governor is based on the importance to the party of capturing that office. The advantage of this type of party chairmanship is continuity.

The third type of chairman is also independent of the governor, because his party does not control that office. He obtains the position either through his own political maneuvering or as the choice of the unsuccessful gubernatorial candidate. In areas of one-party control, the out-party chairman becomes the party leader. This is the case for the Republican party in the South, where Republican chairmen are the party's spokesmen. Some do little else, but about half the Republican chairmen are actively working to build their organizations to contest state and local elections. Southern Republican senators and congressmen have evinced little interest in the nuts-and-bolts organizational work that the more aggressive chairmen have undertaken.

The role of the out-party chairman in the more competitive states varies according to the initiative shown by the individual occupying the office. Some take on the responsibility of rebuilding their party's strength so it can recapture the state offices lost. These chairmen are more likely to work with the state committees because they are the only power base available. However, the traditional inactivity of some state committees leaves the chairmen to their own devices. Although some out-party chairmen are active, others assume no greater obligation than presiding over a dormant organization. In these cases, organizational activity must await a change in the party's fortunes.

Regardless of either the status or the initiative of the chairman, political parties are functioning units in most of the states. They are expected to perform certain activities, among them fund-raising, recruiting candidates, planning electoral strategy, turning out the voters, and distributing patronage.

Some of the development of a state party can be gleaned from the headquarters staff it maintains. All but ten of the hundred state parties have a state party headquarters; over half of these were opened since 1960. In the early 1970s, the median staff employed was five workers during a nonelection year, and ten during campaign periods. Office personnel ranged from a single secretary-receptionist to thirty employees organized into division specialties. The annual median expenditure was $100,000 in a nonelection year and $225,000 in an election year. One chairman reported operating costs of over $2,000,000.[19]

Headquarters operations are becoming more professional.[20] Sixty-five percent of state chairmen reported using some form of public opinion polling to plan long-range party strategy or to develop issues for a campaign. Automatic data processing was employed by half the party organizations, mostly in the larger and competitive states. More chairmen than before are recognizing their responsibility for fund raising and are experimenting with such devices as sustaining memberships, telethons, and large-contributor "clubs" to supplement the traditional fund-raising dinners. Frequently they hire expert consultants for these tasks.

If there is a continued weakness in state party organizations, it is in the tenure of the state chairman.[21] During the period from 1962 to 1974, Democratic chairmen served an average of thirty-seven months in office, their Republican counterparts only thirty-three months.

This short tenure is primarily voluntary. Many leave the post to accept an appointive office, manage a political campaign, or seek elective office. A substantial portion, however, relinquish the chairmanship because of financial hardship. Only a third of state party chairmen are paid a salary, and in many states, the unpaid status of the post is a matter of choice, not party poverty. Some state leaders retain faith in the citizen chairman who is dedicated to his task for other than pecuniary gains. Others argue against this policy because it restricts recruitment to those who are financially well off and can afford to take time away from their regular occupations. An acceptable compromise may be developing in the trend toward paid full-time executive secretaries or directors who manage the headquarters staff. Approximately two-thirds of the state parties employ such a staff director to aid the chairman in running the party.

Local Party Organizations

The comprehensive legislative statutes outlining the state party system often specify the local units to be organized, the method of selecting party officers, and their tenure. Although it would be unfair to conclude that energetic state chairmen have no effect in building an organized state party, it is far from realistic to suppose that this legally ordained hierarchy is under their control. Since local organizations do not depend for their existence upon cooperation with their state leaders, they can often afford to ignore them.

State laws specify a variety of local committees built around town, city, county, or state legislative and congressional districts. The committees spring directly or indirectly from the precinct and ward committeemen ("captains" and "heelers" in the argot of machine politicians), who are commonly selected in an open party caucus or a primary election.

The reality of American party politics, however, is that most of the minor party posts are unwanted and, if staffed, demand little time and effort from the incumbent. Well-organized precincts, the basic American electoral unit, are the exception rather than the rule.

The most important local party organization generally is the county (in a few states, it is the congressional district). The classical political machine that once existed in many American cities was organized around the wards and precincts of the county organization. The "courthouse crowd" of rural machines was also county based.

There are several logical explanations for the dominance of the county organization.[22] A number of officials are elected countywide, which invites the attention of political parties. Moreover, the patronage available at the county level provides one of the incentives for party work. County lines have been observed historically in carving out other political jurisdictions such as congressional districts (although recent court reapportionment decisions have divided many of them). The county is also an important administrative unit of the state as well as a center of commercial activity. And as the number of cities using the nonpartisan ballot has increased, the county has become the logical focus of partisan activity.

The strength of local party organizations has been exaggerated by images of urban political machines herding voters to the polls. The urban machine was always more popular in the northeastern quadrant of the nation, principally in its larger cities and always in their poorer wards. The "silk-stocking" or "newspaper" wards were never effectively organized, at least by the machine politicians. Today, not only have the machines lost power, but many county organizations scarcely exist except on paper. One or two party stalwarts will meet periodically to perform those duties required of the party by the state's election laws but shun any other activity. Most local organizations fall somewhere between the old-style machines and the paper organizations.

The fact is that there has been little systematic work of a comparative nature on party activities at the local level.[23] County chairmen are presumed to be important cogs of the party machinery and their responses to surveys of presidential candidate preferences are considered important indicators of the professionals' choice for their party's nomination. Yet county chairmen rarely receive a salary, seldom have staff assistance, and only a quarter of them command a regular annual budget. Still, their activity levels are higher than what might be expected from local party chieftains lacking staff, salaries, and budgets.[24]

Some idea of the tasks the local parties perform can be gleaned from the few case studies that have been undertaken. It must be stressed that these studies illustrate only some organizations; they are not universally applicable.

The foot soldiers of the local party organizations are the precinct chairmen or, sometimes, the ward leaders. Their activities are an important gauge of how well a party is organized at the local level. One can get an idea of their work by asking them what tasks they perform and how important they perceive these tasks to be. A survey by Lewis Bowman and G. R. Boynton in three Massachusetts and two North Carolina communities did just that, and the results can be seen in Table 4-1.[25]

The party workers believed their most important duties were campaign related. Organizational activities were also recognized as significant, but no other tasks were emphasized. This is just what one would expect at the level of party worker surveyed. Though organizational development and maintenance activities are important for a party that has traditionally held minority status, the job of building the party is largely the responsibility of those in higher leadership posts. Still, the results of an effective organization show up over the long run in the vote turn-out, and the responsibility for getting the voters to the polls rests with those who work at the precinct and ward levels.

If local party officials believe in the importance of campaign activities, is this a sufficient incentive to turn them out

Table 4–1
ACTIVITIES UNDERTAKEN BY LOCAL PARTY OFFICIALS

Type of Activity	Description of Job	Rated Most Important
Campaign related	58.3%	67.8%
Party organizational	27.6	19.9
Ideological	8.3	9.6
Nomination related	5.7	3.5

SOURCE: Adapted from Lewis Bowman and G. R. Boynton, "Activities of Grassroots Party Officials," *Journal of Politics* 28 (February 1966), p. 126.

during the election season? Bowman and Boynton asked the party officials if they had performed six standard campaign activities: "personally talking to voters, door-to-door canvassing, transporting voters to polls, collecting money, distributing campaign literature, and organizing telephone campaigns." Table 4-2 shows their responses.

The results are rather surprising. The overall level of activity is quite high, considering that North Carolina is classified as a one-party Democratic state and Massachusetts has been characterized by Duane Lockard as having weaker parties than many competitive states. The activities most commonly engaged in were talking to voters, distributing campaign literature, and organizing telephone campaigns. Door-to-door canvassing, more likely a task of the local candidate, and transporting voters to the polls were not as common. Fund raising, scarcely a responsibility of the lower rung of party officials, was the activity least frequently undertaken.

Although the local officials were probably correct in naming electioneering as their primary responsibility, this was not the extent of their involvement in party affairs. Partly as a consequence of their campaign role, a majority of the local officials (80 percent in the Massachusetts communities) reported that candidates had consulted with them before announcing their decision to run.[26] Most of the office seekers were candidates for local office or the state legislature. The exception was the North Carolina Republicans. As members of the minority party, their gubernatorial and congressional candidates apparently found it advantageous to consult with the emergent

Table 4–2
NUMBER OF CAMPAIGN ACTIVITIES PERFORMED BY LOCAL PARTY OFFICIALS

No. of Activities	Mass. Rep.	Mass. Dem.	N.C. Rep.	N.C. Dem.	Total
6	72%	52%	47%	29%	50%
5	20	35	18	32	25
4	5	4	20	34	17
3	3	9	12	3	6
2 or less	0	0	3	2	2
	100%	100%	100%	100%	100%
N =	(40)	(23)	(34)	(41)	(138)

SOURCE: Lewis Bowman and G. R. Boynton, "Activities of Grassroots Party Officials," *Journal of Politics* 28 (February 1966), p. 129.

local Republican organization in what was for them hostile territory.

Other studies undertaken in Oregon, Oklahoma, and Detroit confirm the fact that local party activity is alive and well in many places. Of course, a party organization that only exists on paper will not attract the attention of political analysts, so the studies may be biased. At least it can be confidently stated that some officials undertake party-related activities in every state. The extent of these activities varies, but there do not appear to be any insuperable barriers to their further development if the party leaders have the will and skill to undertake the assignment. Indeed, most local chairmen report that their organizations have grown stronger over the past five to ten years.[27]

The Federated Party Organization

The tasks of a political party operating in a federal environment would appear to be straightforward. At each level, the party organization would actively seek to elect as many of its candidates as possible. Since they are committed to the same basic cause, the professionals at all organizational levels would work together to broaden their base of power. Expressing such a philosophy in its first article, the charter of the Democratic party provides that "the Democratic Party of the United States of America" shall:

1. Nominate and assist in the election of Democratic candidates for the offices of President and Vice President of the United States.
2. Adopt and promote statements of policy.
3. Assist state and local Democratic Party organizations in the election of their candidates and the education of their voters.

Such a party goal is not beyond the grasp of American parties, though to achieve it, they would have to place their emphasis on the electioneering activities of party organizations rather than on the promotion of programmatic uniformity. In reality, though, the several organizational levels of the political parties have not shown such a spirit of cooperativeness on any sustained basis. Each has proved sufficiently self-centered to thwart all efforts at an integrated party.

NATIONAL-STATE RELATIONS

The national headquarters of the political parties are the obvious centers from which to direct a party's electioneering activities. The problem is they have seldom been able to perform such a role because their activities have been dominated by presidential politics.

Presidents have shown more concern for their personal power stakes than for fostering party goals. It is the custom for presidential nominees to place their own people in key roles at party headquarters to work on the presidential campaign. Although the election of a presidential candidate is of great importance to the life of a party, a party's overall strength is not measured by its ability to capture that office. A better gauge is whether its national headquarters provides the leadership for building effective grass-roots organizations throughout the nation. Over the long term, all the party's candidates will benefit by professionally staffed organizations.

The limited cooperation between national and state party organizations is not solely the fault of the national parties. Many state party officials resent outside interference, especially when, in their judgment, the national party has no knowledge of the local political terrain. Utah Republicans bitterly complained about the political management firm the national party recommended to develop their congressional campaign strategies in 1970. In a letter to national party leaders, state officials charged that it was a classic case of "not knowing the territory."[28]

At other times, presidential goals conflict with state party interests. It was no secret that Richard Nixon favored the reelection of Democratic senators who supported his Southeast Asian policies and directed the national party to give informal support to the reelection bid of Democratic Senator Henry M. Jackson of Washington in 1970. The Republican state chairman dismissed his entire state finance committee because of its reluctance to build a campaign fund to oppose Jackson.[29] Republicans who challenge the southern Democrats who supported Ronald Reagan's economic package also may have cause to believe that national party aid will not be generous.

State party leaders maintain communications with national party figures, but their principal lines of communication are not through the formal party structure.[30] Rather, they seek out their own officeholders on party or policy matters that may affect their state. On pending legislation, state leaders approach congressmen, and presidential aides when their party is in the White House. U.S. senators often clear presidential appointments with state patronage committees.

The national party chairman, the nominal head of the official party apparatus, was considered a primary contact by less than 10 percent of state chairmen. That state party officials overlook their fellow professionals at the next higher level is not surprising because it is the officeholders who wield the real power over a party's policy goals. The national headquarters is of interest only when it can service the state organization in its electioneering tasks. Providing campaign-related services to local units has been a neglected feature of the national party organizations.

Lack of communication between levels of the official party characterizes American party organizations. National party officials are overlooking an untapped potential in the revitalized state parties. On the other hand, state party officials refuse to define the common problems they face in sustaining or building their organization and appear suspicious of external interference. Given a federal governmental structure, American parties will probably always be loosely articulated. Nevertheless, under the leadership of national chairman William Brock, Republican national headquarters made a useful beginning in aiding state party organizations by providing professional campaign services that had a measurable impact. The demonstrated usefulness of these services did much to allay state leaders' fears of bungling outsiders. The Republican national committee's keys to success have been the quality of the services it offers and the sensitivity of its field coordinators to local pride. It must be recognized, however, that Republican initiatives, while important, are only a first-stage development, not a comprehensive program of aiding state organizations.

STATE-LOCAL RELATIONS

Part of the folklore of American party organizations is that there are no cohesive organizations above the county level. Like most folk knowledge, this contains a kernel of truth: there are no state political organizations that equal the urban political machines in discipline and singleness of purpose. But as with most myths, this one is largely composed of imagined truths. Strong state organizations remain the exception, but they have existed. The Republican organization in Connecticut run by J. Henry Roraback and the Virginia Democratic party under Senator Harry F. Byrd were efficient machines. Republican Chairman Ray Bliss of Ohio and Democratic Chairman John Bailey of Connecticut presided over state organizations that brought them national attention and, later, the chairmanships of their national parties. Organizations that languished in the early postwar years have begun to shake off their lethargy. They have not succeeded in organizing all parts of their states, nor have they brought all local units under central direction, but their very real accomplishments too often go unrecognized.

A little under 14 percent of state chairmen report basically inactive local units.[31] It is difficult to fill local party offices in a state where the opposition party has long monopolized local offices. After winning an award for meeting his fund-raising goal, a Republican county chairman in Georgia explained, "There are four of us around Soperton who will admit to being Republicans—me and my wife, and another fellow and his wife."[32] Elsewhere local units have deteriorated because statewide campaigners have formed their own campaign units and bypassed regular party channels.

The existence of local party organizations does not mean that they function under central direction. In some cases, they receive no direction from above because the state leadership chooses to ignore them. In other cases, it is the local leadership that does not respond to prodding by state leaders. Most commonly, however, the local units that operate autonomously are the rural and urban organizations that are powerful in their own right and jealously guard their independence. John Fenton described the Ohio Democratic party in the 1960s as a collection of city machines with little interest in statewide elections. The Cuyahoga County chairman, Ray Miller, declared that his organization had neither legal nor moral ties to the state organization.[33]

The typical pattern, nevertheless, is one of some cooperation between state and local leaders.[34] In a small number of cases, it is the governor who manages party operations out of his own office. Usually it is the state chairman who works with local party units, either as an agent of the governor or as an independent chairman. Sometimes chairmen deal with local officials selectively, concentrating on those who are most useful to the governor in his legislative endeavors. Other chairmen try to reach out equally to all local organizations. Whatever the style, almost three-fifths of the state chairmen do work with their subordinate units.

The most widely practiced activity is patronage clearance, but it is followed closely by research assistance. Obviously the quality of this kind of assistance varies considerably, but the better organized state research units can put together sophisticated packages for use by local candidates and party workers. One-fifth of party chairmen assist in fund raising, either by securing name speakers or by providing preprinted mailing labels or envelopes for a finance drive. Considering the scant resources of most local units, these undertakings are of no little consequence.

With get-out-the-vote and registration drives, training sessions for local campaigners, and the provision of information on complex legal regulations, state parties are attempting to aid their local organizations. Some state chairmen still provide no services. Few provide all services. Yet there is definite movement in the direction of rendering more aid to local organizations.

The Contemporary Parties: Visions of an Integrated Party Effort

At the present stage of party development, a nationally integrated party effort is not yet a reality. The organizational ties of the national headquarters to state parties historically have been weak. State organizations are in a better position to provide leadership to local party organizations because their relatively smaller jurisdictions facilitate more effective communications. Nevertheless, factional rivalries within state organizations and the separatist tendencies of some local organizations hinder a concerted party effort. These problems are not likely to vanish.

If there is a trend today that suggests cooperation among party levels is improving, it is the technological innovations that have transformed political campaigning. The new campaign style emphasizes the private poll, media advertising, computer analysis of voting data, and the hiring of private consultants to manage campaigns. Although slow to respond at first, party leaders are now beginning to recognize that they must adapt to the modern method of political campaigning. The professionalization of party organizations' headquarters staff may lead to a revitalized party structure.

Assistance in fund raising, the conduct of polls, and the analysis of election data are not likely to cause friction among party levels. The Republican national headquarters and a number of state organizations have shown that technical services can be successfully provided to lower-level organizations. As long as the national party effort is built along lines of service, the future of the extra-governmental party does not appear so bleak. Such a role falls far short of the goal of responsible party government because it emphasizes the technical aspects of campaigning rather than the forging of common ideological goals. Even so, such a circumscribed role remains important. If two-party competition is introduced or maintained throughout the nation, then all of a party's candidates will have a better chance at winning. The programmatic drift of a party will remain principally in the hands of the officeholders, where it always has been.

SUMMARY

It is hard to describe the structure of American parties because the several elements that compose them—officeholders, professionals, and rank and file—are so loosely associated. This chapter has focused on party organizations outside of government, the justification being that these party organizations provide the institutional setting for contesting elections.

American party organizations have been characterized by Maurice Duverger as cadre or skeletal in form. They are unlike the mass membership European socialist parties in that they do not have formally enrolled, dues-paying members who actively participate in party affairs. Duverger would consider Americans who identify themselves as Democrats or Republicans to be supporters but not members of a party. Although Duverger underestimated the role played by American party supporters in nominating politics, he correctly perceived that most citizens are not otherwise active in party affairs.

Other attributes of the cadre organizational style also apply to American parties. They are loosely articulated and basically decentralized, their leaders are the officeholders in government rather than the party officials outside, and they are more electorally than doctrinally oriented. Although Duverger's characterizations would place both American parties in the center of an ideological continuum in the European sense, the Democratic and Republican parties do differ in the social composition of their supporters and in the central thrust of their policy initiatives. Changes in social and economic policies, usually incremental in nature, have had a substantial effect over the long term. Still, the American parties' organizational status is set and does not yield easily to change.

American party organizations follow the federal pattern of our governmental system. Insofar as the parties can be characterized as national political forces, the national convention is their primary institution. The convention adopts rules governing party affairs, drafts national platforms, and selects candidates to head the national tickets. This process affords an opportunity to forge a truly national coalition, but only if the contending candidates and their supporters are willing to compromise their differences to achieve party unity.

National party committees, created in the middle of the nineteenth century, are nominally in charge of party affairs in between conventions. Actually, they exercise little real power. They do not direct the activities of state organizations, nor do they sponsor all campaign-related activities in federal elections. Each party also maintains a separate campaign organization in each house of Congress. These organizations assist in funding party candidates, but only House Republicans undertake a broader role in electing party officeholders.

Managing the national party headquarters is the responsibility of the national chairmen. In-party chairmen are chosen by the president and are loyal to him and his policies; generally they neglect the state parties. Out-party chairmen have a freer hand to develop their party organizations, but their headquarters staff have not provided effective leadership to the state organizations. Recent efforts by the Republican National Committee to supply money and campaign-related services to state and local candidates are a significant step forward. Partly because their party has been burdened by debt, and partly because they have been able to count on labor organizations for significant electioneering aid, Democrats have not kept pace with Republican initiatives. The 1980 election losses, however, made the Democratic National Committee and its staff resolve to match Republican campaign services.

Like the national committees, state committees have formal powers over their party's organizations but seldom choose to exercise them. The headquarters is run by state chairmen, whose role, unlike the national chairman's, is not determined solely by in-party/out-party status. Three types of state party chairmen have been identified: those who act as an agent of the governor; those who are independent because their party does not hold the governor's chair; and those who are independent because they achieved the office without gubernatorial assistance. The last type of chairman is more likely to bring continuity to the office and to emphasize the long-term success of the party.

State party organizations are becoming more professional. All but a handful now maintain a party headquarters (over half were opened in the last twenty years) and the median staff employed is five in an off-year, ten in an election year. Public opinion polling and computer analysis of election and registration data are becoming increasingly common, along with a variety of new techniques of fund raising. The gradual spread of two-party competition among the states has strengthened state party organizations.

Although the party at the local level is sometimes conceived of as a tightly knit machine-style organization, that type of organization was never typical and now exists in only a limited number of wards in some of the larger cities of the Northeast and Midwest. Local organizations are dormant in many jurisdictions, active in others. Where they are active, they engage in campaign and electioneering activities designed to get their supporters to the polls. This is still valuable work despite the media appeals of the new campaign style.

Neither the Democrats nor the Republicans have achieved a nationally integrated party because national leaders have only sporadically undertaken party-building efforts at the grass roots and state leaders have resisted being brought under national supervision. If there is a trend toward centralization, it is to be found in the increasingly sophisticated methods of electioneering. Although the new campaign style initially posed a threat to the parties, many political leaders learned to adapt to it by providing expert technical support to local parties as an inducement to cooperation. The professionalized staff of the Republican National Committee has pointed the way.

Notes

[1]Chapters 6 and 7 discuss the declining influence of party professionals in nominating politics; Chapter 10 describes the weakening of partisanship in electoral decisions.

[2]James L. Gibson et al., "Assessing Institutional Party Strength" (paper delivered at the 1981 annual meeting of the Midwest Political Science Association, Cincinnati, Ohio, April 16–18), pp. 18–19.

³Leon D. Epstein, *Political Parties in Western Democracies* (New Brunswick, N.J.: Transaction, 1980), pp. 380–381.

⁴Maurice Duverger, *Political Parties* (New York: Wiley, 1954).

⁵Ibid., pp. xxiii–xxxvii.

⁶See William Nisbet Chambers, "Party Development and the American Mainstream" in *The American Party Systems*, 2nd ed., William Nisbet Chambers and Walter Dean Durham, eds. (New York: Oxford University Press, 1975), p. 10.

⁷Duverger, *Political Parties*, pp. 63–71.

⁸Duverger believed that the cadre organization was archaic, destined to be replaced by parties with a mass-membership base. For a contrary point of view, see Epstein, *Political Parties in Western Democracies*, pp. 126–129 and 368–377.

⁹Duverger, *Political Parties*, p. 364.

¹⁰419 U.S. 477 (1975). In 1981, the Supreme Court held that the Democratic National Convention did not have to seat the Wisconsin delegation selected in open primaries in violation of party rules. See *Democratic Party of U.S. v. LaFollette*, 101 S.Ct. 1010 (1981).

¹¹For a more complete discussion of national conventions, see Chapter 7.

¹²For a description of the episode, see William J. Crotty, *Decision for the Democrats: Reforming the Party Structure* (Baltimore: Johns Hopkins University Press, 1978), pp. 173–181.

¹³*Congressional Quarterly Weekly Report*, November 1, 1980, p. 3238.

¹⁴John S. Saloma III and Frederick H. Sontag, *Parties* (New York: Knopf, 1972), p. 99.

¹⁵Quoted in ibid., p. 101.

¹⁶*Washington Post*, May 5, 1981, p. A3.

¹⁷Information Bulletin of the Democratic Conference, March 1981.

¹⁸Robert J. Huckshorn, *Party Leadership in the States* (Amherst: University of Massachusetts Press, 1976), chap. 3. The discussion that follows draws heavily on Huckshorn's study.

¹⁹The data are reported in ibid., pp. 254–256. As Huckshorn cautions, however, the figures reported for costs of a headquarters staff may include some campaign expenditures.

²⁰Ibid., chap. 6.

²¹See the discussion in ibid., chap. 3.

²²See the discussion in Malcolm E. Jewell and David M. Olson, *American State Political Parties and Elections* (Homewood, Ill.: Dorsey, 1978), p. 60.

²³The work of Gibson et al., whose preliminary findings are reported in "Assessing Institutional Party Strength," is an important exception.

²⁴Ibid., pp. 37–38.

²⁵Lewis Bowman and G. R. Boynton, "Activities of Grassroots Party Officials," *Journal of Politics* 28 (February 1966), pp. 121–143.

²⁶Ibid., p. 136.

²⁷Gibson et al., "Assessing Institutional Party Strength," p. 42.

²⁸Huckshorn, *Party Leadership in the States*, p. 213.

²⁹Ibid., p. 214.

³⁰See the discussion in ibid., pp. 204–207.

³¹Ibid., p. 234.

³²Ibid., p. 239.

³³John H. Fenton, *Midwest Politics* (New York: Holt, Rinehart and Winston, 1966), p. 137.

³⁴See Huckshorn, *Party Leadership in the States*, pp. 239–244.

5

Party Members and Party Supporters

In Chapter 4, American parties were described as cadre organizations run by a limited number of political activists. In the analysis of Maurice Duverger, the men and women who fill party posts and work for partisan goals are the *members* of a political party, and the voters who profess an identification with a party and commonly support its candidates are its *supporters*. The differences are not always clear-cut, however. Some party officers devote little time to their official duties; some party identifiers are active in their support of their party and its candidates, contributing time and money to partisan causes. Nevertheless, the distinction conforms broadly to the realities of American party organizations. The great mass of party identifiers give only passing thought to problems of organizational maintenance.

The distinction between party members and party supporters provides an analytic perspective for viewing the role of each.[1] Whatever their motivations, political activists are the people who sustain the formal party organizations—they dedicate time and effort to party affairs. Those who merely identify with a political party incur no obligations—they do not formally enroll to achieve their status, nor do they have to pay dues or subscribe to any set of party principles. They do not even have to vote for the candidates of their chosen party. Under these circumstances, one might suppose that the activists would control all important decisions made in the name of the party.

In fact, party officers do not possess the power that would seem to flow from their commitment to their party. They may influence but they cannot control who becomes the party's standard bearer, for example. That decision is now shared with party supporters who participate in the selection process through the various primary election contests. This voter participation is mandated by state law or party rules and reflects a conceptualization of the political party as *an association of party voters*. The anomaly of such a view is that it creates a set of party members without partisan obligations but possessing "rights" that cannot easily be set aside. Most reforms that aim to democratize the internal processes of the party are based on the concept of party supporter as party member.

It is not our purpose here to evaluate the consequences of obliterating the distinction between an organization's members and its following. That discussion will be undertaken in later chapters. This chapter has two objectives: (1) to discuss the reasons why some individuals are willing to serve as party officers and to perform party-related tasks; and (2) to consider the role of supporters in sustaining the life of the parties.

Party Activists as Party Members

Party organizations are not withering away, despite the claims that we live in an antiparty age. The collapse of the city political machine has been widely heralded but, as we have seen, it was never the universal model of party organizations in this nation. Indeed, party organizations have continued active, and in some cases have increased the level of their activity, over the past twenty years.

But how do the parties recruit their workers? What incentives do they offer to those who work at party tasks? What satisfactions do workers gain from their participation? Do the different incentives motivating workers affect the style of politics? It is to these questions that we now turn.

INCENTIVES FOR PARTY WORK

No voluntary organization can survive unless it attracts members to support the activities for which it was created. And to attract members, the organization must provide incentives. A business organization pays its employees to perform the tasks necessary to its operations. A country club is sustained by the social and recreational opportunities it offers its members. Those who have joined the National Organization of Women have been brought together by their common concern for the rights of women. In each example cited, a basically different incentive holds the organization together.

Political parties provide a variety of incentives to induce their workers to contribute time and skills to party-related activities. The principal incentives have varied over time and by place, but at least three distinct types can be identified:[2]

1. Material rewards.
2. Solidary satisfactions.
3. Purposive incentives.

To be sure, the three incentives are not mutually exclusive as motivations for party work. Separate discussion, however, will convey more precisely the characteristics of each.

Material Incentives. Material incentives are money or other things of value. The staple of the classical political machine, material reward is still important for staffing and financing party operations in many locales. Opportunities for rewarding the party faithful are extensive. Jobs must be filled and candidates selected to run for public office. Contracts must be let for construction, printing, insurance, equipment, and other governmental needs. Probate courts must appoint appraisers and trustees of estates. Laws governing vice, the regulation of commerce, and the assessment of property must be applied to individual cases. Whatever form they take, material incentives all have one thing in common: party members either are materially rewarded for their partisan connections or expect to be.

The party organization built on material incentives is on the decline.[3] Although patronage and other perquisites of officeholding still flourish in some states and cities, civil service reforms and the unionization of public employees have provided job security for many state and city employees. The estimated sixty-three thousand jobs the governor of Pennsylvania once could fill, for example, have been reduced to below a thousand. A recent Supreme Court decision places additional restraints on the patronage system. In *Branti v. Finkel*,[4] the Court held that the hiring authority has the burden of proof to show that "party affiliation is an appropriate requirement for the effective performance of the public office involved."

There are other indications that patronage appointments no longer have the appeal they once did. Separate studies of the uses of patronage in a rural and an urban setting showed that the political party was only perfunctorily rewarded for the appointments it secured. Frank Sorauf found that only half the laborers with highway patronage jobs in a rural Pennsylvania county felt an obligation to the party that gave them their jobs, and of these, less than half reported voting a straight ticket.[5] Michael Johnston concluded that 670 federally funded patronage jobs in New Haven, Connecticut, did not produce a marked increase in party activity.[6] In both studies, however, the patronage jobs that produced little partisan return were at the lower employment levels. Supervisory appointments did have the effect intended according to Sorauf's study. One may surmise that the attractiveness of patronage positions used to staff minor posts such as precinct workers has declined as alternative opportunities for employment have become available.

At the higher party levels, material incentives may still play an important role in financing and staffing party organizations. Although no systematic evidence has been collected on the material rewards business and professional people obtain from their party connections, we do know that party service is a frequent stepping-stone to both elective and appointive office.[7] Of the forty-three state chairmen of each political party who served in the ten-year period prior to 1972, fully a third later sought elective office, many successfully. Others were appointed to high government positions. Of course, material incentives may not have been their primary motivation, but the necessity of earning a living while pursuing one's chosen career cannot be discounted either.

Discussions of material incentives for party work often overlook the professional staff who work for national and state party organizations. Many are salaried employees who are hired because of their expertise in electioneering and organizational tasks. Although they constitute only a small proportion of all party workers, their skills are needed to maintain party operations as the older patronage-based organizations continue to decline. If funding is available, the paid employee or consultant may play an increasingly important role in party affairs. Modern political campaigning is so complex that the parties need technical experts to keep them abreast of changes.

Solidary Satisfactions. Although the material incentive has received special attention in the literature of American party organizations, it is not the most common form of incentive offered. Coming together to work at politics, according to a leading student of organization theory, is intrinsically enjoyable.[8] Anyone who has worked on a political campaign and suffered through the minor and major crises that develop over its course knows that a camaraderie develops among the workers that is recalled years later. The election night party, whether it is a joyous or tearful occasion, is emotion packed. Even the ward leader and precinct captain of the machine-led city enjoyed the conviviality of their required attendance at wakes and weddings. But while the satisfactions of working in a campaign with like-minded people are appealing, the more active party workers seldom are motivated by sociability alone. It is either material incentives or commitment to a cause that prompts their dedication.

To the social rewards derived from working with one's partisan colleagues must be added the satisfactions that come from holding positions of influence within the party organization. Mere sociability accrues to all who join in the party effort, even workers who are lackadaisical in the performance of their assigned tasks. The rewards of holding a party office, however, can only belong to some. Thus those who wish to enjoy the power and status that go with holding office must be willing to do more than others. Once they obtain office, they can use it as a stepping-stone to still higher positions of influence.

Purposive Incentives. Yet another incentive offered by political parties in recruiting workers is the nonmaterial satisfaction of working toward some desired goal or end. Every party organization, including the urban machines, has to emphasize its record of accomplishments, if for no other reason than to attract supporters who do not want favors. Party workers, as political scientist James Q. Wilson has observed, may be no more susceptible to motivation by causes than the salesman working on commission who is told by his sales manager that he is marketing a socially desirable product.[9] At the same time, some party workers receiving material rewards may like the reassurance that they are acting not out of self-interest alone, but are serving a larger cause.

The so-called amateur clubs that are part of the regular Democratic and Republican parties in some states are the purest examples of purposive organizations. Members join these clubs to advance either specific issue goals or vague general principles. Material benefits are seldom, if ever, realized. Social satisfaction plays a role, but it is secondary compared to the main reason for participation, which is to support some worthy cause. The Beverly Hills Democratic Club held a monthly dance at a Sunset Strip nightclub, provided excursions to Catalina Island, Las Vegas, and Mexico City, and

DOONESBURY   by Garry Trudeau

organized elaborate preelection parties at expensive hotels. These affairs were important fund raisers, but relatively few club members or officers attended.[10]

The party activist who is motivated by issue concerns is probably on the increase. Partly this is a consequence of the limited availability of material incentives and the lower value placed on them. Partly it is a consequence of the middle-class reformist ideal that there is a distinction between "doing good" and "playing politics."[11] Finally, issue-oriented activism has become more prominent because the social satisfactions of party work are less appealing today when sociability is available from countless nonpolitical clubs and associations.

ORGANIZATIONAL INCENTIVES AND POLITICAL STYLES

The type of incentives a political party offers to its workers is reflected in the attitudes these activists hold toward the nature of their work. The party organization that relies on material incentives tends to produce workers for whom winning is the ultimate aim of politics, for only through victory can they secure the advantages that prompted their participation. On the other hand, workers motivated by causes are more likely to view winning elections as a means to achieving some larger goal. Mere victory is unsatisfactory to them; the victory must advance their cause. The contrasting styles are those of the "professional" and "amateur" politicians.[12] Falling between these two extremes are workers who receive social satisfactions from their party work: these benefits accrue to them whether the organizations they work for are electorally or ideologically oriented.

Professionals and Amateurs. Political professionals are willing to compromise issue stands in order to place their party's candidates in office. They do not believe in the desirability of voter involvement in internal party affairs. Popular participation may be useful at times to unify the party, but they do not view it as intrinsically valuable. The label "political amateur" was coined to describe a very different type of worker. Amateur here does not mean a dilettante or dabbler in politics who lacks political sophistication. The amateur may be, and often is, as knowledgeable about political affairs as his professional counterpart. But where professionals emphasize winning elections, amateurs are unwilling to back just anyone for public office. The issue commitments of the candidates are important to them. Amateurs also emphasize popular participation in party affairs to ensure their control over party policy. Historically, they have opposed the close control political machines have imposed on party operations.

Distinctions between amateur and professional politicians cannot be drawn so clearly in the real world as in the world of political analysis. The two styles reflect tendencies rather than sharply differentiated types. Some of the professionals who thrived on patronage politics have been shrewd enough to pursue the image, if not the substance, of a politics of principle.[13] For their part, many political amateurs who have been actively engaged in politics for a time take on some of the coloration of the professional. Enduring a succession of defeats can turn a confirmed Brahmin into a practical politician. Nevertheless, winning is not everything for all who play the political game. Whether a party organization supports each of its candidates with equal enthusiasm may turn on the attitudes of its workers toward the goals that will be served: the workers' self-interest or some larger cause.

At the higher levels of party and officeholder ranks, the differences between amateur and professional tend to blur. The opportunity to gain office is a powerful spur for candidates to design campaign appeals to fit their audience. At the same time, party leaders cannot afford to disregard the motivations of workers at lower organizational echelons. An organization based on material incentives frees the party candidates to devise any strategy capable of winning. (That strategy, of course, will consider issue appeals to the voting public.) But an organization manned by workers who hold purposive goals limits the flexibility of its candidates, no matter what compromises they would like to make to ensure their election. As James Q. Wilson has written, "the ultimate source of the amateur spirit is found in the expectation of the followers, not in the motives of the leaders."[14]

Influence of the Amateurs on Modern Campaigns. The growth of the middle classes, who espouse an interest in the politics of principle while denigrating a politics of accommodation, is likely to keep the amateur style alive. Political amateurs have not been capable of remodeling the structure of American parties along the lines of the responsible party model that would achieve their twin goals of participation and principle. What they have developed, however, is the candidate-centered campaign that attracts an issue following. The

Barry Goldwater, Eugene McCarthy, George McGovern, and John Anderson presidential bids showed that substantial numbers of political activists were available to work for losing political causes. The danger of such candidacies to the political party is that people give their loyalty to the candidate rather than to the party. In such a process, the collective cover the party label provides its candidates could lose its meaning.

Recruiting Workers

It is evident from our discussion so far that incentives for party work are most easily distinguished at the lower party levels. At the higher party levels, particularly at the level of officeholder, it is difficult to disentangle motives for party service. A senator or governor may believe in the causes he fights for at the same time that he receives considerable satisfaction from occupying a position of power. Nor can he be unconcerned with the necessity of providing an income for himself and his family, unless he is independently wealthy. On the other hand, the motivations of party activists at the local level sometimes fit more neatly into categories of political machines and amateur clubs, conforming to the principal incentives offered by each.

The fact that a party organization is characterized as a particular type does not mean that all its workers are similarly motivated. Nor does it mean that a single incentive provides the motivation of every worker. The parties have the task of matching the incentives they have available to what motivates individuals to work at party activities. Our knowledge of this recruitment process is limited. Again, we must rely on case studies to get a feel for this phase of party operations.

The first question to consider is the extent to which the party leadership cadre is active in recruiting party workers. The notion of a political machine that coopted its workers to sustain party operations was widespread at one time. But patronage jobs used to staff lower-echelon party offices are no longer as attractive as they once were. So how do today's party leaders cope with the loss of a once effective method for staffing minor party posts? Do they actively seek out party workers, or do they rely on the personal initiative of the volunteers who come their way?

Table 5-1 provides the answers for three Massachusetts and two North Carolina communities. Of interest is the relative importance of the political party in recruiting workers. The leaders were active in staffing party posts, but a substantial portion of the "self-recruited" were motivated by party causes. A study of Detroit in the late 1950s revealed a similar recruitment pattern.[15]

But what of the motivations that sparked the interest to serve in the first place? Data from the Massachusetts and North Carolina communities are reported in Table 5-2. In each community, the ranking of incentives was the same. Purposive incentives were the most important, material incentives the least important, with solidary incentives falling in between. The patterns found in Table 5-2 were not unlike the incentives that produced the political activists in Detroit,[16] in a rural community of Illinois,[17] and in a suburban community in Maryland.[18] In each case, purposive incentives were the principal inducements for party work, with the importance of solidary and material incentives varying among the communities.

But the initial incentives that turned supporters into party activists willing to serve in precinct positions were inadequate to sustain their interests. In Detroit, more than two-thirds of the precinct leaders who became active because of a sense of civic duty or in behalf of some cause reported that such motivations were no longer central to their work.[19] They continued in office because of more personal reasons—the social contacts

Table 5-1
THE RECRUITMENT OF LOCAL PARTY OFFICIALS

	N.C. Reps.	N.C. Dems.	Mass. Reps.	Mass. Dems.	Total
Asked by the party	59%	51%	69%	67%	60%
Self-recruited	35	26	27	33	29
For personal gain	(4)	(3)	(12)	(13)	(6)
For the good of the party	(31)	(23)	(15)	(20)	(23)
Asked by other groups	6	23	4	0	11
	100%	100%	100%	100%	100%
	(34)	(41)	(40)	(23)	(138)

SOURCE: Lewis Bowman and G. R. Boynton, "Recruitment Patterns Among Local Party Officials," *American Political Science Review* 60 (September 1966), p. 674.

Table 5–2
THE IMPORTANCE OF PURPOSIVE, SOLIDARY AND MATERIAL
INCENTIVES

	Categories of Incentives (Grand Mean Score)*		
	Purposive	*Solidary*	*Material*
North Carolina Republicans	1.17	2.14	3.15
North Carolina Democrats	1.10	1.96	2.85
Massachusetts Republicans	1.21	2.15	3.39
Massachusetts Democrats	1.43	1.87	3.08
Total	1.18	2.01	3.12

*The possible ratings are (1) "very important"; (2) "somewhat important"; (3) "not very important"; and (4) "not important at all." Thus the higher the grand mean, the lower the incentive category in importance.

SOURCE: Lewis Bowman, Dennis Ippolito, and William Donaldson, "Incentives for the Maintenance of Grassroots Political Activism," *Midwest Journal of Political Science* 13 (February 1969), p. 133.

enjoyed or the fun of playing the game. Similar findings emerged from the study of the rural Illinois and suburban Maryland communities.[20] The argument that reformers were unsuccessful politicians because they could not sustain the initial energy of their reform crusade appears to have received some validation.

Nevertheless, after the first blush of enthusiasm has paled, most precinct workers continue to ply their trade. The camaraderie of associates and the intrinsic excitement of politics may constitute their primary satisfactions. But the sociability and fun of competing would not be attractive if these were for the wrong party or the wrong candidates.

Such a detailed examination of the recruitment process and the motivations of party workers should not obscure one central fact concerning those who staff party organizations. Democratic party workers differ from Republican party workers in ideological orientation at all party levels.[21] Republican party workers are more conservative; Democratic workers are more liberal. That the two groups differ in their central tendencies, however, does not mean that each group is ideologically homogeneous—there are dissenters from the dominant party line in each party's organizational cadre. Nevertheless, ideological dissension is not the mode for party workers. No matter what their motivations, they commonly bring to their jobs a preference for their party's general ideological perspectives.

Party Identifiers as Party Supporters

The place of the party identifier in the American party structure is somewhat ambiguous. To start with, the great majority of party identifiers are not heavily involved in their party. If they were, the many precinct posts that remain unfilled could be staffed and the party organizations would be invigorated. Table 5-3 suggests the type of political participation undertaken by ordinary citizens. The activities reported are probably on the high side, for surveys reveal that most citizens believe they should be more actively politically, a belief that may inflate the positive responses.

Table 5–3
A PROFILE OF CITIZEN INVOLVEMENT

Type of Political Participation	Percentage
1. Report regularly voting in presidential elections	72
2. Report always voting in local elections	47
3. Active in at least one organization dealing with community problems.	32
4. Have worked with others in trying to solve some community problems	30
5. Have attempted to persuade others to vote	28
6. Have actively worked for a party or candidates during an election	26
7. Have contacted a local government official about some issue or problem	20
8. Have attended at least one political meeting or rally in last 3 years	19
9. Have contacted a state or national government official about some issue or problem	18
10. Have formed a group or organization to attempt to solve some local community problem	14
11. Have given money to a party or candidate during an election campaign	13
12. Presently a member of a political club or organization	8

SOURCE: Sidney Verba and Norman H. Nie, *Participation in America: Political Democracy and Social Equality* (New York: Harper and Row, 1972), p. 31.

All the same, the fact that most citizens do identify with a political party and commonly support its candidates is of enormous importance to the life of the parties. This fact imparts a durability to American politics that allows us to avoid the hazards of an unorganized political competition. A more fluid electorate would elevate candidates to office on the basis of media blitzes that depend on a fortuitous grouping of voters or the temporary passions of the moment. An electorate structured along partisan lines provides the basic support that party candidates need to continue the debate on public issues.

If party identifiers are essential to the stability of electoral competition, two important questions surface: (1) How do the parties obtain their loyal supporters? and (2) Are there signs that the electoral bases of the parties are crumbling? It is these questions we shall now explore.

THE CONCEPT OF PARTY IDENTIFICATION

As ordinarily used in political analysis, *party identification* is a psychological attachment an individual feels toward a political party.[22] It does not require formal enrollment or registration, nor any other conscious act. It does not even necessarily signify that identifiers are acquainted with the ideological references of their party or are consistent in their approval of them. It does suggest an emotional commitment or sympathetic attraction to a party that is remarkably durable over an individual's life span. Most Americans have such an attachment to one or the other of the major parties.

The measurement of partisan identification is uncomplicated. It rests upon self-classification: voters are asked whether they consider themselves Democrats, Republicans, or Independents. The intensity of partisan feeling is ascertained by follow-up questions. Those who say they are Democrats or Republicans are asked whether they consider themselves a strong (Republican or Democrat) or a not very strong one. Independents are asked whether they regard themselves as closer to either the Democratic or the Republican party. Leaving aside the tiny minority who are totally apolitical, citizens can be arrayed across a seven-point scale of partisanship as follows:

Strong Dem.	Weak Dem.	Ind. Dem.	Independents	Ind. Rep.	Weak Rep.	Strong Rep.
			0			

The fact of identification is not meaningless to the citizen. It provides a psychological screen through which he or she perceives and evaluates objects of political concern. Removed as ordinary citizens are from the workaday world of politics, they need guides in making their voting choices. The mere fact that a political party has nominated certain candidates is reason enough for many Americans to view them in a favorable light and to vote for them. The political party reduces the complexities of government and politics for citizens who lack the personal knowledge upon which to base their political judgments.

The importance of party identification as a cue giver varies with its intensity. Strong identifiers normally provide overwhelming support for their party's candidates. Weak identifiers are more likely to defect to the opposition, though they commonly give their votes to the party they favor. Attachment to a party is not broken by occasional bolting. For this reason, partisan affiliation is considered a "long-term" influence on the vote, while candidates and issues are considered "short-term" forces.

The reservoir of goodwill expressed toward a party may be temporarily overcome by short-term forces. Many Democrats voted for Richard Nixon in 1972 because they were dissatisfied with George McGovern and his policies, just as a sizable number of Republicans rejected Barry Goldwater and supported Lyndon Johnson in 1964. In neither case, however, did the votes signify a long-term switch in partisan loyalties. Party identifiers manifest a durable allegiance that can withstand temporary dissatisfactions, and this lends stability to the party system.

The classification of voters as Independents is more complex. At one time their virtues were extolled because they did not accept partisan tutelage but, rather, weighed the evidence carefully before deciding how to cast their vote. This image of the Independent was destroyed when survey research showed that, in comparison to partisans, they were less knowledgeable about issues, less involved in political activities, and less concerned about the outcome of election campaigns.[23] Still more recently, the image of the Independent has been partially resurrected. Gerald Pomper has argued that the Independent is not indifferent toward politics, "he is simply—and tautologically—unconstrained by partisanship."[24] Because they do not identify with a party, Independents should not be expected to be concerned with the outcome of party contests. "It is still possible for an Independent to be concerned about the political world, and knowledgeable about its issues and contexts, yet rationally to decide that he is indifferent specifically to the Democrats and Republicans."[25] Pomper then provides evidence that the Independents' general political activity, on such matters as voting on bond referenda, writing letters to public officials, and talking to people about politics, is generally superior to that of weak party identifiers and not far short of the activity of strong identifiers.[26]

The crux of the contemporary controversy concerning Independents is not whether they have been unfairly denigrated by early voting studies. Most analysts now concede that Independents who lean in a partisan direction compare quite favorably to the weakly identified partisans in fulfilling their citizenship obligations.[27] Pure Independents conform to the early descriptions, but they are a minority of all Independents. The most intriguing question today is the significance of these self-declared Independents to party politics. If Independents of all stripes are truly unconstrained by party, then they constitute a pool of uncommitted voters that could provide a "mass base for independent political movements of ideological tone and considerable long-term staying power."[28] Such a development would portend the eventual dissolution of the parties. On the other hand, if there are hidden loyalists among the Independents, the threat to party stability is less severe. The issue will be explored later in this chapter.

THE ACQUISITION AND PERSISTENCE OF PARTY IDENTIFICATION

Most Americans are born "little Democrats" or "little Republicans," or so it would seem from the early age at which children report political party preferences. According to separate studies in New Haven[29] and the Chicago area,[30] a majority of fourth-graders had already taken partisan sides. Although most schoolchildren, even in the early grades, knew the political party of the president, they knew little else about politics. Only a few of the older elementary schoolchildren recognized any issue differences between the parties: some of the eighth-graders perceived the upper-class support of the Republican party and the working-class base of the Democratic party. Nevertheless, the emotional responses of the schoolchildren to who won the 1960 presidential election followed partisan lines.[31]

Though a majority of all schoolchildren reported party preferences, the proportion who ignored parties in defining good citizenship increased with age.[32] Almost half the fourth-graders believed that one should join a political party and always support its candidates. By the eighth grade, three-quarters of the children felt that citizens should not join either political party but should vote for the best candidates running. Inasmuch as the latter view was held overwhelming by their teachers (87.4 percent), the change in the children's attitudes is hardly surprising. Partisan guidance in voting choices is apparently an unacceptable attribute of good citizenship.

Despite the best efforts of elementary school socialization, however, the influence of the family on the child's party preferences remained strong. Approximately three-fourths of the children whose parents agreed politically tended to adopt their parents' party affiliation. Of course, the more active the parents, the greater their influence on the child's partisan preference. The anomaly is that the correspondence in party affiliation between child and father increased slightly over the grade-school levels at the very time that an increasing proportion of schoolchildren said they should make up their minds independently of parental influence.[33]

Family influence on a child's partisan orientation is not a product of conscious indoctrination. Some political values will be taught, particularly those the parents believe are valuable for the child to hold. But these are likely ones dealing with the obligations of citizens that reflect general community standards. Partisan preferences are more commonly learned by parental examples that the child emulates. A surprising number of schoolchildren in the Chicago area, for example, had become politically involved at an early age. Half the eighth-graders wore campaign buttons, and a third had passed out campaign literature.[34] The children undertook these activities even though only a handful recognized issue differences between the parties.

Children's ambiguous attitudes toward political parties parallel those held by many adults. On the one hand, the notion of citizenship that calls for voting the person and not the party has a considerable intellectual appeal. On the other hand, the attachment many people feel toward a party is a potent influence on their choice of candidates to vote for. The two attitudes are compatible only if voters believe their favored party ordinarily nominates the superior candidates. Party cues are most valuable when they convey in a more generalized way what is to be expected if the candidates of one party rather than the other are elected. The fact that the party can cue the voter in this fashion is, at best, only implicitly recognized and contributes to the low estate to which the parties have fallen.

Partisan identification, once acquired, tends to persist through adult life and grow stronger over time. Nevertheless, some voters do change their partisan affiliations. Changes may be produced by either *personal* or *social* forces.[35] Examples of personal forces are marriage, a new job, or a change in place of residence. Since these changes are idiosyncratic, they are unlikely to affect the overall balance of partisan strength within the electorate. Changed personal circumstances are as likely to move a voter toward one party as the other. In contrast, social forces affect large segments of the population more or less simultaneously. Cataclysmic events such as the Civil War and the Great Depression, for example, produced new party alignments. Less profound disturbances can also cause groups of voters to alter their party attachments. Despite the potential for change, however, the distribution of partisan identification has shown considerable stability over the past three decades (see Table 5-4).

THE WEAKENING OF PARTY TIES

Despite evidence of general stability, the partisan electorate has not remained the same over the years.[36] The changes that have occurred are of three sorts. First, the strength of identification has weakened. There are proportionately fewer strong identifiers today than in the past, while the proportion of weak identifiers has remained virtually unchanged. The strong identifiers provide the parties with their most dependable electoral support. Second, the loyalty of both the strong and weak identifiers diminished during the sixties and early seventies. Although partisanship made a comeback in the 1976 presidential election, it fell again in the three-way contest of 1980. Third, there has been a growth in the proportion of self-declared Independents.

The Rise of the Independents. The potentially most important secular change in the distribution of partisan identifica-

Table 5–4
PARTISAN IDENTIFICATION OF THE ELECTORATE

	1952	1956	1960	1964	1968	1972	1976	1980
Strong Democrat	22%	21%	21%	26%	20%	15%	15%	16%
Weak Democrat	25	23	25	25	25	25	25	23
Democrats	47	44	46	51	45	40	40	39
Independent Democrat	10	7	8	9	10	11	12	11
Independent	5	9	8	8	11	13	14	12
Independent Republican	7	8	7	6	9	11	10	12
Independents	22	24	23	23	30	35	36	35
Weak Republican	14	14	13	13	14	13	14	14
Strong Republican	13	15	14	11	10	10	9	10
Republicans	27	29	27	24	24	23	23	24
Apolitical	4	3	4	2	1	2	1	2
Total	100	100	100	100	100	100	100	100
Number of Cases	1614	1772	3021	1571	1553	2705	2875	1379

SOURCE: Survey Research Center of the University of Michigan. Data made available through the Intra-University Consortium for Political Research.

tion has been the proportionate increase of Independents. The cause is not so much that older identifiers are abandoning their party ties as that youthful voters are entering the electorate without a partisan commitment.[37]

This change began to take place sometime after the 1964 elections. The impact of replacing older cohorts with new voters was exaggerated because the electorate of the late 1960s and early 1970s was younger than that of the 1950s. The "youthing" of the electorate was partly a consequence of the World War II baby boom, but more importantly, the result of enfranchising millions of young Americans by lowering the voting age to eighteen. In 1952, only 7 percent of the voting-age population was under twenty-five years of age, and of these, roughly a quarter were Independents. By 1974, 15 percent of the electorate was under twenty-five, and somewhat more than half were Independents.[38]

The numbers of Independents among the young can be explained partially by their limited political experience. Traditionally, partisan identification has been weaker among youth, and then grows in strength over the life span of the individual. Yet the greater youthfulness of the electorate does not fully explain the rise of Independents. Today more young people than formerly are eschewing partisan ties. Their coming of age during a turbulent political period might hold the key to their seeming aloofness. Many were active in or sympathetic to the antiwar movement, and neither political party seemed capable of ending the conflict. The number of Independents seems to have leveled, even declined slightly, since 1974.

Partisan-Leaning Independents. The bulge among Independents in recent years does not tell the complete story, for at least two-thirds of all Independents lean in a partisan direction. It is important to inquire into the partisan behavior of those Independents who lean to one party or the other because they exhibit a striking amount of loyalty in presidential elections.[39] Unlike pure Independents, these partisan-leaners did not switch dramatically from election to election. Unaffiliated Independents gave 83 percent of their votes to Dwight Eisenhower in 1956, but switched sides eight years later when 77 percent supported Lyndon Johnson. Partisan Independents have always given a majority of their votes to the presidential candidate of their preferred party. Their loyalty was not equal to that of strongly identified partisans, but their support of the presidential candidates whose party they favored was often superior to that of weak partisans. The average loyalty of partisans in presidential elections from 1952 through 1980 was:

Strong Democrats . . . . 86 %
Weak Democrats 65
Independent Democrats 68
Independent Republicans. 85
Weak Republicans. 83
Strong Republicans. 96

The partisanship of leaners, however, may not be the same as that of party identifiers. Gerald Pomper has argued that Independents are indifferent to partisan references, but are quite knowledgeable about contemporary issues and as capable as partisans of relating their issue stands to those of presidential candidates. If this is the case, leaners may have no long-term commitment to a party per se, but lean toward one party rather than the other because of essentially short-term forces—the personal qualities of a candidate or the issues that have gained the political agenda. This would mean that parties could not count on durable support from leaners.

Are Independent leaners aware of party symbols and traditions? And do they rely on party cues in their voting choices? If leaners are indifferent to party labels, one would expect them to vote split tickets at least more frequently than party identifiers. However, the incidence of straight-ticket voting in federal elections provides little evidence to support such a contention. Although they do not measure up to strong partisans, Independent leaners are distinguished by only marginal differences in party regularity from weak identifiers. Furthermore, the direction of their voting does not show the sharp swings of the pure Independent. The average proportion of straight-ticket voters in federal elections from 1952 through 1980 was:

Strong Democrats . . . . 80 %
Weak Democrats 57
Independent Democrats 56
Independent Republicans. 63
Weak Republicans. 67
Strong Republicans. 86

Our analysis of the Independent leaner thus far has not addressed whether the same leaners are a constant force across elections . The missing link is provided by evidence from panel studies, that is, studies that interview the same respondents over two or more time periods. Richard A. Brody, using data from 1956–1958 and 1972–1974 panels, found that approximately seven out of ten leaners were directionally stable in their loyalties.[40] The long-term commitment of Independent leaners was not the equal to that of partisan identifiers, but it was hardly insignificant. Independent leaners do not switch parties from election to election. In the 1972–1974 panel, which reflects the increasing youthfulness of Independents, only one in ten leaners had changed party sides.[41] Others who were no longer loyal became uncommitted Independents.

The Contemporary Parties: The Partisan Base of Electoral Support

The implications of our analysis are that the American electorate continues to be structured along partisan lines. The recent growth among Independents has been partially offset by the inclinations of most of these voters toward one or the other of the parties. Independent leaners are behavioral partisans almost the equal of weak party identifiers. At the same time, the strength of party identifications has declined throughout the electorate, and with it the aggregate loyalty of all stripes of partisans.

If those who refused to identify with a party and those who voted in disregard of their party identification did so because of ideological or issue reasons, the usefulness of the political party might be called into question. Such a trend would suggest that voters are listening to what the candidates are saying and no longer find the party label useful in distinguishing candidates. But the evidence does not support such a conclusion. Independents show no greater propensity to evaluate presidential candidates on issue grounds than do partisans. Nor do those identifiers who defect differ from those who remain loyal in the sophistication of their candidate assessments. In other words, the decline in the strength of party identification is not due to disenchantment with the major parties by a quality electorate.[42] Political parties may not be held in high esteem, but there are no clear signs pointing to a more logical grouping of electoral forces. In fact, loyalty in the 1976 presidential contest was higher than at any time since 1964. And party regularity in 1980, with John B. Anderson attracting votes from Republican and Democratic party identifiers, was the equal of 1968, when George C. Wallace also cut into the party vote. Whether voters realize it or not, parties continue to cue them on their candidate choices.

SUMMARY

According to Duverger's analytically useful distinction, the men and women who hold party posts and participate actively in party affairs are party *members*, while those who identify with a party but seldom do more than vote for its candidates are *supporters*. Party members staff the formal party organizations and perform party-related tasks. Party identifiers incur no responsibilities: they do not have to pay dues or contribute money to party candidates; they do not even have to vote for their party's candidates. Still, they have an important power in that they participate in the nomination of party candidates through the primary system.

Party members and party supporters each play an important role in the life of the political party. The party workers sustain the formal organization and help keep alive the party's symbols and traditions. Party identifiers, because they normally vote for their party's candidates, lend stability to political contests. How each group comes to play the role it does has important consequences for the political party.

The motivations of party workers are commonly categorized into three types: material, solidary, and purposive. Material incentives are money or some other thing of value, solidary incentives are the social satisfactions derived from belonging to a party organization, and purposive incentives are issue concerns.

These incentives are not mutually exclusive, particularly at the higher party levels. A state chairman, for example, may be simultaneously motivated by the cause he serves, intrinsically enjoy the clash of arms his party post involves, and hope to use his position as a bridge to an appointed or elective office. However, at lower party levels, the different incentive categories do distinguish some party organizations.

The old-time city machine relied heavily on material incentives to recruit its party workers. Winning was the ultimate goal of the organization, because if the party candidates lost, the party workers were deprived of the patronage and contracts that came with victory. Under such an organizational style, party candidates are free to make any election appeal they think will win them office. By contrast, party organizations that rely heavily on purposive incentives view winning as only a means to an end. Unless their cause is advanced, placing their candidates in office is to them a hollow victory. Workers who are motivated by solidary incentives can adapt to either organizational style.

The party organization that is built out of patronage and the other perquisites of officeholding is on the wane. Civil service reform, unionization of public employees, and court decisions have combined to provide job security for the government worker. Purposive incentives for party work are on the increase, if for no other reason than the decline in the availability of material incentives, at least at the lower party levels. There are two important qualifications: Studies of local party workers suggest that the purposive incentives that led many into party work do not suffice to keep them at their job; because of this, solidary incentives are increasingly important. And the professional staff who work for national and state party organizations are salaried employees who are hired because of their organizational and electioneering skills. Although a small proportion of all party workers, they are playing an increasingly important role as the parties adapt to modern campaign methods.

Aside from incentives, there is another central fact about party workers that should be noted. Republican workers are distinguishable in their ideological and issue perspective from Democratic workers at all party levels. That the two sets of party workers differ in their central tendencies does not mean that each party is ideologically homogeneous. Given the decentralized character of American party organizations, dissension from the dominant party line will always exist. At the same time, the disharmony within party ranks should not be overstated.

An individual becomes a party supporter by identifying with a political party. Party identification involves a psychological attachment to a party that serves as a perceptual screen for evaluating candidates and issues, and it is ordinarily acquired at an early age. Many schoolchildren are emotionally committed to a political party before they are aware of its issue or ideological references. Once acquired, party identification tends to persist throughout life, even though the voter does not always support the party's candidates. For this reason, party identification is considered a long-term influence on the vote, while candidates and issues are considered short-term influences.

Though the aggregate distribution of party identification has been relatively stable over the past three decades, it has not remained unchanged. The proportion of strong identifiers has declined, and the proportion of self-declared Independents has grown. Because this suggests the rejection of the party system by a sizable minority of the voting public, the growth of Independents deserves special attention.

When asked, most Independents indicate they feel closer to one of the parties. These Independent leaners exhibit many partisan characteristics: they are usually more loyal to the party they favor in presidential elections than are weakly identified partisans; they are almost as likely to vote a straight ticket in federal elections as are weak party identifiers; and they do not switch sides from election to election as do the pure Independents.

Still, there has been an increase in unaffiliated Independents and a decline in the strength of party identification, as witnessed by the rise in the number of partisan defectors. If these trends were associated with a quality electorate, they would suggest that parties were no longer needed as voting guides. But the evidence does not support such a finding. Neither Independents nor those who break party ranks show any greater sophistication in evaluating presidential candidates than do loyal party adherents. The obvious conclusion is that party identification still structures the American electorate.

Notes

[1]See, for example, the discussion in E. E. Schattschneider, *Party Government* (New York: Holt, Rinehart and Winston, 1942), pp. 53–61.

[2]The classification is essentially that of James Q. Wilson, *Political Organizations* (New York: Basic Books, 1973), pp. 33–35. Wilson's categories are material, specific solidary, collective solidary, and purposive.

[3]For a contrary view, see Raymond E. Wolfinger, "Why Political Machines Have Not Withered Away and Other Revisionist Thoughts," *Journal of Politics* 34 (May 1972), pp. 365–398.

[4]445 U.S. 507 (1980).

[5]Frank J. Sorauf, "State Patronage in a Rural County," *American Political Science Review* 50 (December 1956), pp. 1046–1056.

[6]Michael Johnston, "Patrons and Clients, Jobs and Machines: A Case Study of the Uses of Patronage," *American Political Science Review* 73 (June 1979), pp. 385–398.

[7]Robert J. Huckshorn, *Party Leadership in the States* (Amherst: University of Massachusetts Press, 1976), pp. 36–42.

[8]Wilson, *Political Organizations*, p. 110.

[9]Ibid., p. 101.

[10]James Q. Wilson, *The Amateur Democrat* (Chicago: The University of Chicago Press, 1962), p. 167.

[11]Wilson, *Political Organizations*, p. 96.

[12]See Wilson, *The Amateur Democrat*, esp. pp. 2–13. The term "professional" is also used in a generic sense to designate the men and women who hold party positions. The specific connotation given the term has to be ascertained by the context of its use.

[13]Ibid., p. 19.

[14]Ibid., p. 5.

[15]Samuel J. Eldersveld, *Political Parties: A Behavioral Analysis* (Chicago: Rand McNally, 1964), pp. 126–128. Although Eldersveld reports that only 38 percent of the precinct leaders were "co-opted" by the party, an additional 27 percent were "cajoled into becoming the candidate in the absence of competi-

tion and against their will" (p. 128). Presumably, party officials provided the arm twisting.

[16]Ibid., pp. 131–134. Eldersveld, however, recognizes the complexities of determining objectively the motivations of workers.

[17]M. Margaret Conway and Frank B. Feigert, "Motivation, Incentive Systems, and the Political Party Organization," *American Political Science Review* 57 (December 1968), pp. 1165–1166.

[18]Ibid.

[19]Eldersveld, *Political Parties*, Table 11.6, p. 287.

[20]Conway and Feigert, "Motivations, Incentive Systems, and the Political Party Organization," p. 1169.

[21]See, for example, Eldersveld, *Political Parties*, p. 216; Herbert McCloskey, Paul J. Hoffman, and Rosemary O'Hara. "Issue Conflict and Consensus Among Party Leaders and Followers," *American Political Science Review* 54 (June 1960), pp. 406–427; and Jeanne Kirkpatrick, "Representation in the American National Conventions: The Case of 1972," *British Journal of Political Science* 5 (July 1975), pp. 313–322.

[22]Angus Campbell et al., *The American Voter* (New York: Wiley, 1960), p. 121.

[23]Ibid., p. 143.

[24]Gerald M. Pomper, *Voters' Choice* (New York: Harper and Row, 1975), p. 32.

[25]Ibid.

[26]Ibid., Table 2.5, p. 33.

[27]See, for example, John R. Petrocik, "An Analysis of Intransitivities in the Index of Party Identification," *Political Methodology* 1 (Summer 1974), pp. 31–47.

[28]Walter Dean Burnham, *Critical Elections and the Mainsprings of American Politics* (New York: Norton, 1970), p. 130.

[29]Fred I. Greenstein, *Children and Politics* (New Haven, Conn.: Yale University Press, 1965), Table 4.3, p. 73.

[30]Robert D. Hess and Judith V. Torney, *The Development of Political Attitudes in Children* (Chicago: Aldine, 1967), Table 23, p. 90.

[31]Ibid., p. 204.

[32]Ibid., Table 18, p. 204.

[33]Ibid., p. 90.

[34]Ibid., Table 21, p. 88.

[35]See Campbell et. al., *The American Voter*, pp. 149–153.

[36]See, for example, Norman H. Nie, Sidney Verba, and John R. Petrocik, *The Changing American Voter* (Cambridge, Mass.: Harvard University Press, 1976), chap. 4.

[37]Ibid., pp. 59–65; Warren E. Miller and Teresa E. Levitin, *Leadership and Change* (Cambridge, Mass.: Winthrop, 1976), pp. 247–250.

[38]Miller and Levitin, *Leadership and Change*, p. 249.

[39]On the partisan behavior of Independent leaners, see Hugh L. LeBlanc and Mary Beth Merrin, "Independents, Issue Partisanship and the Decline of Party," *American Politics Quarterly* 7 (April 1979), pp. 240–256; and Bruce E. Keith et al., "The Myth of the Independent Voter" (Paper presented at the annual meeting of the American Political Science Association, Washington, D.C., September 1–4, 1977).

[40]Richard A. Brody, "Stability and Change in Party Identification: Presidential to Off-Years" (Paper presented at the annual meeting of the American Political Science Association, Washington D.C., September 1–4, 1977), Table 4, p. 17.

[41]Ibid., Table 10, p. 29.

[42]David B. Hill and Norman R. Luttbeg, *Trends in American Electoral Behavior* (Itasca, Ill.: Peacock, 1980), pp. 66–68.

6

Nominations in the States

No activity is so critical to the continued vitality of the parties as selecting the candidates who will act in their behalf. What candidates say or do on the campaign trail will affect the party's image and determine its electoral successes. The decisions victorious candidates make on public business will define the policy thrusts of the parties they represent. Thus, the nominating process offers the parties an opportunity to screen the candidates who will ultimately determine their internal cohesion and unity.

Two Views of the Political Party

Before we take an in-depth look at this nominating process, it is important that we determine who in the political party bestows the party label. Is it the political activists who run the official party machinery? Or is it rank-and-file supporters?

In contrast to the practice in most democracies, candidates in the United States are not named by a caucus of party leaders acting privately. They are nominated under rules, frequently prescribed by state law, that involve the party following in the selection process. Clearly, political parties in the United States are legally conceived to be associations of party supporters. Why else would they be entrusted with such an important responsibility?

For most major elective posts in the United States, only Democratic and Republican party candidates have a realistic chance of winning. In some states, the dominance of a single party almost ensures the victory of its candidates. Given this situation, it is not surprising that major reform efforts have centered on the nominating process. Because the American political party is conceptualized as an association of party supporters, reform has meant the democratization of the nominating process by enlarging popular participation. Yet there are other ways to view the political party and to undertake reform.

E. E. Schattschneider, mentor to an older generation of political scientists, has forcefully argued a contrary notion of the political party. "Whatever else the parties may be," he wrote, "they are not associations of the voters who support the party candidates."[1] Schattschneider preferred to think of the party as a political enterprise undertaken by a group of working politicians. He did not include those who merely identified with a party as among their number. It follows from his thesis that party supporters have no rightful claim to be included in internal party affairs.

But would the recognition of the private character of the party affect its responsiveness to the needs and wishes of the voters? Schattschneider thought not. He likened the party to a commercial undertaking: parties would need no "laws to make them sensitive to the wishes of the voters any more than we need laws compelling merchants to please their customers."[2]

Schattschneider believed in strong national parties.[3] He excoriated the power of local political bosses and the divisive effects of political interest groups. Only party government, he argued, could bring order to the system. Strong national parties would supplement the presidency as the sole rallying point to meet the great issues of the day; they would exert discipline on the Congress to make it more responsible for its own legislative record. The ability to overcome the parochial and special interests that dominate Congress, Schattschneider believed, was the ultimate test of the strength of the parties. If the parties were successful, party government would be achieved.

The Schattschneider thesis sounds politically naive today when the principal trend visible to most political analysts is the declining strength of the parties. Nevertheless, Schattschneider's conceptualization of the political party cannot be dismissed out of hand. At the core of his thinking is the idea of a political party run by political activists who control its internal affairs, including the naming of candidates. This view of the political party is widely recognized elsewhere in the world. In most democratic nations, democracy consists of a choice among competing parties; it does not include a choice of who are to be the party's candidates.

Schattschneider's argument has been presented here to show there is another way of viewing the party reforms that have seen the adoption of the direct primary by every state in the nation and the spread of the presidential primary to almost three-quarters of the states. There were ample reasons for the development of each. Nevertheless, the democratization of the nominating process has not been without costs to the strength of the parties. In this chapter, we will trace the development of nominating techniques within the states and consider the effects of the direct primary on political parties. Presidential nominations will be considered in the next chapter.

The Evolution of Nominating Practices

The history of nominating practices in the states is one of increasing democratization.[4] Early reforms attempted to loosen the oligarchic control exercised by successive party leadership cliques. The aim of securing more representation in choosing nominees led, step by step, to the direct primary, the full flowering of popular participation. Each step along the way was based on a concept of the political party as a representative institution that should reflect its rank-and-file following.

THE INFORMAL CAUCUS

In any setting in which citizens vote on who is to hold elective office, some device must be employed to limit the number of people who seek office and to mobilize support behind particular candidates. During pre-Revolutionary days, small groups of community leaders would come together in informal caucuses to agree on the candidates and policies they would support. A favorite meeting place in colonial Boston was the garret of Tom Dawes where, as described by John Adams, "they smoke tobacco till you cannot see from one end of the room to the other. ... and selectmen, assessors, collectors, firewards, and representatives are regularly chosen before they are chosen in the town."[5] From its earliest beginnings, the behind-the-scenes negotiating to put together a winning slate was viewed by some with the suspicion that is conveyed in the "smoke-filled room" metaphor of nominating politics.

THE LEGISLATIVE CAUCUS

The informal caucus was suited to the needs of local communities but was unsatisfactory for nominating candidates for statewide office. That responsibility was assumed by groups of like-minded members of the state legislature who, as in the case of the local caucus, would meet in private and agree on the candidates they would back. By 1800, the legislative caucus was the principal nominating device used in the states.

The legislative caucus had certain natural advantages. State legislators were men of substance who enjoyed local if not national eminence. Since they were the leaders of their state, they were in a position to ascertain the qualifications of potential office seekers. And in an era when travel was difficult, the legislative caucus had the advantage of involving those who were already assembled in the state capital for their legislative duties. The development of the congressional caucus as a nominating device for presidential candidates paralleled the legislative caucus. Thus was "King Caucus" enthroned.

But the legislative caucus had built-in representative deficiencies that became all the more noticeable as the nation began to divide along Federalist and Republican lines. A local party had no representation in its legislative caucus unless it managed to place its candidates in the legislative assembly. Soon districts controlled by the opposition began the practice of sending a delegate to sit with the legislative caucus. The shift to the "mixed" legislative caucus was not merely an exercise in the abstract logic of representation. Adding delegates from hitherto unrepresented districts affected the outcome of nominating contests.[6]

The reign of the legislative caucus lasted through the 1820s, and its history was always intertwined with the role of the congressional caucus. When the popular war hero Andrew Jackson succeeded in winning the presidency after boycotting his party's congressional caucus, that institution collapsed. Soon after, the state legislative caucus also disappeared. At both levels, the delegate convention became the new method of making nominations.

The conflict that ultimately destroyed the legislative caucus signified a shift in the balance of political forces in the nation. Suffrage was broadening and power was shifting westward from the seaboard states. Symptomatic of this process of democratization was the popular election of members of the electoral college—by 1824, eighteen of the twenty-four states of the Union had provided for popular election, and by 1828, only three state legislatures still selected electoral college members. When Jackson swept into power on the basis of a popular campaign that owed nothing to those members of the Republican party who had refused him its congressional caucus nomination, his victory signaled the passing of an older, more aristocratic leadership centered in the nation's legislatures. The replacement of the legislative caucus by the delegate convention symbolized the growing spirit of egalitarianism. The delegate convention—or so it was supposed—meant grass-roots control of the party's nominating processes.

THE DELEGATE CONVENTION

Delegates to state conventions were elected at open caucuses or conventions held in cities, towns, and counties. This was a system designed to represent the party membership, but despite its original intent, the convention system soon displayed a susceptibility to abuse. In some of the local caucuses, delegate slates were offered with little opportunity of challenge. In others, "snap" caucuses were called with inadequate public notice to limit participation to those who would meekly accept the prepared slate. If the machinations at the local party level were inadequate to secure control for the dominant party faction, the matter was handled at the state convention. Duly elected delegates were refused seats and their credentials were handed over to organizational stalwarts.

The convention system was not everywhere corrupt, but after the Civil War, abuses were widespread. This was an era in which the railroads were expanding westward and required rights of way; public utilities wanted franchises and freedom from public regulation; and the directors of giant corporations were determined to promote their interests without governmental interference. To achieve their goals, these groups sought to control public offices at their source—the nominations made by the parties.

THE DIRECT PRIMARY

Reaction to widespread corruption and the domination of the nation by corporate giants gave rise to the Progressive movement, whose goal was to restore power to the people. Rather than the indirect voice the people had in selecting candidates under the convention system, the Progressives proposed that voters be allowed to participate directly in naming the party candidates. Although the rise of Progressivism at the turn of the century assured the adoption of the direct primary in many states, there was another pressing reason for its acceptance. Under the sectional pattern of politics that produced broad regions of one-party control, citizens would have no direct voice in who was to govern them unless party nominations were subject to *popular* control.

Today most nominations within the states are made through the direct primary. There are states, however, in which a convention role is legally preserved. Connecticut, for instance, employs a so-called challenge primary. Nominations are made in conventions, subject to the right of a losing candidate who receives 20 percent of convention votes to demand a primary election. Utah holds a preprimary convention to narrow the primary contest to the top two convention choices; however, if any candidate wins 70 percent of the convention votes, he or she is declared the nominee. In Colorado and New Mexico, all candidates receiving 20 percent of the convention votes of their party are automatically placed on the primary ballot. Although candidates also can get on the ballot by nominating petitions, party leaders frown on the practice.[7] New York illustrates still another primary variant. The state central committees initially make the selections for statewide nominations. Losing candidates can request a primary if they receive 25 percent of committee votes or collect twenty thousand petition signatures.

In the South, the dominance of the Democratic party made for a unique situation. The Republican party did not even hold primary elections there until recently. State laws either left the choice of how nominations were to be made to the party leadership or required the primary only for those parties receiving a certain proportion of the vote in general elections. Since the Democratic nomination for so long was tantamount to election, any Republican primary contest would have been meaningless. Now that the Republican party is a stronger competitor, the direct primary is more widely employed by both political parties. However, Virginia Democrats took advantage of the legal options available to them in 1978 to nominate their U. S. senatorial candidate by convention, a practice they continued in selecting a gubernatorial nominee in 1981. This decision was taken to promote unity after the Democratic party had been battered by several primary contests.

The historical hegemony of the Democratic party has led to another unique feature of southern primary elections. If no candidate receives a majority of votes cast in the initial primary, a second, or runoff, primary is held between the top two candidates. This plan, which is used in ten southern and border states plus the District of Columbia, was designed to secure majority support for nominees who traditionally encountered only token opposition in the general election. The fear of a minority-backed nominee is still well grounded because southern primaries generally attract more nominees than primaries elsewhere, and the vote in the first primary is often dispersed as a consequence.[8] The front runner in the initial primary is by no means assured of eventual election.

The Direct Primary as a Nominating Device

Adoption of the direct primary was undoubtedly spurred by the shortcomings of the party system that prevailed in the second half of the nineteenth century. Corrupt state and urban party organizations were common enough to stimulate reform, and as sectional politics hardened after the 1896 election, many states were left with a single party dominating their political life. The more recent abandonment or modification of the convention system in Connecticut, Delaware, Indiana, and New York occurred under somewhat different circumstances. Each of these states had strong two-party competition and none had parties as blatantly venal as some that existed at the turn of the century. In these states, it was a more general belief in the intrinsic value of popular participation that prompted the shift to the direct primary. If the parties belong to the people, why shouldn't people name the candidates who will run under the party label?

The logic of popular participation in nominating politics springs from the concept of the party as an association of its

electoral supporters. Nevertheless, some state laws do not recognize that each party has a separate following. The relative
openness of primary elections to all who desire to participate
is explored in the following section.

CLOSED, OPEN, AND WIDE-OPEN PRIMARIES

Direct primaries may be classified according to the restrictions placed on popular participation. There are two basic
types, closed and open, with important variants of each.

Closed primaries are used in thirty-nine states. This plan
supposedly preserves the integrity of the party because it
limits participation to those who claim party affiliation. The
critical issue, however, is the test of party membership. In approximately half the states using the closed system, the voter
need do no more than declare his or her preference at the polls.
The declaration is subject to challenge, of course, but objections are seldom made and even more rarely upheld. In a
Virginia gubernatorial primary, for example, a Republican
precinct leader known to Democratic poll watchers was unsuccessfully challenged when she requested a Democratic ballot.
A more effective test of party membership, designed specifically to block crossover voting, is the requirement of prior
registration as a Democrat or Republican. Under this system, a
ledger is kept at the polls listing qualified voters by their partisan affiliation so voters cannot change their allegiance at the
last moment simply to vote in a contested primary.[9]

In open primary states, no test of affiliation is used to exclude those who are not adherents of a party. As employed in
eight states—Idaho, Michigan, Minnesota, Montana, North
Dakota, Utah, Vermont, and Wisconsin—the open primary permits voters to cast a vote in either party's primary. This system
violates the concept of a party as an association of its loyal supporters by removing all restrictions on who may participate.
The effect is to weaken the distinctiveness of the party labels
conferred.

Party regulars fear that the open primary (and the closed
system without effective tests of affiliation) encourages opposition party members to enter their primary in order to nominate candidates who are not the best or strongest party representatives. Are these fears justified? True, if one party has no
real primary contest, its members may decide to enter the
other party's primary, particularly if it is a close race. But the

practice of "raiding," a deliberate and organized attempt to invade the opposition party to nominate the weakest candidate, has never been supported by evidence. Still, crossovers do occur, and the effect on the party is often the same as with raiding. Even though most opposition party voters who cross over vote for the person they believe will make the best candidate, their choice is not necessarily the same as that of long-time party loyalists.

Party activists find the open primary frustrating for other reasons. If the party organization does choose sides in nominating contests, it is confronted by an unknown electorate. The "street sheets" professionals maintain to locate loyal party followers are an inaccurate guide to who may ultimately participate in their primary. Candidates are also handicapped in devising their electoral strategy, for the appeals one might choose to make to one's own partisans are not necessarily attractive to opposition party members. Candidates prefer an electorate they know to a more fluid one.

Three states—Alaska, Washington, and Louisiana—have variations of the open primary that destroy even further the separate identity of the parties. Alaska and Washington use the "blanket" or "wide-open" primary, which allows voters to participate in *both* party primaries, although not for the same office. These states use a consolidated ballot grouping the candidates of both parties by office. A voter may choose, for example, a Democratic nominee for governor and a Republican nominee for attorney general. After the votes are tallied, the Democratic winners take on the Republican winners for their respective offices in the general election contest.

Louisiana has a system all its own. It is similar to that used by Alaska and Washington in that it employs a consolidated ballot grouping party candidates by office and allows the voters to choose from the list under each office. The unique feature of the Louisiana system is that if a candidate receives the majority of all votes cast in a primary, he or she wins the office without having to go through a general election. If no candidate receives a majority vote, a runoff is held between the two front runners, regardless of their party affiliations. The Louisiana plan would be similar to a nonpartisan election were it not for the fact that candidates are identified by party label.

There is a certain logic to the Louisiana electoral system. If the voters, regardless of partisan affiliation, are to be allowed to choose a party's candidates, why go through the charade of a general election contest between party nominees? The candidates who receive an absolute majority of votes cast in a primary are obviously the people's choices, so why incur the expense of a *pro forma* campaign? Again, if the two front-running candidates happen to belong to the same party, why shouldn't they compete in a runoff election? To award ballot space to a lesser candidate because of his or her partisan affiliation is to deny the popular will.

The Louisiana plan is only one step removed from the nonpartisan primary. Under the nonpartisan system, the candidate's partisan affiliations do not appear on the ballot and the candidate receiving a majority of votes cast is declared the winner. If the primary produces no winner, a runoff is held between the two top vote getters. Nonpartisan elections, which are more overtly antiparty than wide-open primaries, are widely used in municipal elections and for the selection of the judiciary in some states. Nebraska is the only state that still selects members of its legislative body in this fashion.

THE EFFECTS OF THE DIRECT PRIMARY ON POLITICAL PARTIES

Involvement of the rank and file in party nominations has not been universally acclaimed. Those who have taken a position in opposition, implicitly or explicitly, cling to the concept of the party as a group of working politicians. If their power is diluted, then the party is necessarily weakened. "If the strivings to construct party systems more nearly commensurate with the needs of the states are to bear fruit," the late V. O. Key, Jr., wrote, "a sober reconsideration of the direct primary procedure of nomination will have to be made."[10] At issue is the appropriate relationship between the party professionals and the rank and file. Put simply, who is to be in charge of the political party? This question cannot be resolved to everyone's satisfaction, but the arguments against the direct primary are too important to ignore.

Destruction of Party Responsibility. The meaning of "responsible" political parties varies considerably according to those who interpret the phrase. We use the term here in a loose fashion to denote the belief that Democratic officeholders should band together to oppose Republican officeholders on questions of public policy. Citizens may then judge the performance of each party and cast their votes for its candidates accordingly. When working politicians control nominations, it is argued, they can ensure that those receiving the party label are committed to the traditional stand of the party. In contrast, candidates who obtain their nominations through primary elections are not beholden to the party professionals and are free to resort to any stratagem they think may prove successful in garnering votes, regardless of whether it is compatible with party traditions. Party professionals, this argument continues, are more familiar with the ideological references of their party than the average party follower. Furthermore, they are often better judges of political talent than primary voters, who acquire their knowledge of candidates through paid political advertisements.

The problem with this argument is that when the professionals did have power over nominations, they seldom used it to build cohesive parties. Before the advent of the direct primary (and before the popular election of U.S. senators), the congressional parties had been reduced to a state of impotency. Writing in 1885, Woodrow Wilson observed; "Our parties marshal their adherents with the strictest possible discipline for the purpose of carrying elections, but their discipline is very slack and indefinite in dealing with legislation."[11] Although the parties did manage to bring order to the U.S. House in the 1890s, before the enactment of primary laws, they did it initially through rule changes that enhanced the power of the speaker. First Thomas "Czar" Reed and then Joseph "Uncle Joe" Cannon ran the House with an iron fist. After Cannon was replaced by Champ Clark, and the direct primary was spreading throughout the nation, congressional caucuses were used with effectiveness to build support for each party's legislative program.[12] It was not until the 1920s that the caucus fell into disuse. In other words, it was the state of the party organizations within Congress, not the professionals of state and local party organizations, that determined congressional party cohesion.

Even during the period when party professionals were able to engineer the outcome of primary elections, party regularity in the Congress was far from perfect. Franklin Roosevelt scored an impressive victory in 1936, but his popular mandate did not unify congressional Democrats behind his programs. The unsatisfactory state of party unity led to a call for more disciplined parties and the appointment in 1946 of a prestigious committee of the American Political Science Association to study and report on "the condition and improvement of national party organization."[13]

Of course, the degree of party unity is a relative matter. The parties of the 1930s were more cohesive than the parties of today, but the political environment has also changed. In the thirties, partisan sides were more clearly drawn. One either favored the use of government power to correct social and economic ills, or one did not. But the issues are not so easily joined in contemporary America. That government power should be used to manage the economy and alleviate the distress of the needy is no longer seriously debated. *How* that power should be used, however, is a matter of controversy. Yet economic issues are so complex that clear Democratic and Republican alternatives have been slow to emerge. In his first year in office, Ronald Reagan did clarify the Republican position, but the Democrats were unable to agree on an opposition strategy. Nor have moral issues that divide the country—such as abortion and school busing to achieve racial balance—been fought along partisan lines. It is difficult to see how restoring control over nominations to political professionals would work a dramatic change in how officeholders vote.

Nevertheless, political professionals are committed to their party. They may be motivated by the causes they serve, a desire to win, or both. Most are still willing to compromise specific issue stands to place their candidates in office. Perhaps it is their role as political brokers that should be stressed. A party organization that officeholders have to reckon with may not produce the party regularity hoped for by the adherents of the responsible party doctrine, but it might eliminate maverick officeholders with no concern for party fortunes. It would probably also encourage legislative members to work with their governor or president to carve out an acceptable record to run on. The more extravagant claims for the professionals' role appear unwarranted. Yet strengthening their power could counteract some of the divisive tendencies of the antiparty mood of contemporary America.

Unbalanced Tickets and Unpopular Choices. The political party as an organization survives best when it is able to compete effectively for the offices of government. If it is habitually deprived of electoral successes, the party will encounter difficulty in recruiting workers for a hopeless mission. In order to win, however, the party must put forward capable and attractive candidates. Political professionals would argue that they are in the best position to nominate winning tickets. They know how to negotiate with the major ethnic, regional, and ideological elements of the party's normal coalition, and then prepare a balanced slate of candidates. Primary contests do not afford a similar latitude for negotiating a balanced ticket. Electoral strategies are limited to voting for or against individual candidates.

Another problem inherent in primary elections is that the winning candidates are selected by voters who are not necessarily representative of the party's entire following. The turnout in primary elections is commonly lower than in general elections, but this would be of little consequence if primary voters accurately represented the party's following in the general election. Often, however, they are a distorted reflection of a party's following. Primary voters may consist disproportionately of "people of certain sections of a state, of persons chiefly of specified national origin or religious affiliation, of people es-

From *Herblock on all Fronts* (New American Library, 1980).

pecially responsive to certain styles of political leadership or shades of ideology. . . ."[14]

V. O. Key, Jr., described the effect of introducing the direct primary on Democratic choices for statewide office in Massachusetts.[15] Under the convention system, approximately one out of four Democratic nominees came from Boston and its immediate vicinity. Under the primary system, by the end of the 1940s almost 83 percent of the statewide nominees resided in the Boston area. This preference for Boston candidates was not a consequence of the growth of the Democratic electorate there, for it remained approximately the same for the convention and primary periods that Key studied. For each period, the Boston area contributed 20 percent of the Democratic party's general election vote. But Bostonians constituted better than 50 percent of the party's primary vote; hence the lopsided preference for Boston nominees. Because he was a favorite of the Boston Irish, the legendary James Michael Curley often won statewide Democratic nominations but gained office only once, as governor in 1934, the year in which Democratic party strength reached its peak. In 1936, also an advantageous year for most Democratic candidates, Curley lost the U. S. Senate race to Henry Cabot Lodge. Two years later, he was defeated by Leverett Saltonstall in a second try for the governor's office. Curley may have mirrored his Boston constituency, but he was a poor choice for statewide office.

It is also argued that political professionals would reject obviously unqualified candidates or candidates whose political views are embarrassingly opposed to the ideological image the party has striven to maintain. Although the professionals may show a willingness to accept internal dissent in their desire to win, there are limits to their tolerance. In the Ohio contest for congressman-at-large in 1962, the Democratic nomination was won by a political newcomer from Cleveland, Richard D. Kennedy. An avowed segregationist, Kennedy was not backed by the Democratic party in the general election and was easily defeated by the Republican candidate, Robert A. Taft, Jr. Maryland Democratic voters similarly embarrassed their party in 1966 by nominating George Mahoney as their gubernatorial candidate. Campaigning on a segregationist theme of "your home is your castle," Mahoney caused many loyal Democrats to break ranks and support the Republican candidate, Spiro Agnew. And Tom Metzger, state leader of the Ku Klux Klan, won the Democratic nomination in California's forty-third congressional district in 1980 when his two opponents split the anti-Klan vote. Disavowed by Democratic party leaders, Metzger was overwhelmed by incumbent Republican Clair W. Burgener.

Party professionals do not always repudiate what they consider a poor choice of the primary electorate. In 1954 in Massachusetts, a minor clerical employee of a safety razor company filed in the Democratic primary for the post of state treasurer. His name happened to be the same as the then junior senator from Massachusetts, John Kennedy. Although not endorsed by his party in the preprimary convention that Massachusetts employed at that time, Kennedy won his party's nomination. The Democratic State Committee then stated that his primary victory afforded "proof that in Massachusetts democracy works and that Americans invariably draw their best talent for leadership from the rank and file of the people."[16] Kennedy was elected to the office he sought.

The citation of selected examples is not always the best way to support a given viewpoint. The most solid case for giving party professionals a greater role in the candidate selection process rests on the fact that they have private knowledge of the candidates they back, while party supporters often make their choices on candidates' public appeals. In a competitive party setting, the professionals' concern for putting together a winning slate also makes a persuasive argument in their behalf. The contention that they should have more influence in the party's selection process cannot be dismissed as a last ditch grab by a moribund party establishment.

Divisive Primaries and Election Outcomes. A primary election is a contest held within the party family. As so often happens in family rivalries, the contest may open deep wounds. The contestants may each be loyal to the party, but they are competing in a race in which only one can obtain the prize. Under the stress of a campaign, they may level charges and countercharges that are not easily forgotten by the time of the general election. Even if the losing candidate is magnanimous in defeat, his campaign staff and loyal following may not be so forgiving. If the primary contest is bitter enough, the party may lose whatever electoral chances it had at the outset.

One of the functions of the "smoke-filled rooms" of delegate conventions was to avoid the public airing of internal party disputes. Bargaining and compromising were the stock in trade of a party leadership that wished to maintain or enlarge its electoral coalition. Private negotiations offered a wide latitude for reaching a settlement in which each contending faction could emerge with half a loaf. In contrast, a forensic battle among candidates contending to establish their claim for the nomination in a primary election by its nature is designed to divide the party. The party professionals fear that such primary disputes will spill over to general election contests.

The most recent evidence supports the contention that divisive or contested primaries do hurt a candidate's chances of winning in a general election when his opponent is not similarly handicapped. The harm is of two sorts. Fratricidal contests may cause the supporters of the losing candidate to stay away on election day or, worse, drive them to the opposition party in a fit of pique. The successful primary candidate may also find that the ranks of party workers are depleted because the defeated candidate's activists have lost their zeal for campaigning. In either case, the party and its candidate are deprived of important support.

Defining a divisive primary as one in which the victor has less than a 20 percent edge over the next leading candidate, Robert A. Bernstein examined U. S. senatorial primaries from 1958 through 1972.[17] As Table 6-1 shows, both incumbents and challengers were less successful when they had to battle to se-

© 3/26/80, The Philadelphia Inquirer/The Washington Post Writers Group. Reprinted with permission.

Table 6-1
DIVISIVE PRIMARIES AND THE FATE OF INCUMBENTS

	Only Incumbent Had Divisive Primary	Neither or Both Had Divisive Primary	Only Challenger Had Divisive Primary
Won	8	139	45
Lost	4	23	3
Percentage of races won by incumbent	67%	86%	94%

SOURCE: Robert A. Bernstein, "Divisive Primaries Do Hurt: U.S. Senate Races, 1956–1976," *American Political Science Review* 71 (June 1977), p. 541.

cure the nomination and their opponent did not. Although the data in the table are for races involving incumbents, the pattern was the same for open seats. In the pure one-party states, of course, the candidate of the dominant party seldom lost in the general election. In other states, the harmful effects of divisive primaries remained after controls were entered for partisan tendencies of the state.

The effects of primary campaign losses upon party activists were studied by Donald Bruce Johnson and James R. Gibson.[18] Both the Republican and Democratic primaries in Iowa's first congressional district were contested in 1970. After the primary, the campaign workers did not close ranks to prepare for the November elections against the opposition party. Three out of four campaigners on the losing side stated that they did not intend to be very active in the fall. One out of five losers said they planned to work for the opposition party to help defeat the candidate who had defeated *them* in the primary. These disgruntled losers tended to be both less politically experienced and less strongly identified with their party than those who remained loyal.

The Costs of Winning. Political campaigns today are costly undertakings. Money is not the sole determinant of who wins primary contests, but it can purchase the campaign expertise to turn a politically inexperienced contender into a formidable candidate. Professional consultants are available for hire to manage all phases of a candidate's campaign. With appropriate financial backing, almost any credible candidate can mount a serious challenge for a party nomination.

The effects of this situation upon the party are threefold. First, it gives a distinct advantage to candidates who are personally wealthy and can thus afford their political ambitions. Able but less financially secure candidates may have their political hopes dashed because they cannot match their rival's spending. Second, well-financed primary candidates have a wider latitude in the type of campaign they will conduct because they are not dependent upon party resources. Organizational regulars may prefer a candidate who has demonstrated party loyalty, but their counsel may go unheeded in the face of a free-spending party outsider. Third, candidates who face stiff primary opposition may exhaust their funds in winning the nomination. With their financial resources depleted, they are less able to carry the fight to the opposition in the general election.

The personal wealth of a candidate, even in the convention days, was no small matter in the calculations of political professionals deciding whom to back. Yet under the convention system, the political professionals could husband their resources for the general election. In this regard, convention nominations are less costly to the contending candidates and money is less influential in determining the outcome. In Virginia's Republican convention of 1978, the party's state chairman, Richard Obershain, received the U.S. senatorial nomination although he was outspent by his rival, John Warner. When Obershain was killed in a tragic plane accident while campaigning, the Republican State Committee nominated Warner, who went on to win the Senate seat for the Republicans.

Weakening of the Party Organizations. The major political parties still control access to the principal elective offices of the nation. Few independents are elected to high government offices. Yet the party label is rather freely bestowed upon candidates who are able to muster the necessary pluralities in primary elections. Their successes do not always depend upon past work for the party or agreeable relations with those who staff the regular party organizations. If the route to public office does not include loyal party service, an important incentive is removed for party work. To the extent that those seeking the party nomination can afford to ignore the party professionals, the concept of the party as a group of working politicians is vitiated. Political activists may find working for individual candidates more rewarding than staffing party posts. In these circumstances, the fate of the parties rests more and more upon the officeholders alone.

Organizational Adaptations to Primary Nominations

So entrenched is the direct primary in American party politics that few organizational regulars openly advocate abandoning it. Virginia Democrats did take advantage of legal provisions that gave them discretionary authority to employ either the delegate convention or the direct primary in making party nominations. Following a series of bitterly contested primaries involving the populist candidate Henry E. Howell, the Democratic State Committee reverted to the convention form to nominate candidates for major offices. But Virginia has been the exception, not the rule. Indiana and Delaware, the last convention states, succumbed to the direct primary for statewide nominations in the mid-1970s.

PREPRIMARY ENDORSEMENTS

Although they have been unable to block it, party organizations have not docilely submitted to the reformist spirit embodied in the primary election. In some states, a preprimary convention is held to endorse a slate of candidates or to weed out a number of primary contenders. Any candidate who receives 20 percent of the vote in the Colorado convention appears on the primary ballot. If more than one candidate qualifies, their names are listed in the order of the size of their convention vote. In the rare event that a candidate qualifies by petition, his or her name follows that of the convention contenders. In Connecticut, if a challenge primary is sought, the name of the convention-endorsed candidate appears first on the ballot and is marked by an asterisk. The Utah convention selects the two candidates who compete in the primary contests, and no other names appear on the ballot. The names of the candidates endorsed by the Rhode Island state committees are listed first on the ballots, and are designated by an asterisk. In other states, either state conventions or state committees formally endorse a slate of candidates, though their selections do not receive any ballot preferences.

The practice of endorsing slates of candidates, with or without ballot preferences, is indicative of the strength of the formal party apparatus. Preprimary endorsements give party leaders a better chance of controlling the nomination outcome.

One study has found that gubernatorial candidates who receive preprimary endorsements do much better than those who do not.[19] Candidates endorsed by a system mandated by state law do marginally better than candidates who are backed under party rules. For example, the Connecticut challenge primary took effect in 1958, but no convention choice had to fight a primary contest before 1970.[20] The Colorado parties are neither so strong nor so disciplined as those of Connecticut, but from 1928 through 1967 only one gubernatorial candidate who collected the most convention votes was defeated in his party's primary.[21] It is probably safe to say that where the parties endorse candidates, they are confident of their organizational power. Though they cannot always ward off a primary challenge, they usually do back a winner.

CANDIDATE RECRUITMENT

In only fifteen to twenty states do one or both parties formally choose preferred nominees for major state offices. More often, the activity is behind the scenes. Approximately three-quarters of the state chairmen in one study reported that they engaged in some form of regular candidate recruitment.[22] And their task is not simply to ensure that able and attractive candidates enter the primary; they must also dissuade undesirable candidates from making the race. One Democratic state chairman described his recruiting activities in the following way:

> It's important to recruit because that is the only way you can keep self-proclaimed candidates from gaining a spot on the ballot, and that can do you in. You simply have to have the clout to tell a self-starter, "No, you cannot be a candidate and if you go ahead and try we will give you no support at all." I have gone so far as imply that the party will work against a guy if he persists in running. One has to be brutal about it with some of them.[23]

The recruitment patterns of state organizations vary.[24] Sometimes the state chairman works with a recruitment committee selected from members of the state committee. The committee prepares candidate lists and then contacts prospective candidates to determine their interest in running. Most state chairmen get personally involved in the attempt to persuade potential candidates to run. In some states, however, it is the governor or other elected leaders who solicit candidates for statewide or congressional offices. Some state chairmen believe they should be officially neutral and delegate recruiting responsibilities to party leaders at the county or congressional district level.

Prospective candidates frequently consult party workers before they make their decision to run. In a study of selected communities in North Carolina and Massachusetts, from 60 to 80 percent of the precinct and ward committeemen interviewed reported that candidates had consulted them.[25] In most cases, the candidates were seeking local or state legislative posts, but aspirants for higher office, particularly in North Carolina, also spoke to local party officials. Although it is risky to generalize on the basis of limited case studies, securing the support of party regulars seems to be important. The winners in two contested Iowa congressional primaries were supported by a significantly higher proportion of workers who held official party posts than their losing opponents.[26]

INTERVENTION IN PRIMARIES

Party leaders' attempts to control who enters a primary are not always successful. If they were, the direct primary would not be the headache it is to party organizations. Many candidates whose own resources are sufficiently strong are unfazed by the pleas of the party leadership to give way to the organization's choices. Others make political capital out of running against an entrenched political machine. In a contested primary, the organizational leaders are confronted by an additional choice. Do they intervene in behalf of the candidates they would prefer to see win? Or do they maintain a posture of neutrality and let the party supporters select the party nominee?

Most state chairmen will attempt to influence the outcome of primary elections under selected circumstances (see Table 6-2). The decision is not always an easy one to make because backing the wrong candidates in major state races can cost chairmen their positions. One state chairman recalled the fate of a predecessor who regularly intervened in primary contests:

When _____ was chairman in 1966 he announced his support for _____ for governor. Now, that did not seem to be an important problem at the time because everyone expected him to win hands down. Unfortunately, he proved to be a dull and lackluster candidate, and a relative unknown, _____, actually won the primary. Just about everybody ran for cover, but the chairman was left

standing there holding the bag. He was immediately asked to resign, which he did, and _____'s campaign manager was designated as chairman. They went on to lose the election but that
wasn't much consolation to [the former chairman].[27]

Despite the risk, state chairmen who are concerned with their
party's image want to slate credible candidates. Intervening in
a primary may be their only recourse when preprimary activities fail to ward off an embarrassing entrant.

The Contemporary Parties: Primary Competition and Organizational Power

On the surface, it may appear that party professionals
have exaggerated their fears of the direct primary. Available
evidence suggests that most gubernatorial, U. S. senatorial,
and congressional primaries are not seriously contested. This
is probably true of state legislative races as well, although the
data are more spotty. If the party organizations are able to
achieve their objective of avoiding disruptive nominating battles much of the time, why has the primary been singled out as

Table 6-2
STATE CHAIRMEN'S ATTITUDES TOWARD INTERVENTION IN PRIMARY CONTESTS

Response to Question: Should Chairman Intervene?	Democrats (N=39)	Republicans (N=41)	Total (N=80)
Yes, only if candidate is endorsed by party	7.7%	7.3%	7.6%
Yes, if necessary to protect caliber of candidates	25.6	31.7	28.7
Yes, but only by recruiting strong candidate	7.7	4.9	6.2
Yes, open intervention	15.4	14.6	15.0
No, never under any circumstances	28.2	29.3	28.8
No, in local races; yes, in state races	0.0	4.9	2.5
No (but has intervened when necessary)	5.1	0.0	2.5
Not ascertainable/Don't know	10.3	7.3	8.7

SOURCE: Robert J. Huckshorn, *Party Leadership in the States* (Boston: University of Massachusetts Press, 1976), p. 107.

a major cause of party weakness? The reasons are to be found in why some primaries are contested more than others.

DETERMINANTS OF PRIMARY CONTESTS

The influence of the party organization is important in avoiding contests. If the state organizations are strong enough, would-be candidates will work through established party channels to get their name on the primary ballot. Where state law recognizes a party endorsement with preferential ballot treatment, as it does in Colorado, Connecticut, or Rhode Island, primary elections are less likely to be seriously contested. Legal backing for the party organizations in this role, of course, reflects party influence within a state. The effect of more informal party activity in reducing the number of contested primaries is not so surely known, but it requires no great leap in logic to surmise that success varies with the strength of the organizations maintained.

Organizational strength is not the only determinant of contested primaries. The politically ambitious are reluctant to take on incumbents, possibly for fear such a challenge will bring an early end to their career. Since the primary electorate is not structured by party labels, it is less predictable in its choices. The candidate whose name is best known enjoys an advantage, and incumbents are more likely to be recognized than challengers. Added to name recognition is the stance of the party organization—few organizational leaders wish to repudiate their incumbent officeholders. The incumbency factor goes a long way toward explaining the relative absence of primary competition involving members of Congress.

Yet another factor that explains why primaries are contested is the likelihood that the party's nominee will go on to win the general election. The nomination of a party that historically has been on the losing side in state contests is not a prize that is eagerly sought, and a token candidate may have to be persuaded to undertake the assignment to maintain the party's stake in electoral politics. On the other hand, the party that has dominated its state politics is more likely to have contested primaries because the primary victor, barring unusual circumstances, will gain the office. States with reasonably competitive elections fall somewhere in between in the degree to which their primaries are contested. Table 6-3 shows the proportion

Table 6–3
PERCENTAGE OF CANDIDATES IN DIVISIVE PRIMARIES BY PARTY ORIENTATION AND INCUMBENCY

	Party Orientation		
Type of Candidate	Candidates of Dominant or Stronger Party	Candidates of Equally Competitive Party	Candidates of Minor or Weaker Party
Incumbents	8% (120)*	6% (65)	3% (37)
Open races	38% (52)	32% (38)	17% (52)
Challengers	32% (37)	26% (65)	18% (120)

*Figures in parentheses are N's.
SOURCE: Robert A. Bernstein, "Divisive Primaries Do Hurt: U.S. Senate Races, 1956–1976," *American Political Science Review* 71 (June 1977), p. 542.

of U.S. senatorial elections from 1956 to 1972 that were subject to serious challenges. Although incumbency is a powerful influence in limiting competition, the relative strength of the parties clearly is a significant factor.

POWER OF THE PROFESSIONALS

We can now return to the question posed earlier: have the critics of the direct primary exaggerated its impact? We think not for the following reasons. Although many primaries are not subject to serious challenge, the proportion that are is substantial. Not all party organizations intervene in primary contests, and those that do are not always successful in electing their choices. Moreover, if the antiorganization candidate does win office, the effects of incumbency are such that the party may have to live with them for a long time. One state chairman complained bitterly about the results of primary races in a key county he had targeted:

> The primary was held about three weeks ago and we got a Bircher nominated in one, a housewife with no experience in another, and we got our own guy nominated in the third. How in hell are we to go to the people with that? To make matters worse, the Bircher is probably going to win and will be around to embarrass us for the next two years, if not forever.[28]

Party organizations do not have the freedom over candidate selection under the primary that they did under the convention form. Even a lack of serious challenges in primary contests does not necessarily mean that the party organization was instrumental in closing the competition. Political outsiders sometimes have the resources to intimidate potential opposition, and the party may be powerless to counteract their claim to the nomination. On the other hand, the leaders may so fear that a bitter primary battle will leave their party splintered that they will intervene to avoid a contest, even if that means advancing a candidate who was not their preferred choice.

The power of political professionals has certainly diminished in this era of the direct primary. Though their worst fears may not have been realized, they no longer have a free hand in naming candidates. Nor have the goals of the Progressive reformers been fully achieved. The proportion of uncontested primaries is evidence that the people do not always have a voice in conferring the party label.

If neither the professional nor the party follower can be entirely satisfied with the results, some candidates have less reason for complaint. Although the financial costs of obtaining the nomination have escalated, the party dissident or political outsider now has a better chance of getting on the general election ballot as a party nominee. Once elected, officeholders are relatively unconstrained by either party professionals or party followings. Their own sense of party loyalty may encourage them to cooperate with their partisan colleagues, but the ability of incumbents to retain their party's nomination suggests that they are seldom reprimanded by the primary electorate for either lack of party loyalty or achievement in office.

The primary was introduced in a period of widespread corruption in American political life and it gave voters a voice in selecting their leaders in one-party states. However, party organizations of today are vastly different from the corrupt machines of the past, and two-party competition is slowly spreading to areas of former one-party hegemony. Perhaps it is time for a reexamination of the professionals' role in nominations. There is little chance of abolishing the popular voice in the nominating process, but it is possible to enhance the professionals' role. Having party agencies formally endorse candidates might clarify the professionals' job and the candidates' relationship to them. While it would work no miracles, this could be a step toward restoring to the professionals some of the brokerage functions they are adept at handling.

SUMMARY

Nominating candidates for public office is the first stage in the process by which political parties organize the electorate. The choice of nominee is of crucial importance, for it may well determine the party's electoral success. In addition, what candidates and officeholders say and do affects the party's public image as well as its cohesion and unity.

The history of nominations in the United States is one of increasing democratization. The informal caucus of self-appointed leaders gave way to the legislative caucus, at least for statewide nominations. The legislative caucus was altered to seat voting delegates from districts without representation, and finally it was replaced by the delegate convention, which signaled the triumph of popular forces over entrenched and aristocratic state legislatures. The full flowering of popular participation came with the direct primary.

There was ample justification for instituting the direct primary. State and local party organizations of the latter half of the nineteenth century were tainted by fraud and corruption, and party conventions were no exception to the general rule. Progressive reformers proposed the direct primary to restore power to the people. Another reason for adopting the primary was the hardening sectional alignment at the turn of the century that left many states under one-party control. Without the primary, voters would have had almost no voice in selecting their leaders.

The primary spread rapidly and is now used in some form in all the states. As a nominating device, it reflects a conceptualization of the political party as a loose association of its more or less loyal following. It blurred the distinction between party member and party supporter, and consequently reduced the power of political professionals and, many believe, weakened the parties. For this reason, not everyone judges the primary an unqualified success. Implicitly or explicitly, critics cling to a concept of the party as a group of working politicians.

Direct primaries are commonly classified according to their openness to popular participation. Closed primaries are supposedly limited to loyal supporters, but whether a closed primary successfully restricts participation depends upon the test of affiliation. A simple declaration at the polls is ineffective in preventing crossover voting, whereas prior registration as a Democrat or Republican does have the effect intended. Open primaries allow all voters to participate, regardless of their partisan attachment. This system undermines the concept of a party as an association of loyal supporters. Open primaries have certain practical consequences: party distinctiveness is lost because of crossover votes; candidates are uncertain of the electorate they are addressing; and party regulars have little control over opposition party votes.

Because the direct primary limits the influence of political professionals, it is said to crode the concept of responsible parties. Candidates who address their appeals to the electorate are less certainly tied to the party they represent. Although party professionals seldom used their power to build truly cohesive parties, under the convention system, they did have the ability to block the nomination of political mavericks and candidates who would embarrass the party. Today that power is severely restricted.

The direct primary also affects party fortunes by giving nominating power to voters who are often unrepresentative of the party's normal support. Candidates nominated under such circumstances may fare poorly in the general election. The primary has also made it impossible to negotiate a balanced slate that represents the major ethnic, factional, regional, or ideological elements of the party's customary coalition. The brokerage function of the professionals gives way to a more limited strategy of voting for or against individual candidates.

Political professionals also worry about the divisive effects of contested primaries. Charges and countercharges leveled during a bitter primary battle may so divide a party that its ranks become hopelessly splintered. Furthermore, primary contests are costly, which not only works to the benefit of the wealthy candidate, but may also exhaust the sources of party money for the general election campaign.

As the power of the professionals over party affairs has eroded, political activists have found it more rewarding to work for individual candidates than for parties. The danger of this trend is that the party may soon be held together by little more than the willingness of those who share a label to work together for common causes.

The political professionals have not docilely accepted this situation. Where their ranks are strongest, they have adapted to the primary, in some cases by using party agencies to endorse candidates who are then given preferential ballot space, in other cases by working informally with the candidates they prefer.

One measure of the professionals' success in retaining some power is the extent of contested primaries. Most primaries for major offices are not seriously contested. Of course, the absence of contests is not solely a consequence of the professionals' influence. The primaries of a dominant party are more likely to be contested than those of a weak party. Incumbents are less likely to encounter opposition than nonincumbents, and the effects of incumbency are cumulative over the years. Also, an uncontested primary may simply result from intimidation of potential opposition by a party outsider with financial resources.

Although the professionals have learned to live with the primary, they have been constrained by it. At the same time, the primary has not fully achieved the goals envisioned by the reformers. Too many primaries are uncontested; too many incumbents, whatever their record, are never seriously challenged. Since the party organizations of today bear little resemblance to the corrupt machines of the past, and since the areas of one-party dominance have receded, now may be the time to restore some power over nominations to the professionals. Without restricting popular participation, party agencies might formally endorse primary candidates. Such a step could clarify the relationship of candidates and professionals and enhance the brokerage function that is the professionals' forte.

Notes

[1] E. E. Schattschneider, *Party Government* (New York: Holt, Rinehart and Winston, 1942), p. 53.
[2] Ibid., p. 60.
[3] His argument is summarized in ibid., chap. 9.

[4]For brief accounts of early nominating procedures, see V. O. Key, Jr., *Politics, Parties, and Pressure Groups,* 5th ed. (New York: Crowell, 1964), pp. 371–376; and Austin Ranney, *Curing the Mischiefs of Faction* (Berkeley: University of California Press, 1975), pp. 12–21.

[5]Quoted in Key, *Politics, Parties, and Pressure Groups,* 3rd ed., (1952), p. 218.

[6]Key, *Politics, Parties, and Pressure Groups,* 5th ed., p. 372.

[7]Colorado Secretary of State Mary Estill Buchanan, however, was placed on the ballot through the petition route and won the Republican nomination for the U. S. Senate. She was defeated in the general election by incumbent Gary Hart.

[8]Malcolm E. Jewell and David M. Olson, *American State Political Parties and Elections* (Homewood, Ill.: Dorsey, 1978), p. 130.

[9]In a five-to-four decision, the U. S. Supreme Court upheld the practice in New York of requiring registration of one's partisan affiliation some months before primary elections, thus precluding any last-minute change of identification. Speaking for the minority, Justice Powell felt the practice "runs contrary to the fundamental rights of personal choice and expression which voting in this country was designed to serve." *Rosario v. Rockefeller,* 93 S. Ct. 1245 (1973), quoted in Ranney, *Curing the Mischiefs of Faction,* p. 166.

[10]V. O. Key, Jr., *American State Politics* (New York: Knopf, 1956), p. 130.

[11]Quoted in George B. Galloway, *History of the House of Representatives* (New York: Crowell, 1961), p. 131.

[12]Ibid., pp. 136–144.

[13]Ranney, *Curing the Mischiefs of Faction,* p. 43.

[14]Key, *American State Politics,* p. 153. Austin Ranney and Leon D. Epstein disputed Key's claim in "The Two Electorates: Voters and Non-Voters in a Wisconsin Primary," *Journal of Politics* 28 (August 1966), pp. 598–616. Ranney and Epstein, however, placed their emphasis on the absence of differences in the issue attitudes of primary voters and nonvoters. Ranney later wrote, following a study with Epstein of the New Hampshire and Wisconsin presidential primaries, that "there is some smoke to be seen in the vicinity Key predicted; how hot and dangerous is the fire producing it we cannot say. . . ." Ranney, *The Mischief of Faction,* p. 129.

[15]Key, *American State Politics,* pp. 154–161.

[16]Ibid., fn. 16, p. 216.

[17]Robert A. Bernstein, "Divisive Primaries Do Hurt: U. S. Senate Races, 1956–1972," *American Political Science Review* 71 (June 1977), pp. 540–545. On p. 544, Bernstein explains why an earlier study by Andrew Hacker—"Does a 'Divisive Primary' Harm a Candidate's Election Chances?,'" *American Political Science Review* 59 (March 1965), pp. 105–110—was faulty.

[18]Donald Bruce Johnson and James R. Gibson, "The Divisive Primary Revisited: Party Activists in Iowa," *American Political Science Review* 68 (March 1974), pp. 67–77.

[19]Sarah McCally Morehouse, "The Effect of Preprimary Endorsements on State Party Strength" (Paper presented at the annual meeting of the American Political Science Association, Washington, D.C., August 28–31, 1980).

[20]Jewell and Olson, *American State Political Parties and Elections,* p. 99.

[21]Ibid.

[22]Robert J. Huckshorn, *Party Leadership in the States* (Amherst: Unversity of Massachusetts Press, 1976), p. 103.

[23]Ibid., p. 105.

[24]See ibid., pp. 102–109.

[25]Lewis Bowman and G. R. Boynton, "Activities and Role Definitions of Grassroots Party Officials," *Journal of Politics* 29 (February 1966), p. 136.

[26]Johnson and Gibson, "The Divisive Primary Revisited," p. 71.

[27]Huckshorn, *Party Leadership in the States,* p. 107.

[28]Ibid., p. 108.

7

Nominating a President

Party followers participate only indirectly in the selection of presidential candidates. Although some form of presidential primary is in use in thirty-eight states and the District of Columbia, the ultimate choice of a party's presidential candidate rests with the national convention delegates. Recent changes in delegate selection procedures have constrained the convention's deliberative functions, but some bargaining over platform proposals or rules changes still takes place in the context of selecting a nominee. More importantly, it is always possible that no candidate will receive a first-ballot nomination, and as the balloting continues, the delegates will be released from their pledge to support a particular candidate. In that case, negotiations to win the nomination for one of the contenders would be intense.

So far, the nation's leaders have not yielded to proposals periodically submitted to Congress[1] for a one-day national primary, despite the fact that Gallup polls reveal a majority of the public favor its use.[2] This lack of enthusiasm in Congress for a national primary is evidence of the staying power of the political parties. Efforts at making the parties more popularly representative have significantly changed the convention's role without abolishing it. Its continuance, even in altered form, is of considerable importance to the future of the parties, for the convention is the closest approximation to a national organization that the parties maintain. It is the only party assembly that brings together party representatives from all over the nation and attempts to unite them behind a candidate and a platform. If the parties abandoned this forum, they would be without a mechanism for brokering the interests of the diverse and sometimes fragile elements of their electoral coalitions.

The evolution of the national convention as a nominating device is intertwined with the development of the president's independent base of political power. Once presidential aspirants didn't have to submit to a screening by congressional caucus leaders, those from a wider spectrum of American political life could hope to satisfy their ambitions. That development was congenial to the concept of separated powers, but a system built upon clearly separated powers is not always conducive to the enactment of a president's legislative program.

A president's difficulties with Congress are magnified if he does not enjoy the respect of the professionals and office-holders who are his party's colleagues. Part of his standing is determined by how he obtained the nomination in the first place. The president whose route to the White House avoided established party channels may find upon arrival in office that his tasks are unduly troublesome. And the ease with which a political outsider can win his party's nomination is determined by the nominating procedures employed. Although the national convention has been in use since the first half of the nineteenth century, both its composition and its role have substantially changed. We will briefly review the development of the convention in order to place contemporary practices in a historical context.

The Rise and Fall of King Caucus

The Constitutional Convention provided for the selection of a president by an ad hoc electoral college. The college was originally intended to serve as a nonpartisan deliberative body to choose the president from among the nation's preeminent statesmen. In the elections of 1789 and 1792, the electoral college performed according to form, and George Washington was the unanimous presidential choice. As the military leader of a successful revolution and the presiding officer of the Constitutional Convention, Washington's qualifications for the highest office were well established. But as early as his first administration, there were signs that the deliberative functions of the electoral college could not be kept free of partisan considerations.

The battle lines were first drawn within Congress. Federalist forces were led by Alexander Hamilton, whose fiscal measures were the source of much of the partisan controversy. The anti-Federalist opposition was led by Thomas Jefferson in the Cabinet and James Madison in the House. Following the 1790 congressional races, the Federalists held a majority of seats in both houses.[3] With their sympathizers in a minority position within Congress, Jefferson and Madison took to the hustings to build support for their philosophy of government. Their reasoning was simple: to build majorities within Congress, popular majorities had to be created at the grass roots. Hamiltonians countered with their own organizational efforts, and in the early 1790s, a party system began to emerge out of the struggles taking place within Congress. To signify their opposition to the "monarchical" tendencies of the Federalists, the anti-Federalists soon adopted the label "Republican."

The electoral college was not immune to the developing partisanship. In the election of 1796, the leading Federalist candidate, John Adams, received seventy-one votes to overcome the sixty-eight votes cast for Jefferson, his principal Republican rival. Party support was only imperfectly mobilized, however, because ballots were cast for thirteen candidates. Not only were the ballots dispersed, but Adam's running mate, Thomas Pinckney, received only fifty-nine votes. The Constitution gave each elector two votes, but did not provide for separate balloting for presidential and vice presidential candidates. Since not all of Adam's supporters cast their vote for Pinckney, Jefferson won the vice presidency as the candidate with the second highest electoral college vote. Had the Federalist electors been more disciplined, the Adams-Pinckney ticket would have prevailed.

To plan their strategies and to continue their party-building efforts, the leaders of each partisan group in Congress met in private session or caucus. The caucuses were also used for the first time in 1800 to nominate each party's presidential and vice presidential candidates. That the caucuses were effective in mobilizing party support is indicated by the outcome of the balloting. The Republican candidates, Jefferson and Aaron Burr, each received seventy-three votes. Federalist unity was only a shade less complete. Adams received sixty-five votes, Charles C. Pinckney sixty-four, and John Jay one vote. Although party discipline within the electoral college was truly remarkable, it also produced an electoral absurdity—no winner! Jefferson was clearly the Republican choice for president, but he had received the same electoral vote as Burr. Burr did little to clarify the situation as the contest was transferred to the House of Representatives for a decision, where, largely through the efforts of Hamilton, Jefferson ultimately emerged victorious. Shortly after this episode, the Twelfth Amendment, providing for separate presidential and vice presidential balloting, was passed.

The Federalists were the first to abandon the congressional caucus as a nominating device. Their ticket was overwhelmed in the 1804 electoral college vote at the same time that their representation in Congress was sharply reduced. In the next two presidential races, Federalist leaders met privately in New York to name their candidates.[4] Although they showed signs of a comeback in 1812, their fall from power thereafter was precipitous. They made no nationally organized effort to mobilize electoral college votes in 1816 and soon disappeared as an opposition party.

Republicans were successful with the congressional caucus through the 1816 election. Because there was no organized opposition to the incumbent president, no caucus was held in 1820 and James Monroe easily won the electoral college vote. In the meanwhile, dissatisfaction with the congressional caucus was growing and came to a head with the candidacy of Andrew Jackson in 1824. Knowing that his chances of receiving the nomination from the Republican congressional caucus were slim, Jackson's supporters began a campaign to discredit its use. The caucus was only sparsely attended and its nominee, William Crawford, ran a poor third behind Jackson and John Quincy Adams. Jackson's suspicions of his congressional support were verifed when the election was thrown into the House, and Adams, who had run second behind Jackson, received the vote of a majority of the state delegations.

By 1828, the Republican party had split into two factions, the National Republicans of Adams and the Democratic Republicans of Jackson. There was no congressional caucus, nor was any other national party mechanism used to nominate candidates in that year's election. Martin Van Buren, the leader of antiadministration forces in the U. S. Senate, had proposed a national convention, but his recommendation went unheeded. Van Buren guided Jackson's well-organized electoral campaign to an easy triumph over Adams. That members of the electoral college were popularly elected in all but two states was a distinct advantage to Jackson's cause. Jackson's triumph symbolized the growing egalitarianism of the nation. Access to presidential power was freed from the more aristocratic legislative leadership and became rooted in the support of voting masses.

Origins of the National Convention

The collapse of the congressional caucus as a nominating device left the parties without a nominating authority. In a series of steps, the caucus was replaced by national delegate conventions. The anti-Mason party, which had evolved from anti-Jackson groups in New York and Pennsylvania, was the first to employ the modern convention in 1831. As a new party with few public officeholders, it found the delegate convention well suited to its aims of building a national following.

The ranks of the National Republicans in Congress had been depleted, and they also turned to the delegate convention to provide a broader representation of their following. The Democratic Republican party of Jackson had been successful with a decentralized method of nomination, but Jackson's strength lay with the people and not with either congressional or state legislative leaders. A split within Democratic Republican ranks had developed between Vice President John C. Calhoun and Secretary of State Martin Van Buren. As Jackson's chief lieutenant, Van Buren counseled the dumping of Calhoun from the ticket. Since Calhoun was strong both within state legislatures and the Congress, a national convention suited Van Buren's plans. The convention that was called in 1832 balloted only for the vice presidential choice and selected Van Buren.

National conventions in their modern form were thus in place for the 1832 election. At this point in history, however, they did little more than ratify the obvious presidential choices. Vice presidential selections were not always accepted by party leaders as equally authoritative. In 1840, the Democratic party (successor to the Democratic Republicans) did not name a running mate for Van Buren. Gradually, however, the national conventions took on the task not only of choosing the heads of the ticket but of reconciling factional disputes and building party unity as well. It is the convention's role in creating party consensus that has been its unique contribution, and it is precisely that deliberative role that has eroded in recent years. How this erosion came about will be discussed later in this chapter.

Making the Conventions Representative

If the demise of the congressional caucus opened opportunities to candidates out of favor with the national legislative leaders, another problem soon arose that was equally troublesome for those who believed that the president should be a man of the people. National conventions were dominated by state and local oligarchies—or so it was said—and the rank-and-file party adherents had little voice in selecting their party's nominee.

Representing the popular following of a party presents vexing issues for which there are no pat solutions. Two distinct processes are involved in sending delegates to the quadriennial nominating conventions. First, the national party must determine the number of delegates to which each state party is entitled. Then, once the quotas are set, the men and women who will serve as convention delegates must be selected. Each process can affect the outcome of presidential nominations.

APPORTIONING DELEGATES

Throughout most of their history, national conventions have apportioned delegates by a formula tied to each state's electoral college vote. The pattern was set by the anti-Mason party and followed by subsequent party conventions. So long as the major objective of the parties was to provide an organizational mechanism to win presidential elections, the precise apportionment formula was of secondary significance.[5] But as a method of accurately representing a party following, the formula was defective on two counts. In the first place, electoral college votes are not apportioned among the states precisely in accordance with population size. In the second place, and of greater significance, the formula gave no recognition to the partisan characteristics of a state. A state party received its allotment of convention delegates whether or not it had much of an organized following.

The Republican Formula. The initial response of the parties to the issue of representation was to award "bonus" delegates to those states that had supported their presidential and other major candidates. The Republicans were the first to change. At the Republican convention of 1912, the states of the Old Confederacy held 23 percent of Republican delegate votes although they had contributed but 7 percent of the popular vote for the Republican ticket in the preceding presidential election.[6] Partly because of his southern support, incumbent President William Howard Taft was able to beat back the challenge of the still popular Theodore Roosevelt and be renominated for a second term. Miffed at the turn of events, Roosevelt led a third-party movement that split Republican ranks and handed the election to the Democrats. In the call for the 1916 convention, steps were taken to cut back on the number of southern Republican delegates. The party adopted a plan to award additional delegates to states that were sympathetic to Republican officeholders. This plan, begun in 1916, has been periodically strengthened. The current Republican apportionment formula provides:

1. Six delegates for each state.
2. Three delegates for each congressional district within a state.
3. One additional delegate for each Republican governor or U. S. senator elected by a state.
4. One additional delegate if Republicans hold at least one half of a state's congressional delegation.
5. Four and one-half delegates plus 60 percent of its electoral college vote (rounded to the nearest whole number) if a state cast its vote for Republican electors in the preceding presidential election.

The Republican formula, even in its award of bonus delegates, is still weighted toward the electoral college vote,[7] and the practical effect is to give an edge to smaller states and, as it happens, more conservative delegations. The large and generally more liberal Republican following in such northeastern states as New York, Pennsylvania, and New Jersey is relatively underrepresented at Republican conventions. It was for this reason that the liberal Ripon Society challenged the Republican apportionment formula in the federal courts. However, the Supreme Court refused to enter the political thicket of deciding how national conventions should be apportioned.

The Democratic Formula. The Democrats left their apportionment formula untouched until 1944. In that year, they followed the Republican lead by awarding bonus delegates to those states that had gone Democratic in the preceding presidential election. Thereafter, they expanded their system of bonus awards, while managing never to reduce a state's allotment from one convention to the next.

The most sweeping reapportionment in either party was adopted by the Democrats for their 1972 convention. Though the new apportionment formula was not the centerpiece of the extensive reforms undertaken that year, it did result in a significant modification of prior state allotments. Under the 1972 plan, approximately 53 percent of each state's apportionment was based on its electoral college vote. The remaining 47 percent was apportioned in accordance with the average size of a state's popular Democratic vote over the three preceding presidential elections. Unlike the Republican bonus system, the Democratic plan distributed additional delegates to the states on the basis of the size of the party's popular following in those states. The immediate beneficiaries were the large industrial states with a traditional Democratic following.

After their disastrous defeat in 1972, the Democrats further tinkered with their apportionment formula. Much of the controversy surrounding the electoral debacle centered on the effects of quotas for women, blacks, and youth (discussed later in this chapter), but the resulting changes also recognized a role for party professionals and officeholders. The call for the 1980 Democratic convention stated the apportionment formula in a far from simple mathematical equation, but, fortunately for state leaders who may have been more politically than mathematically inclined, each state's delegate strength was listed in tabular form. The formula now gives equal weight to electoral college votes and past voting patterns, but adds 10 percent to the number of delegates allocated to each state for party and elected officials.

SELECTING DELEGATES

Once a state's allotment is known, procedures can be set in motion to select the national convention delegates. Three principal methods of selection, singly or in combination, have been used in the past: (1) state conventions; (2) state committees; and (3) primary elections.

State Conventions. A state convention was the common method employed before the recent proliferation of presidential primaries. Under the older convention system, party professionals and elected officeholders controlled delegate selection. Delegates to the state conventions sometimes served *ex officio* because of their party posts. More commonly, they were selected through processes that began with open precinct meetings. Though the general public rarely turned out for these, and the selection procedures were not always faultless, the system was defended as broadly representative of a state's partisan interests.[8]

The convention states of today are more commonly designated caucus states in the popular press and professional literature. But the difference involves more than a name. Only a handful of Republican caucuses (Arizona, Arkansas, Delaware, and Montana) are restricted to party officials. Most Republican and all Democratic caucuses begin with well-publicized mass meetings, and rank-and-file participation has increased. Those who turn out are no longer just the party stalwarts gathered together by local party leaders. Today's caucuses include voters who are urged to attend by candidate organizations. The delegates they elect are more interested in furthering the nomination of a candidate than they are in representing their state party.

State Committees. A second method of delegate selection used in the past, although never widespread, was even further removed from popular participation than the older convention system: some state committees selected the entire slate of national convention delegates. The McGovern-Fraser Commission found Democrats using such a practice in six states; in two of them, the committees did little more than ratify a slate prepared in the governor's office.[9] Democrats currently authorize a state-level committee in the primary states to appoint up to 35 percent of a state's delegation: 25 percent to achieve affirmative action goals and 10 percent to award delegate credentials to party leaders and elected officeholders. But the committees making appointments must be representative, and their selections must fairly reflect the candidate preferences shown in the primary balloting. The abuses of the past can no longer be repeated.

Primary Elections. The selection process that involves the most widespread participation of the rank and file is the presidential primary. Its earliest use was justified on the same grounds as those of the direct primary—it would provide a greater voice in party affairs for the party's following. However, the presidential primary differs from the direct primary in one important respect: the direct primary actually results in the nomination of a party's candidate, whereas the presidential primary can do no more than elect national convention delegates who are instructed to vote for a candidate until released from their pledges. The distinction is more apparent than real if the nomination is secured on the first ballot. On the other hand, if no candidate receives a majority on the initial roll call of states, the delegates could play a creative role in nominating a candidate.

The Development of Presidential Primaries

Presidential primaries were introduced in the heyday of the Progressive movement shortly after the turn of the century. They were part of a set of reforms that included the direct primary, nonpartisan elections, the initiative, referendum, and recall, and the direct election of U. S. senators. These reforms reflected the view that politics could be purified if power could be wrested from party bosses and returned to the people, where it belonged. Although it spread rapidly in the first two decades of the century, the presidential primary did not play a determinative role in the early nominating contests.

The Republican nomination of 1912 must have been particularly disheartening to primary proponents. When Theodore Roosevelt issued his challenge to incumbent President William H. Taft, only seven states had enacted primary laws. An additional five states joined their ranks in anticipation of the clash. In the ensuing contests, Roosevelt defeated Taft in nine, including Taft's home state of Ohio, and lost to him in two. (Both major contenders lost to Robert LaFollette in one primary.) Although clearly the popular choice in these primary states,

Roosevelt was denied the nomination. Nor did the Democratic primary races provide solace to those who had high hopes for the primary. Champ Clark garnered 423 delegates votes in the primary states to Woodrow Wilson's 274, but the convention chose Wilson anyway.

And so the story went. Supreme Court Justice Charles Evan Hughes received the Republican nomination in 1916, although, as a matter of principle, he engaged in no preconvention campaigning. Hiram Johnson and General Leonard Wood were the principal opponents in the Republican primaries four years later, but the nomination went to Ohio's favorite son, Warren G. Harding.

From 1920 to 1948, the presidential primary went into eclipse. Eight states abandoned it, and only one state adopted it—to enable its senior senator to run as a favorite son and to name his own convention delegates, it was said.[10]

A number of causes could be cited for the loss of confidence in the primary. Regular state organizations, of course, were opposed to its use. Reform sentiment made few inroads in the wide-open twenties, was preoccupied with economic and social problems in the thirties, and was subordinated to the war effort in the forties. Most importantly, serious candidates did not see the presidential primaries as the route to convention success. Al Smith and Herbert Hoover in 1928, and Roosevelt in 1932, each won primary elections and received his party's nomination, but none had personally campaigned in the primary states. Candidates often withheld their names from contests they were not certain of winning, or refused to enter against favorite-son candidates. Since the convention would make the ultimate choice, major contenders did not wish to antagonize state delegations that had rallied around a state leader (who had usually only entered the race to tie up his delegation for later bargaining purposes). Voter interest in one-sided or uncontested primaries was low, yet the costs of election administration were significant. For all these reasons, the number of primary states had been reduced to sixteen plus the District of Columbia by 1948.

A popular interpretation of the presidential primary at that time was that it could thwart but not enhance a candidate's chances for the nomination. Yet the presidential aspirant who did not have the ear of the party's professionals had little alternative but to enter the primaries to advance his candidacy. The primary was used in this fashion sporadically from

1948 through 1968. Harold Stassen is easily dismissed today as a peripheral figure, but in 1948, he was a person to be reckoned with. Cut in the Progressive mold, the youngest governor in Minnesota's history, Stassen had the resources to run a serious campaign. However, his political strength lay more in the general electorate than among Republican party leaders. Knowing that he had only an outside chance for the nomination, Stassen committed himself early to a strenuous schedule of primary battles.[11] He scored upset victories over the front runner, New York Governor Thomas E. Dewey, in Wisconsin, Nebraska, and Pennsylvania. As he did, Stassen replaced Dewey as the leader in the Gallup polls. Dewey headed west to campaign in Oregon, shrewdly leaving the Ohio contest to Stassen and "Mr. Republican," Senator Robert A. Taft. By dividing his time between Ohio and Oregon, Stassen managed to make a respectable showing in each state, but he lost both races. These losses shattered his winning image, and with it his hopes for the nomination.

Stassen had showed the potential of the primaries, but it was John F. Kennedy who most successfully exploited them. It is questionable whether Kennedy would have received the Democratic nomination had he not shown his mettle in selected primary races. Many Democratic party leaders, including those of the Catholic faith, doubted that a Catholic could be elected president of the United States. Kennedy had other drawbacks. In the Senate, he had voted in favor of the Republican plan for a sliding scale of parity payments to farmers. The so-called Benson Farm Plan, named after President Dwight Eisenhower's secretary of agriculture, was anathema to midwestern farmers. And lingering in the background as a challenge to his liberal credentials was the senator's controversial father, Joseph P. Kennedy. The Camelot legend that was later to surround the Kennedy family was not in evidence in early 1960.

Selecting his primary states carefully, Kennedy opened his campaign in New Hampshire with a one-sided victory over token opposition. Moving to the Midwest, he challenged Hubert H. Humphrey in Wisconsin, a farm state in Humphrey's political backyard, and beat his major rival in the presidential preference balloting. To show that his Catholicism was not a handicap in a predominantly Protestant state, Kennedy entered and easily defeated Humphrey in the West Virginia primary. He had now scored his decisive victory; the later primary contests were anticlimactic. As the clearly established front runner, and with his religion very much discussed, Kennedy could not have been denied the nomination without seriously alienating the Catholic vote that had already shown a restiveness with Democratic presidential candidates in the 1950s. Although later analysis showed that his Catholicism was more an asset than a liability in the general election, Kennedy's primary forays were unquestionably necessary to convince the convention delegates they could afford to support a Catholic nominee.

It was still said that primary victories were more valuable as an indication of popular support than as a source of delegate strength. Hubert Humphrey won the Democratic nomination in 1968 without entering a single primary. He was able to do this because he had strong organizational backing and because three-fifths of the Democratic delegates were then selected by state conventions or state committees. Even where the primary was in use, the balloting did not always result in a clear commitment of delegates to a major contender. Some primaries were only advisory; others chose delegates who had not stated their candidate preferences. And favorite sons could still tie up a state's delegation for bargaining purposes.

Reliance on the backing of political professionals to secure the nomination came to an end with the 1968 conventions. The number of primaries spread as Democrats sought to comply with their party's new delegate selection rules. The new laws allowed few of the uncertainties and ambiguities of older practices. A handful of primaries are still advisory, and in these, the popular winner does not always receive a proportionate share of a state's delegates. Even these victories, however, are important to the winner's "momentum" as interpreted by the media. In most of the primary states, the candidates of both parties clearly add to their delegate strength as well as their popular image as the race moves toward the convention.

Candidates can no longer rely on the professionals to control even the remaining caucus states because participation in the mass meetings has increased dramatically. The effect of the reforms has been to enhance the popular voice in nominations. Candidates may still concentrate their resources more in some states than in others, but it is impossible today to gain the nomination of either party without doing some serious preconvention campaigning. Even an incumbent president cannot refuse to accept a primary challenge.

Reforming Delegate Selection: The Crucial Issues

We have made reference more than once to Democratic reforms that have transformed the presidential nominating process. Although the Republican party has also altered its delegate selection procedures, the Republicans have been more affected by legislative responses to Democratic rules changes than by their own reforms.[12] Republican modifications have been neither so novel nor so sweeping as those of the Democrats. For this reason, the discussion that follows will stress Democratic actions.

The spadework of Democratic reform was undertaken by a commission appointed early in 1969 and headed first by George McGovern and later by Donald M. Fraser.[13] The effects of its delegate selection changes were felt in the 1972 conventions. A second commission was chaired by Barbara A. Mikulski and governed selection procedures in 1976.[14] Morley A. Winograd led a third commission, whose rules changes went into effect for the 1980 convention.[15] As each successive commission wrestled with the questions of representation posed by delegate selection, conflicting views were exposed and, to an extent, reconciled. There is no better way to understand the debate over what type of party best suits the American temperament than to follow the reforms recommended by these commissions.

OPENING THE DELEGATE SELECTION PROCESS

If one begins with the premise that the political parties are associations of their rank-and-file adherents, it is easy to make the case that the national conventions were in need of reform. Under the older convention model, state and local political leaders took charge of the delegate selection process, sometimes by quite arbitrary methods. The control the party regulars exercised enabled the dominant leadership factions to bargain as cohesive units with other state delegations and candidate organizations. Rather than a process open to all who identified with the party, delegate selection was subject to oligarchic control.

The initial call for reform by the Democrats made it clear that the power of the established party leaderships over the delegate selection process was to be curtailed. In a move that caught the 1968 convention leadership by surprise, the minority report of the innocuous-sounding Committee on Rules and Order of Business came to the floor.[16] The crux of the brief resolution offered was the proposal that the 1972 Democratic convention be selected in a manner "in which all Democratic voters have a full and timely opportunity to participate." National Chairman John M. Bailey rushed to his Connecticut delegation to urge it to vote no. Other states with strong party organizations also voted against the resolution. The proposal nevertheless carried by a vote of 1,350 to 1,206, and the forces led by Eugene McCarthy and Edward Kennedy scored their only clear victory in the convention that year. Delegations from New York, California, and other primary states were solidly in favor of the call for reform.

The McGovern-Fraser Commission was empowered to develop guidelines for the states to follow in selecting delegates to the national convention. In making the case for reform, the commission laid bare practices that limited popular participation. In many states, party leaders were in a controlling position because the rules governing delegate selection were either inadequate or nonexistent. They enjoyed discretion in organizing the delegate selection process and used it to their advantage. For example, almost one-third of the delegates to the 1968 convention were selected before the calendar year of the convention. Since Eugene McCarthy had not announced his candidacy that early, his supporters were unable to compete for those delegate positions.

A number of other practices used by party leaders to retain control over delegate selection were condemned. Among them was proxy voting—empowering one person to act in behalf of another. A Missouri party official once cast 492 proxies in an open caucus meeting, three times the number of people physically present, and in behalf of a candidate whose supporters were a minority of those assembled. In Hawaii, a proxy vote was cast for an unorganized precinct that consisted largely of vacant lots in an urban renewal tract. Nor was timely notice always given for scheduled caucuses. Only organization insiders would turn out for poorly publicized meetings. Even where delegate selection was unaccompanied by such overtly irregular practices, participants did not always exercise a free choice in naming the delegates. They were often presented with a slate of candidates that could be altered or challenged only with difficulty.

The first step in opening the process, of course, was to ensure that fair and formal rules were adopted by the state parties. Toward this end, the committee urged that state parties be required to give adequate and timely notice of caucuses, that proxy voting be abolished, and that slate making become more open and subject to challenge. These procedural safeguards were the least controversial of the McGovern-Fraser proposals, yet they signified a profound change in the selection process. The reforms were not aimed at ensuring that state party leaders were properly installed in their offices. Rather, their intent was to encourage popular participation and thereby to limit the power of organization leaders.

The McGovern-Fraser Commission did not mean to extend the number of presidential primaries. Yet its guidelines provided eighteen new ways to challenge the credentials of state delegations, and to avoid such a threat, several state parties followed the path of least resistance and turned to the primary as the safest way to select delegates.[17] Others followed when they found their caucuses captured by delegates who favored candidates who were unpopular in their states.[18] Whatever the intent, the result was a rapid spread of presidential primaries.

The logical extension of the movement toward a greater popular role in presidential nominations is a national direct primary. If it were enacted, a party's following would participate directly, not indirectly, in the selection of the nominee. Yet none of the Democratic reform commissions urged that additional step. The Winograd Commission expressed a fear that a national primary would "favor candidates who already had national reputations and who would buy large chunks of media,"[19] and in an argument reminiscent of traditional criticism of popular participation, it argued that a one-day national primary "would spell the end of the national party system as we know it."[20]

Preserving the Integrity of the Party. Two steps were taken to preserve the integrity of the Democratic party as an institution. One was to limit participation in the selection process only to Democratic party identifiers. The second was to reserve a role for the party's professionals and officeholders in choosing a presidential nominee.

If the national convention delegates were to be selected by the party following, then only bona fide Democrats should be allowed to participate. Open primaries that allowed crossover voting by Republicans would blur the distinctiveness of the two party groups. Although earlier commissions recognized the problem, the Winograd Commission submitted the strongest proposal. Participation in the delegation selection process was to be limited to Democratic voters who "publicly declare their party preferences and have their preferences publicly recorded."[21] Because their state laws mandated open primaries, Michigan and Idaho Democrats shifted to the caucus method in 1980. Democrats in Wisconsin and Montana ignored their party's rules and continued to select delegates in an open primary. When they carried the issue to the courts, however, Wisconsin Democrats were unsuccessful in their challenge of national power. The Supreme Court upheld the right of the national Democratic party to prescribe the rules under which the delegates to its national convention are selected.[22] Elsewhere, state Democratic parties made various attempts to restrict crossover voting.

Mandating "closed" caucuses and primaries was a satisfactory solution to Republican invasions of the Democratic party's candidate selection process, but these reforms hardly enhanced the influence of the party leadership. Yet it is a curious party system that shows so little deference to its leaders that it ignores their role in the nominating process. The Mikulski Commission met strong opposition when it considered granting voting rights to elected officials and party officers who did not run as delegates. The debate continued under the Winograd Commission, which offered a number of options to reserve a place at the national convention for party leaders. The proposal that was finally approved directed that 10 percent be added to each state party's delegation, with the additional delegates to be chosen from elected officeholders and those holding party positions. Even though the proposal ensured that the candidate preferences of the leadership delegates would reflect the candidate preferences shown in earlier caucus or primary voting, it preserved the idea that a political party was more than an association of its adherents in the electorate.

Republican Reforms. Having captured the presidency in 1968 and 1972, Republicans were not under similar pressure to reform their nominating practices. Nor did the Republican party have any significant groups within its ranks lobbying for reform. Antiwar protestors, civil rights advocates, and other social activists, insofar as they were involved in party politics at all, gravitated toward the Democratic party as the vehicle to transform the nation's priorities. The 1968 Republican convention, however, did authorize an examination of its delegate selection procedures. Appointed by the national chairman in 1969, the Committee of Delegates and Organizations (dubbed the "DO" Committee) was headed by Missouri Committeewoman M. Rosemary Ginn. The DO Committee went about its business without the fanfare of the McGovern-Fraser Commission. Though its deliberations were neither so thorough nor so open, many of its recommendations paralleled those of its Democratic counterpart.

The new rules adopted at the Republican convention of 1972 to go into effect for the 1976 nominating season called for more open delegate selection procedures in the convention states. Public information systems were urged, and proxy voting was banned. Delegates could no longer receive their credentials *ex officio* for the party leadership posts they held. Meanwhile, of course, state legislatures had already reacted to the Democratic reforms by enacting primary laws that accounted for two of every three Republican national convention votes in 1976. Although popular participation increased in their convention and caucus states, the Republican party leadership was not encumbered by the rules changes and compliance commissions that troubled Democratic state leaders.

Effects of the Reforms. The justification for increasing rank-and-file participation in delegate selection is to achieve a convention that is more representative of a party's following. A representative convention is then supposed to nominate a candidate who would begin his campaign with a large popular following.

Two measures are commonly employed to gauge the representativeness of national conventions. One standard is how well the demographic characteristics of the delegates mirror their party's constituency. As we shall see later, the Democrats were successful in increasing the proportions of minority, women, and youth delegates at their conventions, but did not otherwise move to reflect their constituency base. Nor do Republican delegates more accurately mirror the demographic composition of their following since the reforms. To state the obvious, both conventions, now and earlier, overrepresent well-to-do, college-educated professionals and underrepresent clerical and blue-collar groups. Most representative institutions have a similar bias, and delegate selection reforms have not avoided it.

A second way to measure how well delegates represent their party constituencies is to compare their attitudes on issues with those of their following's. New delegate selection rules have produced mixed results. At the 1956 conventions, under the old rules, the attitudes of Democratic delegates fairly reflected those of their rank-and-file adherents, though this was not true of Republican delegates. The convention Republicans were distinctly more conservative than their following. The reverse was true in 1972 under the new rules. Republican delegates were much more in tune with their following, and Democratic delegates were well to the left of their supporters. The curiosity is that the Republicans won both presidential elections by landslide proportions.

That the Republicans won in 1956 in a year when their delegates poorly reflected the issue attitudes of their following is consonant with the professionals' role in mediating a convention and backing a winner. Ohio Senator Robert Taft may have earned the respect of Republican professionals for his conservative record, but the Republican convention picked a winner in Dwight Eisenhower in 1952 and stayed with him in 1956. Republican identifiers gave the general overwhelming support. On the other hand, the 1964 Republican delegates voted their convictions and supported Barry Goldwater in a losing cause that saw widespread defections from Republican ranks. Democratic delegates who nominated McGovern in 1972 out of zeal for his liberalism were the match of the Goldwaterites in the purity of their beliefs. The result was that many Democratic supporters deserted their party's nominee to vote for the Republican ticket. Neither the old nor the new rules guarantee the ultimate goal of selecting a candidate who can appeal to a widespread following. But the older system provided greater flexibility in making the choice.

REPRESENTING CANDIDATE PREFERENCES

Democratic reforms went further than merely opening the door to popular participation. They also tried to ensure that the candidate preferences of the party's following would be accurately represented. This goal was partly achieved at the 1968 convention when the unit rule (which allowed the majority of a delegation to cast a bloc vote, regardless of minority positions) was abolished.

But did the unit rule prohibit winner-take-all primaries? Technically, a winner-take-all primary did not violate the unit rule ban, yet insofar as it did not allow for the expression of minority candidate preferences, it was clearly in violation of the spirit of the unit rule prohibition. The McGovern-Fraser Commission tiptoed around this issue. It endorsed the principle of proportionality, but required only that state parties using the convention system select 75 percent of their national convention delegates at a level no higher than the congressional district. This provision, unless a contender swept every district, would allow some representation of minority preferences.

The equivocation of McGovern-Fraser on winner-take-all primaries resulted in a confusing array of delegate selection plans in 1972. In the twenty-two states using presidential primaries, there were eighteen distinct plans for awarding delegates to the primary contenders.[23] The differences were not all trivial, and in the aggregate, they could have affected the convention's choice. Table 7-1 shows what the outcome of the fifteen primaries held in 1972 before the crucial California winner-take-all vote would have been if every state had adopted either: (1) a statewide winner-take-all system; (2) a proportional plan, distributing delegates according to the popular strength of the candidates; or (3) a congressional district winner-take-all plan.

The debate over methods of reflecting candidate preferences is similar to the debate over electoral college reform. The electoral college features a winner-take-all vote, and like all such plans, it enhances the influence of large and politically diverse states.[24] A candidate cannot ignore them in his campaign strategies. Under proportional or district plans, however, the larger states are politically weakened. The *margin* of a contender's victory becomes the measure of success, and consequently, presidential campaigners are encouraged to concentrate on smaller and less diverse states where they can gener-

Table 7–1
THE DIFFERENTIAL IMPACT OF PRIMARY PLANS, 1972

	Winner-Take-All	Proportional	Districted	Actual Results
Humphrey	446	314	324	284
Wallace	379	350	367	291
McGovern	249	319	343	401.5
Muskie	18	82	52	56.5
Others	0	27	6	59

source: James I. Lengle and Byron Shafer, "Primary Rules, Political Power, and Social Change," *American Political Science Review* 70 (March 1976), pp. 29–30.

ate the greatest vote differences. The district plan holds the greatest rewards for candidates who are attractive to the smaller states, because they might not have to share any delegates with their opponents. Gerald Ford carried Maryland's 1976 presidential primary with 60 percent of the vote cast and, under the district plan, won fifty-eight pledged delegates. Had a proportional plan been in use, Ford would have received only thirty-five delegates.

Although the general public may have been unaware of the effects of different candidate preference systems, the consequences were not lost on later reform commissions. Adopting the recommendations of the Mikulski Commission, the 1976 Democratic convention operated under more clearly specified formulas for awarding delegates to contending candidates. Statewide winner-take-all primaries were prohibited, though congressional district plans were allowed. Otherwise, any candidate who received 15 percent of the popular vote in a caucus or primary received a proportionate share of delegates. The Winograd Commission prohibited the congressional district plan for 1980 and provided the most precise guidelines to date.

Democratic practices to ensure that the national convention accurately reflects the candidate preferences of the rank and file are of three sorts. First, all delegates are required either to state their candidate preferences or to run uncommitted at all stages in the delegate selection process. Presidential candidates have the opportunity to approve the national convention delegates committed to them to ensure that they are their bona fide representatives. (In the past, some delegates were lukewarm to the candidates to whom they were formally pledged and awaited the opportunity to break ranks.) Second, under rules adopted at their 1980 Democratic convention, delegates are required to vote on the first ballot for the candidate whom they were elected to support, unless they are released in writing by that candidate. Third, delegates are to be apportioned among the contending candidates according to candidates' popular strength. To qualify for a share of delegates, however, a candidate must receive a threshold vote in a caucus or primary that was near 15 percent for most states in 1980.[25] In the midst of their reforming mission, the Democrats have been mindful that a scattering of support among several contenders could deadlock a convention and lead to the very thing the reforms were designed to avoid—a convention brokered by political professionals. Some analysts feared this would happen in 1976 because of the number of Democratic contenders, but it did not because of the sequential nature of the primaries. Carter's early victories established him as a serious candidate and his campaign gathered strength along the way.

Unless bound by state law, Republican state organizations are allowed to set their own candidate apportionment formulas. The chief difference between the Republican and Democratic practices is that the Republicans still permit state or district winner-take-all plans. In only fifteen Republican primary states are delegate votes allocated among the candidates according to their popular strength. The potential effect of the Republican plan is to allow a clear front runner to amass the necessary votes for nomination long before the close of the selection process. This did not happen in 1976, when Ford's lead in the early primaries of the East and Midwest was equalized by Reagan's capture of the sunbelt states. In 1980, however, despite George Bush's reluctance to step aside, Reagan's commanding lead in committed delegates set the stage for a unified convention.

QUOTAS FOR THE UNDERREPRESENTED

The most controversial of the Democratic reforms was the requirement by the McGovern-Fraser Commission that women, blacks, and youth be accorded representation at the convention "in reasonable relationship to their presence in the population of the state."[26] Everyone agreed that the three groups had long been underrepresented and that white middle-aged males had dominated earlier conventions. But other groups also had been underrepresented. There were, for instance, fewer labor leaders and farmers at the 1968 Democratic Convention than college professors and clergymen.[27] Apparently the claim for fairer representation of these other groups was not pressed within the commission as an argument against giving special consideration to blacks, women, and youth.[28] The proposal carried by a narrow ten-to-nine margin.

A majority of commission members obviously felt that quotas were needed to advance the interests of selected categories of Democratic supporters. They supposed that other groups were adequately represented by party regulars. Opponents of a quota system contended that it clashed with the other reform goal of free and open access to the delegate selection process by the granting of special privileges to some. The McGovern-Fraser Commission denied that its guidelines were to be accomplished by the imposition of mandatory quotas, but nonetheless the guidelines had that effect. In an attempt to soften the impact of the guidelines, the Mikulski Commission required affirmative action, but placed the burden of proof on those charging discriminatory practices. The change resulted in a slight diminution in the representation of the preferred groups in 1976. The Winograd Commission recommended the continuance of affirmative action programs for an extended list of minority groups (women, blacks, youth, Hispanics, native Americans, and Pacific-Asians are now included under Democratic party rules), while returning to mandatory quotas in the case of women. Thus half the 1980 convention seats were reserved for women delegates. The pattern of delegate representation is shown in Table 7-2.

The effect of the quotas upon a fair representation of candidate preferences was alleviated somewhat by a plan first suggested by the Mikulski Commission for the primary states and extended by the Winograd Commission to all states. Twenty-five percent of a state's delegation had to be selected at large, and this percentage was to be used, where necessary, to meet affirmative action goals. However, the at-large delegates still had to reflect candidate preferences shown in the popular votes at the earlier caucus meetings or primary elections.

The issue of giving special consideration to some but not all of the traditional Democratic following has created problems for the candidates. At the 1972 convention, many of George McGovern's supporters organized into special caucuses of women, blacks, Latinos, and youth. At issue was not

Table 7–2
DELEGATE REPRESENTATION IN DEMOCRATIC CONVENTIONS

Year	Minority	Women	Youth (under 30)
1968	5.5%	13.0%	3.0%
1972	15.0	40.0	22.0
1976	11.0	33.0	15.0
1980	15.0	49.0	11.0

SOURCE: Commission on Presidential Nomination and Party Structure, *Openness, Participation, and Party Building: Reforms for a Stronger Democratic Party* (Washington, D.C.: Democratic National Committee, 1978), p. 19. The 1980 data were taken from Warren J. Mitofsky and Martin Plissner, "The Making of the Delegates, 1968–1980," *Public Opinion*, October/November 1980, p. 43.

only their loyalty to McGovern the candidate but also the compatibility of their interests with the concerns of potential Democratic supporters in the general election.[29]

The special caucuses formed in 1972 did not displace other bargaining units at the convention.[30] Since they were scattered throughout hotels in the convention city and had to contend with a concentrated schedule of events, the special caucuses had little time to plan their strategies. The candidate organizations continued to work through the network of communications established with state delegations, and many in the newly formed groups were willing to compromise their issue stands to ensure McGovern's nomination. Nevertheless, floor fights on twenty separate minority planks undermined McGovern's candidacy and left the Democratic party in disarray.

At the 1976 convention, the caucuses made demands on the candidate and platform, but were otherwise quiet as the delegates rallied behind their nominee in an effort at party unity.

The 1980 convention, however, was once again marred by noisy floor fights. Although the caucus groups did not cause the political infighting, they did contribute to the discord within the convention. For example, feminist forces moved to strengthen the platform that endorsed the Equal Rights Amendment (ERA) and approved in principle of freedom of choice on abortions. They successfully lobbied for minority planks, unwanted by the Carter camp, that specifically approved of Medicaid funding of abortions and withheld financial and other aid from Democratic candidates who would not support ERA.

The Republican party did not approach the question of representing the unrepresented with the passion shown by the Democrats. The 1968 Republican convention did provide that participation in the delegate selection process "shall in no way be abridged for reasons of race, religion, color or national origin." To implement the resolution, the DO Committee recommended that each state seek to represent men and women equally, and youthful delegates in accordance with their voting strength. The 1972 convention accepted the proposal for women, but rejected proportionate representation of youth as an attempt to "McGovernize" the GOP.[31] Instead the convention authorized a second committee to develop "positive action programs" for the Republican party aimed at increasing participation of women, youth, the elderly, and minority and ethnic heritage groups.

Chaired by Representative William Steiger, the committee was popularly labeled the "Rule 29 Committee" after its enabling resolution. The Rule 29 Committee required the states to develop plans to increase representation of the selected groups and to submit them to the Republican National Committee for review. Unlike the Democrats, the Republicans did not set any standards of compliance. Even this timid approach was modified by the national committee which made the submission of positive action programs voluntary. Republicans think of their party as an association of state parties, and the national committee did not wish to infringe upon their authority. Though they committed themselves in principle to broadening delegate representation, the Republicans took no further steps to accomplish their stated goals. Blacks accounted for 3 percent of Republican delegates in 1980; women, 29 percent; and youth under thirty, 5 percent.

The special caucuses common to recent Democratic conventions surfaced at the Republican conventions of 1976 and 1980, but the Republican groups were far less active. There are a number of reasons why they played a more restricted role. For one thing, the conventions were preoccupied with the selection of presidential nominees, and the Republican groups subordinated their aims to the interests of their presidential candidates. For another, logistical problems and a heavy convention schedule plagued the Republican groups, as they had the Democratic special caucuses in 1972. Perhaps the most telling reasons why the Republican groups were less active than their Democratic counterparts were the widespread feeling among the delegates that the Republican party was not an interest group party and the wariness of party regulars toward nonstate caucuses. In all likelihood, Democratic caucuses will continue to argue their causes more aggressively.

Delegate Selection and Organizational Power

Criticisms of the contemporary delegate selection process are much the same as those made of the direct primary. At their core is the contention that the party professionals no longer are in charge of presidential nominations.

When presidential primaries were not so widespread, and when the primary mandate was sometimes ambiguous, the use of primaries was not sharply questioned because they afforded an opportunity to assess a candidate's campaign style at first hand and they stimulated popular interest in party politics. Political professionals may even have approved of the primaries as a useful candidate testing ground. But before the 1970s, a candidate's vote-getting ability in the primaries did not assure him of the nomination. He also had to enter the smoke-filled rooms of the convention and negotiate with state and big city party leaders.

The spread of the presidential primary and the opening of caucus meetings have changed the fundamental rules of how to win the nomination. Lining up the support of officeholders and organization leaders remains important but is not crucial for success in an era in which presidential contenders can take their case directly to the voters. Jimmy Carter was scarcely known outside his native state of Georgia and was lightly regarded as a presidential possibility in 1976 before his early successes in Iowa (a caucus state) and New Hampshire (a primary state). As a newcomer to the national political scene, Carter was free to project whatever image his political strategists felt would win him votes. In fact, he gained the nomination of his party "by running against it as an antipartisan outsider."[32]

Carter was clearly unable to unify the party he had ignored in gaining the presidency. Consequently he had to expend enormous resources in beating back a formidable challenge for the Democratic nomination in 1980 and later suffered a disastrous defeat at the hands of Ronald Reagan in the general election. Since it is reasonable to surmise that Carter would never have received the 1976 nomination under former selection procedures, we may ask: Are the political professionals a better judge of talent than the voters?

Critics of the present selection system argue that the turnout in caucus states provides only token representation of the public (see Table 7-3). Though contests in the primary states brought out a substantial popular vote, it nevertheless fell far short of the general election vote (see Table 7-4). It is known that primary participants are better educated, wealthier, and more interested in issues and political personalities than are voters in the general electorate, but whether their attitudes or candidate choices significantly differ from those of people who do not vote in primaries is disputed. A fair conclusion is that the extent of differences between the two electorates varies from election to election.[33]

Table 7–3
ESTIMATED TURNOUT IN PRECINCT CAUCUSES, 1976

State	Estimated Voting-Age Population	Attendance at Precinct Caucuses	
		Estimated Number of Persons	Percent of Voting-Age Population
Alaska	231,000	1,000	0.4
Arizona	1,555,000	26,700	1.7
Colorado	1,773,000	30,000	1.7
Connecticut	2,211,000	106,600	4.8
Hawaii	600,000	3,000	0.5
Iowa	2,010,000	45,000	2.2
Kansas	1,610,000	N.A.	—
Louisiana	2,532,000	120,000	4.7
Maine	741,000	6,500	0.9
Minnesota	2,721,000	58,000	2.1
Mississippi	1,544,000	60,000	3.9
Missouri	3,348,000	20,000	0.6
New Mexico	771,000	10,000	1.3
North Dakota	432,000	3,000	0.7
Oklahoma	1,937,000	65,000	3.3
South Carolina	1,933,000	63,000	3.2
Utah	783,000	16,300	2.1
Vermont	327,000	2,500	0.8
Virginia	3,528,000	20,000	0.6
Washington	2,536,000	60,000	2.4
Wyoming	266,000	600	0.2

SOURCE: Austin Ranney, *Participation in American Presidential Nominations, 1976* (Washington, D.C.: American Enterprise Institute, 1977), p. 16.

The question goes beyond representation of the party following. Since voters cannot use party labels to distinguish candidates in primary contests, they must make their decisions on the basis of the information that comes their way. Inevitably, this means that the media play a dominant role in what the voters see and hear about the presidential contenders. Again, the 1976 Carter candidacy is illustrative. Through intensive organizational efforts, Carter emerged the victor in the Iowa caucuses early in the year. Whether ready for it or not, the public could scarcely have been unaware that the race was now under way and that a relative unknown was an early winner. When Carter ran ahead of other contenders in the New Hampshire primary, he was dubbed the front runner and his picture appeared on the cover of national magazines and he was sought out for television interviews. At this point, his achievement was gaining the support of several thousand participants in the

Table 7–4
TURNOUT OF VOTERS IN PRESIDENTIAL PRIMARIES, 1976

State	Total Votes Cast	Estimated Voting-Age Population	Percent of Voting-Age Population Voting
Alabama	665,855	2,501,000	26.6
Arkansas	534,341	1,503,000	35.5
California	5,709,853	15,294,000	37.3
Florida	1,910,149	6,326,000	30.2
Georgia	690,843	3,375,000	30.5
Idaho	164,960	567,000	29.1
Illinois	2,087,807	7,718,000	27.0
Indiana	1,245,715	3,640,000	34.2
Kentucky	439,534	2,374,000	18.5
Maryland	757,717	2,863,000	26.5
Massachusetts	911,950	4,173,000	22.6
Michigan	1,771,480	6,268,000	28.3
Montana	196,620	518,000	37.9
Nebraska	395,390	1,080,000	36.6
Nevada	122,991	424,000	29.0
New Hampshire	187,312	574,000	32.6
New Jersey	602,961	5,514,000	11.7
North Carolina	798,559	3,847,000	20.7
Ohio	2,083,207	7,459,000	27.9
Oregon	730,167	1,653,000	44.2
Pennsylvania	2,183,122	8,441,000	25.9
Rhode Island	74,700	648,000	11.5
South Dakota	142,748	469,000	30.4
Tennessee	574,359	2,958,000	19.4
Texas	1,979,001	8,503,000	23.3
Vermont	72,270	327,000	22.1
West Virginia	528,269	1,281,000	41.2
Wisconsin	1,333,373	3,211,000	41.5
Total	28,925,253	103,149,000	

Mean turnout 28.2

SOURCE: Austin Ranney, *Participation in American Presidential Nominations, 1976* (Washington, D.C.: American Enterprise Institute, 1977), p. 20.

Iowa caucuses and twenty-three thousand voters in New Hampshire. Although these people were hardly representative of the nation's Democratic supporters, their early support made Carter's candidacy. Surely, it was a shrewdly calculated and well-orchestrated strategy, but that is beside the point here. The question left unanswered by Carter's early successes was whether the selection process provided an adequate screening of his talents beyond his ability to campaign effectively in small states.

A candidate's chances of ultimate success are unduly influenced by the results of caucuses and primaries held early in the nominating season. The measure of success is more than just winning or losing, for candidates are handicapped by the media much as the thoroughbreds in a stakes race and the media announce whether their performance has lived up to their initial ratings. Eugene McCarthy lost to Lyndon Johnson's organized write-in candidacy in the New Hampshire Democratic primary of 1968, but the outcome, being much closer than anticipated, was called a moral victory for McCarthy and Johnson withdrew from the race shortly afterward. Edmund Muskie won the New Hampshire Democratic primary in 1972, but his victory was the start of his downfall because, with 48 percent of the vote to his nearest rival's 37 percent, he had not won convincingly enough.

Candidates with the correct combination of financial resources, effective organization, forensic skills, marketable personality traits, and luck are the ones who make the most serious challenge for the nominating prize. True, anyone who does survive the primary hurdles and wins convention approval must possess a formidable array of talents. Nevertheless, it is a candidate-centered organization that has made his success possible. A candidate who has not been compelled to negotiate with other elements of his party to strengthen his grip on the nomination may find himself viewed as an outsider by his partisan colleagues. Should he go on to win the presidency, he may discover that his lack of organizational ties hinders his ability to govern.

DOONESBURY   **by Garry Trudeau**

After stating all these criticisms of the contemporary selection processes, we must acknowledge that they do broaden
the selection of presidential candidates. An aspirant can throw
his hat in the ring even though he is viewed with suspicion by
party regulars. This is particularly important during times
when the party's leadership is unresponsive to the party's constituency and new blood is required to redirect the party
toward issues that have been ignored. This is how Democratic
reformers saw their party after the 1968 elections.

The Role of the National Convention

The national convention is more than an institution for
nominating the president. In many respects, it *is* the national
party, the forum that brings together men and women from
throughout the nation to tend to the party's business. The delegates have the responsibility of making rules that not only govern the convention proceedings but the more general affairs of
the party as well. They must adopt a platform that reveals how
the party proposes to deal with issues that arouse public concern. The nominations for the presidency and vice presidency
are only the culmination of a process that defines the national
party and reveals the coalitions that compose it.

National conventions have always been a political spectacle whose proceedings have been conducted in a carnival atmosphere. Today they are also media events. The television
cameras search out the colorful, the bizarre, and the controversial aspects of convention activities to hold the interest of an
audience whose favorite programs have been preempted. For
their part, the parties welcome such national exposure and try
to schedule their proceedings for maximum impact. Despite all
the hijinks and hoopla, however, the business of the convention
is seriously undertaken.

ORGANIZING FOR WORK

Much of the preliminary work of the convention is conducted through four major committees: permanent organization, credentials, rules, and resolutions. Months before the
convention, the national leadership designates the chairs of the
committees, who then consult with state leaders to complete

the rosters. This early appointment of committees is necessary because the short duration of the convention does not allow time to prepare for the sometimes complex issues that must be resolved.

The Permanent Organization Committee. The least controversial of the committees today is that on permanent organization. Its major responsibility is to select a permanent chairman (co-chairpersons for the Democrats in 1976) to preside over the convention proceedings. At one time, the person who wielded the gavel occupied a position of considerable power. In the 1956 Democratic convention, for example, Sam Rayburn avoided a floor fight over civil rights by the simple expedient of refusing to recognize the state banners calling for a roll call vote. Today, because of rules changes and sophisticated communications equipment linking the rostrum and the floor, the convention chairman has little discretionary power. Nevertheless, the 1980 Democratic chairman, Speaker of the House Thomas P. "Tip" O'Neill, skillfully orchestrated convention approval of compromises that had been worked out between the Kennedy and Carter organizations on minority economic reports. Calling for voice votes, O'Neill was greeted with a chorus of boos when he ruled that a minority report combining a $12 billion jobs program with wage and price controls had failed to carry. The jobs program, part of the compromises reached, had passed earlier in a separate minority report.

The Credentials Committee. The credentials committee has the responsibility for making recommendations to the convention on delegates whose credentials have been challenged. Given the very imprecise rules that once governed the delegation selection process, and the arbitrary fashion in which they were applied, challenges were not uncommon. The disputes commonly centered less on the merits of the delegates' claims than on whose candidacy they would advance. Thus the floor vote on credential fights was often a prelude to the presidential balloting. In the 1952 Republican convention, the credentials committee recommended the seating of southern delegations favoring Senator Robert A. Taft. Delegates supporting General Dwight D. Eisenhower overturned the decision on a roll call vote that displayed the general's strength.

The Democratic party's complicated delegate selection procedures produced bitter contests at its 1972 convention. An Illinois delegation led by Chicago Mayor Richard Daley had been selected in conformity with state statutes but contrary to

McGovern-Fraser guidelines. Whether California's winner-take-all primary of that same year conformed to the new Democratic rules also was hotly debated. The credentials committee refused to seat the Daley delegation and allowed McGovern only 151 of the 271 California delegates. In the floor fight that ensued, pro-McGovern forces sustained the Illinois decision and returned the rest of the California delegates to their candidate. The outcome of the convention might very well have hinged on these contested seats. By comparison, credentials controversies have been relatively quiet since the 1972 Democratic bloodletting.

The Rules Committee. Both the Republican and Democratic conventions operate under a set of rules adapted from those governing the House of Representatives. The responsibility for proposing changes in the rules, as well as in the methods of apportioning and selecting delegates to the conventions, rests with the rules committees. Though their handiwork is procedural by definition, their decisions have a substantive impact. It was a minority report of the rules committee at the turbulent 1968 Democratic convention that touched off the very substantial changes made in the party's delegate selection process. On other occasions, rules changes are aimed at securing immediate tactical advantages. Fearing that some of his backing was "soft," delegates in favor of Gerald Ford at the 1976 Republican convention backed a so-called fair play rule that bound delegates to the presidential choices expressed in their primary or caucus votes. A similar issue arose at the 1980 Democratic convention, only its outcome had more far-reaching implications. Carter delegates defeated a minority report sponsored by the Kennedy camp that would have overturned a proposed rule binding delegates to the candidates to whom they were pledged. Pointing to Carter's low standing in opinion polls, Kennedy supporters argued that conditions had changed since the delegates were selected. An "open convention," they contended, could nominate a candidate stronger than Carter. To have allowed the delegates this freedom of choice, however, would have undone the work of Democratic reformers.

The Resolutions Committee. The work of the resolutions committee in drafting a platform is second in importance only to the naming of the presidential and vice presidential candidates. To compile an acceptable draft for consideration by the convention delegates (the 1972 Democratic platform ran to twenty-four thousand words) is no mean literary achievement.

Hearings are held months in advance of the convention to solicit a variety of views on what should and should not go into the document. Democrats have recently started earlier and heard testimony from a greater variety of groups and individuals wishing to press a point. Although they hold regional hearings, the Republicans have not sought to make the initial drafting a public process. Each party's committee spends hours in arduous labor to find a phrase that will arbitrate competing claims, or at least allow each side to claim victory. The care that is taken in drafting key planks is not misspent. Floor fights disrupted the 1964 Republican convention and the 1968, 1972, and 1980 Democratic conventions. Carelessly worded or hastily drafted resolutions only invite additional controversy and doom the party's hopes of achieving unity before the convention closes.

Despite all the efforts expended on the platforms, their significance is often denigrated. Party platforms, it is said, are deliberately ambiguous on all the contentious issues, mere campaign documents full of promises no one ever intends to keep. They are seldom read and soon forgotten. There is unquestionably some truth to these charges, yet convention delegates feel strongly enough about some planks to engage in acrimonious debate over their adoption. To the careful analyst, platforms are more meaningful than is popularly supposed.

Much of the criticism of the platforms derives from a conception of the parties as two ideologically distinct groups competing for power whose platforms should reflect their programmatic differences. But, as we have seen, the American parties do not differ along such ideologically pure lines. In his study of twelve platforms covering the years 1944 through 1964, Gerald M. Pomper found that the parties took opposing sides on only 10 percent of their pledges.[34] They stood on the same side in approximately one-third of their planks. The remaining planks differed simply because the two parties had designed their platforms to appeal to different groups of voters.

Party platforms reflect the nature of American parties. The similarity of Democratic and Republican platform appeals suggests an overlap between the two parties' followings and broad areas of consensus in American political thought. Still, the two parties are directly opposed on some issues, which means that programmatic differences are not always submerged. Also, each party feels compelled to make individual appeals to certain constituent groups of its normal electoral

coalition. Ultimately, however, both parties try in their platform to appeal to as many groups within the electorate as possible.

Pomper found that the platforms were not simply meaningless exercises in semantics.[35] Of the nearly fourteen hundred specific pledges in the platforms he studied, Pomper
found that slightly over half were fulfilled. If one includes
measures that partially redeemed platform promises as well as
appropriate inaction, almost three fourths of the pledges were
kept. That is not a bad record. As one might expect, it was the
bipartisan pledges that were the most likely to be fulfilled by
later congressional or executive action. Winning the presidency also had an effect. The in party delivered on about four
fifths of its pledges, twice the rate of the losers. So, contrary to
the popular wisdom, platforms should be taken seriously.

DELEGATE SELECTION AND THE BARGAINING PROCESS

Under the classic model of the convention, the basic bargaining units were the state delegations. They could act as cohesive units because of the way the delegates were selected
and, in the case of the Democratic party, because the unit rule
prohibited the expression of minority views. The delegations
were led by senior elected officials or prominent party leaders.
To build a national coalition behind the convention's choice,
state delegations would bargain with one another and with
candidate organizations. In the process, a basically decentralized party system could become national in scope.

The Waning Power of Professionals and Officeholders.
Bargaining at the convention has not disappeared, but its
character has altered because the new delegate selection rules
have changed the type of participants and thus the methods of
convention decision making. Critics have charged that the
reforms have weakened the party. By this they mean that the
professional and officeholder wings of the party no longer play
a dominant role. Democratic officeholders have seen their role
diminished to the point where many no longer bother to attend
(see Table 7-5). Republican officeholders have a better record
of delegate service. The different participation rates reflect the
stricter Democratic requirement for an early commitment to a
presidential candidate. Many officeholders prefer to hold back
a decision until they see how the contest is shaping up. Only
half the Republicans in Table 7-5 were committed at the time of

Table 7–5
REPRESENTATION OF MAJOR ELECTED OFFICIALS AT
NATIONAL CONVENTIONS

	1968	1972	1976	1980
Democrats				
Governors	96%	57%	44%	74%
U.S. Senators	61	28	18	14
U.S. Representatives	32	12	14	14
Republicans				
Governors	92	80	69	68
U.S. Senators	58	50	59	63
U.S. Representatives	31	19	36	40

Note: Figures represent the percentages of Democratic or Republican Office-holders from each group who served as delegates.
SOURCE: Data are derived from Warren J. Mitofsky and Martin Plissner, "The Making of the Delegates, 1968–1980," *Public Opinion*, October/November 1980, p. 43.

their selection in 1980, compared to all but two of the Democrats. That so many Democratic governors turned up at the 1980 convention was the result of the Carter strategists' skillful use of the powers of incumbency.[36]

Though a high rate of turnover characterized both Democratic and Republican conventions before the new selection procedures were put into effect, more convention delegates are new to their tasks than ever before. In the recent past, only a third of all delegates had attended prior conventions, but the effects of inexperience are more keenly felt today than when the delegations were hierarchically controlled. At the 1972 Democratic convention, only 16 percent of the delegates were experienced, at the very time when the power of organizational leaders was being severely curbed. The 1972 Democratic delegates were also much less committed to their party than their Republican counterparts, as Table 7-6 shows. A party's integrity is threatened when it leaves the selection of its presidential candidates to those whose loyalty to it is lukewarm.

Amateurs vs. Professional Delegates. New delegate selection procedures benefit the political amateur to the detriment of the political professional because the process is so open. As we discussed in Chapter 5, the distinguishing characteristic of amateurs is that they are motivated by a cause whose advancement is often tied to the candidacy of a particular contender. Because they so often see issues in moral terms, they are unwilling to compromise their stand. Professionals, on the other hand, view accommodation and compromise as neither im-

Table 7–6
PARTY IDENTIFICATION STRENGTH OF 1972 CONVENTION DELEGATES

Party Identification	Democratic Delegates	Republican Delegates
Strong Democrats	47.7%	0.0%
Democrats	20.8	0.0
Independent Democrats	30.4	0.0
Independents	0.7	0.0
Independent Republicans	0.4	12.0
Republicans	0.0	14.9
Strong Republicans	0.0	73.1
N=	(283)	(242)

SOURCE: Adapted from Joseph H. Boyett, "Background Characteristics of Delegates to the 1972 Conventions: A Summary Report of Findings from a National Sample," *Western Political Quarterly* 27 (September 1974), p. 477.

moral nor hypocritical but as necessary conditions for building a party and running a nation. The real-world presence of both types in their ideal form may be exaggerated, but there is ample evidence to support the contention that convention delegates may be usefully classified as leaning to one or the other type.

The importance of the distinction lies in the willingness of delegates to compromise their differences in the name of party unity. By the nature of their support, issue candidates are limited in the kinds of compromises they can afford to make. McGovern's support at the 1972 convention was composed of more amateurs than professionals.[37] The amateurs were not only purer in their ideological beliefs but were also less identified with the Democratic party. They strongly endorsed McGovern's candidacy at the same time that they identified with such groups within the national constituency as blacks, women, and youth. The professionals, who were somewhat more experienced and thought of themselves as representing the rank and file of the party in their home states, tended to support the candidacy of Hubert Humphrey because his long record of service to the Democratic party and strong ties to its traditional constituency made him a "safer" candidate.

McGovern's attempt to moderate his liberal image and to extend an olive branch to those Democrats who had opposed his candidacy ultimately failed. It had been the practice for the winner of the California primary to provide delegate credentials to his opponents in the interests of party unity. The McGovern campaign staff was unsuccessful in convincing the

senator's California supporters to offer more than token representation to his former adversaries. Organized labor, for example, was left virtually unrepresented in California's delegation.[38] On the other hand, the McGovern organization was successful in keeping certain planks out of the platform that year.
Stands on abortion, homosexuality, and drug legalization were
not included. Busing to achieve racial balance was described
as only "one tool" to deal with school integration. And the goal
of a guaranteed annual income was not mentioned, much less
the figure of $6,500 proposed by the National Welfare Rights
organization.[39] Although his convention supporters may have
gone along with this strategy reluctantly, they were "professional" enough to know that McGovern's nomination would be
best advanced by some compromise.

The 1972 Democratic convention did not close ranks behind their candidate.[40] The amateur supporters of McGovern,
once they had secured his nomination, were unwilling to make
any further compromises to unify the party. The professionals,
blaming their loss on the new delegate procedures, refused to
accept McGovern as their party's leader. Perhaps the crux of
the intraparty struggle was each side's expectations in November. Most McGovernites were confident that their candidate
would win. Party regulars were just as confident that they had
nominated a losing candidate.[41] There was thus no compelling
incentive offering mutual advantages to unite the party.

Front-running candidates with professional backing have a
better chance of bargaining with issue enthusiasts without endangering their own support. The 1976 Republican convention
is a case in point. The setting was one that might have wrecked
the party in a manner reminiscent of the 1972 Democratic convention. The delegate count was closely divided between the
Ford and Reagan camps, with Ford holding a slim edge.
Reagan supporters were overwhelmingly conservative (85 percent), while Ford delegates, on the whole, were moderates (77
percent).[42] Over half of Reagan's supporters reflected the ideological purity of the amateur, but only a fifth of the Ford delegates were similarly classified.[43] Yet the eventual victory of
Ford provoked little of the disharmony that the McGovern
nomination caused the Democrats. Not all Reaganites were
willing to work actively for Ford's election, but few publicly
disclaimed his candidacy.

The Republicans emerged from their convention relatively
unscarred because Ford allowed his opponents little opportunity to rally behind any potentially divisive issue. More con-

cerned with winning the nomination, the Ford camp left the writing of the platform to the delegates. Since the document was basically conservative, the Reaganites got much of what they wanted. Even a minority plank that was critical of their leader's foreign policy was unopposed by the Ford organization. Ford made a further concession to the Reagan delegates when he passed over more liberal or moderate vice presidential choices to name Robert Dole as his running mate. The success of the Ford strategy may have been aided by the waning spirit of conservative Republican purists, dimmed over the years as they fought so many losing battles. Their hopes of winning had been pinned on Reagan, and they accepted his leadership when, first, he announced that the liberal Richard Schweiker was his vice presidential choice, and later, when he called upon them to support Ford as the Republican nominee.

Jimmy Carter also had little difficulty with the liberal issue advocates of his party in 1976. Having wrapped up the nomination in a campaign that avoided clear issue stands, he next moved to strengthen his support for the November election. He met individually with blacks, women, and Hispanics to reassure them of his concern for their interests and to claim their support.[44] Because he was successful in his efforts, the Democrats managed to avoid the dissension that had splintered party ranks four years earlier. The Carter strategy was aided by the candidate's sure grasp on the nomination and polls that showed he was a likely winner over either Reagan or Ford. It was probably also aided by the memory of what had occurred in 1972 when issue controversies were taken to the floor for resolution.

Carter's political fortunes had changed dramatically by the 1980 convention. Although he came into the convention with all the delegate votes he needed to be renominated, he either acquiesced in or was unable to prevent a series of minority platform reports that he did not want. In his public statement on the platform, Carter neither rejected the amendments nor embraced them; he merely indicated he could live with them. His chief rival, Edward Kennedy, endorsed the platform and then pledged his support for Carter. This show of unity at the convention's end only thinly veiled the rancorous debate that had taken place.

By comparison, the 1980 Republican convention was a love feast. The platform called for tax cuts, spending restraints, and less government regulation of industry, measures that most Republican delegates enthusiastically supported. Although he was personally opposed to the Equal Rights Amendment, Reagan, in a gesture to moderates, suggested that the platform take no stand on the issue. Overtures were made to blacks, labor, and the poor with promises of vigorous enforcement of civil rights laws, assistance to workers in industries threatened by foreign competition, and a pledge to revitalize America's inner cities. A more hard-line approach was taken on the abortion issue: the platform endorsed a constitutional amendment banning abortions and also pledged the appointment of judges who respect "the sanctity of innocent human life." Although Republican moderates were not altogether pleased with the outcome, the platform was adopted in its entirety by voice vote. Sensing their chance at capturing the presidency, Republican delegates were more interested in a winning strategy than in a definitive statement of party policies.

Old vs. New Delegate Selection Procedures. Contemporary methods of delegate selection are not an insuperable barrier to a unified convention. And it should be remembered that the conventions run by political professionals were not always able to compromise their differences. Yet the reformed selection procedures of today are more conducive to the nomination of ideologically oriented candidates who are opposed to or incapable of accommodation.[45] Popular participation in delegate selection now requires the presidential aspirant to begin his campaign at an early date and build a personal following that will endure the lengthy course of the campaign. Those most likely to join a campaign early and last the course are issue enthusiasts who find a candidate committed to their cause. Party professionals are more inclined to stand on the sidelines until they see how the race is developing and what the contest means to them and to their state. The professionals excel at bargaining, compromising, and coalition building, but by the time of the convention, these skills are not much wanted because the nomination has usually been determined.

As the newer methods facilitate a policy of advocacy, the older delegate selection procedures encouraged a politics of accommodation.[46] In the past, the conventions brokered intra-party disputes, avoided divisive issues, and tried to unite the party behind a winning candidate. In the process, they seldom offered the voters a clear programmatic choice. An alternative approach would have the candidate use the nominating process to build a national following behind his vision of society's needs. Even if his candidacy is ordained to lose, he may confront the nation with issues that have been avoided for too long and educate the voters as he does. The difficulty with achieving a more programmatic politics by appealing directly to the electorate is that most voters are not doctrinally oriented.

The overall effects of the delegate selection reforms have been to reduce the power of professionals to broker the interests of the party's following without substituting any other institutional mechanism for that purpose. The deliberative functions of the convention have diminished, but more responsible parties have not been realized.

NAMING THE CANDIDATES

The culmination of the convention is the naming of the presidential and vice presidential candidates. First, the roll of states is called to nominate "the next president of the United States." The nominating and seconding speeches represent political oratory at its baroque best. When a contender's name is offered to the delegates, his supporters create a din that resounds throughout the convention hall. After the nominations are completed, the roll call is repeated for balloting by state delegations. More displays of enthusiasm greet votes cast by large delegations and doubtful states. Convention leaders must frequently request the sergeant-at-arms to clear the aisles. To control the furor of past conventions, the "Star-Spangled Banner" often has been played, and if all else fails, the lights of the convention hall have been dimmed.

One may find in the outbursts at a convention either the charm of old-fashioned politics or the vulgarity of a spectacle unsuited for the serious business at hand. What one won't find is much suspense in the proceedings. Democrats have not needed more than one ballot to nominate a president since 1952. Republicans have selected their candidate on the first ballot since 1948. The candidates' showings in the primary states, their support in the caucus states, and their standing in the preconvention polls, singly or in combination, allow anyone who follows politics to predict the outcome.

Just because recent conventions have lacked suspense does not mean that the convention is a useless appendage to the selection process. If a race is close enough, the projected winner may not receive a first-ballot nomination and a winning combination will have to be negotiated. The front runner always has to round out his support and make peace with former opponents. The more flexible the candidate and his organization can be about the platform and rules changes that affect the party organization, the more assurances they can give to group leaders, and the more likely the delegates will leave the convention city satisfied with their nominee.

The Naming of a Vice President. One device presidential nominees use to unify the convention behind them is their choice of a running mate. Although the selection may not be universally acclaimed, the delegates will accede to the presidential candidate's wishes. The choice may already have been determined as part of a bargain the nominee made to win the nomination. Franklin Roosevelt promised second place on the ticket in 1932 to House Speaker John Nance Garner (who later reported the office was not worth a bucket of spit) in return for the delegate votes he controlled. More commonly, a nominee's choice of running mate has been designed to lend geographical, factional, or ideological balance to the ticket. John F. Kennedy asked his major convention opponent, Senate Majority Leader Lyndon Johnson, to accept the job in 1960. Californian Richard Nixon selected Maryland Governor Spiro Agnew in 1968 as part of a "southern strategy" to capture the White House. Southern moderate Jimmy Carter picked liberal midwesterner Senator Walter Mondale to run with him. The moderate and bland Gerald Ford chose Robert Dole, who was not only more conservative but was also known for his "slashing" campaign style. And Ronald Reagan showed his political flexibility when, after negotiating with his 1976 rival, Gerald Ford, he turned to his chief opponent in the 1980 primaries, George Bush.

The Vice President's Changing Role. The manner of choosing vice presidential candidates has been a source of dissatisfaction to some students of the presidency. For a long time, balancing the ticket meant binding together two incompatible politicians. If their campaign was successful, the vice president was inevitably isolated within the administration,[47] relegated to a political limbo from which he seldom returned unless the president died in office, in which case he moved into the White House. Though vice presidents still stand in the shadow of the president, the office is no longer a political dead end.

Harry S. Truman was the first modern president to appreciate the plight of the vice president. When he succeeded to the presidency upon the death of Franklin Roosevelt, he was ignorant of most of the commitments that Roosevelt had made at the

WELL, I GUESS I'M STUCK WITH HIM ... HOWEVER, HE DOES UNDERSTAND THE ROLE OF A VICE PRESIDENT.

I'LL TAKE IT! I'LL TAKE IT!

BUT (SOB) JERRY VOSS MY BEST TICKET!

THERE, THERE HENRY

various wartime conferences with other Allied leaders. He was also unaware of the development of the atomic bomb, although shortly after he assumed office, he had to decide whether to use its destructive power. Shaken by this experience, Truman ensured that his own vice president, Alben Barkley, was fully briefed on current White House operations.

It was under President Dwight Eisenhower, however, that the vice presidency came into its own. Vice President Nixon not only sat in on meetings of the Cabinet and the National Security Council but also traveled on international missions that were more than ceremonial. Presidents since Eisenhower have tried to find assignments for their vice presidents that are more significant than presiding over the Senate (the vice president's only constitutional role), and the office is now viewed as a stepping-stone to the presidential nomination.

Two Novel Plans for Nominating a Vice President. The upgrading of the vice presidency has made no difference to the issue of how vice presidential candidates are selected. Two novel solutions have been offered by major presidential contenders of the recent past. At the 1956 Democratic convention, Adlai Stevenson refused to name his running mate, insisting instead that the convention make the choice. Stevenson's stratagem was to show that the Democratic convention was "open," in contrast to the Republican convention of that year when the Eisenhower-Nixon ticket was assured of renomination despite some disgruntlement with Nixon. Stevenson's ploy was of added significance because of the widespread speculation over Eisenhower's health. Should Eisenhower fail to serve out his term, the Republican convention would, in effect, select Richard Nixon as president.

Ronald Reagan announced his vice presidential choice in 1976 before the balloting for the presidential nomination. Then his backers proposed a rules change that would have required each presidential contender to announce his running mate so that the convention would know the ticket they were backing. At that stage, Gerald Ford wanted no part of any decision that would have revealed his hand and possibly cost him convention votes. His supporters defeated the proposal on the floor.

Although obviously self-serving, the Reagan and Stevenson maneuvers deserve more consideration than they got. Either plan, by strengthening the power of popularly elected delegates, is in keeping with the goals of the new nominating reforms. However, both plans would tie the hands of the presidential nominee in making peace with his opponents and unifying the convention.

The Contemporary Parties: A Need for Further Reform in Presidential Selection?

The choice of presidential and vice presidential candidates completes the process that defines the national parties. The way that process has evolved affects the fortunes of those who would use the party to win office and to govern. Reformers achieved many of the goals they sought, even if the reforms they enacted brought with them unintended consequences. Still, one important question remains: is the reform spirit itself compatible with organizationally strong parties?

Few reformers approve of the lengthy and complicated process by which presidential candidates are selected. They did not decide that the nominating campaign should be expanded to a year's duration, nor did they mean to give any advantage to the states that began the selection process. They did wish to enlarge popular participation, but they did not forsee or approve of the proliferation of primaries. By calling for citizen involvement, they did not intend to exclude party officials and elected officeholders from the process. Reformers did mean to curb the power of party leaders in picking a president, but not so that the media could assume that same power. Yet these results all flowed from the reforms enacted.

Ironically, it is the Democratic party, which started the reform movement, whose leaders are the most dissatisfied with the changes that have been made. At the nub of the continuing controversy over delegate selection procedures is how to ensure a fair representation of the party's rank and file without impeding the ability of traditional leaders to unify their party. The incentives are strong for the Democrats to bring more orderly procedures to their nominating process. Battered by the 1980 elections and confronted by prospects of minority status, they are seeking ways to avoid the internal dissension that contributed to their downfall.

Partly in reaction to their defeat, a fourth reform commission, headed by Governor James B. Hunt, Jr. of North Carolina, was appointed in 1981 to recommend selection procedures for the 1984 Democratic National Convention. Commission members promised not to tamper with rules that give half of the delegate seats to women and "fair representation" to blacks, Hispanics, and other minorities through affirmative action plans. Serious discussion is likely to take place on proposals that would concentrate the primary schedule to limit the influence of the early starting states; increase the participation of elected officeholders—particularly congressmen—as well as party officials; and revise the system of proportional candidate representation that, some allege, prolongs divisive campaigns and contributed to the disruptive fights at the 1972 and 1980 conventions.

A decade's experience with reformed procedures is ample time to judge their effectiveness. The authority of the national party to determine its delegate selection rules, even where state legislatures have refused their cooperation, has been firmly established by Supreme Court decisions.[48] The Hunt Commission cannot avoid meeting headlong the question of how much power should be restored to party leaders. How the issue is resolved will determine whether only the reforms that democratize party processes are capable of success.

SUMMARY

Presidential candidates are nominated at national conventions. Although the deliberative functions of the convention have been constrained by recent reforms in delegate selection, it is still possible that no presidential candidate will receive a first-ballot nomination. Were this to occur, delegates would be released from their pledges as the balloting continued, and they, not the voters, would select the nominee.

Before the national conventions were established, nominations were made in congressional caucuses. The early caucuses were effective in mobilizing support for their candidates in the electoral college, but they died under a growing egalitarianism. Andrew Jackson's supporters, knowing that their candidate was weak in the congressional caucus, boycotted the affair in 1824. Although Jackson was unsuccessful in his bid for the presidency that year, he swept to power in 1828 and established an independent base of presidential power in voting masses.

After 1828, national conventions became the vehicle for making nominations. Setting up a national convention involves two distinct processes: apportioning delegates among the states, and then selecting those who will attend. Over most of the history of the conventions, delegates have been apportioned among the states on the basis of their electoral college vote. Such an apportionment formula ignored the strength of a party's popular following within a state, and for this reason, each party devised new formulas to add delegates from those states that favored its candidates. The present Republican plan benefits the smaller and usually more conservative states, while the Democratic apportionment gives greater weight to larger and politically diverse states.

The delegate selection process has undergone dramatic reform. Three methods have been used to select national convention delegates: state conventions, state committees, and presidential primaries. The most widespread method of the past, the state convention, was run by party and elected officeholders with little popular participation. Today, states that use the convention method are referred to as caucus states, and they select their delegates in well-publicized local caucuses attended by a party's rank-and-file following.

The presidential primary appeared around the turn of the century, at the same time as the direct primary, as a reform to encourage the widest popular participation. In fact, though, the early presidential primaries were disappointing and the winners of these contests did not go on to win the nomination. Many states abandoned the primary because of its poor record.

For the candidate out of favor with party regulars, however, the primaries were the only hope of capturing the nomination. Harold Stassen showed how primaries could be exploited, and John Kennedy shrewdly used selected Democratic primaries in 1960 to establish his claim for the nomination. Kennedy's success revitalized the primaries by proving that a candidate's primary performance could be significant, but primary winners still had to negotiate in smoke filled rooms to obtain the nomination.

Through 1968, the professionals retained control of the selection process. Hubert Humphrey won the Democratic nomination in 1968 without campaigning in any of the primary states, but the turmoil that characterized themocratic convention that year set in motion a series of reforms that would fundamentally change the way the nomination was to be won. The Democratic reforms in delegate selection ultimately encouraged the adoption of some form of presidential primary in thirty-eight states, the District of Columbia, and Puerto Rico, and their effects touched the Republican party as well.

Democratic objectives were threefold. In the first place, they wished to make delegate selection more open to rank-and-file participation. States that did not employ a presidential primary had to select their convention delegates in timely, well-publicized open caucuses. Second, they decided that delegates sent to the national conventions had to reflect the candidate preferences of participants in primaries and caucuses. Winner-take-all primaries were banned, and the unit rule was prohibited. Third, they mandated affirmative action to assure representation of minorities, women, and youth in proportion to their presence in the voting population. The effect of all these reforms was to increase the number of presidential primaries as the state parties tried to comply with the new rules.

With less fanfare, the Republicans also revamped their delegate selection rules. Like the Democrats, they called for well-publicized and more open procedures in selecting convention delegates and urged their state parties to seek increased participation by women, youth, the elderly, minorities, and ethnic heritage groups. But because Republicans view their party as an association of state parties, the national committee did not set up any machinery to ensure compliance with these stated goals. And unlike the Democrats, the Republicans do not require that a candidate's delegate strength be proportionate to the popular vote he received in caucuses and primary elections.

The road to the White House now leads through the open caucuses and primaries; even an incumbent president has to battle for renomination. Critics of the reforms charge that the voters who turn out for caucuses and primaries do not represent a party's following in the general election. They also argue that a candidate's performance in the early primaries unduly influences the outcome of a contest because the media interpret primary and caucus results and declare when a candidate has stumbled or won a moral victory. And despite the numbers who now participate in delegate selection, they contend, the American people are still dissatisfied with the alternatives presented to them.

At the core of the controversy is the role that political professionals can and should play in the nominating process. Are their talents and knowledge useful in deciding on a nominee? Or should the people themselves judge who their party's nominee should be? So far, the Congress has rejected a single national primary to determine a party's candidate, despite polls showing support for such a primary.

Under the older convention method, state delegations bargained among themselves and with candidate organizations, each delegation looking after its own interests. In the process, the convention was usually able to avoid sharply programmatic stands and to broker internal disputes. Though the earlier conventions were not always successful in uniting behind the winner, some observers believe they offered more opportunities for resolving differences than the present system. Others approve of the new selection procedures because they allow a candidate to appeal directly to the people and to call attention to pressing problems that party regulars tend to ignore for fear of disturbing the equilibrium of a party's coalition.

The difference between the old and the new selection procedures is between a politics of accommodation and a politics of advocacy. The professionals who dominated earlier conventions were adept at the art of bargaining, compromising, and coalition building. Bargaining has not disappeared from today's conventions, but it has been sharply constrained. The contemporary selection process gives an advantage to the candidate with an ideological following, who may be unwilling to take the steps necessary to unify his party for fear of seeing his support erode.

The culmination of this lengthy process is in the naming of presidential and vice presidential candidates. The presidential choice wins the nomination by arduous campaigning, but the vice presidential choice is the personal selection of the presidential nominee. Chosen to lend geographical, ideological, or factional balance to the ticket, the vice president of the winning team must stand in the shadow of the president.

In sum, nominating a president is a party process that can affect party unity and the ability of the president to govern. Recognizing that reforms have had unintended consequences, Democrats have once again appointed a reform commission to examine their presidential selection procedures. The problem the commission must address is how to maintain active participation by the rank and file while increasing the power of traditional party leaders.

Notes

[1]Over a hundred bills have proposed some form of national direct primary since 1911. See Austin Ranney, *The Federalization of Presidential Primaries* (Washington, D.C.: American Enterprise Institute, 1978), pp. 7–8.

[2]A January 1980 Gallup poll, for example, reported that 66 percent of respondents favor abolishing the conventions and substituting a one-day national primary.

[3]Paul T. David, Ralph M. Goldman, and Richard C. Bain, *The Politics of National Party Conventions*, ed. Kathleen Sproul (Washington, D.C: Brookings Institution, 1960), p. 7. Chapter 1 provides a good summary of the origins of the national conventions.

[4]Some have called these meetings the first national conventions. However, they were held without public notice and in closed sessions. The first modern national convention was called by the Anti-Masons in 1831. See David, Goldman, and Bain, *The Politics of National Party Conventions*, pp. 11 and 14.

[5]Austin Ranney, *Curing the Mischiefs of Faction* (Berkeley: University of California Press, 1975), p. 105.

[6]David, Goldman, and Bain, *The Politics of National Party Conventions*, p. 100.

[7]Providing each state with six delegates-at-large and three district delegates for each congressional district, of course, is just another way of saying that each state will receive three times its electoral college vote.

[8]V. O. Key, Jr., *Politics, Parties, and Interest Groups*, 5th ed. (New York: Crowell, 1964), p. 408.

[9]Commission on Party Structure and Delegate Selection, *Mandate for Reform* (Washington, D.C.: Democratic National Committee, 1970), pp. 18–19.

[10]James W. Davis, *Presidential Primaries: Road to the White House* (New York: Crowell, 1967), p. 28.

[11]See the account in ibid., pp. 57–60.

[12]Austin Ranney, *Participation in American Presidential Nominations, 1976* (Washington, D.C.: American Enterprise Institute, 1977), p. 6.

[13]Commission on Party Structure and Delegate Selection, *Mandate for Reform.*

[14]Commission on Party Structure and Delegate Selection, *Democrats All* (Washington, D.C.: Democratic National Committee, 1973).

[15]Commission on Presidential Nomination and Party Structure, *Openness, Participation and Party Building: Reforms for a Stronger Democratic Party* (Washington, D.C.: Democratic National Committee, 1978).

[16]See the account described by John S. Saloma III and Frederick H. Sontag, *Parties* (New York: Knopf, 1972), pp. 14–15.

[17]James I. Lengle and Byron Shafer, "Primary Rules, Political Power, and Social Change," *American Political Science Review* 70 (March 1976), p. 26.

[18]Ranney, *Participation in American Presidential Nominations, 1976*, p. 6.

[19]Commission on Presidential Nomination and Party Structure, *Openness, Participation and Party Building*, p. 33.

[20]Ibid., p. 32.

[21]Ibid., p. 70.

[22]*Democratic Party of U.S. v. LaFollette*, 101 S. Ct. 1010 (1981).

[23]Lengle and Shafer, "Primary Rules, Political Power, and Social Change," fn. 3, p. 26.

[24]See the discussion in ibid., pp. 32–35.

[25]The Winograd Commission had recommended an escalating threshold as the primary season unfolded, rising from a 15 percent cutoff during the first third of the delegate selection period, to 20 percent during the second period, and to 25 percent during the final third. Together with recommendations for early filing dates, the proposed rules were designed to benefit the Carter camp by flushing out their opposition early, discouraging less well known candidates from entering, and preventing a late entry by a candidate who used others to test the waters. Carter's use of the Winograd Commission to help his renomination prospects is unsurprising, since this was the first reform group to meet under an incumbent Democratic president.

[26]Commission on Party Structure and Delegate Selection, *Mandate for Reform*, p. 40.

[27]Saloma and Sontag, *Parties*, p. 60.

[28]Ranney, *Curing the Mischiefs of Faction*, p. 114.

[29]William Cavala, "Changing the Rules Changes the Game," *American Political Science Review* 68 (March 1974), pp. 36–39.

[30]See Dennis G. Sullivan et. al. *The Politics of Representation* (New York: St. Martin's), chap. 3.

[31]Charles Longley, "Party Reform and the Republican Party" (Paper presented at the 1978 annual meeting of the American Political Science Association, New York, August 30–September 3, 1978).

[32]Garry Orren, "Candidate Style and Voter Alignment in 1976," in *Emerging Coalitions in American Politics*, ed. Seymour Martin Lipset (San Francisco: Institute for Contemporary Studies, 1978), p. 129.

[33]Commission on Presidential Nomination and Party Structure, *Openness, Participation and Party Building*, p. 15. See also Austin Ranney, "Turnout and Representation in Presidential Primary Elections," *American Political Science Review* 66 (March 1972), pp. 21–37.

[34]Gerald M. Pomper, *Elections in America* (New York: Dodd, Mead, 1968), pp. 193–194.

[35]Ibid., pp. 185–192.

[36]Warren J. Mitofsky and Martin Plissner, "The Making of the Delegates, 1968–1980," *Public Opinion*, October/November, 1980, pp. 42–43.

[37]See the discussion in Sullivan et al., *The Politics of Representation*, pp. 122–127. For a similar treatment of the 1968 Democratic convention, see John

Soule and James Clark, "Amateurs and Professionals: A Study of Delegates to the 1968 Democratic National Convention," *American Political Science Review* 64 (September 1970), pp. 888–899.

[38]See Cavala, "Changing the Rules Changes the Game," pp. 36–39.

[39]Sullivan et al., *The Politics of Representation*, p. 113.

[40]See the discussion in ibid., pp. 125–132.

[41]Ibid., p. 114.

[42]Dennis G. Sullivan, "Party Unity: Appearance and Reality," *Political Science Quarterly* 92 (Winter 1977–78), p. 638.

[43]Ibid., p. 641.

[44]Stephen J. Wayne, *The Road to the White House* (New York: St. Martin's, 1980), p. 138.

[45]Nelson W. Polsby and Aaron Wildavsky, *Presidential Elections*, 5th ed. (New York: Scribner, 1976), p. 280.

[46]Ibid., pp. 279–286.

[47]David, Goldman, and Rains, *The Politics of National Party Conventions*, pp. 40–42.

[48]See, for example, *Cousins v. Wigoda*, 419 U.S. 475 (1975) and *Democratic Party of the U.S. v. LaFollette*, 101 S. Ct. 1010 (1981).

8

Money in Politics

Carrying a message to the voters costs money, substantial sums of it in this era of inflated prices. Some candidates are wealthy enough to foot their own bills, but most who aspire to public office must depend upon contributions from individuals and organized groups. Even friendly students of American politics are dissatisfied with the way in which political money is raised in this country. They fear that politics is becoming closed to all but the few who are wealthy enough to afford their political ambitions or who are willing to sell out to powerful organized interests.

Regulating campaign finances is one way to prevent closure of the political processes, and laws with this intent date from the early twentieth century. To understand the unsatisfactory results of the early laws, one central fact should be kept in mind: legislators themselves wrote the rules under which they sought political office.

Even with the best of intentions, regulating the sources of political money is a thorny undertaking. The encouraging note is that important first steps have been taken, and only the cynical would deny that the reforms of the 1970s have achieved some success. At the same time, it must be admitted that the new regulations benefit some campaigners while harming others. Perhaps that was inevitable. That Congress passed any legislation at all is adequate testimony that reforms were badly needed. How the legislation came about and what form it took reveal the complex nature of money in politics.

The Costs of Democracy

Participation in politics is considered a civic virtue and making financial contributions is a form of political participation that helps pay the costs of democracy. Yet campaign giving has not been extolled in the same way as other citizen political activities, for in this area, egalitarian principles run headlong into the reality of an unequal distribution of wealth. Do the costs of political campaigning limit those who seek political office? Does the side with the most money enjoy an unfair edge? Are the big contributors unduly influential in shaping public policies? That political money is regulated in itself suggests affirmative responses to these questions, but regulation hardly solves all the issues involved. The desire to reconcile inequalities must be balanced against the traditionally cherished value of voluntarism in our political system.

THE EXPENSES OF RUNNING FOR OFFICE

In the simpler agricultural society of the nineteenth century, the campaigner went out on the stump to reach an audience of voters. The political campaign, with torchlight parade and courthouse oratory, was an exciting event in an era when entertainment was scarce. The personal stamina of candidates, rather than the size of their bankrolls, limited their activities. It is said that Abraham Lincoln won his first race for the U.S. House of Representatives on a campaign budget of 75 cents.[1] The story is probably apocryphal, but certainly political campaigning was not financially draining in an earlier age.

All that has changed. Campaigning in modern urban America is depersonalized in all but local races. Sophisticated techniques are necessary to reach a mass audience, and these techniques are costly. True, some campaigners for statewide office have been known to walk their state to meet its people. But it is also true that they know their trek will be recorded by television cameras and displayed to an audience much wider than any they could hope to meet personally. Rather than a throwback to the past, such a stratagem is an artful way to meet the rising costs of campaigning.

The exact costs of running for office were unknown before federal laws tightened reporting requirements in federal elections. Even now, the amounts spent in state and local races are uncertain because state laws vary in the strictness with which they require expenditures to be reported. Herbert E. Alexander has compiled the best estimates of total election year expenditures before the public funding of presidential contests in 1976.[2] The cost of all political campaigns increased gradually from $140 million in 1952 to $155 million in 1956, $175 million in 1960, and $200 million in 1964. Then expenditures jumped by 50 percent in 1968 to $300 million, and moved up over 40 percent in 1972 to $425 million, heightening concerns about "buying" offices.

The dramatic rise in campaign costs was not altogether the result of inflation and the growth of the electorate, for campaign expenditures rose more than twice as fast as the consumer price index over the twenty-year period from 1952 to 1972, and over two and a half times faster than the growth in the number of voters.[3] Clearly it was costing more to hold public office than at any time in the nation's history. The lion's share of the 1972 expenditure dollar (33 percent) went to the presidential campaigns, followed by congressional races (23 percent), state-level contests (22 percent), and local campaigns (22 percent).[4] If costs were left unchecked, many who otherwise desired a political career would be discouraged from running.

Television and Other New Techniques. The causes of increased campaign costs are to be found in the new techniques by which the candidate reaches the voter. Of all the technological innovations that have affected modern campaigning, television is the leader. It penetrates over 95 percent of the nation's households and is an incomparable instrument for projecting a candidate's style, image, and campaign theme. The cost of air time is the most expensive, but not the only, television-related expenditure. To fully exploit television's potential, candidates must spend additional dollars to ensure that their messages get across. Production costs for political programming can run half as high as broadcast time.[5] To produce film clips that present the most favorable image of the candidate while stimulating viewer interest is a skill of no mean importance, and the talented producers who possess this skill do not hire themselves out cheaply.

The care with which candidates prepare their television commercials is symptomatic of the specialization that now attends political campaigning. Professional consultants aid candidates in all phases of their campaigns. Public opinion polls gauge the mood of the electorate and reveal the issues that can be exploited. Direct-mail requests for financial contributions or voter support are replete with personal touches designed to disguise the broadcast nature of their appeal. Writers with a talent for the deft turn of phrase prepare the candidate's speeches. All these new skills and technology enable the modern candidate to reach a mass audience, but they have also escalated the costs of campaigning.

WHICH SIDE HAS THE ADVANTAGE?

The mounting cost of political campaigns raises questions about the influence of money in determining the outcome of election campaigns. Does the side that spends the most win the election? It would be foolhardy to associate electoral success with any single determinant. The credibility of candidates, events that transpire between elections, the distribution of partisan identification within a constituency, and the incumbency factor all may influence the outcome of an election. Nor is the absolute amount of dollar outlays the only indicator of money's role. How efficiently the money is used is also important. Despite all qualifications, however, money does make a difference in some elections. It may not guarantee victory, but few candidates with a thin war chest relish the prospects of taking on a lavishly financed opponent.

The surface record of winners and losers tends to support the influence of money. In the twenty-nine presidential campaigns held between 1860 and 1972, the last year before public funding, the candidate who spent the most won twenty-two times (see Table 8-1). In the 1978 Senate races, winners outspent their rivals in twenty-six of the thirty races held. The candidate with the largest purse won 366 of the 435 House elections in the same year.[6] But do the victorious candidates win because they spend more money, or do they attract more money because they look like winners? Probably there is a little of both elements in election contests. In what has to be a classic case of overkill, twenty-six House candidates spent a total of $1.2 million to be elected to office in 1978, despite the fact that they had no opponents in either the primary or the general election.[7] At the same time, of the only nineteen challengers who won over sitting House members, eleven outspent the incumbent—in seven cases, by as much as $100,000.[8] The winning pattern established by candidates with the

Table 8–1
COSTS OF PRESIDENTIAL GENERAL ELECTIONS, 1860–1972

Year	Republican		Democratic	
1860	$ 100,000	Lincoln*	$ 50,000	Douglas
1864	125,000	Lincoln*	50,000	McClellan
1868	150,000	Grant*	75,000	Seymour
1872	250,000	Grant*	50,000	Greeley
1876	950,000	Hayes*	900,000	Tilden
1880	1,100,000	Garfield*	335,000	Hancock
1884	1,300,000	Blaine	1,400,000	Cleveland*
1888	1,350,000	Harrison*	855,000	Cleveland
1892	1,700,000	Harrison	2,350,000	Cleveland*
1896	3,350,000	McKinley*	675,000	Bryan
1900	3,000,000	McKinley*	425,000	Bryan
1904	2,096,000	T. Roosevelt*	700,000	Parker
1908	1,655,518	Taft*	629,341	Bryan
1912	1,071,549	Taft	1,134,848	Wilson*
1916	2,441,565	Hughes	2,284,590	Wilson*
1920	5,417,501	Harding*	1,470,371	Cox
1924	4,020,478	Coolidge*	1,108,836	Davis
1928	6,256,111	Hoover*	5,342,350	Smith
1932	2,900,052	Hoover	2,245,975	F. Roosevelt*
1936	8,892,972	Landon	5,194,741	F. Roosevelt*
1940	3,451,310	Willkie	2,783,654	F. Roosevelt*
1944	2,828,652	Dewey	2,169,077	F. Roosevelt*
1948	2,127,296	Dewey	2,736,334	Truman*
1952	6,608,623	Eisenhower*	5,032,926	Stevenson
1956	7,778,702	Eisenhower*	5,106,651	Stevenson
1960	10,128,000	Nixon	9,797,000	Kennedy*
1964	16,026,000	Goldwater	8,757,000	Johnson*
1968	25,402,000	Nixon*	11,594,000	Humphrey
1972	61,400,000	Nixon*	30,000,000	McGovern

*Indicates winner.
SOURCE: Herbert E. Alexander, *Financing Politics* (Washington, D.C.: Congressional Quarterly, 1976), p. 20.

greatest financial resources has to be disquieting news for those who believe political office should be won by merit alone.

Money, then, is an important ingredient of electoral success, but does this fact imply partisan advantages? Do the candidates of the Republican party, as the party of business and society's well-to-do, find it easier to raise money than Democratic candidates? Before a cap was placed on campaign contributions, the Republicans did enjoy a financial edge in presidential elections. Republican presidential candidates outspent their Democratic rivals in twenty-five of the twenty-nine elec-

tions held between 1860 and 1972. The Republican advantage
stemmed from the party's ability to tap wealthy donors for
large sums. For example, of the record $60.3 million raised by
Richard Nixon's campaign in 1972, almost a third came from
153 donors who gave $50,000 or more.[9] If contributions had
been limited to $3,000, according to Alexander W. Keema,
George McGovern would have raised more money than
Nixon.[10] Partisan advantages in presidential fund raising, however, have been neutralized by the public funding features of
present law.

Private contributions to congressional campaigns reveal a
somewhat different pattern. In 1972, the last election before individual donations were limited, Democratic House candidates
raised more money than their Republican counterparts. The
reverse was true of Senate races in that year, when Republicans proved to be more successful fund raisers. Even after reform legislation restricted political giving, a mixed verdict was
returned. In the 1978 contests, Democratic House candidates
and Republican senatorial aspirants outspent their rivals in a
repeat of the 1972 pattern. Of greater significance than partisanship in the congressional races, however, was the incumbency factor. Senate and House incumbents, in the aggregate,
outspent their challengers by wide margins.

The edge in seats held by Democratic House members may
partially explain their success at fund raising. Individual and
group donors apparently believe they will see a greater return
on their investment if they spend it on incumbents. Nevertheless, such a cynical view cannot explain the pattern of giving in
open races. Well over half the Democrats contesting open seats
in 1978 collected more money than their Republican opponents
for both primary and general election races.[11] Incumbency
may be a contributory factor, but it is not the only reason Democratic candidates receive money.

WHO GIVES AND WHY

The political parties and their candidates have always
been embarrassed by their dependence on wealthy contributors. Although some campaigners who were electorally
secure did limit the size of gifts they would accept, most candidates could not afford to be so noble. Big money was particularly important in federal elections until Congress acted to
restrict the size of individual contributions in 1974. Even a

campaigner like George McGovern, whose direct-mail solicitation of small donations produced a sizable campaign chest, benefited from the large dole. Moreover, the large gifts McGovern took were particularly significant because they constituted the "up-front" money he used to get his campaign under way.[12] Table 8-2 lists the top contributors to McGovern and Nixon in 1972, a year of unprecedented campaign expenditures.

Candidates' dependence upon wealthy donors raises questions concerning the commitments they may have to make to get this money.[13] The public suspicion is that he who pays the piper calls the tune. Yet most of those who give to a candidate are probably not motivated by the simple desire to obtain a material benefit once the candidate is elected. Nor, contrary to

Table 8–2
MAJOR CONTRIBUTORS TO 1972 PRESIDENTIAL CAMPAIGNS

Nixon	Amount	McGovern*	Amount
W. Clement Stone	$2,051,643.45	Stewart R. Mott	$407,747.50
Richard Mellon Scaife	1,000,000.00	Max Palevsky†	319,365.00
John A. Mulcahy	624,558.97	Anne & Martin Peretz	275,016.44
Arthur Watson	303,300.00	Alejandro Zaffaroni	206,752.76
Ruth & George Farkas	300,000.00	Nicholas Noyes	205,000.00
John J. Louis, Jr.	283,360.22	Daniel Noyes	199,317.11
John Rollins	265,523.50	Alan & Shane Davis	158,872.25
Roy Carver	263,323.77	Richard Saloman	137,752.02
Sam Schulman	262,574.56	Joan Palevsky	118,616.86
Daniel Terra	255,000.00	Miles Rubin	108,000.00
Walter Annenberg	254,000.00	Bruce Allen	100,000.00
John Safer	251,000.00	John Lewis	100,000.00
Kent Smith	251,000.00	Henry Kimelman	82,533.00
Leon Hess	250,000.00	Albrecht Saalfield	82,000.00
Saul Steinberg	250,000.00	Diana & Salim Lewis	74,950.00
Jack Massey	249,999.96	Howard Metzenbaum	72,416.98
Max Fisher	249,773.05	Abner Levine	69,452.53
Ray Kroc	237,000.00	Alva Ted Bonda	67,454.73
Jack Dreyfus	231,000.00	Carol Bernstein	63,926.03
F. L. Cappeart	213,000.00	Robert Meyerhoff	63,486.52
Raymond Guest	200,000.00	Frank Lautenberg	57,955.48

*Includes loan amounts that were converted.
†Includes contributions from 1970.
SOURCE: Herbert E. Alexander, *Financing the 1972 Election* (Lexington, Ky.: D. C. Heath, 1976), p. 377.

popular myth, are candidates often willing participants in *quid pro quo* arrangements as a price for financial support.[14] The relationship between donor and recipient is a complex one that is not easily reduced to rule-of-thumb generalizations.

Some individuals offer contributions without attaching any strings to them, particularly people who give out of a sense of civic duty. Their motive in giving money to political campaigns is to share in the costs of democracy. Most small contributors are civically motivated: they give to the candidate whose party or policy views they agree with, but expect no special favors in return. Others give for ego fulfillment and want nothing more than the social contacts their contributions make possible. To have a senator attend their son's bar mitzvah or their daughter's wedding is repayment enough. Or perhaps a donor wishes to taste the excitement of a campaign and is allowed to ride a few stops on the campaign plane.[15] Like civically motivated donors, these people give their money to preferred candidates but impose no obligations that are difficult to perform.

Others who give large sums of money are seeking to buy access. These donors may have no special problem in mind that they wish the candidate to address. Rather, they are investing in the future. If a time comes when they do wish to discuss some matter with the officeholder, they are virtually assured of a receptive audience. Officeholders do not close their doors to those who have regularly contributed to their campaigns.

Still other large contributors give money because they want to advance a special interest. These are the donors who pose a delicate problem for candidates. On the one hand, a financial contribution made in expectation of some public policy return is quite legal. After all, that is what election contests are all about. On the other hand, a contribution made to obtain some special favor is a bribe, and quite possibly legally actionable. The difference hinges on the specificity of the pledges exchanged and the character of the favors asked.

For their part, most candidates to public office resist incurring specific obligations to their donors. Some turn over fund raising to their campaign staff, claiming they do not wish to know the sources of their money. It is hard to believe in the realism of such a tactic, since contributors usually insist that the candidate recognize their donations. Other candidates have been known to refuse contributions because of the donor's expectations. Nevertheless, officeholders do become locked into policy positions because of their established sources of campaign money. Contributors view candidates as either friends or foes and give or withhold their donations accordingly. It is impossible for officeholders to be unmindful of the sources of their political money, and this makes them ever more sensitive in taking public stands. Thus, in a subtle way, they become the captives of those who pay their campaign bills.

SPECIAL-INTEREST MONEY

Organized groups have also been prominent in financing political campaigns. Although such money originates in the form of individual contributions, the manner in which the funds are collected and disbursed indicates that they are intended to serve group objectives.

Business. Private corporations have been forbidden to make contributions to federal election campaigns since 1907, but nothing prevents their officers or board members from making private donations. Although before 1974, few corporations had auxiliary organizations (now called political action committees) to finance political campaigns, their executives did make concerted contributions. In 1952, executives of the twenty-two largest oil companies reported giving $300,000 to Republican candidates and committees after Dwight Eisenhower announced his support of legislation to return the tidelands oil to the states, a move the oil industry favored. By contrast, Democratic gifts from oil-related sources amounted to a mere $6,000.[16]

Despite the proscription of contributions from corporate treasuries, Watergate-related investigations revealed a pattern of illegal giving in 1972 that involved officers of twenty-one corporations. The total amount of questionable contributions was a little under $1 million, a modest portion of the record-breaking political expenditures of that year. The bulk of the money went to Richard Nixon's campaign, but illegal gifts were also made to George McGovern, Hubert Humphrey, Wilbur Mills, Henry Jackson, and Edmund Muskie.[17] Of probably greater significance in the past were contributions in kind made by business firms. Billboards, company airplanes, stamp meters, and office space were offered to candidates, as well as personnel on retainer who spent part of their time campaigning.[18] Always a gray area of the law, these indirect aids from the corporate treasury are prohibited under present regulations.

Contributions from officers and members of the boards of the nation's largest corporate enterprises have gone predominantly to the Republican party. An analysis of top-level giving from corporate sources in 1972 revealed that Republican candidates and committees received 85 percent of the donations.[19] Included in the study were the executives of the twenty-five largest contractors of the Department of Defense, the Atomic Energy Commission, and the National Aeronautics and Space Administration, and the twenty-five largest industrial companies on the "Fortune 500" list. Nevertheless, Democratic backing had to come from somewhere, and most of it came from people engaged in business.[20] The formation of political action committees by corporate enterprises under today's law allows a better accounting of business money and reveals that, although Republicans are favored, Democratic candidates are not ignored. At the same time, the limitations placed on individual contributions have cut back on the size of donations from the executives of the corporate giants who so heavily favored the Republican party in the past.

Labor. Unlike business contributions, labor money was not significant in national politics until the 1930s and was left unregulated until 1944.[21] Labor sources contributed $770,000 to Franklin Roosevelt's 1936 campaign, thus beginning its long-term association with the Democratic party. Labor's growing role in political campaigning led to the Smith-Connally Act of 1944, prohibiting contributions from labor organizations to federal campaigns. The act did not apply to nominations nor did it explicitly forbid expenditures (as opposed to contributions) made in behalf of candidates. These loopholes were plugged by the Taft-Hartley Act, which prohibited both unions and corporations from making either contributions or expenditures in behalf of candidates in federal elections, including nominating contests. The Taft-Hartley law remains applicable today.

Still, labor money finds its way into political campaigns. Union members may contribute voluntarily to their auxiliary political action committees, which can make campaign contributions. Of equal or greater significance, however, are the union funds that still can be legally used in behalf of candidates friendly to labor. Under First Amendment protections, labor organizations can use dues money for such "educational" expenditures as registration drives, get-out-the-vote campaigns, and the distribution of information sheets. Labor organizations registered 4.6 million voters in 1968 and distributed over 100 million pamphlets and leaflets. Local chapters of labor deployed over 100,000 people to make phone calls and engage in door-to-door canvasing. Some 94,000 labor volunteers worked on election day to get out the vote.[22] This last-minute effort almost put Hubert Humphrey over the top in his close race with Nixon that year.

CORRUPT PRACTICES LEGISLATION

The laws that regulated campaign finances prior to the 1976 election were largely ineffective, and the ease with which the regulations could be flouted contributed to public cynicism toward government leaders. The early laws were adopted during the Progressive era, chiefly in reaction to the millions of dollars national banks and corporations poured into the Republican campaign of 1904—a pattern of organized giving designed by Republican Chairman Mark Hanna for the earlier campaigns of William McKinley. The widespread involvement of business corporations in corrupt state and municipal governments at the turn of the century also gave impetus to reform. Thus in 1907, national banks and corporations chartered under federal law were prohibited from contributing to any political campaign, and all other corporations were forbidden to support candidates in federal elections. A 1910 law required congressional candidates to report their campaign receipts and expenditures. A year later, ceilings were placed on expenditures by Senate and House candidates. Limitations on the amounts that individuals could contribute and national committees could spend were set in 1940. Controls on contributions by labor unions were enacted in 1944, and strengthened in 1947. In reference to the ills they were designed to treat, these laws were labeled "corrupt practices legislation." But what did all the reform mean?

The manner in which labor and corporate money found its way into political campaigns has already been described. Limitation of the amount that national committees could spend ($3 million) had its intended effect of preventing the Republican and Democratic national committees from centralizing party finances, but did not affect the total amount each party spent. It was easy to establish new committees to receive and spend political money. The limitations on the amounts that House and Senate candidates could spend were ludicrously small, and remained unchanged during an era of skyrocketing campaign costs. No matter. Those who supported the candidates could spend unlimited amounts in their behalf, without even having to report the sums if the committees they formed operated in only one state. As to the limitations placed on individual contributions, they scarcely mattered either. Not only could wealthy individuals make donations to as many candidates and committees as they chose, but they also could funnel more than the legal amount to single candidates through gifts made in the name of family members, friends, or institutions. In short, the old campaign laws exemplified political hypocrisy at its worst.

The Move to Reform

Dissatisfaction with the existing laws eventually touched off new efforts at reform. Sensitive to charges that he had bought his office, President Kennedy appointed a bipartisan Commission on Campaign Costs in 1962.[23] The commission dutifully came up with a comprehensive plan for limiting and disclosing campaign costs, but its recommendations were ignored by a Congress jealous of presidential initiatives in a field it traditionally regarded as its own. The censure of Connecticut Senator Thomas Dodd for the misuse of campaign funds in 1966 led to a bipartisan bill that called for a Federal Election Commission to receive, audit, and publicize campaign finances. It failed to pass. In an unexpected move, however, Senator Russell Long sponsored and shepherded through a bill calling for federal subsidization of presidential elections. Although the bill was passed by both houses in 1966, the Long Act was never implemented and its provisions were allowed to die the following year. In the meanwhile, President Lyndon Johnson's plan for placing limits on media spending and using tax incentives to encourage political contributions was shelved when the Long Act was passed. Although these initial efforts at reform were unsuccessful, they did provide the legislative foundation for the acts that were to follow.

The first effective laws were passed in 1971. The Federal Election Campaign Act eliminated most of the ceilings on campaign expenditures but set limits on the amounts that could be spent in media advertising in federal elections. It also restricted the amount that candidates and their immediate families could spend on their own campaigns, and tightened reporting laws. A separate act that same year provided tax credits and tax deductions to encourage political giving.

The 1971 legislation was a modest effort at reform. Tax incentives to encourage the small contributor undoubtedly eased the burden of those wishing to give. Placing limits on media spending, however, did not prevent record-breaking expenditures in 1972. No steps were taken to curtail the influence of the big contributor, other than putting a limit on expenditures candidates made in their own behalf (later declared unconstitutional). Nor did the legislation place any additional restrictions on labor, business, or other organized groups. What proved to be the most significant provision of the 1971 reforms was the improved reporting procedures. Watergate-related investigations relied on them in part to trace the tangled and sometimes sordid web of money in the 1972 campaign. Confronted by an aroused public, Congress then moved to put teeth into the campaign finance laws. Amendments made to the Federal Campaign Act in 1974 and again in 1976 and 1979 now govern campaign finance.

LIMITS ON INDIVIDUAL CONTRIBUTIONS

To curb the influence of the "fat cats" of political finance, limitations were placed on the sums that individuals can contribute to federal election campaigns. Up to $1,000 may be donated to any one candidate or his organization in a primary battle, and an additional $1,000 may be given for the general election contest. Up to $5,000 may be given to any one political action committee, and up to $20,000 may be contributed to a party's national committee. An individual's total political gifts cannot exceed $25,000 in any election year.

Loopholes available under the old corrupt practices legislation were effectively plugged. Contributions in behalf of others are now forbidden, and candidates cannot set up additional committees to escape the limitations imposed. The new regulations were written with the clear intent of preventing a few individuals from exerting undue influence on electoral politics. The figure of W. Clement Stone, who with his wife Jessie contributed $7 million to the Republican cause between 1968 and 1972, must have loomed large in the minds of congressmen writing the legislation. The Congress's Democratic majority probably also recalled that the Republicans were able to outspend them in the 1972 presidential race by a two-to-one margin, largely because they received so much money from wealthy donors.

Some critics believe the legislation was too successful. The contribution limits, unlike the expenditure limits, are not indexed to inflation. As campaign costs soar, the value of the individual contribution wanes. Foreclosed from raising up-front money from a few wealthy backers, some candidates have had difficulty in getting their campaigns under way. Others have turned increasingly to alternatives sources of money: their personal wealth or corporate, labor, or other political action committees. In 1972, House candidates received 14 percent of their funds from political action committees; by 1978, that figure had risen to 25 percent. The reforms had been sincere, but they raised additional problems.

THE FORMATION OF POLITICAL ACTION COMMITTEES

Political action committees (PACs) are formed to make political contributions. To qualify as a PAC, an organization must register with the Federal Election Commission six months in advance, receive contributions from more than fifty persons, and make contributions to at least five candidates. Although any individual or group can set up a PAC, there are four principal types:

1. Corporate PACs set up by business corporations.
2. Labor PACs established by labor unions.
3. Trade, membership, and health PACs set up by such groups as the American Medical Association, the National Rifle Association, and the National Association of Realtors.
4. So-called nonconnected PACs established by conservative and liberal ideological groups.

PACs can contribute up to $5,000 to any candidate in a primary election and an equal amount to his or her general election campaign. There are no limitations on the total amount a PAC can give to all candidates, nor are there any restrictions on the amount a PAC can *spend* to elect any candidate, so long as the expenditures do not have the consent or cooperation of the candidate. A 1976 Supreme Court ruling held that independent expenditures were protected by the First Amendment's freedom of expression, while contributions to a candidate could be

restricted.[24] Although most money raised by PACs is contributed to the candidates, independent expenditures are on
the rise.

The number of PACs increased from 608 in 1974 to over
2,600 by 1981. The balance is tilted in favor of corporate and
trade, membership, and health PACs, groups that generally
have conservative political leanings. Together they outspent
the labor PACs by a five-to-two margin in 1980 (see Table 8-3).
There were some surprises, however, in the way the money was
doled out. As expected, labor PACs gave almost exclusively to
Democratic party candidates, but the funds contributed by
other PACs that made sizable donations, although favoring Republicans, were more evenly spread between the two parties.
Overall, the Democrats emerged with a modest advantage in
PAC money.

The more striking pattern of PAC-giving in 1980 was the
preference shown to incumbents. Congressmen running for reelection received $33.8 million, while their challengers were
given $14.3 million. The edge Democrats held in aggregate PAC
contributions was a reflection of the loyalty shown to them by
labor groups plus their status as the majority party in Congress. Evidently a variety of corporate groups and professional
associations were buying access by contributing to incumbents
without regard for partisan labels.

Table 8-3
PAC CONTRIBUTIONS TO 1980 SENATE AND HOUSE RACES
(in $ millions)

	Total Contri- butions*	Party Affiliation		Candidate Status		
		Demo- crat	Repub- lican	Incum- bent	Chal- lenger	Open
Corporations	$19.2	$ 6.9	$12.2	$11.0	$ 5.8	$2.4
Labor	13.1	12.2	0.9	9.3	2.2	1.6
Nonconnected organizations	4.8	1.5	3.3	1.5	2.4	0.9
Trade, Membership, Health	16.1	7.1	9.0	10.3	3.7	2.1
Cooperatives	1.4	0.9	0.5	1.1	0.1	0.2
Corporations without stock	0.7	0.4	0.3	0.5	0.1	0.1
Totals	$55.3	$29.0	$26.2	$33.8	$14.3	$7.2

*Row and column totals do not always equal because of rounding.
SOURCE: Federal Election Commission news release, August 4, 1981, p. 30.

The overall role of PAC money is not awe inspiring. PACs accounted for under 14 percent of the funding of Senate campaigns in 1978, but a more sizable 25 percent of House contests.[25] In a nation that is best described as pluralistic, political groups should be an expected source of campaign funds. Such political money is tainted only if it is presumed that organized groups should have no role in electoral politics. Moreover, PAC money does not ensure electoral success. Of the twenty-one House candidates who received $100,000 in PAC contributions in 1978, nine were defeated, including six incumbents.[26]

The alarm over the rise of PACs is caused by the way some PAC money is clearly targeted. In 1979, for example, more than 130 PACs affiliated with oil and gas interests were registered with the Federal Elections Commission, nearly seven times the number in 1976.[27] Involved in the stakes was the "windfall profits" tax backed by President Jimmy Carter. According to a survey by the *Washington Post*, twelve of the twenty members of the Senate Finance Committee considering Carter's tax proposal had received a total of $370,000 in oil industry contributions.[28] Members of key House committees involved in writing tax and energy policies also were beneficiaries of oil-related money.

Another worrisome issue is the growing use of independent expenditures as a means of escaping limitations imposed on PAC contributions. The three top-ranking PACs in the 1980 elections (all ideological groups of the right) together spent $8.7 million in selected campaigns, over six times the amount of their direct contributions.[29] A well-publicized effort spearheaded by the National Conservative Political Action Committee (NCPAC) was undertaken to unseat liberal Democratic senators in 1978 and 1980. Whether NCPAC deserved credit for turning out the senators they had targeted for defeat is disputed. For example, former Republican Representative James Abnor, who defeated Democratic Senator George McGovern of South Dakota, not only discounted NCPAC's influence but filed a complaint with the Federal Election Commission charging NCPAC with using his name without authorization. Republican National Chairman Richard Richards worried that the so-called New Right groups would create a backlash sympathy for the candidates they marked for defeat, and compared their tactics to the Committee to Reelect the President that led to the Watergate scandals. White House political adviser Lyn Nofziger, however, defended NCPAC because it softened up the opposition. Whatever role ideological PACs played in the defeat of Democratic congressmen, their independent role in the electoral process worries the leadership of both parties. Democrats are disturbed because they are being outspent by the conservative PACs as well as by the regular Republican organizations. Republicans are displeased because NCPAC and similar groups appeal to the same sources of political money as they do, and because NCPAC is not subject to party control.

LIMITS ON EXPENDITURES

Curtailing the influence of large donors and special interests was not the only goal in regulating campaign finance. The cost of campaigning had skyrocketed and Congress attempted to place a lid on further rises. The restrictions of the 1971 act on media advertising had been ineffectual in reducing total costs. The intentions of the 1974 legislation were to open competition to candidates formerly discouraged from running by limiting campaign expenditures, and at the same time make the large contribution unnecessary. The two-pronged strategy had much to commend it in the abstract, but left many questions unanswered. At what level should spending be set to allow the candidates adequate access to the voters whom they were calling upon for support? More practically, how much money does a challenger need to have a fair opportunity to unseat an incumbent?

The answers provided by Congress in the 1974 amendments, insofar as its own membership was concerned, were hardly satisfactory. House candidates were limited to $70,000 for a general election run. Senate candidates could spend $150,000, or 12 cents per eligible voter, whichever was larger. Neither provision was particularly generous. Twenty-one Senate candidates spent over $1 million in their 1978 campaigns, and nine House candidates spent over a half a million dollars.[30] It was the incumbents who would have reaped the advantages of the act's provisions. They have a staff, paid for by public funds, to assist them in organizing a campaign, they enjoy superior name recognition, and, not least among their advantages, they have the franking privilege. The flow of mail from the Capitol's postal service increases dramatically in the summer and fall months of an election year before a clamp is placed on political mailings twenty-eight days before an election.

"Senator, according to this report, you've been marked for defeat by the A.D.A., the National Rifle Association, the A.F.L.-C.I.O., the N.A.M., the Sierra Club, Planned Parenthood, the World Student Christian Federation, the Clamshell Alliance . . ."

Drawing by Dana Fradon; © 1980 The New Yorker Magazine, Inc.

In *Buckley v. Valeo,* the Supreme Court struck down spending ceilings on congressional campaigns as an unconstitutional restraint on free speech.[31] The Court's pronouncement effectively means that federal controls on congressional campaign costs are invalid, unless candidates are supplied with money from the federal treasury. The restrictions imposed on presidential campaigners are valid only if the candidates agree to them in return for public funding. That the limitations on presidential campaigns withstood a constitutional test did not render them immune to criticism.

A presidential candidate who accepts a public subsidy in seeking the nomination is limited to an outlay of $10 million, plus an additional 20 percent for fund raising. The ceiling is indexed to inflation, and in the 1980 races came to just under $15 million. Not all the money spent on prenomination campaigns, however, is controlled. A contender may actively seek the nomination before he files with the Federal Election Commission to commence the official nominating season. To finance his speaking engagements about the country, the yet-to-be-declared candidate may rely on his personal finances. Jimmy Carter did so in preparing his candidacy in 1976, and so did several Republican aspirants in the 1980 race.[32] Others have set up PACs that, while conforming to the campaign laws, can be used as vehicles to launch a presidential contender. Ronald Reagan's Citizens for the Republic disbursed over $4.5 million in 1977–1978, less than 15 percent of which went to support federal candidates. Most of the remainder was used to support a large staff, send out a newsletter, conduct seminars, finance direct-mail operations, and finance the undeclared candidate's travels.[33] One suspects that the contributors to the Reagan PAC were called on again when the nominating battle began in earnest.

The spending limits placed on candidates seeking a nomination were set at a time when the delegate selection process was undergoing transformation. More states have adopted the presidential primary and popular participation in the caucus states has increased. All these changes have added to the costs of campaigning, but the spending ceiling (except for adjustments for inflation) has remained the same. The advantage necessarily rests with an incumbent seeking renomination because he can gain the support of state and local leaders through the judicious use of appropriated funds he has at his command. His official acts are newsworthy and can be exploited to keep his name before the public, and he can schedule "official trips" to further his campaign interests.

Presidential candidates who accepted public funds were limited to spending a little under $30 million on their campaigns in the general election of 1980. (The sum is adjusted for inflation each presidential election year.) Is such a sum sufficient to allow each candidate to build an effective organization and to buy the media advertising he needs to get his message across? Any figure set should consider the inherent advantages of incumbency, which are the same whether a candidate is seeking renomination or reelection. What constitutes adequate in these circumstances is hard to divine. Herbert Alexander, the foremost student of campaign finance, set a minimum figure of $32 million for the 1976 general election, a year in which each major party candidate spent approximately $22 million in his campaign. Nevertheless, the funds provided Jimmy Carter in 1976 and Ronald Reagan in 1980 were adequate to defeat incumbent presidents.

PUBLIC FUNDS FOR PRESIDENTIAL RACES

The 1974 amendments devised two plans for assisting presidential aspirants in their bid to occupy the Oval Office, one for the nominating process and the other for the general election contest. In seeking the nomination, candidates can finance their campaign by a combination of private donations and public funds. But in the general election, candidates who accept public funds cannot take private contributions.

The contender who elects to receive public funds in his nomination bid must first qualify by raising $5,000 in each of twenty states in sums of $250 or less and collect a total of $100,000. Thereafter, the candidate is eligible for federal matching funds of up to $250 for each individual contribution received. The law's intent was to open the nominating battle to more contenders, while at the same time discouraging frivolous candidacies. This goal has been largely met. The combined effect of the ceiling on expenditures, restrictions on individual giving, and the availability of matching funds has equalized opportunities. Morris Udall was neither independently wealthy nor a nationally known figure, but he stayed in the 1976 Democratic party sweepstakes to the end. With a campaign chest of $4.5 million, $2 million of it from matching grants, Udall campaigned actively in a third of the primaries and, although unsuccessful, carried the liberal banner into the convention.[34]

Candidates without a serious chance of winning have qualified for matching funds, but they have been unable to stay the course. Ellen McCormack, who ran on a "prolife" (antibortion) platform for the Democratic party nomination in 1976, was criticized by some as a single-issue candidate who was more interested in her cause than the nomination. When she failed to receive 10 percent of the vote in two successive primaries, her matching funds were cut off in accordance with amendments added in 1976. Lyndon LaRouche, the former head of the U.S. Labor party who ran as a Democrat in 1980, also gained and then lost his eligibility for federal campaign aid.

In the general election, each candidate of a major party receives the same amount of aid. A major party is defined as one that received at least 25 percent of the popular vote in the preceding presidential election. Minor party candidates who received between 5 and 25 percent of the vote in the last election are given a proportionate share of funds. The candidate of a newly created minor party may claim matching funds retroactively by winning at least 5 percent of the vote in the current election.

Grumbling over the quasi-public funding of candidates seeking the nomination has been subdued in comparison to complaints voiced over the public subsidies paid to general election candidates. Conceived as private voluntary associations, the American political parties traditionally have been supported by private giving. To provide major party candidates with funds from the federal treasury cloaks the parties with a public character and gives them an official status. It hardens the political status quo. Nor does the provision for assigning a pro rata share of public funds to minor party candidates solve the problem. Their candidates are given a "Catch-22" alternative: they must earn 5 percent of the popular vote before they can receive public funds, but they may need the public funds in order to obtain their share of the votes cast.

Of course, a candidate does not have to accept public funds and, with them, limits on campaign expenditures. Nevertheless, restrictions on private giving make it difficult to finance a campaign through private sources alone. To date, only John Connally, in his quest for the Republican nomination in 1980, struck out on his own. In refusing public funds, Connally hoped to build momentum for his campaign by spending more than otherwise would be allowed in early primary states where he needed to do better than others to establish a credible candidacy. His strategy proved unsuccessful, and he dropped out of the race after a poor showing in the South Carolina primary. The principle of federal funding in presidential races survived its initial test.

PUBLIC DISCLOSURE OF CAMPAIGN MONEY

Some analysts have argued that public disclosure of the sources of a candidate's campaign money is the best safeguard against financial abuses. The timely filing of public reports apprises the voter of a candidate's financial backing and can be an important guide in weighing an electoral decision. Although the argument has merit, it is questionable whether many voters bother to learn whose money is behind a candidate's bid for office. Nevertheless, the figures issued by the Federal Election Commission are reported, by the print media in particular, and can shape general impressions, particularly when a candidate is charged with "buying" an election. No doubt many factors contributed to the defeat of eleven of the nineteen candidates who spent over $400,000 in 1978 House races, and overspending was possibly one of them.[35]

Current laws have tightened reporting requirements. Candidates and political committees must report contributions of $50 or more, expenditures in excess of $100, and aggregate receipts and expenditures. Quarterly reports are required, as well as reports ten days before and thirty days following an election. Expenditures of $1,000 made within fifteen days of an election must be reported within twenty-four hours. The Federal Election Commission prescribes the forms on which the reports are made.

Aside from the specificity of who is to report what type of receipts and expenditures, the major breakthrough in the law was the requirement that each candidate for federal office had to establish a central campaign committee to accept all campaign gifts and approve all disbursements. No longer can candidates escape the law's provisions by having others spend money in their behalf. Individuals may still spend unlimited amounts advocating the election or defeat of any candidate, but they must state, under penalty of perjury, that the expenditures were not made in collusion with the candidate. One other disclosure-related feature of the act has practical and symbolic importance. Cash donations in excess of $100 are forbidden. Satchels stuffed with hundred-dollar bills are no longer a part of the election scene.

Reporting requirements have proved a headache for campaigners, even those who don't doubt their necessity. One consultant advises his clients to reserve from 5 to 10 percent of their campaign budgets for complying with the law's disclosure provisions.[36] Volunteer treasurers whose only qualifications for office were their willingness to work in behalf of their candidate are now being replaced by paid lawyers and accountants. Although time-consuming and tedious, the reports are an essential part of campaign regulations, for they provide the information necessary to evaluate the success of the reforms.

ENFORCEMENT OF THE ACTS: THE FEDERAL ELECTION COMMISSION

A bipartisan Federal Election Commission (FEC) was created to administer the various provisions of the campaign reform laws. Its early history was clouded by constitutional issues. Initially composed of two members appointed by the president and four by the Congress, the FEC's method of selection was successfully challenged in *Buckley v. Valeo* as a violation of the separation-of-powers doctrine. Critics charged that congressmen had known the FEC's makeup would be ruled invalid but had advanced it anyway because they hoped to implant enough doubtful provisions in the bill to invite the courts to rule all its reforms unconstitutional. Although some presidential candidates suffered in their 1976 primary races because the FEC could not certify matching payments, the Congress acted quickly to restore its legal basis. It authorized the president to appoint, subject to Senate confirmation, all six voting members of the FEC. The clerk of the House and the secretary of the Senate sit *ex officio* as nonvoting members.

The FEC is charged with the responsibility of authorizing public funds, ensuring compliance with reporting provisions, and issuing regular and special reports on campaign finance. To accomplish these objectives, the commission is empowered to issue regulations governing campaign practices that have the force of law unless disapproved by either house of Congress. The Commission also investigates campaign irregularities and can impose civil penalties for violations. Any criminal violations it discovers are turned over to the Justice Department for prosecution.

The creation of the FEC represents a distinct step forward in campaign reform legislation. For the first time, a specific agency has the responsibility for ensuring compliance with campaign financial regulations. The FEC has had minor problems in establishing its independence from the Congress, and several of its proposed rules have been rebuffed by one or both houses, but it should have been expected that some of the regulations issued by the commission would prove controversial. First of all, Congress did not always clarify its intent in the laws it enacted. Moreover, the effect of the commission's rulings fall on the very legislators who must acquiesce in their adoption. For example, an issue that developed early was how to treat "constituent service funds" used to supplement a congressmen's office expense allowances.[37] Were the private contributions received to assist legislators in sending out newsletters or traveling to their home districts to be considered campaign or office related? The commission originally ruled that they were campaign related, but then, after strong congressional objection, relented and said they would be considered office related.

On the whole, the FEC has been successful in securing voluntary compliance with its regulations. It provides information to candidates on its campaign guidelines and issues advisory opinions on questionable practices. Although some believe its regulations are unnecessarily narrow and legalistic,[38] the commission is acquiring a reputation for an even-handed application of its powers, and compliance with the legal provisions of reform is no longer a major issue.

THE ROLE ASSIGNED POLITICAL PARTIES IN FINANCING CAMPAIGNS

Most of the foregoing discussion has centered on reporting requirements, expenditure limits, and regulations to curb the influence of large donors and special interests. These aspects of reform have deservedly received considerable public attention. Almost unnoticed, except in the halls of Congress, has been the limited role given to political parties in financing campaigns.

The Long Act of 1966 was the first legislation to pass the Congress that provided for public subsidization of presidential elections. Although its provisions were never implemented, it was novel in respects other than its public funding features. The money that was to be paid out of the public treasury was to go to the national parties, not the individual candidates. State party leaders traditionally have feared that the centralization of campaign spending would lead to the centralization of the parties, and one of the purposes behind the earlier $3 million limitation on expenditures by national-level committees was to check the influence of the Republican and Democratic national committees. The provisions of the Long Act would have superseded that requirement. In arguing for the law's repeal, Senator Robert F. Kennedy contended that it placed excessive power in the hands of national party chairmen. Even the presidential choice of a party, Kennedy argued, could be influenced by a chairman's promises of how he would distribute the allotted money.[39]

Party Aid to Candidates. Under today's law, public funding of presidential campaigns goes directly to the candidates. The party's participation in campaign funding is not proscribed, but it *is* limited. The law permits the national committees to spend 2 cents times the voting age population (adjusted for inflation, approximately $4.6 million in 1980) on the presidential campaigns. Because the national chairmen are effectively controlled by the presidential nominees, party spending amounts to little more than an extension of presidential expenditure limits.

If the parties have the money, they may aid Senate and House candidates in two ways: by making contributions to a candidate to spend as he pleases, and by spending money in behalf of a candidate—for example, paying his polling or television costs. The latter is often referred to as "coordinated spending" and gives party committees a greater voice in how the money is used. Allowable expenditures are indexed to inflation, while contribution limits are set at fixed amounts. Current regulations of general election contests provide the following:

1. *Contributions*

   a. The national committee, the congressional campaign committee, and a state committee may each contribute $5,000 to a House candidate.
   b. The national committee and the senatorial campaign committee may make combined contributions of $17,500 to a senatorial candidate. A state committee may contribute $5,000.

2. *Expenditures*

   a. The national committee and the congressional campaign committee may spend a combined $10,000 ($14,720 in 1980 dollars) to support a House candidate. A state committee may spend an equal amount.
   b. The national committee and the senatorial campaign committee may spend a combined $20,000 ($29,440 in 1980 dollars) or 2 cents per eligible voter, whichever is larger, to support a senatorial campaign. A state committee may spend an equal amount.
   c. State and local committees may spend unlimited amounts on certain campaign materials (buttons, bumper stickers, posters, handbills, and lawn signs) to promote any federal election candidate.

Current laws also permit the parties to give unlimited indirect aid to candidates. They are allowed to conduct party schools to advise candidates and their staffs on campaign techniques, and to finance research units that provide information on issues and incumbent voting records. They may also undertake registration drives and get-out-the-vote campaigns that benefit all party candidates. The most significant recent development that does not fall within expenditure limits imposed on the parties was the institutional advertising the Republicans mounted in 1980. Jointly sponsored by the Republican National Committee and the Republican Congressional Campaign Committee, the advertisements were aired in three separate waves during the campaign at a cost of $9.6 million. Reminding viewers that Democrats had been in power for twenty-five of the past twenty-seven years, Republican strategists appealed to the television audience to "Vote Republican—For a Change." A Republican-commissioned postelection survey undertaken by Market Opinion Research in thirty-one competitive congressional districts involving over six thousand interviews confirmed the success of the advertisements.

Party Funding as an Alternative to PACs. The direct support political parties give to federal election candidates is puny in comparison to the sums they receive from business, labor, and other PACs. If the reform goal is to check the influence of special interests, the parties are the best alternative source of funding available. The political money they would raise would probably come from the same donors tapped by the candidates under today's laws, but an important difference is that the candidates would be one step removed from the sources. It follows that candidates would then be indebted to the leaders who dole out party funds, instead of to private donors.

The question of party funding, however, does have certain partisan considerations. Although Democratic candidates raise money as readily as Republican candidates in federal elections, the Democratic party as an organization has not been able to match the Republican party at fund raising. In 1978, Democratic House leaders attempted to set a $10,000 limit on contributions that House candidates could receive from all party sources. One out of three Republicans in 1976 would have been affected by the bill's provisions, but only one out of nine Democrats. In a moment of levity, Republican Charles E. Wiggins presented the Democratic chairman of the House Administration Committee, Frank Thompson, with an engineer's cap to compliment him on the way he had railroaded the bill through committee.[40] Republicans took the issue seriously, however, because it threatened their ability to unseat entrenched Democratic incumbents.

The attempt to limit party giving was probably part of a Democratic strategy to induce the Republicans to support public funding of congressional races. The proposed limitations would have been used as a bargaining chip, to be cashed in when the Republicans voted for public financing. The stratagem backfired, however, when Republicans united against significant change in the campaign laws.[41]

Congressional Public Funding Proposals. Former President Carter, the Democratic congressional leadership, the Democratic Study Group, and a number of outside organizations, including Common Cause, have backed public funding of congressional races. The bills submitted would have provided matching grants similar to those now given presidential candidates who seek their party's nomination. Because the proposals also include spending ceilings, Republican party officials have been vocal in their opposition. They charge that the bills are hand tailored to protect Democratic incumbents from losing their seats. Republican opponents of public subsidies are joined by some Democrats who fear that the plan will invite challenges in districts that have had only token opposition in the past.

Although it remains a live issue, a public funding bill for congressional races has yet to pass. The stakes involved are real enough. Allowing for some hyperbole, to decide how campaigns should be financed is to pass judgment on who should be given an edge in winning.

Activity at the State Level

Investigations arising out of the Watergate scandals highlighted the role of political money in the 1972 elections and created a political climate favorable to election reform. Within a four-year period, almost every state seized the opportunity to revise its elections laws.[42] Not all the states enacted laws that were drawn as tightly as the federal regulations, but many took significant steps toward reform, and some states experimented with novel methods of financing campaigns that, when sufficiently evaluated, may point the way to further reform of federal campaign practices.

PUBLIC DISCLOSURE OF RECEIPTS AND EXPENDITURES

Public disclosure of receipts and expenditures is the most common feature of state regulations. The rationale is that campaign abuses will wither in the full glare of publicity. To be effective, however, reports must be filed before an election so voters can make timely use of the information. Every state but one requires financial reporting, although Alabama and Wyoming do not demand preelection disclosure.[43] The usefulness of the financial reports depends on how stringently the regulations are enforced and how well former loopholes have been closed. A ten-state study concluded that there were no "significant unreported cash contributions" in the 1974 campaigns other than cash outlays on election day ("walking-around money") in Maryland and Georgia.[44]

BIPARTISAN COMMISSIONS

Twenty-nine states have established independent bipartisan commissions to administer their campaign election laws.[45] The appointment of such commissions represents a good-faith effort to insulate the regulation of campaign finance from partisan politics. Formerly the administration of corrupt practices legislation was in the hands of elected or appointed officials whose partisan ties cast doubts on their evenhandedness. Some state commissions have powers to issue subpoenas and to assess civil penalties to election law violators. Criminal violations, of course, must be turned over to partisan prosecutorial authorities who decide whether to pursue the referrals.

LIMITS ON CONTRIBUTIONS

Well over half the states had imposed limitations on campaign expenditures by the time the Supreme Court declared such ceilings invalid. Limitations on the size and sources of contributions have been less common. Twenty-five states limit the amount of individual contributions, with considerable variations in the curbs imposed. Most limitations fall within a $1,000 to $3,000 range for statewide campaigns, but New York's law, based on the number of registered voters, is considerably more generous.[46] There is a comparable disparity among state laws controlling special interest money. Twenty-four states prohibit outright contributions from corporations, while seven others merely limit the size of the corporate donation.[47] Only ten states prohibit labor unions from contributing to candidates for state office. As in federal elections, however, business and labor money finds its way into state elections through the donations of individual contributors.

PUBLIC FUNDING

Seventeen states provide public grants to state campaigners in general elections. Thirteen of these states raise the money through a tax checkoff system modeled after federal practice, while four permit taxpayers to add a dollar surcharge to their tax bill to be used for public subsidies.[48] In what has to be a disheartening commentary on the electorate's contributory habits, the two plans have produced decidedly different results. For example, less than 1 percent of Maine's taxpayers have been willing to *add* a dollar to their tax bill to support political campaigners. On the other hand, up to 25 percent of those filing Minnesota returns have *diverted* a dollar of their tax bills to an election campaign fund.[49]

Public funding of state campaigns has other unique features. In five states, the taxpayer designates the party he or she wishes to support. In eight other states, tax money is paid into a general election fund to be distributed to major party candidates according to statutory provisions. In four states, taxpayers may designate their money for a specific party or for the general election fund. With few exceptions (Utah in 1976 and 1977), Democrats have been the beneficiaries of the party designation plans. Unsurprisingly, Republicans have opposed public funding plans that have rendered them financial losers. However, they are likely to oppose any public subsidies because of their accompanying expenditure limits. Often in the minority, Republicans believe they have to outspend their rivals to gain office.[50]

On the issue of whether to fund party committees or individual candidates, the states are equally divided. Eight states make grants to the parties, eight other states give to candidates, and one state (Oklahoma) offers aid to both parties and candidates.[51] Providing grants to party committees gives them greater flexibility in party-building efforts. They can use the public subsidies to hire staff, conduct campaign training sessions, and finance registration drives and get-out-the-vote campaigns. Although sometimes restricted by allocation formulas, party committees can also attract able candidates by promises of campaign aid.

Subsidies that go directly to candidates tend to weaken party organizations. So long as the public monies go only to general election races, bypassing the party may have little effect on its organizational presence because candidates must receive their party's nomination before they can receive public money. New Jersey, Massachusetts, and Michigan, however, provide subsidies to gubernatorial candidates running in the primaries, and this kind of public funding weakens the party's grip on its nominees.

In New Jersey, for example, candidates qualify for state matching funds by first raising $50,000, after which they receive $2 for every $1 they collect from individual donations (limited to $800). Used for the first time in 1981, the public subsidies appeared to keep candidates in the race who might otherwise have dropped out along the way. New Jersey gubernatorial primaries often have crowded fields, but the number who stayed the course in 1981 was unusual. The legislature had earlier rejected a proposal to raise the qualifying threshold to $150,000, as well as a plan calling for a runoff primary. As a result, the electorate was confused by the number of contenders. Michigan and Massachusetts had smaller fields in 1978, but in each case, an incumbent was running. The presence of an incumbent often tends to keep down the number of challengers in both parties' primaries.[52] In open races, public money may lure candidates who have not earned the blessings of party leaders.

Though the focus of public attention is generally on Washington, the state efforts at regulating political money offer an opportunity for comparative analyses that could provide answers to difficult questions of how best to finance political campaigns. Their experiences should be carefully monitored for the effects the several plans have on electoral politics. No plan will ever be universally acclaimed, but the unintended consequences of imperfectly drawn laws can be avoided as more information is accumulated.

The Contemporary Parties: The Effects of Financial Reforms

The campaign reform legislation of the 1970s has had considerable impact. Unlike older corrupt practices legislation, the new laws have teeth in them. Wealthy contributors cannot finance federal elections to the extent they once did, for they are restricted in the amount they can give to individual campaigners and in their aggregate contributions. The principle of public funding of election campaigns has been established. Although public subsidies are now used only in presidential campaigns, they have been considered by recent Congresses as a means of financing all federal election campaigns. Public disclosure of campaign receipts and expenditures has been vastly improved under the new reporting requirements, and for the first time, a bipartisan commission with no other responsibilities is charged with enforcing federal campaign laws. These are considerable accomplishments.

Reform legislation has not solved all the problems associated with political money. Except in presidential races, there is no lid on total campaign outlays, and general election spending in congressional campaigns in 1978 increased by over 50 percent from 1976.[53] As one source of political money dries up, others are found to keep the funds flowing. One consequence of the limits placed on individual contributions has been the proliferation of PACs. The rise in the number of corporate PACs, in particular, has been spectacular. While the haziness of the old laws permitted some corporate officers to make illegal donations, the new laws actually invite the business community to participate in fund raising. Thus wealthy donors are able to have a cumulative effect on American politics, and their interests are even more clearly identified.

Independent expenditures by ideological PACs, most of them supporting conservative causes, also have proved worrisome. Such expenditures not only get around the legal limitations on PAC contributions, but are beyond the control of the preferred candidates or their parties as well. Compounding the problem has been the tendency of the ideological PACs to conduct negative campaigns against targeted candidates, sometimes accompanied by reckless charges, rather than mounting positive efforts in behalf of candidates of their choosing. The problem is so serious that both the Republican and Democratic national chairmen called for an examination of the electoral role of PACs after the 1980 elections.

Congressional candidates can still spend as much of their own money as they wish to finance their campaigns. This exception to the more general curbs on the well-to-do donor was not made by Congress but by the Supreme Court, which declared that restrictions on personal expenditures by a candidate were valid only if they were tied to acceptance of public funds. A little more than 10 percent of total congressional expenditures in 1976 were financed out of the candidate's own pocket.[54]

The reform goal of increasing the contributions of the small donor has been partially realized. Contributions under $500 provided in the neighborhood of 45 percent of all congressional spending in 1976 and 1978,[55] significantly more than the sums from other individual categories: the candidate's personal expenditures, contributions of PACs, gifts of $500 or better, and the money provided by party committees. Candidates are also the indirect beneficiaries of small gifts made to PACs and the political parties.

Increasing the role of the small donor is not an insurmountable task. Direct-mail appeals have produced large campaign chests for the Republican National Committee in sums that averaged $26 in 1979. McGovern raised $12 million through direct mail in his 1972 general election campaign, and most of the $7.5 million Jesse Helms spent on his 1978 senatorial campaign came from mail solicitation. Unfortunately, the costs of preparing lists and mailing requests may eat up one quarter to one half or more of the donations received. Moreover, because loans in federal elections must be repaid by legally acceptable contributions, borrowing to meet the starting-up costs of a mailout makes the technique a risky undertaking for many campaigners.

Two avenues are open to reformers who wish to open access to public office more widely, while at the same time curbing the influence of special-interest money. One is the route of public funding. If public support of presidential races is justified, then the same rationale can sustain subsidization of congressional candidates. Drawing the legislation will be more complex because congressmen from safe districts do not wish to encourage competition where none exists and Republicans fear that the spending limits associated with public subsidies will impede their efforts to unseat Democratic incumbents. So far these controversies have stalled legislation embodying public support of congressional candidates.

A second avenue to reform, which has received less public attention, is strengthening the party role in financing campaigns. This route would require two types of changes in existing laws. First, restrictions on the amounts individuals and groups can give to political committees would have to be raised. This step would increase the overall availability of party money and supply the Democratic party in particular with the seed money its national committee needs to build a more solid direct-mail fund-raising program. Second, the financial contributions parties could make to individual candidates would have to be increased, and more flexibility would have to be permitted in the direct services party staffers could provide for individual campaigns. If this were done, the parties could concentrate their aid on key races and assist candidates who were targeted for defeat by PACs. Of course, there would be political costs. Undoubtedly some races would be selected for party spending and others written off as lost causes, the influence of party professionals would be enhanced, and party officeholders might well be brought under more central direction. Nevertheless, making election contests more of a collective undertaking led by the parties would combat the divisive tendencies now evident in the spending and contribution patterns of single-issue groups and other organizations of limited policy objectives.

Watergate and related scandals spurred the reforms of the 1970s, and a great deal was accomplished in a relatively short time span. Now that it feels under less pressure, Congress will probably move much more slowly toward any additional reforms. Perhaps it is wise to await further analyses before deciding on the directions any new reforms should take. Public funding of congressional races holds enormous significance for the parties. It would further free campaigners from the organization whose label they wear and contribute to the continued decline of the parties. Such a step should be taken only after careful consideration of its full implications, and after the parties are afforded the opportunity to demonstrate their fund-raising capabilities.

SUMMARY

The costs of political campaigning are higher today than at any time in the nation's history. After adjusting for inflation and an enlarged electorate, the real costs of seeking public offices have dramatically increased over the past three decades. The causes of the soaring expenses are to be found in the new techniques by which the candidate reaches the voter. Modern political campaigning makes use of expensive technological innovations, not the least of which is the paid television advertisement.

The mounting cost of campaigning raises a fundamental question: Does the side with the most money win? Not always. The credibility of candidates, events, and the distribution of partisan identification all influence an election outcome. Nevertheless, money is an important ingredient in most contests, and in some, it is the determinative element.

Money, then, is an important resource, but does this imply partisan advantages? Before a limit was placed on presidential spending, Republicans did enjoy a clear advantage in fund raising—they outspent their rivals in twenty-two of the twenty-nine races held between 1860 and 1972. The pattern has not been so clear in congressional races, at least in recent years. House Democrats have spent, in the aggregate, more than their Republican counterparts, but the reverse has been true of Senate contests, with Republicans outspending Democrats. Perhaps of greater significance has been the financial advantage incumbents have enjoyed over their opponents.

Fear that political competition might become limited to the personally wealthy and those who are the captives of powerful organized interests led to the regulation of campaign finance. The early laws prohibited contributions from national banks and corporations, required financial reports from congressional candidates, and placed ceilings on House and Senate campaigns. Later legislation limited individual contributions and expenditures made by national committees, and the 1947 Taft-Hartley Act prohibited contributions from labor organizations. All these laws did little to curb expenditures, limit individual contributions, or reveal the sources of campaign money.

Ineffective regulation of campaign funding was a continuing source of dissatisfaction to observers of the American political scene. The mere fact of raising enormous sums to compete for office cast doubt on candidates' independence from their financial contributors. Most candidates are wary of accepting money as part of a *quid pro quo* agreement, and most donors do not demand such an understanding. Nevertheless, officeholders often find themselves locked into certain policy positions because they depend on generous contributions from individuals and organizations that demand they hold to those positions.

Further attempts at reform fell before an unresponsive Congress until the Watergate-related scandals shocked the

American conscience. Urged on by the media and an aroused public, Congress passed a series of laws and amendments that effectively regulated campaign finances. The "fat cats" of political finance were limited to $25,000 in aggregate contributions, presidential aspirants who accepted government subsidies had to agree to limits on their campaign expenditures, and reporting and disclosure laws ensured an exact accounting of political money. A bipartisan Federal Elections Commission was created to administer and enforce the new laws.

Though it was unquestionably effective in tightening the laws regulating campaign finance, the reform legislation did not solve all the problems of money's role in politics. Some critics charged that the $1,000 limit on individual contributions to a candidate was too low and prevented some candidates from mounting an effective campaign. Others asserted that the limit placed on candidates seeking the presidential nomination was also too low because of the increased number of presidential primaries since the law's enactment. Many critics dislike the idea of any limits on expenditures on the grounds that they benefit an incumbent, who can draw upon the resources of his office to improve his chances of election. The public-funding features of presidential elections also came under attack. Subsidizing the Democratic and Republican parties cloaks them with a public character and tends to freeze the status quo, making it harder for minor party candidates to compete.

Reform legislation has not been successful in holding down the costs of campaigning in congressional elections. Legislation that limited House and Senate campaign expenditures was declared unconstitutional because it was not tied to an acceptance of public funding, and bills to provide matching funds for House candidates, accompanied by limits on expenditures, have become embroiled in a partisan controversy. Republican critics believe expenditures limits would make it more difficult for them to unseat entrenched Democratic incumbents.

Another effect of the new legislation has been the proliferation of PACs. Neither corporations nor labor organizations can make contributions from their own treasuries in federal election campaigns, but both can set up auxiliary organizations to receive and dole out private contributions. With individual giving restricted, PACs have risen sharply in numbers and importance. PACs make only modest direct contributions to Senate races, and account for only 25 percent of the costs of House campaigns. Nevertheless, PAC money is often targeted to key committee members, and this is one source of concern. A second is that independent expenditures made by ideological PACs are not subject to restrictions.

There is no doubt that the political parties have been weakened by the recent financial regulations. Party contributions to candidates are restricted by law and amount to less than the aggregate contributions of PACs. Candidates who are provided with public grants or who raise their own funds can afford to act independently of their party both in the type of campaign they can run and the public stands they take. The more independence candidates achieve, the less the party resembles a collective undertaking.

The same forces that spurred the reform of federal elections also activated the states. Almost every state now regulates campaign finance, although the effectiveness of the legislation varies. Every state but one requires public reports of receipts and expenditures, and nearly half the states limit individual contributions. Corporate giving is also commonly restricted, labor donations less so. Seventeen states provide public funding for campaigns, which, interestingly, goes to party committees as often as to individual candidates. That half the states administer their acts through bipartisan commissions suggests a serious attempt at reform.

Financial reforms have not achieved all that their sponsors had hoped, but effective regulation of money was new to American politics and not all of its consequences could be foreseen. Reformers wish to place even more controls on political money and hope that state experiences with various types of plans will point the way. But it is unclear at this juncture whether the political parties will be allowed to resume the role they once had in financing their candidates.

Notes

[1]Delmar D. Dunn, *Financing Presidential Campaigns* (Washington, D.C.: Brookings Institution, 1972), p. 26.

[2]Herbert E. Alexander, *Financing Politics* (Washington, D.C.: Congressional Quarterly, 1976), p. 17, Fig. 2-1.

[3]Ibid.

[4]Ibid., p. 18, Fig. 2-2.
[5]Ibid., p. 29.
[6]*Congressional Quarterly Weekly Report*, September 29, 1979, p. 2152.
[7]Ibid., p. 2157.
[8]Ibid., p. 2156.
[9]Herbert E. Alexander, *Financing the 1972 Election* (Lexington, Mass.: D.C. Heath, 1976), p. 7.
[10]Quoted in ibid., p. 380.
[11]*Congressional Quarterly Weekly Report*, September 29, 1979, pp. 2154–2155, 2158–2163.
[12]Alexander, *Financing the 1972 Election*, pp. 122–123.
[13]For a discussion of why individuals give money, see Dunn, *Financing Presidential Campaigns*, pp. 14–25.
[14]Although corruption in high places unquestionably occurs, "its reputation for moving the wheels of government is far more potent than its performance." Ibid., p. 14.
[15]Ibid., p. 17.
[16]Alexander Heard, *The Costs of Democracy* (Garden City, N.Y.: Anchor, 1962), pp. 92–93.
[17]Alexander, *Financing Politics*, p. 113.
[18]On indirect corporate giving, see Heard, *The Costs of Democracy*, pp. 115–117.
[19]Alexander, *Financing Politics*, p. 110.
[20]Heard, *The Costs of Democracy*, p. 106.
[21]Alexander, *Financing Politics*, p. 105.
[22]Ibid., p. 107.
[23]See the discussion in ibid., pp. 134–137.
[24]*Buckley v. Valeo*, 424 U.S. 1 (1976).
[25]*Congressional Quarterly Weekly Report*, September 29, 1979, p. 2152.
[26]Ibid., September 8, 1979, p. 1955.
[27]Ibid., November 3, 1979, p. 2455.
[28]Quoted in ibid., p. 2456.
[29]*Washington Post*, January 27, 1981, p. A4.
[30]*Congressional Quarterly Weekly Report*, September 29, 1979, p. 2152.
[31]424 U.S. 1, 1976.
[32]Stephen J. Wayne, *The Road to the White House* (New York: St. Martin's, 1980), p. 44.
[33]*Congressional Quarterly Weekly Report*, February 17, 1979, p. 309.
[34]Wayne, *The Road to the White House*, p. 44.
[35]*Congressional Quarterly Weekly Report*, September 29, 1979, p. 2155.
[36]Alexander, *Financing Politics*, p. 34.
[37]See ibid., pp. 145–147.
[38]Ibid., p. 164.
[39]Ibid., p. 137.
[40]*Congressional Quarterly Weekly Report*, March 18, 1978, p. 721.
[41]Ibid., p. 718.
[42]Alexander, *Financing Politics*, p. 169.
[43]Herbert E. Alexander, *Financing Politics*, 2nd ed. (Washington, D.C.: Congressional Quarterly, 1980), p. 127.
[44]David S. Broder, "Epilogue: Assessing Campaign Reform: Lessons for the Future," in *Campaign Money*, ed. Herbert E. Alexander (New York: Free Press, 1976), p. 311.
[45]Alexander, *Financing Politics*, 2nd ed., p. 134.
[46]Ibid., p. 129.
[47]Ibid.
[48]Ruth S. Jones, "State Public Campaign Finance: Implications for Partisan Politics," *American Journal of Political Science* 25 (May 1981), p. 348.

[49]Alexander, *Financing Politics*, p. 182.

[50]Jones, "State Public Campaign Finance," pp. 345, 349, and 352.

[51]Ibid., p. 345.

[52]See the discussion in *Congressional Quarterly Weekly Report*, May 16, 1981, p. 861.

[53]Ibid., September 29, 1979, p. 2153.

[54]Ibid.

[55]Ibid.

9

Political Campaigning and the "New Politics"

The political campaign is the vehicle candidates for public office use to present their qualifications to the voters. Under ideal conditions, campaigners would identify the problems that need addressing and offer solutions for them. They would also try to convince the voters that they possess the leadership skills necessary to be effective in the offices they seek. For their part, voters would listen to the campaign discussion and cast their ballots for the candidates with the most convincing arguments and imposing credentials. In short, the ideal contest would represent an honest effort to provide the voters with a rational choice. Unfortunately, the candidate who conformed to such an idealized version of political campaigning in most election races would be left at the starting gate.

Realistically, political campaigns are designed to win elections. They may inform the voter along the way, but that is not their major purpose. The goal of campaigners is simple—to defeat their opponents at the polls. As a result, campaign debate bears little resemblance to a dispassionate discussion of issues. Campaigners distort facts, sloganize, use half-truths to justify a doubtful position, and equivocate on the tough issues. They contrive personality appeals of an excessively sentimental or emotional nature to play on the susceptibilities of the public. It is not that there are no limits on how far candidates will go to realize their ambitions—most do observe some moral and legal limits—but the ground rules of political campaigning are sufficiently flexible to permit one-sided arguments and the projection of false candidate images.

Only the romantic believes that the politics of an earlier age produced statesmen who were both gifted orators and deep thinkers. Candidates for public office have always reduced solutions to complex issues to pat formulas and exploited people's hopes and fears for partisan advantage. And they have always carefully cultivated their image. What *is* different in political campaigning today is a technology that has transformed all the old tricks and tactics into a new art form. The campaigns of major officeholders are now guided by professional campaign consultants. Whether their skills are as great as claimed is beside the point. As long as it is believed that they hold the key to electoral success, they will continue to control the style and content of campaign communications.[1] The fact that a cadre of professional consultants has risen to such status in political campaigning is of considerable consequence to the political system and to the strength of political parties.

The Effects of the Campaign

Political campaigners spend enormous sums on winning elections, justifying these expenditures as necessary in order to convince the voters that they are worthy of holding public office. Yet some campaigns, no matter how well planned or financed, are doomed from the outset. If this is the case, it necessarily follows that some candidates can win office by paying only desultory attention to normal campaign activities. Political campaigning may tilt the balance in reasonably close contests, but its overall impact is not so great as popularly imagined.

SAFE DISTRICTS

Democrats have enjoyed unusual success in congressional races since Franklin Roosevelt brought his party to power in 1932, a pattern of victories so consistent that the Republican takeover of the Senate in 1980 was a notable achievement. The Democrats' dominance is not the result of superior campaign abilities in the normal sense, for many of them start with fixed advantages before their campaigns get under way. There are also many Republicans comfortably ensconced in office who need not fear the campaign trail. In recent Congresses, from 60 to 70 percent of House candidates have won elections with over 60 percent of the vote, margins that qualify as landslide elections.[2] The reason some campaigners have an easy go at winning office is that they run in safe districts. Such districts impose limits on the effects of political campaigns, and must be examined in that light.

A district is safe if voters have developed a habit of supporting only the candidates of one party. Although some incumbents enjoy widespread support in what would be hostile country for others who wear the same party label, most major party candidates who win by large margins are running in friendly territory. They win big because their party can claim a larger share of identifiers within the electorate. Although partisan attachment does not always dictate the choice of a voter, it does so often enough to render some districts immune to challenge by any kind of campaign.

PARTISAN IDENTIFICATION

Because partisan identification is an accurate gauge of how many voters will cast their ballots, it is commonly referred to as a long-term force on the voting decision. The candidates who run and the issues they raise are considered short-term forces, because they change more frequently from election to election. Campaigners can overcome the long-term partisan predispositions of the electorate during the campaign by taking the popular side on issues and making the most of their personal traits. Successful candidates usually adapt their campaign strategies to the partisan characteristics of the constituency.

Even in a contest of high visibility, when the effects of party identification are most likely to give way to candidate appeals, the partisan leanings of the electorate remain important. Most voters know how they will vote in a presidential election before the campaign begins.[3] Indeed, as Table 9-1 suggests, many voters have made up their minds before the conventions have selected the nominees. Others make their choice as soon as they know who the candidates are. Only somewhat near a third of all voters decide whom they will vote for during the campaign and are potentially subject to its influences.

Table 9–1
WHEN VOTERS MAKE THEIR CHOICES IN PRESIDENTIAL ELECTIONS

Time of Decision	1948	1952	1956	1960	1964	1968	1972	1976	1980
Before conventions	37%	34%	57%	30%	40%	33%	43%	33%	40%
During conventions	28	31	18	30	25	22	17	20	18
During campaign	25	31	21	36	33	38	35	45	39
Don't remember, or not ascertained	10	4	4	4	3	7	4	2	2
Total	100%	100%	100%	100%	101%*	100%	99%*	100%	99%*

*Does not add to 100% because of rounding.
SOURCE: William H. Flannigan and Nancy H. Zingale, *Political Behavior of the American Electorate*, 4th ed. (Boston: Allyn and Bacon, 1979), p. 171. Copyright © 1979 by Allyn & Bacon, Inc. Reprinted by permission. 1980 data are derived from Survey Research Center of the University of Michigan, and made available through the Inter-University Consortium for Political Research.

THE UNDECIDED VOTE

That one out of three voters delays choosing a presidential candidate means that there are sufficient votes available at the start of a campaign to determine the election outcome in ordinary circumstances. The late deciders become a principal target of political campaigners. Other voters are not neglected—partisans who already lean toward the candidate must have their inclinations reinforced—but the primary emphasis of the campaign must be on those voters who are either wavering in their allegiance or have not yet come to a decision.

If undecided voters can turn an election, their characteristics are of crucial importance to the campaigner. Most analysts agree that the hard core of party loyalists will have reached a decision before the campaign begins and will be unmoved by its tactics. They also agree that independents and the less firmly committed partisans are often among the late deciders. There is less agreement on other attributes of undecided voters, though the conventional interpretation has been that they are the voters least interested in and informed about politics.

There is considerable truth to the belief that the campaign has the greatest effect upon the disinterested and uninformed electorate. Nevertheless, in some recent presidential elections, those who reported a high interest in the campaign did not always make an early decision.[4] There are two plausible explanations for such a pattern.

Many Independents who lean in a partisan direction also express high interest in a political campaign. As we discussed in Chapter 5, these Independents are more appropriately characterized as partisans, but their loyalty is not so certain as that of strong identifiers. Since they are less firmly committed to a party, they may withhold a final judgment until the campaign is under way and the candidates clarify their positions.

The second explanation concerns the more committed partisans. They are predisposed to their own party's candidate, yet they may have doubts concerning his personal attributes or issue stands. Thus they are subject to cross pressures. Liberal elements of the Democratic party coalition, suspicious of the southern background and religious fundamentalism of Jimmy Carter, did not immediately join the Carter bandwagon in 1976. In 1980, with his popularity plummeting as the election neared, the choice of Carter led even more Democrats to question their partisan loyalty. Republican moderates in 1980, at least initially, were also torn between their desire to see a Republican in the White House and their fear of Ronald Reagan's ideological rigidity. In circumstances like these, a voter may wish to weigh the alternatives before deciding on how to cast a vote.

A useful typology of campaign targets, based on campaign interest and time of decision, has been summarized by Dan Nimmo[5] (see Table 9-2).

Attentive Voters. The attentive voters who decide early are often the most committed partisans. They are unlikely to defect to the opposition, and the task of the candidate they favor is to ensure that they turn out in numbers. The opposition candidate knows that it would be a waste of resources to try to win them over.

The attentive voter who is a late decider is frequently subject to cross pressures. The goal of the campaigner is to resolve whatever conflicts exist in the minds of these voters. No campaign is likely to change deep-seated voter attitudes. What a campaign can hope to change is voters' perceptions of the candidates. To use an earlier illustration, most Republican moderates in 1980 did not embrace the ultraconservative philosophy of the right wing of their party, but they apparently were persuaded that Reagan was not the uncompromising ideologue his detractors had pictured him to be.

Indifferent Voters. The early deciders who are inattentive to campaigns are somewhat puzzling. Their effect on the campaign depends upon their rate of turnout. The candidate they back must see that they are mobilized on election day, and the opposition party candidate must avoid antagonistic tactics that could stimulate their resolve to vote. Since they are basic-

Table 9-2
A TYPOLOGY OF CAMPAIGN TARGETS

	Attentive Voters	Indifferent Voters
Early Deciders	Reinforce attitudes	Mobilize or immobilize voters
Late Deciders	Change attitudes and mobilize	Motivate turnout

SOURCE: Dan Nimmo, *The Political Persuaders* (Englewood Cliffs, N.J.: Prentice-Hall, 1970), p. 25.

ally indifferent voters, their preferences are likely based on fortuitous circumstances. It is more difficult to devise a rational campaign strategy to capture these voters.

Voters who are both indifferent to the campaign and late deciders are ripe for recruitment. In many elections, they yield the margins of victory. The campaigners must search for the appeal that can motivate these people to turn out in their behalf. In the hope of sparking some interest among the marginally involved, campaigners often artfully reduce political issues to their most simplistic levels. Some of the most questionable campaign communications result from the felt need of campaigners to make extravagant appeals to turn out the disinterested.

The Changing Style of Political Campaigns

Over the course of the past thirty years, the way in which candidates campaign for public office has undergone dramatic change. A new group of professionals, who developed their skills in nonpolitical fields, have brought their expertise to the management and conduct of campaigns.[6] These new specialists are adept at exploiting the technological innovations of the past few decades. They were quick to see that the computer would prove invaluable in the systematic type of research and organizational efforts that characterize modern campaigning. And, of course, they saw the potential of televised political advertising for revolutionizing the way in which candidates present their case to the voters.

The contemporary campaign style is candidate centered rather than party oriented. Party leaders, comfortable with the patronage-based organization that traditionally delivered a vote, were slow to adapt to the changes, clinging to their traditional methods even though their organizations had become materially weakened. Confronted by the tasks of mobilizing mass support and finding the party organizations ineffective, candidates for major offices turned to the new specialists to organize and manage their campaigns. The passage of legislation that limited the aid parties can give candidates in federal elections further eroded the party role. Only recently have party organizations begun to modernize the services they offer candidates in an attempt to regain their former prominence.

THE RISE OF THE NEW EXPERTS

In an earlier age, adroit party politicans counseled candidates on the strategies that would win them public office. Like all good salesmen, they knew their territory. Though their knowledge was more intuitive than systematic, some gained a deserved reputation for their political acumen. Mark Hanna skillfully directed William McKinley's campaigns at the turn of the century, and Jim Farley was no less successful as a campaign adviser to Franklin Roosevelt. Such legendary party professionals have slowly been replaced by the new group of campaign managers and consultants.

Modern political managers are the descendants of the public relations consultants who advised industry groups during the twenties on how to counteract a rising criticism of business practices.[7] Their mission was to create a favorable climate for the pursuit of business goals, which, in turn, would bolster the position of business executives when they pleaded their case before legislative bodies. Early on, the public relations experts directed their campaigns through the mass media, and the techniques of mass advertising they devised were soon found suitable for use in political campaigns.

The Democratic party was the first to hire a full-time public relations adviser. A California newspaperman, Charles Michelson, was added to the staff of the Democratic National Committee in 1929.[8] Trained at the *San Francisco Examiner* and the *New York American*, he had the kind of experience at dramatizing the popular or sensational news item that built the Hearst empire and gave it a reputation for "yellow journalism." To Michelson, the tarpaper shacks built by the unemployed were "Hoovervilles," and the catastrophic Depression was the "Hoover panic." Largely responsible for the propaganda output of the Democratic party in its presidential campaigns of 1932, 1936, and 1940, Michelson demonstrated the usefulness of the public relations counsel and justified his annual salary of $25,000.[9]

The first firm created solely to manage political campaigns is credited to Clem Whitaker and Leone Baxter, a California husband and wife team who formed Campaigns, Inc., in 1933.[10] No more providential political locale than California could have been selected to test the new campaign style. The initiative and referendum, legacies of the Progressive era, required

Californians to settle major public issues at the polls. Weak political parties were ineffectual in guiding popular choices, so Campaigns, Inc., was developed to assist voters in reaching a decision. Its record of successes is testimony to the effectiveness of a systematic attempt to mold voter attitudes. Between 1933 and 1965, before their profession became crowded, Whitaker and Baxter won seventy of the seventy-five campaigns they managed.[11] A flourishing industry has grown from their pioneering efforts.

Professional campaign consulting is a diversified industry encompassing many technical specializations. The candidate can hire a political manager to oversee his campaign, employ a management firm to undertake all phases of his campaign, or contract with specialists to perform selected campaign tasks.[12] Some campaign consultants can advise the candidate on all features of the campaign. They have broad political backgrounds, and although they specialize in certain areas, they are familiar with overall campaign operations. They serve candidates as managers and hire other consultants to do organizational work, design media advertising, or prepare direct mail appeals. Every campaigner needs such a general manager. As one successful political consultant has written, "the worst choice any candidate can pick for his campaign manager is himself. No one—repeat, no one—can do a competent job in a major campaign if he tried to serve both roles."[13] Most top-level professional managers insist on being given the authority necessary to do a proper job, and this includes control of the campaign budget.

Public relations firms that specialize in political campaigning can also be hired to perform most, if not all, of the services that a candidate requires. At one time, PR firms engaged in political consulting on a part-time basis, earning most of their revenue from business clients and civic groups. As the earlier firms gained a reputation for successful campaigns, the demand grew for the type of professional assistance they offered. More agencies entered the field, and the variety of available services was expanded. Finally, there came the political consulting firm whose principal, if not sole, business was managing political campaigns. One such firm lists the following campaign-related activities it can perform:

Advance and Candidate Scheduling
Bond Issue and Referenda Campaigns

Campaign Counseling
Campaign Management
Demographic and Audience Research
Election Day Activities
Issue Research
Media Planning, Coaching and Buying
Opinion Polls/Survey Research
Political Party Management and Organization
Press Relations
Public Relations
Speech and Script Writing
Staff Recruitment and Organization
Voter Registration Drives
Computer Letters and Direct Mail
Computer Software Services and Data Processing
Direct Mail
Telephone Communications Consultants

Political managers, whether individuals or full-service firms, tend to work for candidates of only one political party. Neither party is handicapped by this policy, since there are talented individuals on both sides of the political fence.[14] However, the major firms will not take on just anyone who has the finances to pay their charges because they wish to protect their reputation for backing only credible candidates. Supposedly the firm of Spencer-Roberts delayed a decision on managing Ronald Reagan's 1966 gubernatorial campaign until they were convinced that, first, he was running on more than his movie-star fame, and second, that he did not intend to conduct a Goldwater-style campaign.[15] Campaign consultants are particularly sensitive to charges that they are political mercenaries and argue that the good people in the business are neither "hustlers nor con men."[16] Joseph Napolitan maintains, for example, that his firm has turned down more clients than it has accepted.[17]

Individuals and firms can also be hired to perform more specialized campaign tasks. There are specialists in purchasing media time and space, producing television documentaries and commercials, preparing radio spots and newspaper ads, canvassing precincts, designing direct-mail campaigns, conducting opinion polls, and raising money. Scarcely any phase of a campaign is uncovered by professional expertise. Not necessarily typical but illustrative of the services available was

"This is the candidate. I think you want the packager."

Drawing by D. Reilly; © 1980 The New Yorker Magazine, Inc.

the reelection team put together by Rhode Island Senator Claiborne Pell in 1972. Pell hired Charles Guggenheim for television ads, Tony Schwartz for radio spots, Matt Reese for organizational tasks and get-out-the-vote drives, Tom McCoy for fund raising, Valentine-Sherman for canvassing lists, and Patrick Cadell for polling and issue analysis.[18] That was a formidable array of talent to assemble for an election campaign.

RESEARCHING THE CAMPAIGN

Political consultants must survey the political terrain before deciding on a strategy for their clients. At one time, the campaigner relied on intelligence gathered by party workers and opinions offered by interest group leaders, journalists, and others active in political and community affairs. Information collected this way, although unquestionably useful, was far from systematic. Modern-day campaigners still make use of such "soft" judgments, but rely more on "hard" information from opinion polls and analyses of demographic data and election returns.

Past Election Returns. The most accessible data of a systematic nature available to the campaigner are past election returns. Caution must be used in interpreting election data because they report aggregate, not individual, behavior. The problem cannot be entirely overcome, but working with the smallest reporting unit is helpful. For example, a county may divide almost evenly between Democratic and Republican candidates, but considerable differences in voting choices may appear by wards or precincts. By examining precinct data, the analyst can determine what the turnout rate has been, which party has been favored, and which areas are likely to split their tickets.

The analysis can be further refined. Election returns for offices of low visibility are good indicators of hard-core party support, and past races with similar campaign issues or candidate styles provide additional clues on how to target resources. Census-type data for voting units give a gross picture of the demographic makeup of pro-Democratic, pro-Republican, and swing precincts. One can then tailor campaign appeals to fit the type of voters one believes will support the candidate.

The Private Poll. Analyses of election returns, no matter how sophisticated, have one important drawback: they reflect past voting behavior rather than the contemporary mood of the electorate. For this reason, the privately commissioned poll is increasingly used to measure voter attitudes. The best way to discern what voters are thinking about at any given time is to ask them. From the respondent interviews, one can learn not only what issues are uppermost in the public's mind but also whether individuals would be "more likely" or "less likely" to support a candidate advocating a particular issue stand. What voters like and dislike about the candidates can also be uncovered through the polling technique.

Some pollsters go beyond such straightforward questions and try to uncover more basic attitudes. Whether the voters are cynical toward government, whether they believe "things are getting better or worse," and whether they have pride in their state and its people offer clues to consultants on how to put over their client. Suppose, for example, the surveys reveal that voters are distrustful of their government but would not wish to live any other place but where they reside. And suppose pollsters find that the candidate, a newcomer to politics, is relatively unknown. One strategy would be to produce a series of thirty-, sixty-, or ninety-second film clips showing the candidate in attractive settings about the state, talking to "ordinary" people. The candidate achieves name recognition and at the same time associates himself with what the voters like about their state. To capitalize on public cynicism, the candidate asks for help in restoring integrity to a government that has for too long been in the hands of unresponsive political professionals. Just such a strategy was devised by a consulting firm for a candidate who was successful in a South Carolina primary contest.

SELECTING THE MEDIA

Once the campaigners have all the information they need, the next step is to create and put across the desired message. Rather than relying on any single method, the experienced manager will match the media to the audiences to be reached. Among the considerations of media selection are the size of the campaign budget and the fixed advantages and limitations of a particular medium. A low-budgeted campaign affords little scope in candidate promotion, whereas a generously financed campaign can use a blend of media to make specialized appeals to particular audiences.

The mass media are particularly associated with the new campaign style. Modern-day campaigners make use of them through controlled and uncontrolled communications. The paid political advertisement is a controlled communication because the candidate can determine its content. News stories, press conferences, and interview shows are not directly controlled by the candidates but may give them useful exposure. Since both forms of communication affect the voter, the candidate must be schooled in how to use each to his advantage. The most careful "packaging" of a candidate can become undone if he is not skillful at handling the press and other media representatives in an uncontrolled environment.

Practitioners of contemporary campaigning, of course, do not confine their advertising to the mass media. Professional campaign managers value the systematic execution of their planned strategies, and they will use whatever medium they think will contribute to a successful race. Although the effects of different advertising media are not surely known, there are certain commonsense rules that apply to each.[19]

Display. Campaign displays—billboards, lawn signs, transit advertisements, window posters, bumper stickers—are used primarily to achieve name recognition, to inform the voters that a particular candidate is running for a certain office. Since the audience may only glance at the display, the message it conveys must be kept short and simple—"a proven leader," "the citizen's candidate," or "time for a change." Or, if it is an advantage, the candidate's party identification will be conspicuously displayed. The hope is that repetition of the candidate's name will impress it on the voter's mind through election day. Displays also set the stage for other media messages.

Direct Mail. Sending out campaign literature in the mails is a time-honored method of reaching voters. Direct mail has received considerable attention recently because such experts as Richard A. Viguerie have used it with great success to raise large sums of money for their clients. The return on investment is easily measured by comparing the costs of the mailout to the donations received. The effectiveness of direct mail as a channel of campaign communication is less surely known. Viguerie believes that "95 percent of the political direct mail that I have seen is a waste of money."[20]

Most campaigners who use direct mail select the audiences they wish to reach and tailor the messages they send. The breakthrough has come with the computer-generated letter. After a voter canvass categorizes the electorate in terms of party identification, candidate support, occupational class, place of residence, and issue concerns, paragraphs of a letter are prepared for each facet of a voter's interests and the computer assembles them in the combinations that will have the maximum effect. The communication will appear as an individually typed letter to the recipient. But direct mail of such sophistication is costly, and its effects on voting are uncertain.

Newspapers. How a medium is used for political advertising depends upon its characteristics. Different media reach different audiences. Attentive readers of newspapers and magazines, on the whole, are better educated, have higher incomes, and hold higher-status jobs than television viewers.[21] The metropolitan daily has a different readership from that of the suburban newspaper or the rural weekly. Other newspapers are more specifically addressed to black audiences or ethnic groups, sometimes in their native languages. The candidate must consider these audience differences in employing the print medium.

Newspaper advertising is a relatively inexpensive channel for mass communication. Space is much easier, and cheaper, to obtain than radio or television time. Production costs are also less expensive and require less design expertise. Most newspaper advertisements are little more than small billboards, identifying the candidate and the candidate's party. Other types include endorsements by prominent citizens or a list of contributors to show the candidate's range of support. Some advertisements use a longer format to provide more detail on the candidate's background and stand on issues. These frequently take the form of a "news" story or a column written by the candidate's advisers (though, by law, they must be labeled as a political advertisement). The nature of the advertisement, and its intended audience, will suggest where in the newspaper it should be placed. More informative advertisements usually appear on news or op ed pages. Other advertisements are placed in sports, business, local news, or women's sections, depending upon the audience to be reached.[22]

Radio. Radio cannot compete with television for audience coverage and has been supplanted by television as a news source. Nevertheless, commuters, housewives, students, and workers on the job still tune in their favorite stations to pass the time. Moreover, because coverage is more limited, radio audiences are more specialized. Station programming is designed to appeal to selected audiences—the young, the middle-aged and older, the blacks, the truckers, the sophisticates, the farmers. And compared to television, production costs are low and the purchase of time is flexible.

Radio advertising has declined in presidential races, but has displayed a resurgence in other political contests. Candidates running in constituencies that make up only a small portion of the local television station's market find the costs of televised advertisements prohibitive. Radio advertisement is more suited to their needs. Radio is also useful to gain attention for candidates who must compete against television coverage of high-visibility campaigns.

Given the negative audience reaction to lengthy formats, campaigners rely heavily on radio spots. The short advertisements are designed to reinforce candidate identification and to convey simple themes and short messages. The spots are repeated, sometimes with slight variations, and reach their saturation point in the declining days of an election. Some candidates use longer formats. Richard Nixon's radio addresses in 1972 were viewed not as an alternative to television, but as a replacement for speeches at dinners or rallies that would draw only a few thousand people.[23] A considerably greater number listened to his radio speeches and, given the commitment of their time, probably had a high interest in the campaign.

Television. No other medium has been so fully associated with the new campaign style as television. It ranks as the most important source of news for the general public and is the medium through which most voters become acquainted with candidates for major offices. But it is not just broad coverage that makes television so attractive as a channel of political communication. Because it combines audio and visual images, television gives its audience a personalized view of the candidate that is unmatched by other media. So-called image merchants rely heavily on television to construct an image of their candidate that can be "sold" to a mass market. The television commercial portrays the human dimensions of candidates, as well as their stand on key issues and their general competency to hold office.

For all its value, television has drawbacks. One is that it is the most expensive medium to exploit. Television time is costly and is not always available when and for as long as desired, and production costs must be added to the expense of buying air time. Another drawback is that the television audience is far less segmented than the radio audience. Although televised spots can be purchased around programs whose viewing audience has been profiled, prohibitive costs rule out the specific type of targeting that other channels provide.

Television is best at reaching a large audience of relatively uninformed and uninterested voters.[24] Its most likely effects are activating latent candidate support and winning over the doubtful. Since many voters decide how they will cast their vote before the onset of the campaign, a strategy aimed at the undecided pays good dividends. It is for this reason that major party candidates are willing to devote such a large portion of their budget to television commercials. In 1980, Carter spent over half of his alloted funds on costs attributed to televised advertisements.

Television commercials tend to be short, at least partly because of the high costs of purchasing time. Ordinarily they stress the candidate's personal strengths and a few overriding issues. The productions are carefully staged to get the maximum effect from the audio and visual dimensions of the medium. If conservation is a campaign theme, for instance, the candidate can be pictured next to a river polluted by industrial wastes. The message may be conveyed by the candidate in conversation with concerned citizens or by a voice-over describing a program of action. A candidate suitably attired for his on-site examination enhances the effectiveness of the ad.

Some consultants question the usefulness of the short slick spot ad. Charles Guggenheim has argued that a longer political program is much more effective. He has himself produced spots, but only because he couldn't buy the time for lengthier formats. On the other hand, William Taylor, who worked on Nixon's 1972 media campaign, thought that short spots got the message across better because "most half-hour stuff is just plain boring."[25] The longer format also preempts established programs and demands extra care to hold the audience. The thirty-minute campaign documentary has been employed, particularly by presidential candidates, to present a broader impression of the candidate to those voters who tune in. It is only reasonable to assume that, as Guggenheim has argued, the voter does get to know the candidate better through the longer format. It is just as reasonable to argue, however, that the spots will continue to be exploited because they cost less and ensure a captive audience. Viewers endure and absorb the short televised message, but many tune out the lengthier political program.

PERSON-TO-PERSON CONTACTS

Before the ascendancy of the electronic media in political campaigning, personal contact was regularly used to solicit votes. Registration drives ensured that eligibles were placed on the voting lists, and election day activities turned them out. Most of these operations were centered in the political party. The machine-led cities were legendary for their ability to turn out the vote, and in other locales, the party organization, with ranks swelled for the election season, had few rivals at the task. Voters were predisposed to vote along partisan lines, and party workers capitalized on this fact in urging them to the polls.

Campaigning in the age of the electronic media has altered the way the candidate tries to reach the voter. Voters have multiple sources of information, many of them candidate rather than party centered. With their limited resources, the parties are no longer looked upon as indispensable by candidates seeking office. Many candidates raise their own money and hire their own campaign experts to place themselves in office. Much of the campaign budget is spent on the mass media and considerable public attention has focused on this fact. Nevertheless, even in this day of image makers packaging a candidate-product, the more prosaic tasks of contacting voters on an individual basis are not neglected.

The goal of individual solicitation is threefold:[26]

1. To increase the turnout.
2. To encourage a vote for lesser offices, often left unmarked on the ballot.
3. To influence the voter's candidate selections.

Where parties are reasonably well organized, their efforts at getting out the vote are not wasted. Some evidence suggests that the party organizations are better at turning out voters than at influencing their preferences, particularly in a race with highly visible candidates. The obvious strategy, then, is to concentrate on voters or neighborhoods that ordinarily support the party. At the same time, personal contact is useful in shaping voter attitudes toward lesser candidates who are ignored by the mass media and cannot afford to advertise in them.

If the party organization does not maintain up-to-date "street sheets" locating its supporters, the candidates' organization must undertake the job. Candidates with the necessary funds can hire specialists to oversee this job, though the skills required for it are not so arcane as those associated with media-related activities. The essential work is preparing lists of voters who will be targeted for registration drives and personal contacts. The computer is helpful in organizing the lists, but manpower is essential for performing the tasks. While well-known candidates may have little difficulty in recruiting volunteers, lesser known candidates have to rely on party or interest group support. Besides the canvassing necessary to prepare lists, typical tasks include: manning phone banks around election time; serving as poll watchers to note who has not voted; providing transportation or babysitting for voters; and passing out literature at the polls. Political campaigns are often won by small margins, and even today, candidates cannot afford to ignore the increments a well-organized program of personal contacts can add to their vote totals.

Myth and Reality in Political Campaigning

An old political saw holds that half the money spent in election campaigns is wasted—only no one knows which half. The saying contains a large kernel of truth, particularly in regard to media campaigns. Stories that relate how a political consultant created a candidate's public image and flawlessly orchestrated his campaign make good reading. Some may even be true, but most exaggerate the precision with which the campaign strategy is executed.

Practitioners of media advertising do not agree upon its conventions. As one student of political campaigning has observed, "political consultants have yet to develop a chemistry of campaigning. As in the old politics, strategy building more nearly resembles alchemy."[27] What works in one campaign may be ineffectual in another. Experienced consultants may develop a sense of what is working for their clients, but still have difficulty in generalizing why the tactics employed are successful.

Consider the example that one consultant cited to illustrate his point that political messages should relate to practical problems.[28] His firm represented a candidate running for secretary of state in California whose principal campaign issue was the elimination of pay toilets. She had worked for three years in the state legislature to secure passage of such a law and was known as the "pay toilet" lady. She even had one commercial filmed inside the ladies' room of the San Francisco International Airport. "The political press said she was a candidate without substance. Everyone laughed except the public which decided that there at least was something they could relate to and someone who wasn't offering pie in the sky solutions."[29] The result: she led the Democratic ticket with a total of more than 1,300,000 votes. If the office was indeed won on the issue stressed, it is hard to believe that the consultant did more than play a hunch on what might temporarily titillate the public.

The same consultant declared that a great deal of public distrust of officeholders was due to a lack of candid communication. Consultants should have the courage, he said, to advise candidates to "tell them what's on your mind—what's really on your mind."[30] This advice was proffered as a practical guide to gain public support because the public no longer tolerates the "art of waffling, dodging and avoiding with meaningless rhetoric."[31] Even allowing for hyberbole, this counsel is scarcely a new truth that governs the advice adroit consultants give their clients.

PRESENTING THE CANDIDATE IN A FAVORABLE LIGHT

Political consultants try to present their candidate's best side to the public. That, after all, is their job. As consultant Joseph Napolitan has argued, job seekers in private industry do not reveal everything about themselves to their prospective employers. They tell only the good things, and the same practice holds for the office seeker.[32] However, the lengths to which some political consultants have gone to present their candidate in a favorable light—and to distort the image of their opponent—has brought sharp criticism of their methods.

A case in point was Nelson Rockefeller's 1966 New York gubernatorial campaign, which has been described as one of the most professional, astute, and imaginative ever conducted. It also has been criticized as one of the most ruthless.[33] Rockefeller was presented as a friend of labor, yet he had vetoed a $1.50 minimum wage the year before. Commercials that called attention to his support of the state university system did not mention that he had killed free tuition.[34] His opponent, Frank D. O'Connor, was accused of opposing the New York State Thruway, when actually he had only been against making it a toll road. The script for a commercial that was shown only in upstate New York read: "Frank O'Connor from New York City is running for governor. He says the subways should be free. Guess who he thinks should be paying for them?"[35] O'Connor had never made such a specific proposal, although he had speculated on the long-term possibilities of providing free public transportation in *all* cities.

THE LIMITS OF MEDIA MANIPULATION

Skilled practitioners of the art of advertising, one commentator believes, "can play upon the voters like virtuosos. They can push a pedal here, strike a chord there. And, presumably, they can get precisely the response they seek."[36] Herein lies the suspect character of present-day political communications. Political consultants, of course, deny that they manipulate an unsuspecting public. They claim instead that they are professionals who know how to capitalize on their candidates' virtues when presenting them to the public. "What we cannot do," said one, "is create. We can't make the voters believe that a dummy is smart, a bent man straight, a follower a leader, a bad man good."[37]

Although it would be foolhardy to discount the influence of well-organized media campaigns on election outcomes, it is just as erroneous to assume that media consultants can work miracles, for candidates are not infinitely malleable. John B. Connally spent millions to gain national television exposure, but his campaign to win the 1980 Republican nomination never got off the ground. Not only are political ad men constrained by the talents of their clients in presenting them in paid advertisements, but they must also contend with the uncontrolled media. Adroit advisers wish to get maximum exposure for their candidates, but they realize the risks are greater in an uncontrolled setting. Edward Kennedy's 1980 nomination bid received an early setback when the senator's performance in a lengthy interview with then-CBS correspondent Roger Mudd received poor reviews in the press.

News events can also affect a candidate's fortunes. Jimmy Carter's 1980 renomination campaign received a spectacular boost when the nation rallied behind his efforts to secure the release of American hostages held by the Islamic revolutionaries in Iran. His early handling of the crisis was approved by media and public alike, and blunted Kennedy's charge that Carter could not lead the nation. Carter strategists took advantage of the unexpected turn of events and sent out surrogates on the campaign trail while the president stayed close to Washington to monitor day-to-day developments in Iran. Initially, the news coverage he received was more valuable than any contrived political advertisement. But by the eve of the general election, after an ill-fated rescue mission and stalemated negotiations, Carter became the victim of events he could no longer control.

EQUAL ACCESS TO PROFESSIONAL COUNSEL

There is yet another reason why political managers cannot take just any candidate and plot a winning strategy. Experts in campaign management are available to candidates on both sides of the partisan fence, and only the size of the campaign

"I'm going to do a flip-flop on Africa. Can you make it look good?"

Drawing by Weber; © 1976 The New Yorker Magazine, Inc.

budget limits the skills that may be purchased. Assuming near equal resources, professional counsel is neutralized as a factor in the campaign except insofar as the credibility of the candidates or the turn of events gives an advantage to one side. Consultants who worked for the winner may justly claim that they helped the candidate to office, just as those who advised the loser may declare they helped their client run a creditable campaign. But being on the winning side does not necessarily mean that one is the more talented adviser.

The new experts do not possess a magic formula. When they have the financial resources, experienced managers can mount a well-organized and systematic campaign effort, and if their client is running against a candidate who is poorly financed and understaffed, they are likely to win. Claims that the shrewdest of them can win with any credible candidate are unfounded.

The Contemporary Parties: Confronting the New Campaign Style

The campaign effort of political parties traditionally relied on personal contact of voters by party workers. Their stock-in-trade was identifying voters, registering them, and getting them out on election day. A well-organized precinct is still an asset to any candidate, particularly those running for low-visibility offices. Candidates for state legislatures, county boards, or city councils seldom employ professional managers or invest heavily in media campaigns. They commonly depend upon the party organization for voter information, volunteer workers, and election day activities.

Candidates for major offices are more inclined to rely upon their own resources, particularly if they want to emphasize a media campaign. They seek out professional consultants to plan their strategy and manage their campaigns. Still, the professional manager will make use of the resources available from the well-organized party, particularly manpower for tasks that require a voter canvass.

Four trends have weakened the role of the party organizations in political campaigning:

1. The old-time political machines that were so effective in delivering a vote have been brought down.
2. Voter ties to the political party have weakened, which encourage candidates to make nonpartisan campaign appeals.
3. The parties initially failed to adapt to the new campaign style.
4. The parties have been legally restricted in aiding candidates in federal elections.

An example of the last trend is that Congress did not permit state and local party groups to purchase, without limit, such campaign materials as buttons, bumper stickers, posters, and yard signs to support congressional and presidential candidates until late 1979.[38]

Candidates discovered on their own that professional consultants with systematic campaign plans often won election contests. While the media-run campaign is most usefully employed in large jurisdictions, the party's campaign effort has traditionally been centered in local organizations. Parties at the state and national levels have lacked the financial resources and the professional staff to compete with the expertise of the professional consultants. Almost before they realized what was happening, party professionals were replaced by the new experts.

MODERNIZATION OF PARTY ORGANIZATIONS

There are signs today that party organizations are modernizing their campaign services. The Local Election Campaign Division of the Republican National Committee conducted training sessions, analyzed election data, provided computer services, and offered on-site advice from fifteen field representatives in an effort to aid state legislative candidates in 1978. The national party's assistance must have played some role in the net gain of three hundred legislative seats the Republicans made that year. State organizations also are beginning to offer a wider range of services to their candidates. Robert Agranoff, a political scientist who is an astute observer of political campaigns, has described how the Democratic-Farmer-Labor party (DFL) of Minnesota used modern techniques to assist its candidates in the 1968 state legislative races.[39] The DFL's media planning was provided by eight professionals with radio, television, journalism, or advertising experience. The research staff consisted of seven persons with a knowledge of polling, aggregate data analysis, and issues research. Other full-time staff members assisted in fund raising. The carefully planned and executed program reversed the losses the DFL had suffered in five consecutive elections and added fifteen new house members to their ranks.

There is no real reason why the political parties cannot provide the same type of services that professional consultants now provide, and at cheaper costs. The skills of managing a campaign and conducting election research can be taught. Opinion sampling is not so arcane a science that it cannot be learned and used more widely. State- and national-level parties can easily maintain computer facilities that are tied together so the data files can be used more efficiently. The Republican Party Data Processing Network (REPNET), set up to assist state parties in preparing for 1980 reapportionment battles, illustrates the great usefulness of a centralized computer facility.

At present, the parties are constrained by law in the services they can provide to federal election candidates. The public subsidization of presidential candidates has tended to isolate them from their parties, and the limits placed on party contributions to individual Senate and House campaigns are not overly generous.[40] Until recently, the question of legal restrictions on party giving was academic because the parties did not have the resources to contribute what the law permitted. The Democratic party still has difficulty raising money, but the Republicans acquired a war chest of $46 million for the 1980 elections. If the Democrats can put their national committee on a sound financial basis, it would be wise to take a second look at federal campaign regulations. After all, the intent of the laws was not to restrict party organizations from providing the type of services now bought from private consultants.

State laws seldom limit the party role in aiding state and local candidates, yet major state officers often seek out professional consultants to aid their campaigns anyway. With funding sources depleted by individual candidate appeals, the party organizations are not in a position to develop the type of expertise offered by private consultants. Where they have been able to offer more modern campaign services, the beneficiaries have been candidates for lesser state and local offices who cannot afford to hire professional consultants. This type of aid lays a base for recruiting future leaders of the party, but a more concerted party role on behalf of all its candidates is still more vision than reality.

POLITICAL ENTREPRENEURS VS. POLITICAL PARTIES

The fact that major officeholders now campaign as individual political entrepreneurs lessens their dependence upon the official party structure. They may depend upon the vote of party identifiers more than they realize, but they no longer rely heavily upon party workers to turn it out. Since they believe that the party contributes little to their campaign success, congressional candidates feel free to adopt whatever strategies promise to earn them votes. Thus campaign appeals by those wearing the same party label vary considerably and the voter is deprived of an easy shorthand in casting a ballot. As a result, the election mandate is ambiguous and governing becomes difficult. In 1932, only 14.1 percent of House districts were carried by a presidential candidate of one party and a House candidate of the opposite party. Significantly, that proportion had doubled by 1976, though this was below the peak of 44.1 percent in 1972 when the unpopular George McGovern headed the Democratic party ticket.[41]

That political campaigning today is more an individualistic than a party-centered activity is bound to influence the character of representation in the nation. The systematic attempt to acquire information on constituents and then devise a strategy based on it, so characteristic of the new campaign style, has quite possibly improved the ability of disparate districts to choose spokesmen for their interests. At the same time, however, it has made the melding of diverse interests into a cohesive set of policies—the traditional function of political parties—more complex. The development of coherent programs, which was never perfectly realized in American practice, is much more difficult when elections place candidates in office rather than empowering parties to govern.

SUMMARY

Candidates use the political campaign to convince voters they are worthy of holding public office. Rather than a forum for the dispassionate discussion of issues, the campaign is the way to beat the other fellow at the polls. In this sense, political campaigning has undergone little change over the years. Campaigners have always tended to simplify issues, sloganize their appeals, and capitalize on their personal traits. What has changed are the methods they use to reach the voter. They now hire professional consultants who are masters of the new technology to advise them on the style and content of their campaign communications.

The effect of campaigns on voters is probably exaggerated. Many candidates who pay little attention to normal campaign activities win office anyway because they run in "safe districts," that is, districts whose voters normally prefer the candidates of one party. This is an example of the long-term influence of partisan identification on the vote.

The campaign is likely to determine the outcome of an election in constituencies where Democrats and Republicans are more evenly divided. Even here, though, the campaign is decisive for only a minority of the electorate. Studies have shown that most voters know how they will cast their ballots in presidential elections as soon as the candidates are announced. Only about a third make up their minds during the campaign, and these late deciders are the principal target of campaign communications because they hold the key to victory in ordinary circumstances.

Analysts agree that late deciders are often Independents and weak partisans, but disagree about whether their delayed decision is caused by poor information and/or disinterest. In some recent presidential elections, voters who expressed a high interest in the campaign were among the late deciders. Perhaps cross pressures made their choice uncertain, or perhaps their partisanship was weak enough that they required more information to make up their minds.

At one time, seasoned party leaders advised candidates on how to win over the doubtful and turn out the faithful. Though their counsel is still sought, a new group of experts who developed their skills in nonpolitical fields have taken over the task of managing campaigns for major political offices. Campaign consulting is a flourishing and diversified industry. There are consultants with broad political experience who manage campaigns, calling on specialists for certain services, and public relations firms that perform most if not all campaign-related tasks. Other experts have specialized competency in purchasing media time, producing television commercials, sampling opinion, manning phone banks, canvassing precincts, preparing direct mail, or raising money. Few phases of campaigning are without skilled practitioners ready to sell their talents.

The new managers and consultants have made modern campaigning for major offices a systematic undertaking. The thoroughness with which they have undertaken their assignments has earned them an enviable reputation. They analyze past election returns to identify Democratic, Republican, and swing districts, and conduct private polls to uncover the mood of the electorate and the issues that concern it most. They develop campaign themes, target identified groups, and use computer-prepared lists to aid in fund-raising and turning out the vote. They are exceedingly skillful at conveying the candidate's message in radio and television commercials.

The new campaign advisers have been criticized as political mercenaries who are willing and able to manipulate an unsuspecting public. The consultants protest that they are professionals, not political con men, and their task is merely to make the public aware of the virtues their candidates already possess.

Although some consultants have gone to dubious lengths in presenting their clients in the most favorable light, they are correct in asserting that they are not miracle workers. Even the best of them cannot take just any candidate, create a public image for him, and then flawlessly direct a campaign to place him in office. In the first place, they are constrained by their campaigner's talents and public reputation. Second, their strategies are often disrupted by the uncontrolled media, whose political analysts are unfazed by paid commercials. Third, political consultants have no control over external events that may make or break a candidacy. And finally, political consultants of equal competence are available for hire on both sides of the political fence, thus neutralizing the effects of the new campaign style. Superior campaign advice is a valuable aid to any candidate, but those who have it are not guaranteed victory.

Since not all candidates can afford the new campaign style, some—particularly those running for lesser state and local offices—continue to rely on party resources. Aiding these candidates is important to the party because is may draw its future leadership from them. Despite this fact, it is undeniable that the campaign role of the party has declined in recent years.

Although party organizations are modernizing their campaign services—and this development should not be minimized—their stock-in-trade is still direct voter contact. Party workers continue to identify potential supporters, register them, and get them to the polls on election day, but the party's ability to deliver a vote has greatly diminished because the machine-run city has all but disappeared and partisan ties within the electorate have weakened. Because the parties were slow to adapt to the new campaign style, candidates went outside them for professional advice, which further weakened the parties. And more recently, the parties have been restricted in the aid they can provide candidates for federal offices.

The result of all these changes is that campaigns for major offices are more candidate centered than party oriented. Voters are confused when candidates wearing the same party label make quite different campaign appeals, and thus the election mandate becomes ambiguous and governing more difficult.

Notes

[1]"Fed a steady diet of buncombe," writes V. O. Key, Jr., "the people may come to expect and to respond with highest predictability to buncombe. And those leaders most skilled in the propagation of buncombe may gain lasting advantage in the recurring struggles for popular favor." *The Responsible Electorate* (Cambridge, Mass.: Harvard University Press, 1966), p. 7.

[2]*Congressional Quarterly Weekly Report*, March 31, 1979, p. 573.

[3]William Flannigan and Nancy Zingale, *Political Behavior of the American Electorate*, 4th ed. (Boston: Allyn and Bacon, 1979), p. 170.

[4]Ibid., p. 175.

[5]Dan Nimmo, *The Political Persuaders* (Englewood Cliffs, N.J.: Prentice-Hall, 1970), pp. 24–25.

[6]For the development of professional public relations, see Stanley Kelley, Jr., *Professional Public Relations and Political Power* (Baltimore: The Johns Hopkins University Press, 1956), chap. 1.

[7]Ibid. See also Nimmo, *The Political Persuaders*, p. 35; and Robert Agranoff, ed., *The New Style in Election Campaigns*, 2nd. ed. (Boston: Holbrook, 1976), pp. 23–24.

[8]Kelley, *Professional Public Relations and Political Power*, p. 30.

[9]Ibid., p. 32.

[10]Nimmo, *The Political Persuaders*, p. 36.

[11]James M. Perry, *The New Politics* (New York: Potter, 1968), p. 10.

[12]For a discussion of campaign personnel, see Nimmo, *The Political Persuaders*, pp. 38–41.

[13]Joseph Napolitan, *The Election Game* (Garden City, N.Y.: Doubleday, 1972), p. 17.

[14]Ibid., p. 10.

[15]Nimmo, *The Political Persuaders*, p. 44.

[16]Napolitan, *The Election Game*, p. 11.

[17]Ibid., p. 12.

[18]Agranoff, *The New Style in Election Campaigns*, p. 8.

[19]For a discussion of advertising practices in the several campaign media, see Robert Agranoff, *The Management of Election Campaigns* (Boston: Holbrook, 1976), chap. 14. The discussion in this section borrows generously from Agranoff's treatment.

[20]Richard A. Viguerie, "Direct Mail: Campaigning's Sleeping Giant," in *The Political Image Merchants*, ed. Ray Hiebert et al. (Washington, D.C.: Acropolis, 1971), p. 165.

[21]Agranoff, *The Management of Election Campaigns*, pp. 318–319.

[22]Ibid., pp. 395–396.

[23]Ibid., p. 394.

[24]Ibid., p. 337.

[25]L. Patrick Devline, "Contrasts in Presidential Campaign Commercials," in *The New Style in Election Campaigns*, ed. Agranoff, p. 338.

[26]Agranoff, *The Management of Election Campaigns*, p. 413.

[27]Robert Agranoff, "The New Style in Campaigning: The Decline of Party and the Rise of Candidate-Centered Technology," in *Parties and Elections in an Anti-Party Age*, ed. Jeff Fishel (Bloomington: Indiana University Press, 1978), p. 235.

[28]Sanford L. Weiner, "The Role of the Political Consultant," in *The New Style in Election Campaigning*, ed. Agranoff, pp. 73–74.

[29]Ibid., p. 73.

[30]Ibid., p. 76.

[31]Ibid.

[32]Napolitan, *The Election Game*, pp. 76–77.

[33]Perry, *The New Politics*, p. 107.

[34]Agranoff, "The New Style in Political Campaigning," in *Parties and Elections in an Anti-Party Age.*, ed. Fishel, p. 239.

[35]Quoted in Perry, *The New Politics*, p. 130.

[36]Ibid., p. 213.

[37]Frederick Papert, "Good Candidates Make Advertising Experts," in *The Political Image Merchants*, ed. Hiebert et al., p. 97.

[38]*Congressional Quarterly Weekly Report*, January 5, 1980. p. 31.

[39]Robert Agranoff, "The Role of Political Parties in the New Campaigning," *The New Style in Election Campaigns*, ed. Agranoff, pp. 127–136.

[40]Party giving in House races is more restricted than in Senate contests. Because of the option of spending two cents times the number of eligible voters, for example, national Republican committees have figured prominently in some Senate races. Nevertheless, in fourteen states, a party's national committees are limited to $17,500 in contributions and $29,440 in coordinated (1980 dollars) spending in Senate elections.

[41]Thomas E. Mann, *Unsafe at Any Margin* (Washington, D.C.: American Enterprise Institute, 1978), p. 105.

10

Electoral Decisions

The greatest responsibility of citizens in a democracy is to choose their leaders. Why is it, then, that some people vote and others do not? Why do voters select some leaders and reject others? According to the classical model of democratic theory, voters go to the polls out of a sense of civic duty. They consider the ideological orientations and issue positions of the candidates in making their choices. From the collective decision of the people, a clear election mandate emerges. The leaders selected to govern know the policy preferences of a majority of citizens.

This rational view of voting has been challenged by election studies employing survey research techniques. The most influential of them, *The American Voter*, written by Angus Campbell and his associates of the University of Michigan, was published in 1960.[1] Basing their book principally on analyses of the 1952 and 1956 presidential elections, the Michigan analysts found that civic responsibility was not equally spread across the electorate's population groups. Their more exceptional discovery, however, was that only a small proportion of voters held an ideological view of politics. Moreover, many voters had *no* opinions on major issues or, if they did, were unaware of where the candidates stood on them. By contrast, a person's party identification was found to be closely associated with how he or she voted.

   The portrait of the American voter drawn by the Campbell team was not a flattering one, but it did suggest why American politics were so stable: partisan identifiers stuck by their parties through minor international crises and domestic turmoil. Only a major upheaval, such as the Civil War or the Great Depression, could cause large numbers to switch their partisan allegiance. Because the American electorate was structured by partisan identification, each party's candidates had a dependable base of support when seeking office. The majority party candidates did not always win office, of course, but party coalitions did not change dramatically from election to election and the relative stability of voting patterns restrained the nation's leaders from sharply revising government policies.

   The American Voter based its findings on data from the 1950s, a period of peace, prosperity, and tranquility. Later research on elections that followed civil rights marches, antiwar protests, and conflagration in the cities uncovered a more restive and less partisan electorate. At least four important trends have been noted since the Michigan researchers first began analyzing voting behavior:

1. The proportion of eligible voters who go to the polls has declined.
2. Partisan influences on the vote have weakened.
3. Issues have become more important to the citizen in making a choice of candidates.
4. A growing number of voters say they no longer trust their government and its leaders.

How these several trends are related and what they mean to the party system are explored later in this chapter. First our discussion will focus on successful efforts to broaden the franchise to include all but a tiny fraction of the adult population.

Suffrage Expanded

   Over most of the nation's history, only a minority of adults were able to cast a ballot. Suffrage was extended by successively removing the legal impediments of property, race, and sex and by lowering the voting age to eighteen. Today only such adults as convicted felons, prison inmates, and residents of state mental institutions are denied the franchise. However, registration requirements may make it inconvenient for some citizens to vote.

ELIMINATING VOTING REQUIREMENTS

During the Colonial period and for a time afterward, suffrage was legally restricted to white males who owned property. Where land was cheap or the laws laxly enforced, the white male electorate was potentially large. In some states, however, property standards were set high and rigidly enforced, which sharply restricted the number of eligible voters. Gradually, one state after the next began to expand the franchise. A taxpaying requirement was often substituted for property qualifications, and then it, too, was abandoned. By 1850, the tax standard was passing out of use and the last state had removed its property-owning requirement. Only the poll tax (used in southern states to restrict black suffrage) persisted into the twentieth century, and it was abolished by a constitutional amendment in 1964 and a judicial ruling in 1966.

The next group legally enfranchised were black males, first by congressional act, then by constitutional amendment. Constitutional safeguards notwithstanding, southern blacks were effectively denied the vote when the Reconstruction governments were disbanded. By a combination of physical threats and legal maneuvers, whites had reestablished their control over the electoral processes in the states of the Confederacy before the last decade of the nineteenth century.

The move to achieve voting rights for southern blacks was fought out initially in the courts. The most formidable and, for a time, legal obstacle to black voting was the so-called white primary. Discriminatory actions by state governments were prohibited by the Civil War amendments, but so long as political parties were viewed as private voluntary associations, no constitutional bar prevented the Democratic party from excluding blacks from its primaries. Since nomination by the Democratic party in the South was tantamount to election, blacks were effectively disfranchised. Then, in a series of cases, the courts held that a political party was cloaked with a public responsibility if its primaries were regulated by state laws or if it, in fact, determined who was to govern.[2]

The invalidation of the white primary did not put an end to the blacks' struggle for voting equality, for soon the southern states instituted literacy tests and complicated registration procedures that were selectively applied against black voters. Although some states were more permissive than others, the rate of black registration remained far below that of whites in the South. The breakthrough came with the passage of the Voting Rights Act of 1965, which has been extended and expanded at periodic intervals. No longer did blacks have to resort to costly court suits to establish their voting rights. Under the act's provisions, federal examiners were empowered to enroll blacks in areas where fewer than 50 percent of them were registered. Black registration in the southern states went from 38 percent of those eligible to vote immediately prior to the act's passage to 62 percent shortly thereafter.[3]

Efforts to enfranchise women began before the Civil War and were related to the abolition movement. The legal position of women under the common law was compared to that of slaves. Concentrating their activities at the state level, women first gained the franchise in school elections. Kansas became the first state to extend the school suffrage to women in 1867, and fourteen states and territories had followed by 1890. Less headway was made in securing a more general franchise. Beginning with Wyoming in 1869, a handful of states, mostly in the West, permitted women the vote in all elections.[4]

Since progress in achieving woman suffrage state by state was so slow, the suffragettes decided to focus on Washington and a constitutional amendment. They drew national attention by setting up pickets around the White House in 1917. After six months of demonstrations, the government moved to arrest the women for obstructing traffic. At their trials, the suffragettes either stood mute or made speeches justifying their cause. They further embarrassed administration leaders by insisting on serving their jail terms. All the while, more women came to Washington to join in the picket lines and take their places in jail. The nationwide publicity had its intended effect: Woodrow Wilson was won over, the Congress passed the Nineteenth Amendment enfranchising women, and two thirds of the states had ratified it by 1920.[5]

The extension of the suffrage to voters under twenty-one years of age was accompanied by little of the agitation required to enfranchise women and blacks. Prior to congressional action in 1970, only four states had lowered the voting age below twenty-one. Georgia and Kentucky permitted voting at eighteen, Alaska at nineteen, and Hawaii at twenty.

The movement to lower the voting age inevitably was tied to the military obligations of the young: eighteen-year-olds could be inducted into military service but could not participate in the selection of officials who might determine their fate. With the Vietnam war at its height and young people active in its opposition, the logic of extending them the franchise was compelling. In 1970, Congress lowered the voting age to eighteen in both federal and state elections. The new eligibility requirements were upheld for federal elections, but the Supreme Court ruled that Congress had exceeded its authority in prescribing the voting age in state elections. The Twenty-sixth Amendment, which constitutionally lowered the voting age in all elections, was quickly passed the following year.

REGISTRATION REQUIREMENTS

Every state requires its citizens to register before they can cast a vote. Because they impose an additional burden on the voter, registration requirements have lowered voter turnout.

Most of the laws requiring registration were enacted toward the end of the nineteenth century to combat fraudulent voting. In the more agrarian pre-Civil War society, formal registration was unnecessary because voters were known to election officials, but as the cities grew and their populations became more mobile, the eligibility of voters was harder to establish. In some machine-run cities, voters moved from precinct to precinct to cast several ballots, and party organizations were not above importing voters from the surrounding countryside to ensure an electoral victory. To prevent these irregularities, reformers succeeded in establishing registration requirements to determine eligibility for voting.

States vary in the permissiveness of their registration systems. According to a study by Steven J. Rosenstone and Raymond E. Wolfinger, the adoption of four practices by *all* the states would expand the electorate by 9.1 percent:[6]

1. Eliminating the closing date for registration.
2. Opening the registration office during the normal work week.
3   Opening the registration office in the evenings or on Saturdays.
4. Permitting absentee registration for the sick, disabled, and absent.

The most important impact on voting would come from eliminating the closing date for registration. Other practices thought burdensome, such as residency requirements, made no perceptible difference in turnout according to Rosenstone and Wolfinger.

One or two states now permit election day registration. President Jimmy Carter proposed it for the nation in an election reform package he sent to Congress in 1977, but neither house responded favorably. Some critics charged the measure was a thinly disguised attempt to enlarge the Democratic electorate, the supposition being that less educated and low-income citizens, more likely Democrats, would find it easier to register. Yet the study by Rosenstone and Wolfinger suggested otherwise. They concluded that the demographic, ideological, and partisan composition of an expanded electorate would be little different from the turnout under current laws.[7]

Who Votes?

Today, though there are few legal and administrative obstacles to voting, many citizens still do not go to the polls. But not everyone who abstains from voting is uninterested in politics. Illness in a family, business travel, lack of transportation, and similar reasons are commonly cited by those who do not cast a vote. For some people, such claims are excuses to hide their political apathy, but for others, they are legitimate explanations. Among citizens who are registered, nonvoters are more likely to name personal problems than lack of interest as their reason for abstaining.[8]

Psychological Motivations. Even if one accepts as legitimate all the excuses people offer for not voting, that still leaves many millions of Americans who voluntarily refrain from voting. Psychological motivations are the immediate determinants of whether a person votes.

A positive motivation springs from several sources. Some citizens have a standing commitment to participate in electoral politics. These individuals have a high sense of political efficacy and citizen duty, that is, they believe that government can be understood and influenced by ordinary people, and that every citizen has a civic responsibility to vote. By contrast, those who believe that government is remote and complex or who have not been instilled with an obligation to vote are less likely to turn out.

Orientation to a specific election also affects whether a person will vote. Some people become intensely involved in an election, while others remain untouched by it. Interest in a campaign and concern over the election outcome are correlated with turnout. For example, presidential contests consistently attract more voters than congressional elections because most people find presidential races far more interesting and believe the results will have a greater impact on them. Heightened interest and concern increase the votes over the normal turnout.

Education, Income, and Occupation. Voters and nonvoters are also distinguished by social characteristics (see Table 10-1). The most educated turn out in greater numbers than those with fewer years of formal schooling, not only because education enables an individual to comprehend the complexities of politics but also because it includes the civic training that instills in a citizen an obligation to vote. Then, too, the educated find it easier to overcome any impediments imposed in registering or casting an absentee ballot.

Income and occupation are related to voting, but their effects are slight if education is controlled. The principal reason why people with high incomes and upper-status occupations vote more regularly is that they are better educated. Income appears to be a factor only among the abject poor, whose struggle for existence occupies their interests and depresses their turnout.

Members of some occupational groups also vote more frequently than others, despite similar educational achievement, because the nature of their jobs engenders in them an interest in politics or confers the political skills that normally come from education. These factors have been found to affect the turnout rate of farm owners and government workers.[9]

Age. Voting also follows phases of the life cycle. The rate of turnout increases from youth to middle age, levels off during the middle years, and then declines with advanced age.

Young people have the lowest participation rate of the life-cycle groups. Although the young are somewhat less interested in politics than their elders, this is not the sole cause of their abstention. Part of the explanation rests with their political inexperience, and part with the unsettled conditions of their lives. Another factor that may be relevant to the recent decline in their turnout rates is the ambivalence toward politics felt by many of those who came of age during a period of political unrest.

Table 10-1
VOTING TURNOUT BY POPULATION CHARACTERISTICS,
1968–1980

	1968	1972	1976	1980
Male	69.8%	64.1%	59.6%	59.1%
Female	66.0	62.0	58.8	59.4
Age				
18–20		48.3	38.0	35.7
21–24	51.0	50.7	45.6	43.1
25–34	62.5	59.7	55.4	54.6
35–44	70.8	66.3	63.3	64.4
45–64	74.9	70.8	68.7	69.3
65 and over	65.8	63.5	62.2	65.1
Education				
8 years or less	54.5	47.4	44.1	42.6
9–11	61.3	52.0	47.2	45.6
12	72.5	65.4	59.4	58.9
More than 12	81.2	78.8	73.5	73.2
Race				
White	69.1	64.5	60.9	60.9
Black	57.6	52.1	48.7	50.9
Spanish origin	Not available	37.4	31.8	29.9

SOURCE: U.S. Department of Commerce, Bureau of the Census, *Statistical Abstract of the United States* (Washington, D.C.: Government Printing Office, 1977), p. 508. 1980 data are taken from U.S. Department of Commerce, Bureau of the Census, *Current Population Reports* (Washington, D.C.: Government Printing Office, 1981), Series P-20, No. 359, p. 4.

The decline in the turnout of older citizens was once blamed on the infirmities of age. This may be a valid explanation for nonvoting among the very elderly, but other factors better explain why the voting rate declines after middle age. Women now outlive men by approximately eight years, and elderly women do not vote as frequently as their male counterparts. Several reasons are behind this phenomenon. Women of advanced age grew up at a time when female education was not stressed, so they received fewer years of schooling than older males. Also, elderly women were socialized during an era when politics was considered a man's business. Finally, women of advanced age are often widows who lack the encouragement to go to the polls that is often found in the marriage relationship. By contrast, men in their seventies actually vote more than middle-aged groups, and their turnout rate does not dip until they reach eighty.[10]

Race. Although many of the legal and administrative barriers they once confronted have been removed, blacks still do not turn out at the polls at the rate of whites. The discrepancy in their turnouts is accounted for by two primary factors: Blacks have not obtained the education or the economic status of whites. If socioeconomic differences are controlled, the voting rate of blacks is actually higher than that of whites. Blacks with less than a college education vote more frequently than whites without college training. Racial differences in voting weaken and then disappear as each group acquires more education. Still, the aggregate turnout rate of blacks has been 12 percent under that of whites in recent national elections because of the continued socioeconomic disparities.[11]

Sex. Differences in turnout rates between men and women have virtually disappeared in national elections. Upon first receiving the franchise, women still encountered an essentially negative view of their role in politics. Gradually, as attitudes changed, they went to the polls in greater numbers. The women's liberation movement gave added impetus to women's participation in politics and has all but removed sex differences in voting turnout. Only among the older and less educated groups of the population does the sexual distinction remain.[12]

The Decline in Turnout

Alarm has been expressed over the recent decline in the proportion of the voting-age population that goes to the polls. From a high of almost 63 percent in 1960, the rate of turnout steadily declined until it fell to 53.3 percent in 1980. The increasing years of education obtained by Americans would seem to suggest just the opposite trend, particularly since the legal obstacles to black voting have been removed and since women have almost matched men in their voting habits. So how does one account for a substantial decline when circumstances appear to encourage voting?

The decline in turnout is too puzzling to permit firm answers, but one piece of the puzzle may be the weakening of partisan ties. The proportion of strong party identifiers within the electorate has been declining, and strength of identification has always been associated with turnout. However, party identification traditionally expressed itself in heightened interest in the campaign, and there has been little falloff in the proportion of the electorate reporting a high level of interest in presidential elections. At best, declining partisanship only partially explains why citizens are staying away from the polls.[13]

Neither can the explanation be found in the low turnout rate of the young people enfranchised by the Twenty-sixth Amendment. In the first place, the eighteen-to-twenty age group constituted only slightly more than 8 percent of the voting-age population in 1976. In the second place, the high level of educational achievement of young people today partially compensates for their traditional propensity to abstain from electoral politics. One estimate is that only one quarter of the drop in voting between 1968 and 1972 could be accounted for by enfranchising voters under twenty-one.[14]

The puzzle becomes even more baffling when it turns out that the American people believe as much as ever in the civic obligation to vote. As Table 10-2 demonstrates, the highest percentage of citizens think they should vote even if the contest is one-sided, involves minor local offices, or is not likely to be much affected by their one vote out of the millions cast. The view that a person should vote even if he or she doesn't care how the election comes out has less popular support, though the proportion of the public holding such an attitude has changed little over the years. Still, the responses on this item may be helpful in explaining recent voting abstention.

More Americans than ever before are reporting that they are little concerned with the outcome of presidential elections and feel that voting is not worth the effort. At the same time, an increasing proportion of voters are reporting that "government is pretty much run by a few big interests," "quite a few of the people running for office are a little crooked," "people like me don't have any say about what the government does," and that the "government in Washington" is to be trusted "only some of the time" or "none of the time." In other words, voters have become more cynical toward their government, and this widespread dissatisfaction with the trustworthiness and responsiveness of government has had an effect on the rate of turnout.

Just how rational is the abstention of nonvoters? Do citizens decline to vote because they do not like the choices presented to them in presidential elections? The evidence does not point to such a conclusion. In 1972, for example, most nonvoters (82 percent) rated either one or both candidates positively. Only 6 percent of nonvoters rated both candidates negatively, and two thirds of them conceded that one candidate was the

Table 10-2
BELIEF IN THE CITIZEN'S DUTY TO VOTE, 1952–1976

	Election Year				
Item and Response	1952	1956	1960	1972	1976
"I'd like to have you tell me whether you agree or disagree with each of these . . . statements."					
"It isn't so important to vote when you know your party doesn't have a chance." "Disagree."	88.7%	90.7%	92.5%	91.4%	91.8%
"So many other people vote in the national elections that it doesn't matter much to me whether I vote or not." "Disagree."	87.7	90.1	92.1	89.9	89.7
"If a person doesn't care how an election comes out, he shouldn't vote in it." "Disagree."	46.0	53.5	55.5	54.1	53.8
"A good many local elections aren't important enough to bother with." "Disagree."	82.1	86.1	88.0	86.3	86.1

SOURCE: Richard A. Brody, "The Puzzle of Political Participation in America," in *The New American Political System*, ed. Anthony King (Washington, D.C.: American Enterprise Institute, 1978), p. 302.

lesser of two evils. The remaining 12 percent of nonvoters either offered no opinion or were neutral in their assessment of the candidates.[15] The same pattern held true in 1976, when fewer than 2 percent of nonvoters were negative toward both Gerald Ford and Jimmy Carter.[16]

The evidence, then, suggests that failure to vote is less a conscious rejection of politics than a drift into indifference. Citizens who evaluate candidates from an ideological or issue perspective have been the most likely to vote in recent elections, while those who are unable to express an opinion are the least likely to turn out. From this evidence, we can state that the downturn in voting is not caused by an informed electorate who no longer believe that voting is meaningful.[17]

The American Voter of the 1950s

No other political activity undertaken by ordinary citizens attracts more interest than the choices they make in the privacy of the polling booth, for the verdict they render there determines who will govern the country. But can the winners be confident that the issue positions they took during the campaign have received popular approval? Or should they presume no more than that a majority of citizens have confidence in their leadership qualities? These questions can be answered only if it is known how voters arrive at their voting choices.

Though there are potentially many components of the electoral decision, most researchers settle on three, singly or in combination:

1. Voters may be guided by their party identification.
2. They may vote on the basis of issue preferences.
3. They may be attracted by the experience, demeanor, or other personal qualities of the candidate.

The weight given each of these factors varies from election to election, but most analysts agree that partisan influences have been declining at the same time that issues and candidate qualities have been becoming more important to the voter. Just how much change has taken place, however, is disputed.

PARTY IDENTIFICATION AND VOTING BEHAVIOR

The starting point of any analysis of voting behavior is *The American Voter*. This classic 1960 study has guided later generations of scholars and is essential to understanding how the American electorate has changed. Campbell and his associates placed primary stress on party identification; they discounted ideological orientation and issue preferences as major forces on the vote.

Party identification was defined as a psychological attachment toward one of the parties that the voter acquired during early socialization and retained through adult life. Generally, the longer the partisan attachment, the more committed the voter became to his or her preferred party. Partisan attachments remained basically stable across elections except when major social or economic upheavals caused periodic realignments.[18]

Party identification acted as a perceptual screen through which the individual perceived and evaluated candidates, parties, and issues. The fact that a party nominated a candidate, for example, was reason enough for many of its identifiers to vote for him. A party's choice also influenced how voters perceived a candidate. Thus Democratic identifiers would have good things to say about Democratic candidates, and Republican adherents would make positive statements about Republican candidates.

Partisan identification did not control political attitudes all the time. In 1956, for example, Dwight Eisenhower was clearly the more popular candidate. Had voters evaluated the nominees solely on the basis of party identification, they would have rated Adlai Stevenson more favorably. In the same year, the electorate accorded Eisenhower and the Republican party high marks on foreign policy matters, and rated Stevenson and the Democrats better on domestic issues. Despite these variations, however, one pattern remained constant: Democrats were the most likely to perceive the benefits of voting for their candidate, and Republicans were similarly disposed toward their nominee.

It might be asked here why the authors of *The American Voter* placed such stress on party identification in shaping political attitudes when, logically, it might be the other way around—that is, an individual's political views could determine his or her party affiliation. Such an intuitively reasonable contention was rejected on two grounds. One was that party identification was acquired at an early age, before the individual was much aware of the political world or had formed mature political judgments. Yet most individuals stuck with the party they acquired during childhood.

A second reason that the Campbell team emphasized the influence of party identification on political judgments was the voters' level of issue awareness. Voters said that they preferred the domestic policies of Stevenson and the foreign policies of Eisenhower, but how much did they actually know about either? To qualify as an issue voter, the Campbell group said, an individual had to meet three conditions. First, the voter had to be aware of the existence of an issue and hold some opinion on it. Second, the issue had to arouse a minimal level of interest in the voter. Third, a person had to perceive that one candidate came closer to representing his or her opinion than the other candidate. It was the inability of most voters to meet these conditions that led Campbell and his associates to assert that issues did not play a major role in a voter's decisional calculus.[19]

It still could be argued that while average voters were not well informed on specific issues, they might have recognized a more generalized difference between the parties. In other words, they understood that the Democratic party was the more liberal party, and the Republican party the more conservative. If this were the case, it would explain the persistence of party identification. Voters would line up behind the party whose ideology matched their own and stick with it even when some of its candidates took issue positions that did not square well with the party's philosophy. Though they did not pay much attention to precise issue questions, the voters counted on their party's ideological orientation over the long term.

The supposition that voters conceived of the parties in ideological terms proved unfounded because few in the electorate engaged in abstract thinking about politics. Most voters were unaware of the philosophical orientations of the parties that distinguished them along such lines as the appropriate role of government in society. On the contrary, most who perceived partisan differences thought in more concrete terms. For example, a blue-collar worker would see the Democratic party as protective of labor interests, while a doctor would count on the Republican party's opposition to government interference in the private practice of medicine. Since neither voter considered the broad government role, neither could appeal to a general set of principles to sort out all his political attitudes.[20]

THE INFLUENCE OF CANDIDATE IMAGE

The one apparent inconsistency in *The American Voter* model was the impressive victories won by Eisenhower in 1952 and 1956, years when the Democrats were the majority party. If party identification was so central to the voter's choice, why did the Republican candidate win? One of the book's co-authors, Donald Stokes, supplied the answer after examining the elections of 1960 and 1964. Party images, he maintained, were relatively stable across elections, but the attractiveness of presidential candidates varied from election to election. Thus either party had a chance of winning if their candidate had sufficient appeal.[21]

Stokes did not challenge the basic conclusions of *The American Voter*, which were that most voters vote their partisan identification and issues are relatively unimportant in presidential contests. Yet he found that if a candidate projected a clearly more attractive image than his rival did, he would be supported overwhelmingly by his own partisans and would pick up support from Independents and the more weakly identified adherents of the opposition party. Eisenhower did this in 1952 and 1956 and therefore was able to win as a minority party candidate. Lyndon Johnson, as the majority party's candidate, won even more impressively in 1964, also because he was clearly perceived as the more attractive candidate. Yet only 17 percent of all partisan identifiers defected in 1956, and only 16 percent in 1964.

SHATTERING THE MYTH OF THE RATIONAL VOTER

The American Voter forever shattered the myth of the rational voter dear to democratic theory by demonstrating conclusively that most citizens followed their partisan identification in voting. Did this mean that election outcomes were determined more by habit than by reason? Not entirely. A minority of voters were issue conscious in making their candidate choices. Others evaluated the parties on how well they served group interests, such as those of workers, businessmen, or farmers. Still others, although vague in their references, commented on the "goodness" or "badness" of the times and associated an incumbent administration with the prospects of war or peace, recession or prosperity. Only about 17 percent of all voters could muster no comments at all about public policy-related topics.

The myth the book demolished was that of the average citizen taking stands on specific public policy alternatives and relating them to a more general political philosophy or ideology. Most people, having neither the interest nor the information necessary to become such model citizens, used party identification to sort out the political world. They had confidence in the ability of their party and its candidates to run the nation. It was an imperfect system for linking citizens to their government, but no better alternative was clearly evident.

The Changing American Voter

The turmoil that characterized the 1960s and the early 1970s stood in sharp contrast to the relatively quiescent 1950s. During the fifties, most citizens may have been only minimally interested in a debate over issues, but was such indifference possible in an era when the nation was mired in a military venture in Vietnam and long-smoldering racial antagonisms exploded in one city after the next? Did partisan identification still guide voting choices as a new set of concerns over the environment, the rights of women, crime in the streets, and the growing use of drugs preoccupied more and more Americans? If the changing political environment had an effect upon the American voter, what was the nature of this effect?

THE DECLINE OF PARTISANSHIP

One widely noted change in American electoral politics is the diminished role of partisanship in shaping a voter's choice. Party voting has declined, it is said, for two reasons: First, the number of self-declared Independents has risen, and thus the number who can cast party votes are fewer. Second, the number of partisans who defect to vote for opposition party candidates has also increased.[22] The erosion of partisan ties is real enough, but the extent of its spread and the meaning of its development are less clear.

The proportion of Independents within the electorate rose steadily from 1964 to 1974, when the increase began to level off. Independents are not a homogeneous group, however. As we discussed in Chapter 5, most Independents acknowledge leaning in a partisan direction and exhibit many of the characteristics of partisans. That is, they usually vote for the candidates of the party they lean toward, and they retain their partisan inclinations across elections. Such Independent leaners are quite capable of casting partisan votes.

The proportion of Independents who disclaim any partisan preference has also increased since 1964, from 8 percent of the electorate to 12 percent in 1980. These Independents show less stability in their partisan choices from election to election, but they are also less interested in political campaigns and less likely to vote. If only voters are considered, the proportion of citizens who are truly independent, that is, who eschew all partisan guidance in their election choices, is more modest. In 1980, they accounted for a little over 8 percent of the presidential vote cast.

Of equal significance to the growth of Independents, however, has been the loosening of party ties more generally. The proportion of weakly identified partisans has remained relatively stable over the years, but the proportion of more committed partisans has declined. In 1964, 26 percent of the electorate were classified as strong Democrats; in 1980, that figure had declined to 16 percent. Comparable figures for strong Republicans were 11 percent in 1964 and 10 percent in 1980. So the partisan electorate has become increasingly composed of Independent leaners and the weakly identified. The causes are less that older partisans are questioning their partisan ties than that the young are entering the electorate with weak or no partisan commitments.[23]

The consequences of loosened partisan ties are seen in the rate of party defections and straight-ticket voting. As Table 10-3 indicates, party voting in presidential and House elections has displayed an irregular but downward trend since the 1950s. In neither case, however, has the drop in partisanship been especially sharp. More convincing evidence of diminished partisanship is contained in Table 10-4, which displays the trend in straight-ticket voting in all federal elections. Because of the combined effect of defections in House, Senate, and presidential races, the proportion of straight-ticket voters has fallen more steeply from its earlier levels. That so many partisans now split their tickets can only mean that their partisan attachments are less firm than before.

THE RISE OF ISSUE VOTING

If voters are relying less on partisan cues than before, what criteria are they using in making a choice among competing candidates? Many researchers believe that issue voting is replacing party voting.[24]

Voting one's party identification and voting on the basis of issues do not have to be incompatible. The two would be in conflict only if partisans did not accept the issue positions normally taken by their party's candidates. Indeed, some scholars

Table 10-3
PARTISAN LOYALTY OF VOTERS

	1952	1956	1960	1964	1968	1972	1976	1980
				Percent				
Presidential Elections								
Strong Dem.	83.6	85.0	90.1	95.3	84.7	73.4	90.6	88.2
Weak Dem.	62.0	62.5	71.7	82.1	57.9	48.5	74.0	60.3
Ind. Dem.	60.0	67.5	87.7	90.0	51.6	60.2	72.3	50.5
Ind. Rep.	93.3	93.5	86.9	75.0	82.2	86.0	83.2	77.4
Weak Rep.	93.5	92.7	86.9	56.1	82.3	90.4	76.8	82.4
Strong Rep.	98.5	99.5	98.4	90.3	95.8	96.7	96.3	96.0
All Partisans	80.7	84.1	86.4	83.4	75.4	73.3	81.9	76.2
House Elections								
Strong Dem.	90.4	94.4	93.0	93.9	88.0	92.4	89.3	86.9
Weak Dem.	77.2	87.0	86.1	84.1	72.7	80.6	78.2	69.9
Ind. Dem.	63.3	83.3	87.1	79.5	62.7	79.5	77.9	79.5
Ind. Rep.	80.8	82.3	74.4	71.7	82.1	72.7	67.8	60.9
Weak Rep.	89.5	88.4	85.4	63.2	78.4	75.6	72.0	72.8
Strong Rep.	94.8	94.9	91.6	91.5	91.8	84.9	85.5	82.3
All Partisans	84.7	82.7	87.5	83.6	79.9	81.3	79.5	75.4

SOURCE: Survey Research Center/Center for Political Studies of the University of Michigan. Data made available through the Inter-University Consortium for Political Research.

Table 10-4
STRAIGHT TICKET VOTING IN FEDERAL ELECTIONS

	1952	1956	1960	1964	1968	1972	1976	1980
	Percent of Those Voting a Straight Ticket							
Strong Dem.	78.4	82.3	85.1	87.0	82.0	66.7	80.4	75.8
Weak Dem.	56.3	58.8	66.2	70.0	54.1	39.0	57.3	44.9
Ind. Dem.	52.4	59.5	73.1	68.2	39.4	46.8	52.9	42.5
Ind. Rep.	78.8	72.3	74.5	52.4	63.8	62.9	46.3	38.6
Weak Rep.	87.3	81.9	76.7	42.5	70.4	68.8	47.2	47.0
Strong Rep.	91.8	92.6	91.4	82.5	87.3	80.2	78.7	74.8
All Partisans	74.3	76.1	78.4	71.4	68.1	58.9	60.9	54.9

SOURCE: Survey Research Center/Center for Political Studies of the University of Michigan. Data made available through the Inter-University Consortium for Political Research.

have argued that parties have sorted out their supporters fairly well so that citizens identify with the party that best reflects their issue attitudes.[25] But if this is so, why have partisan ties weakened?

The more common argument is that issue voting and party voting are not mutually reinforcing. Scholars who advance this argument implicitly assume that party voting in the past was dictated more by habit than by reason. Voters were emotionally tied to a party and supported its candidates regardless of their public stands on the issues. The psychological commitment was broken only when voters suddenly realized that their issue preferences were not being reflected by the candidates of their chosen party. If this argument is correct, issue voting contributes to the erosion of party loyalty.

Just how much more common issue voting is today than in the past is disputed. One could say that the great strides made in education have enabled more citizens to understand and evaluate the issue positions of candidates. But this is not what is being argued. Instead, it is contended that the change in the *political environment* has produced issue voters. Beginning in 1964, politics took on an intensity unknown to the 1950s. Voters could not remain unaware of the great moral issues at stake in the struggles to achieve black equality and to end the Vietnam conflict. And to these dominant controversies of the 1960s could be added other social and cultural issues and, later, a burdensome inflation. The effects were seen, it is argued, in the voting of the less educated as well as the college trained.[26]

An additional development, some suggest, has encouraged issue voting: voters have become more consistent in the attitudes they hold across issues.[27] In other words, voters have become more ideological in their issues orientation and therefore less likely to be torn between liberal attitudes on some issues and conservative attitudes on others.

It is difficult to prove that the electorate has become more consistent than before because the format of questions asked in national surveys has changed over the years. Although the topic has been hotly debated, one experiment conducted in 1973 suggested that the newfound ideological consistency of the American voter was an artifact of questionnaire wording. When the same questionnaire format used in the 1950s and early 1960s was presented to a 1973 national sample, the results showed little difference between the electorate of the 1970s and the electorate of the 1950s.[28]

Cartoon by Gamble, © 1981. Source: *The Florida Times-Union*. Reprinted courtesy of the Register and Tribune Syndicate.

Although complex, the debate over issue voting has important implications for the nation's parties. If voters are capable of evaluating candidates on the basis of their issue stands, they do not need the party label to assist them in rewarding or punishing officeholders. A more precise individual accountability could replace the imperfect collective responsibility offered by the parties. If voters are also grouping themselves into liberal and conservative camps, holding individual candidates accountable would not hopelessly fragment politics. On the contrary, the ideological preferences of the electorate would emerge from election contests.

Few researchers doubt that great national controversies influence how citizens vote. Popular reaction to national political events is not a new phenomenon, although the scope and intensity of the public's response has varied with the nature of the controversies. Differences over issue voting center on the question of how citizens translate whatever issue concerns they have into voting choices.

In *The American Voter*, issue voting was narrowly defined. A voter had to have an opinion on an issue, know what the government policy on that issue was, and perceive a difference in how the parties or candidates proposed to resolve it. In other words, voters had to choose among *alternative policies* with some understanding of the options presented. An undefined discontent with the pace of social change or a general dissatisfaction with the state of the economy, no matter how intensely felt, fell short of what the Campbell team had in mind when they spoke of issue voting.

At least part of the controversy over issue voting turns on how it is defined and how it is measured. The intricacies of the debate need not be dwelled on. What is important is how election results are to be interpreted. Are voters of today capable of providing clear policy mandates to the officeholders they elect? Or do they elect politicians to decide what is in the best interests of nation and state? If the former is the case, citizens tell their leaders what policies they favor. If the latter is the case, voters merely identify the problems they believe need solving.

The 1980 presidential election may be used for illustrative purposes. Surveys conducted in the last year of the Carter administration showed the electorate's dissatisfaction with the president's job performance. Two months before the election, 85 percent of the electorate thought Carter was doing only a fair or a poor job in handling the economy, and 78 percent thought his management of foreign policy merited only a fair to poor rating.[29] The specific reasons for the ratings varied. Inflation, unemployment, and high interest rates contributed to the low rating Carter received on the economy, while the continuing Iranian hostage crisis and the Soviet invasion of Afghanistan figured in the low evaluation of his foreign policy. What did emerge clearly from the surveys was that most citizens were dissatisfied with the way Carter was running the country.

A majority of Americans had obviously lost confidence in Carter, but did that mean that they embraced the policies of Ronald Reagan? Only in a general sense, according to a survey conducted during the early weeks of the Reagan administration. While two thirds of those questioned thought that Reagan's economic program would lead to a rapid improvement in the nation's economy, this faith in Reagan's ability to bring about economic recovery was not matched by approval of his specific economic proposals. For example, a majority approved of wage and price controls, a policy that Reagan had specifically rejected. No more than 15 percent said they favored spending cuts for the poor, for education, or for health—all reductions included in the Reagan administration's first budget. In other areas, opinions were sometimes in line with Reagan policies, at other times at sharp variance.[30] So the public elected Reagan to office, but did not dictate his policies in the process.

That the public does not provide its leaders with specific policy directions does not mean that citizens disregard issue controversies in making their voting choices. Voters blame an incumbent administration for all the problems they believe could be better handled. But do they direct the blame at the incumbent president or the incumbent party?

VOTING THE PERSON, NOT THE PARTY

As we discussed earlier in this chapter, most party identifiers prefer their party's nominees to those of the opposition. Voting in the 1980 presidential election was no different from other elections in this regard: 87 percent of Republicans voted for Ronald Reagan, while 67 percent of Democrats supported Jimmy Carter. But how does one account for the defections that occurred in this and other presidential elections?

Voters may desert their party to vote for the presidential candidate of the opposite party because of his personal attractiveness or because he has promised to solve problems of widespread concern. It is difficult to separate the personal and issue dimensions of a candidate's appeal.[31] Many people attributed Dwight Eisenhower's victory in 1952 to his war hero fame and his genial personality, even though the preceding Democratic administration of Harry Truman was wracked by scandals, charges of communist infiltration in high government places, and an unpopular war in Korea.[32] Many claimed that Richard Nixon won reelection in 1972 because his issue positions more nearly coincided with the preferences of the public. However, his opponent, George McGovern, lost votes even among those who agreed with his issue stands because he was negatively perceived in personal terms.[33]

Early voting behavior theory emphasized that voting shifts were brought about by negative attitudes toward White House policies. The negative attitudes could be accompanied by a favorable feeling toward the opposition party candidate, but positive forces alone were not likely to initiate widespread changes in the party balance.[34] Has the growing issue consciousness of the public had the effect of holding the president rather than his party accountable? More voters than before are making issue references in evaluating presidential candidates. Nevertheless, those who remain loyal to their party are as likely to cite issue reasons in assessing a candidate as those who bolt. In other words, evaluating candidates on issue grounds is as likely to lead to a reaffirmation of partisanship as to a crossover vote.[35]

To summarize, voters often make their choices according to the confidence they have in a candidate to make the right decisions once in office. That confidence is sometimes based on the widely publicized issue stands taken by a candidate, but more often it is based on the perceived strengths and weaknesses of the candidate's other qualifications for office. The perception of candidates, in turn, is often colored by a voter's partisan affiliation. Defections occur when the opposition party nominates a candidate of unusually attractive personal qualities, or when the voter's own party nominates a person who does not inspire public confidence. Voters may be more issue aware than in the past, but they express their issue concerns by voting for the candidate they think has the overall ability to meet the problems that concern them.

Voting Behavior in Congressional Elections

An examination of voting behavior in congressional elections may throw more light on changes in the American electorate and the relative weight to be accorded party, issues, and candidates. Until recently, much of our knowledge of how voters picked their congressmen came from studies of the 1958 off-year elections. Additional data on how members of Congress are elected were collected twenty years later, allowing the analyst to discern what changes took place in the intervening years. These data are especially valuable because political analysts are often tempted to generalize about the electorate's voting habits from the study of presidential elections alone.

THE VOTER OF THE FIFTIES

The earlier studies found the voter possessing little information about House candidates.[36] Of those who went to the polls, 46 percent reported that they had not read or heard anything about either candidate. Voters were almost twice as likely to have had knowledge of incumbents as challengers. Furthermore, the knowledge they did possess was seldom related to contemporary public issues. Only 7 percent stated that issues influenced their candidate choices.

Possessing little information, most voters relied on their partisan identification to guide them. Defections were related to knowledge of the candidates—a crossover vote was most likely if a person had knowledge only of the opposition party candidate, whereas voters who knew only the candidate of their own party almost always voted loyally. That the voters' information was so void of issue content, however, gave little hint that the party label was serving as a surrogate for their issue interests.

Additional evidence confirmed that party voting was not based on an evaluation of the legislative record of a party. When corrected for guessing, probably no more than half of all voters knew that the Congress was controlled by Democrats. Even those who said they knew who had organized the Congress did not seem to apply that knowledge to their choice of candidates. At least those who thought their own party had organized the Congress showed no difference in their loyalty whether they believed that domestic affairs had gone well or badly. Similarly, those who thought the opposition party was in control were unaffected in their voting by how they perceived the state of domestic policies.

THE VOTER OF TODAY

Analyses of 1978 congressional races reveal that the American electorate has changed, in some matters rather considerably, since 1958. The most striking difference is in the ability of voters to recognize and evaluate candidates. In House contests, 93 percent of respondents were able to rate incumbents, and 44 percent could rate challengers. Because contests for House seats involving incumbents are often so one-sided, the discrepancy is not surprising. In more competitive open races, with neither candidate an incumbent, almost three quarters of the respondents could evaluate both candidates.[37]

A second change that took place over the twenty-year period was the declining influence of party identification on the vote. Partisan stability across elections has always been more characteristic of House races than presidential contests, with the presidential vote swinging more widely from one election to the next. However, the proportion of partisans voting loyally in House elections has declined from over 87 percent in 1960 to under 76 percent in 1980. The logical explanation for the growing rate of defections is that voters now possess sufficient information to make a judgment on candidates that contradicts their partisan affiliation.

The incumbent has the advantage in attracting votes from the opposition party mainly because incumbents are more visible and widely perceived as more qualified than their challengers. Almost three fourths of the voters in 1978 made a positive evaluation of incumbents, while only a fifth rated challengers favorably. Crossing over to vote for incumbents is a primary cause of declining party loyalty. Crossovers who voted for challengers accounted for 43 percent of all defections in 1958; in 1978, the comparable figure was a mere 11 percent.[38]

Incumbents are in an enviable position because nine out of ten voters have had some form of contact with them. A surprising 23 percent reported that they had met the incumbent personally. Most voters had read about their congressman in news articles or seen him on television. Seventy-one percent said that they had received mail from him.[39] Apparently the effect of all these ties to constituents is a favorable evaluation.

The data from 1978 confirm that voters form impressions from their contacts with the candidates that influence how they vote. But how much attention do voters pay to the voting record of their congressmen? Few mentioned ideology or issues when asked what they liked or disliked about the candidates. Only 15 percent recalled how their congressman had voted on a bill in recent years, and fewer than half had formed an opinion on his voting record. Most impressions of incumbents were formed on the basis of their experience, their character, or their ties to the community.[40] In this respect, the voter of 1978 differed little from the voter of 1958.

House and Senate Races Compared. Although information on Senate races is more limited, one important generalization can be made: incumbent senators are more vulnerable today than incumbent representatives. Several factors help to explain the difference in their electoral fortunes. Because of its smaller size, a House district is more likely to be dominated by a single party than a state. Prospects of one-sided contests discourage challenges. Also, the mass media cover Senate elections more fully than House contests, and consequently, voters acquire more knowledge of Senate challengers than of House challengers. Finally, because of greater media coverage, incumbent senators are less able than incumbent representatives to control the information voters receive about their performance. As a result, Senators are more involved in controversial national issues.[41]

The Contemporary Parties: Election Outcomes and Party Government

When party government is working properly, the electorate places the same party in control of both executive and legislative branches. It is then possible to judge the party according to its performance while in power. In the ordinary course of events, a successful party is returned to office and an ineffectual one is replaced. The vote is based on a retrospective judgment of how well the nation fared since the last election.

The practice of rewarding or punishing a party for its conduct of government has broken down since the close of World War II. Except for the Eighty-third Congress, which was elected with Dwight Eisenhower in 1952, Republican presidents have been unable to carry a majority of their legislative colleagues to power in both the House and the Senate. Democrats have been more fortunate. Since Franklin Roosevelt led his party to power in 1932, only Harry Truman has confronted a Congress organized by Republicans. Divided control of government is evidence that parties are imperfectly mobilizing the voters.

When voters disregard the partisan affiliation of candidates, election contests become individually fought battles whose victors often have little in common beyond their ability to attract a vote. When voters choose candidates on the basis of clearly staked out issue positions, it is possible for a broad election mandate to emerge. This is unusual in American politics for several reasons. In House elections, voters are more influenced by a candidate's ties to the local community than the great issues of the day. Issue controversies exert a greater influence on presidential elections, but even here it is not so much a candidate's announced stands that attract votes as people's confidence in his ability to lead the nation and solve its problems.

THE "SURGE-AND-DECLINE" EFFECT IN MIDTERM ELECTIONS

Partisanship has not weakened so greatly in recent years that congresssional and presidential elections are completely separated. Party identification remains an important influence on how voters perceive and rate candidates in any election. Moreover, partisan labels sometimes act in aid of national forces that shape the collective outcome of elections. Consider the debate over whether the midterm verdict is a referendum on the stewardship of the presidential party. In every election but one since the Civil War, the party of the incumbent president has lost seats in the House at the midterm. At one time, this pattern was explained on the basis of a "surge-and-decline" effect.[42] It was argued that a presidential election brought out voters who were only marginally interested in politics. Normally, the winner received more than his share of these inattentive voters. At the midterm, peripheral voters did not turn out and the presidential party lost some of the support it had enjoyed in the preceding election. According to this theory, the greater the margin of a presidential candidate's victory, the greater would be his party's loss two years later.

MIDTERM ELECTIONS AS A REFERENDUM ON THE PRESIDENT

Recent research has challenged the surge-and-decline thesis. Some scholars now argue that voters react to congressional candidates not necessarily on the basis of the legislative record of the parties, but on how well the president has been doing his job. They reward or punish the president's party, and thus their actions are more rational than previously thought. For example, Edward Tufte has shown that the popularity of the president and the state of the economy can explain the deviations of the midterm House vote from what would "normally" be expected. The midterm, concluded Tufte, is "neither a mystery nor an automatic swing of the pendulum: the midterm vote is a referendum."[43]

Tufte's findings explain deviations in the party vote from previous elections and are important because they show that election outcomes at the midterm are related to a popular judgment of the president's performance. Nevertheless, his data do not disclose why most people vote as they do. Presidential performance has an impact on enough voters to influence the overall division of the partisan vote, but it is not the principal explanation of how votes are cast. In 1978, for example, 78 percent of Democrats who approved of Jimmy Carter's record voted for Democratic House candidates, compared to 74 percent who were negative; 29 percent of Republicans who approved of Carter voted for Democratic House candidates, compared to 21 percent of those who disapproved of his performance. Although the difference that Carter's performance made on the vote was slight, it was still sufficient to explain the limited national shift observed in 1978.[44]

MAKING ELECTIONS A TEST OF THE PARTY'S RECORD

The most formidable obstacle to making elections a test of a party's record is the ability of incumbent House members to win reelection whether or not a majority of voters are satisfied that the nation's affairs have been well handled. In contrast, presidential candidates are more frequently evaluated according to their competence to solve whatever problems confront the country. The swing of votes from one presidential election to the next is thus better related to the tides of national events. For the same reasons, the popular majorities placing the president and congressmen in power differ in important respects.

If national elections are to be made a referendum on the performance of the presidential party, the advantages held by House incumbents must be equalized. If challengers posed a more serious threat to incumbents, then the national forces described by Tufte would have a greater opportunity to determine the ultimate distribution of House seats. Senate incumbents are more vulnerable to challenges than their House counterparts, and they cannot escape the effects of national political forces. In 1980, for example, the tide that swept Reagan into office also produced a Republican Senate. The electoral edge that accrues to House incumbents will not be easily removed, but it can be partially offset by the recruitment of aggressive candidates who have adequate resources to communicate with voters. Only in this way can the aggregate outcome of elections be more firmly linked to popular judgment on how the nation's problems are being met.

SUMMARY

Throughout most of the nation's history, only a minority of adults were able to cast a ballot. Various movements to broaden the suffrage have enfranchised the propertyless, blacks, women, and persons eighteen years old, so that today the only remaining hurdle for citizens desiring to vote is registration requirements.

Still, many millions of Americans do not go to the polls. Some abstain because of personal problems, but most nonvoters choose not to vote. Those most likely to turn out are people who believe strongly in the political efficacy of voting, are civic minded, and are interested in a campaign and its outcome. People who consider the government remote and complex, have little interest in politics, and do not view voting as a civic obligation are less likely to cast a ballot.

Voting is also associated with certain sociological correlates. Of these, education is the most important because it enables citizens to understand politics and encourages the development of a civic consciousness. Income and occupation are also related to voter turnout, but mainly because they are associated with education.

Blacks are less likely to vote than whites, but only because they have not obtained the educational and occupational status of whites; when socioeconomic differences are controlled, blacks actually turn out at a higher rate than whites. Sex differences in voting have all but disappeared—only among the elderly and the least educated do men vote more regularly than women. Voting does still follow a life-cycle pattern: turnout increases from youth to middle age, and then declines with advanced age, because of the lower participation rate of elderly women.

Although circumstances today would seem to encourage a high voter turnout, participation in national elections has been declining steadily since 1960. Lowering the voting age to eighteen explains only part of the downturn; estimates are that it accounted for no more than one quarter of the drop between 1968 and 1972. Neither the American people's sense of civic duty nor their interest in political campaigns has diminished. What is new is that more citizens believe that government is run for the few, that many office seekers are a little crooked, and that ordinary people have little to say about what governments do. Such widespread cynicism has undoubtedly depressed turnout rates.

Few nonvoters appear to be politically aware citizens who have been turned off by politics. Actually, turnout is highest among voters who possess enough information to evaluate presidential candidates on issue or ideological grounds, and lowest among voters who are unable to express an opinion about the candidates. Moreover, only a tiny fraction of nonvoters are negative in their evaluations of both presidential candidates. The decline in voting appears to result more from indifference than from a rational and conscious rejection of politics.

Three factors are commonly said to influence the choices made by voters: party identification; attitudes on issues; and judgment of the experience, leadership, and other personal qualities of the candidates.

The earliest voting studies stressed the importance of party identification on voting behavior. Party identification, acquired at an early age and frequently persisting throughout life, was a perceptual screen through which the average citizen evaluated the political world. Democratic identifiers tended to perceive Democratic candidates in the most favorable light, and Republican identifiers were similarly disposed toward their candidates. Most voters were unaware of the specific issues in election contests or, if they were, did not know where the candidates stood on them. Most people did not think of parties in ideological terms but in terms of their own group interests or, more vaguely, of the "goodness" or "badness" of the times. Voting preferences were not based solely on habit, but neither did they conform to the rational model of democratic theory.

Much of the early theory of how citizens voted was based on elections in the 1950s, a relatively quiet period in American history. More recent studies, following the civil rights marches, the conflagrations in the cities, and the antiwar protests of the 1960s and early 1970s, revealed a more restive electorate. The changes that occurred over this twenty-year period have had an important bearing on the party system.

The easiest change to document is the diminishing influence of partisanship, although some researchers have exaggerated the extent of the decline. True, the number of Independents has grown, but most of them lean in a partisan direction and exhibit many of the characteristics of party identifiers. Nevertheless, it is undeniable that party identification has weakened, and the results are seen in party defections and split-ticket voting.

As their partisanship has eroded, voters have looked to other guides when casting their ballots. Some analysts believe that voters weigh the issue stands of presidential candidates more heavily than they did in the past. It is intuitively sensible to believe that voters are influenced by major political controversies. When some overriding national issue engages the public's attention, as Vietnam did in 1972, some voters do choose sides on the basis of the alternative positions staked out by the candidates. More often than not, however, citizens react to public policy debates by selecting the candidate whose personal qualities inspire their confidence, which is why it is difficult to disentangle the candidate and issue dimensions of a voter's choice.

National moods are most easily expressed in presidential elections, next in Senate contests, and are least discernible in House races. If each set of elections were governed by the same issue dynamics, election mandates would be more easily interpretable. But since the several contests are subject to different electoral forces, mandates are clouded and the concept of party responsibility is weakened.

Under the most favorable conditions of party government, the same party would control both executive and legislative branches and could therefore be judged on its performance while in office. The greatest obstacle to making elections a test of a party's record is the ability of House incumbents to win reelection whether or not voters are satisfied with the state of national affairs. Some voters, however, do reward or punish the candidates of the presidential party according to their evaluations of the president. If more House incumbents were seriously challenged for reelection, the collective outcome of federal elections would more nearly reflect the public's evaluation of the president and the party he represents.

Notes

[1]Angus Campbell, Philip E. Converse, Warren E. Miller, and Donald E. Stokes, *The American Voter* (New York: Wiley, 1960).

[2]The white primary was declared unconstitutional in *Smith v. Allwright*, 321 U.S. 649 (1944).

[3]David Campbell and Joe R. Feagin, "Black Politics in the South: A Descriptive Analysis," *Journal of Politics* 37 (February 1975), p. 133.

[4]V. O. Key, Jr., *Politics, Parties, and Pressure Groups*, 5th ed. (New York: Crowell, 1964), pp. 614–615.

[5]Ibid., pp. 615–617.

[6]Steven J. Rosenstone and Raymond E. Wolfinger, "The Effect of Registration Laws on Voter Turnout," *American Political Science Review* 72 (March 1978), pp. 35–36.

[7]Ibid., pp. 37–41.

[8]David B. Hill and Norman R. Luttbeg, *Trends in American Electoral Behavior* (Itasca, Ill.: Peacock, 1980), p. 97.

[9]Raymond E. Wolfinger and Steven J. Rosenstone, "Who Votes" (paper delivered at the annual meeting of the American Political Science Association, Washington, D.C., September 1–4, 1977), pp. 22–27, 49–56.

[10]Ibid., pp. 34–42.

[11]Ibid., pp. 31–33.

[12]Ibid., pp. 34–36.

[13]Richard A. Brody, "The Puzzle of Political Participation in America," in *The New American Political System*, ed. Anthony King (Washington, D.C.: American Enterprise Institute, 1978), p. 301.

[14]Wolfinger and Rosenstone, "Who Votes," p. 48.

[15]Brody, "The Puzzle of Political Participation in America," p. 309.

[16]Ibid., p. 312.

[17]Hill and Luttbeg, *Trends in American Electoral Behavior*, p. 104.

[18]Campbell et al., *The American Voter*, chap. 7, treats the development and persistence of party identification; chap. 6 discusses its influence on political attitudes.

[19]Ibid., chap. 7.

[20]Attitude structures and levels of conceptualization are discussed in ibid., chaps. 9 and 10.

[21]Donald E. Stokes, "Some Dynamic Elements of Contests for the Presidency," *American Political Science Review* 60 (March 1966), pp. 19–28.

[22]Norman H. Nie, Sidney Verba, and John R. Petrocik, *The Changing American Voter* (Cambridge, Mass.: Harvard University Press, 1976), p. 164.

[23]Ibid., p. 65.

[24]For example, see the discussion in Arthur H. Miller, Warren E. Miller, Alden S. Raine, and Thad A. Brown, "A Majority Party in Disarray: Policy Polarization in the 1972 Election," *American Political Science Review*, 70 (September 1976), pp. 753–778; and Nie et al., *The Changing American Voter*, chap. 10.

[25]See Gerald M. Pomper, "From Confusion to Clarity: Issues and American Voters, 1956–1968," *American Political Science Review* 66 (June 1972), pp. 415–428.

[26]Ibid., p. 421. See also Nie et al., *The Changing American Voter*, pp. 185–187.

[27]Nie et al., *The Changing American Voter*, especially chaps. 8, 9, and 10.

[28]George F. Bishop et al., "The Changing Structure of Mass Belief Systems: Fact or Artifact," *Journal of Politics* 40 (August 1978), pp. 781–787. See also John L. Sullivan et al., "Ideological Constraint in the Mass Public: A Methodological Critique and Some New Findings," *American Journal of Political Science* 22 (May 1978), pp. 233–249.

[29]The NBC News/Associated Press surveys were reported in "Opinion Roundup," *Public Opinion*, December/January 1981, p. 27.

[30]The Washington Post/ABC News Poll conducted February 19 and 20 as reported in *The Washington Post*, February 24, 1981, pp. A1 and A5.

[31]For a discussion of the relative importance of the issue stands as opposed to the personal qualities of candidates, see Nie et al., *The Changing American Voter*, pp. 166–173; and David E. RePass, "Comment: Political Methodologies in Disarray: Some Alternative Interpretations of the 1972 Election," *American Political Science Review* 70 (September 1976), pp. 814–831. Warren E. Miller and Teresa E. Levitin also note that George McGovern did not get all of the votes from his "natural constituency" in *Leadership and Change: Presidential Elections from 1952–1976* (Cambridge, Mass.: Winthrop, 1976), pp. 144–145.

[32]Campbell et al., *The American Voter*, pp. 526–527.

[33]Miller and Levitin, *Leadership and Change*, pp. 144–155.

[34]Campbell et al., *The American Voter*, pp. 554–555.

[35]Hill and Luttbeg, *Trends in American Electoral Behavior*, pp. 66–68.

[36]The discussion of the 1958 House elections is taken from Donald E. Stokes and Warren E. Miller, "Party Government and the Saliency of Congress," *Public Opinion Quarterly* 26 (Winter 1962), pp. 531–546.

[37]Thomas E. Mann and Raymond E. Wolfinger, "Candidates and Parties in Congressional Elections," *American Political Science Review* 74 (September 1980), Table 4, p. 623.

[38]Ibid., pp. 620–621.

[39]Ibid., Table 2, p. 627.

[40]Ibid., p. 629.

[41]Alan I. Abramowitz, "A Comparison of Voting for U.S. Senators and Representatives in 1978," *American Political Science Review* 74 (September 1980), p. 633.

[42]Angus Campbell, "Surge and Decline: A Study of Electoral Change," *Public Opinion Quarterly*, 24 (Fall 1960), pp. 397–418.

[43]Edward R. Tufte, "Determinants of the Outcomes of Midterm Congressional Elections," *American Political Science Review* 69 (September 1975), p. 826.

[44]Mann and Wolfinger, "Candidates and Parties in Congressional Elections," p. 630.

11

Parties in the Legislative Process

Party voting in legislative roll calls is essential to the linkage function that parties perform. Citizens who cast a partisan ballot are cheated if the legislator they help to elect commonly sides with the opposition party. In the Congress and most two-party state legislatures, the parties do bring a degree of coherence to the divisions that take place over questions of public policy. The ability of legislative parties to act in concert, however, is far from perfect.

A legislator's primary allegiance is to those individuals or groups within his constituency that helped to elect him,[1] and his constituency's interests do not always coincide with those of his party. When the two are in conflict, the legislator will heed his instincts for survival and vote his constituency. Party leaders understand the pull of the electoral connection and are reluctant to ask support for a bill that would endanger a member's chance of reelection. More than anything else, constituency ties explain legislators' deviations from party-line voting.

At the same time, an overwhelming proportion of congressmen have reported that they would like to vote in accord with their party's position.[2] Members are likely to vote loyally when district interests and party positions coincide, or when a bill has little significance for their district. It is under these circumstances that the legislative parties are able to muster their membership behind a legislative program. This is also the reason why so many studies have concluded that a legislator's roll call votes are more closely associated with party affiliation than with any other single factor.

The place to begin an examination of the role of partisanship is with the offices that the parties have established to manage the legislative process. Although limited by the environment in which they operate, party leaders perform important tasks. They inform members of the legislative schedule, provide information that may determine how a vote is cast, serve as a connecting link with the executive when he is of the same party, and interpret legislative actions for the media. They may not control the legislative output, but they do provide for orderly procedures.

Party Organization in the Congress

The party machinery in Congress is better suited for organizing the work of that body than for forging a consensus among party members. In each chamber, the parties provide the mechanisms through which committee assignments are made and leaders are selected. The leaders have the responsibility for scheduling legislation, devising floor strategies, and rounding up votes. They may marshall their forces with considerable success, but they cannot count on a dependable following, for other than their powers of persuasion they have few means of compelling party members to act as a collegial group.

THE CAUCUS OR CONFERENCE

The formal source of a party's power in each house of Congress is the caucus or conference, to which all party members belong. The caucus is the forum used to select a party's leaders and to ratify committee assignments. It may also serve as a mechanism for developing a party's position on legislation, though it is seldom used for this purpose today. Floor leaders and committee chairmen do not want to be told what to do, nor do individual congressmen wish to surrender their independence to the demands of a caucus majority.

At one time, caucuses were effective in building legislative majorities. During the first administration of Woodrow Wilson, they functioned in both houses and were an important factor in the enactment of his legislative program.[3] The Wilson administration, however, proved to be the high-water mark of the legislative party. There was a public outcry against the dictatorial powers of "King Caucus," particularly the practice whereby House Democrats bound members to caucus decisions. As party unity waned, the caucuses found it difficult to establish a party position. At the same time, the practice of awarding committee chairs on a seniority basis insulated chairmen from other power centers in their chamber. By the 1920s, the caucuses retained only the power to select party leaders.

The caucuses remained dormant until the late 1960s, when reform-minded members of the Democratic party moved to strengthen their power in the House.[4] Led by the liberal-oriented Democratic Study Group (DSG), the reformers first obtained a party rule calling for more frequent caucus meetings. With regular sessions, the caucus became the vehicle for a series of reforms that checked the arbitrary power of committee chairmen and strengthened the hand of floor leaders. For a time, House Democrats successfully employed the caucus for selected legislative policy purposes.

As a device for furthering the legislative aims of the party, the House Democratic caucus relied on two principal techniques:[5]

1. Expressing the "sense of the caucus" as guidance for party members.
2. Instructing Democratic members of a committee to take specific actions.

Although used sparingly, caucus actions taken on the Vietnam war issue solidified antiwar sentiment within the House. And in 1975, the caucus used its leverage over Democrats on the Rules Committee to obtain a floor vote on oil depletion allowances. Thereafter, caucus resolutions carried less weight with Democratic House members. Those on the Ways and Means Committee failed to comply with a caucus resolution in 1978 to report a bill rolling back scheduled Social Security tax increases. Nor did Democrats act on their caucus resolution to retain oil price controls in 1979.

The sporadic attempts by Democratic reformers to revive the caucus as a policymaking arm of the party was criticized by Republican leaders, who charged that deciding the fate of bills or amendments in an agency in which Republicans had no representation undermined the legislative process. But it took more than Republican criticism to bring about the decline of the caucus. Democratic chairmen resented caucus actions taken before a committee held hearings on a bill because they undercut the chairmen's authority. The Democratic leadership also found that caucus resolutions endorsing certain party positions reduced their flexibility in seeking compromises on a bill in the full House. And many Democratic members were wary that caucus action might create problems for them in their districts.

Because of all these dissatisfactions, the caucus once again receded into the background (today regular caucus meetings in the House seldom have a quorum), but not before the reformers had achieved many of the goals they sought. Committee chairmen were made more accountable and committee operations more democratic. Most members appear content with the powers that have been won, and the brief revival of the caucus for policy purposes proved its potential.

POLICY COMMITTEES

The creation of party policy committees was one of the recommendations of the Joint Committee on the Organization of Congress in its 1946 report, but since the House leadership did not wish to contend with an additional power center, it deleted the provision from the bill that authorized them. By separate action the following year, the Senate established policy committees for its legislative parties. House Republicans established a policy committee two years later, but it was not until 1973 that House Democrats created a Steering and Policy Committee as part of the reforms designed to overcome the power of committee chairmen.

According to the Joint Committee report, the policy committees were "to formulate overall legislative policy" for their respective parties in each chamber, but the policy committees have never attempted to play such a role. The root causes of this failure are the same as those that have prevented the caucuses from becoming the real sources of party power: effective policy committees would usurp the authority of committee and subcommittee chairmen and limit the independence of individual members. The policy committees now serve principally as forums for discussion and as agencies for disseminating information on pending legislation.

Republican Policy Committees. In both the House and the Senate, the chairmen of the Republican policy committees are elected by their party caucuses. The Senate Republican Policy Committee maintains a research staff that periodically undertakes lengthy policy studies for Republican senators. The House Republican Policy Committee meets more regularly to discuss legislative issues than its Senate counterpart, and when a consensus emerges, it issues policy statements. In neither chamber, however, is the action binding on members, and neither policy committee attempts to develop a comprehensive legislative program.

Democratic Policy Committees. The same conclusions apply with equal force to the Democratic policy committees. However, the Democratic committees are more an arm of its floor leaders because the speaker of the House and the minority leader of the Senate chair their respective policy committees. The committees have responsibilities other than those associated with the development of party policy postures. The House Democratic Steering and Policy Committee prepares the roster of committee assignments and recommends committee chairs to its caucus. The Senate Democratic Policy Committee worked closely with the floor leadership in planning the legislative schedule when Democrats were in the majority. Each of these tasks is important, but neither comes close to providing the type of party government envisaged by the original proponents of the policy committees.

PARTY LEADERS

The key element of the legislative party organization in Congress is the leadership. For the majority party, the speaker of the House and the majority leader of the Senate are the chief figures in their respective chambers. The speaker is assisted by a majority leader and a majority whip, while the principal aide of the Senate majority leader is his whip. Selected in party caucuses, these leaders are frequently distinguished from the seniority leaders or committee chairmen. The elected leaders have the principal function of maintaining party unity, and when their party occupies the White House, they are expected to work closely with the president and his staff. Minority leaders in House and Senate, aided by their lieutenants, perform counterpart functions for their party.

The Speaker of the House. Although his responsibilities are not spelled out, the position of speaker of the House is provided for in the Constitution. The title of "speaker" inevitably invites comparison to the impartial presiding officer of the British House of Commons, but the American office is quite different. In addition to his duties as presiding officer, the American speaker is clearly a partisan figure. He is elected by the full House at the start of each new Congress, and the majority party ranks hold firm behind the nominee earlier selected at their caucus meeting.

The speaker's powers were once formidable. Toward the close of the nineteenth century, he assigned members to committees and named their chairmen. He was *ex officio* chairman of the Rules Committee and in that capacity decided what legislation the House would consider. The speaker used his power of recognition to reward the faithful and punish the disloyal. Two of the most autocratic speakers during this era were Thomas B. "Czar" Reed and Joseph "Uncle Joe" Cannon. When Cannon succeeded to power in 1903, however, the Progressive movement was gaining momentum and sought to challenge the use of the speaker's power to promote a conservative economic and social philosophy. An alliance of liberal Democrats and insurgent Republicans stripped the speaker of his more important powers in 1910. No longer could he sit on the Rules Committee, control the standing committees, or use his power of recognition in an arbitrary fashion. There matters stood until Democratic reformers restored some power to the office in the 1970s.

The speaker today, at least while the Democrats control the House, chairs the Steering and Policy Committee, which makes Democratic assignments to the standing committees. He also makes the appointments to the Rules Committee. Although all committee assignments are subject to caucus approval, members routinely accept the rosters that are submitted. The speaker not only influences the makeup of committees but also has some control over the legislation they consider. Under House rules, the speaker has the authority to send a bill to more than one committee, or to split a bill, sending parts to different committees. He can thus direct a bill to the committee most likely to do his bidding. In these several ways, the speaker is able to circumvent the power of committee chairmen.

At the same time that the Democrats strengthened the speaker's powers, they undertook other reforms that created problems for the leadership. By expanding the number of sub-committees, specifying their jurisdiction, and guaranteeing them adequate funding and professional staffs, Democrats decentralized legislative power. Under the new rules, subcommittee chairmen are elected by a caucus of committee Democrats, where before they were appointed by committee chairmen. Because each House Democrat can hold only one subcommittee chair, an increasing number of members now share legislative power. This diffusion of power has added to the problems of the speaker and his aides in coordinating the legislative work.[6]

The Senate Majority Leader. The Senate majority leader faces many of the same problems as the speaker in managing his party. Over the past two decades, the Senate has become a more individualistic body. Power once securely in the hands of a small "club" is now spread more widely. Committee chairmen continue as important figures in the legislative process, but they share their authority with a growing number of subcommittee chairmen. Because of the Senate's relatively small size, junior senators of the majority party are virtually guaranteed chairmanship of more than one subcommittee, and with these chairmanships comes the power to appoint staff. Having assumed increased responsibilities, more senators are willing to assert themselves on policy matters.[7]

The Senate majority leader, like the speaker of the House, has influence over committee assignments and the scheduling of bills for floor consideration. Since he is not the presiding officer of the Senate, however, he does not have the speaker's power of recognition or of making parliamentary rulings. Although leadership styles vary with the occupants of the offices, both the speaker and the majority leader must assemble their power in much the same fashion. They are the elected leaders of their chambers, and the offices they hold carry power and prestige. Each is in a position to aid the interests and careers of individual members, and by doing so can place them in his debt. The leaders know their way around Washington and can open doors for the member who needs help with some constituency problem. They can assist members in getting desired committee assignments or in advancing legislation of special interest to them. They often attend dinners to raise funds or to honor the achievements of members. For their part, members recognize that the relationship with their leaders is not a one-way street. They expect the leaders to ask for their votes on critical issues.

WHIP ORGANIZATIONS

In both the House and the Senate, whips and assistant whips aid the leadership in rounding up votes. Because of the larger size of the House, the whip organization in that chamber is both more elaborate and more important. The whips are of particular significance when major legislation is being considered, for they provide the intelligence that helps to determine the leadership's strategy. In general, the whip organization performs four important tasks.[8]

Securing Attendance. The first function of the whip's office is to see to it that members attend sessions when important votes are taken. An effective whip organization, for example, will know of members' travel plans so the majority party can schedule legislation on days when maximum attendance by its members is likely. Either party can ask a member to change the date of a proposed trip. The whips don't want a good party turnout so much as a favorable vote. For this reason, they will take extraordinary steps to ensure the presence of those members who are sympathetic to the leadership position.

Providing Information. A second task that the whip organization performs is to provide information to the members of its party. At a minimum, members must be informed of the legislative calendar on a weekly basis. Some whip organizations go beyond this. The House Democratic whip office also circulates "Whip Advisories," which summarize the contents of bills, outline possible controversial features of their provisions, and even include amendments likely to be proposed from the floor. Since the advisories are drafted by supporters of the leadership, the rank-and-file members know how their leaders stand on any major bill.

Polling. The whip poll is a third function undertaken by the whip organization. Party members are asked how they will vote on pending legislation of interest to the leadership. When assistant whips query members on how they stand on legislation, they try to determine what provisions of a bill the members find most troublesome. If a consensus emerges against a particular feature of a bill, the bill may be changed in time to prevent its defeat. The most important use of the whip poll, however, is to inform the leadership of the probable fate of a bill. If a bill has no chance of passage, the leaders may defer consideration to prevent the ignominy of a decisive defeat or to allow time to regroup forces. If the outcome of the bill is uncertain, the leaders will know where to apply pressure to obtain its passage.

Supporting the Party Leadership. The ultimate function of the whip organization is to provide support for the party leadership. Once the trouble spots of a bill are known, the leaders go to work, and it is precisely at this point that the diffusion of power within each chamber makes their tasks difficult. No longer able to command, the leaders and their aides have to try hard to persuade. If they have been of service to certain members in the past, they may be able to prevail on those members to switch their votes to save a bill that otherwise would fail. It is when legislative divisions are close that the leader's parliamentary skills are put to the test. Of necessity, their influence on legislation is exerted at the margins because the structure of the legislative system denies them any stronger role.

TASK FORCES

Because the whip system has failed to produce the desired majorities in recent times, Democratic speaker Thomas P. O'Neill has resorted to ad hoc task forces to aid in the passage of key bills.[9] The idea is not new—in the past, the leadership often worked with committee leaders and representatives of interest groups in devising floor strategies. The task forces employed by O'Neill, however, are more formally constituted, with a chairman and a list of members. The technique is used only on important bills that appear headed for trouble on the floor.

The speaker appoints the chairman of the task force, usually from the committee that considers the bill. Most chairmen are junior members, partly because they are not so burdened with committee responsibilities as senior members and partly because it is the deliberate policy of the speaker to draw them into the leadership circle. By giving them responsibilities, the speaker hopes to foster in the junior members an understanding of the leadership role and the need for cooperative activity. Although he may suggest members, the speaker gives the chairman a relatively free hand in making up the task force membership.

Task force size has varied from sixteen to forty-one, with twenty-eight the average. The first consideration in the appointment of members is their commitment to the bill in question, but within that constraint, an effort is made to obtain regional, seniority, and ideological balance. The task force members are then assigned (or select) names to contact based on friendship, service together on a committee, entry in the same congressional class, or other mutual interests that may assist them in winning over votes. The belief that members will be more successful in influencing their contemporaries explains the heavily junior membership of the task forces.

The overall record of the task forces has been good: targeted legislation has been passed without the crippling amendments feared, even though some of the victories have not been as clear-cut as the leadership had hoped. Still, the task forces have been successful enough in shepherding through controversial legislation that members now request the speaker to establish task forces on bills of importance to them. Although the immediate objective of the task force is passage of a particular bill, the long-term impact of its use should also be considered. Given the interests of junior members in participating more fully in the legislative process, the task force is one way of coopting them to work in behalf of the leader and the party. And as they do, they may come to appreciate the problems of the leadership and be more willing partners in future legislation. At a minimum, the task force has proved a useful strategy in a legislative chamber marked by dispersed power.

INFORMAL HOUSE GROUPS

A number of informal groups have been organized in the House to gain a greater voice in its deliberations. A Black Caucus was formed in 1969 to promote the legislative interests of the nation's black population, and a Congresswomen's Caucus and a Hispanic Caucus were created to promote bills of interest to these groups. There is an Environmental Study Conference, as well as a Steel Caucus and a Textile Caucus. In all, there are about twenty groups, technically called legislative service organizations, each serving as a voting reference for its members. The most influential of them is the Democratic Study Group (DSG), but other strategically placed groups also play key roles in the legislative process.

The DSG was organized formally in 1959 by a group of liberal Democratic congressmen who had been meeting on an ad hoc basis since the early 1950s.[10] For more than two decades, liberal Democrats had confronted a coalition of Republicans and southern Democrats who often dominated the House. Particularly frustrating to the liberals was their failure to marshall all their potential votes. The DSG was formed to turn out their forces and to counter the influence of the conservative coalition.

The size of the DSG has ranged from 115 to over 200 members. It is headed by an elected chairman and executive committee that meets regularly to plan strategy on important legislative matters. The DSG employs a staff to research legislative issues and provides fact sheets for its members that are similar to the whip advisories. It also organizes task forces around major legislative initiatives to guide bills through committee and to prevent crippling amendments on the floor.

The DSG has devoted a substantial portion of its resources to providing adequate information to its members. It also has created its own whip organization to turn out a friendly vote on important legislation. In its "whipping" operations, the DSG has cooperated with representatives of sympathetic interest groups in getting members to the floor and influencing their vote. In recent years, the DSG has provided campaign services to its own members and to Democratic candidates challenging Republican seats. In addition to limited financial contributions, the DSG has held seminars on campaign techniques and has given challengers research reports and information on their opponents' records. These services are often an incentive for new congressmen to join the DSG.

The DSG has unquestionably increased the turnout of liberal-to-moderate Democratic congressmen on important votes, and it has improved the cohesion of this bloc. The inner circle of the DSG is united on most issues and constitutes a formidable group within the House. It was these members who led the fight for reform within the Democratic party caucus in the early 1970s. Now that the caucus is little used to discuss legislative policy, the DSG is increasing its emphasis on electoral activity as a means of enlarging its membership. In this way, it hopes to remain a powerful force in the House.

The conservative counterpart of the DSG is the Conservative Democratic Forum (CDF). Composed of approximately forty southern Democrats, the CDF organized after the 1980 elections to gain better representation of conservative interests within the Democratic party. The southerners occupied a pivotal position in the passage of Ronald Reagan's first budget and were courted by both the White House and the House Democratic leadership. Reminiscent of the older southern Democratic–Republican alliance that dominated House proceedings in the two decades following World War II, the southerners refer to themselves as the "Boll Weevils," a once pejorative label placed on them by liberal House members. The CDF poses a quandary for the leadership of both parties. Democratic leaders resent the southerners' weak party ties, and some Republicans complain that the House seats they occupy should rightfully belong to Republicans.

Conservative and liberal congressional organizations have also surfaced within the Republican party. The Wednesday Club was organized by liberal Republican members in 1963, but since its membership has never exceeded thirty, it has not constituted a major force in the House. Whatever influence it once had was vitiated by the recent conservative trend within the Republican party.

Of potentially greater influence is the more recently organized Republican Study Committee (RSC). Modeled after the DSG, the RSC researches legislative issues and coordinates conservative strategies. Because the 1980 election increased the number of conservative-leaning Republicans, the RSC was able to claim 150 members at the start of the Ninety-seventh Congress. Although too recently formed to be judged, the RSC may figure prominently in House battles of the future.

State Party Groups. State party delegations are another source of influence for House members.[11] Some delegations meet regularly to discuss matters of interest to their states; others rely less on formal meetings and more on informal contacts. New members often consult with the more senior members of their delegation in choosing committee assignments and in learning their way around the House. To the extent that state delegations act cohesively, they improve their chances of getting what they want for their state or district. But they also increase the leaders' difficulties in managing the activities of the House. And so it is with any special group that bands together to argue their interests. The more the House is split into separately organized interests, the more difficult it becomes to legislate.

The Party Role in Congressional Committee Assignments

The major work of the Congress is conducted through the standing committees. Each year, thousands of bills are introduced in one of the houses of Congress, but fewer than 10 percent ever reach the floor. The committees are responsible for deciding which bills are worthy of floor consideration. Knowing the difficulties of trying to write a bill on the floor, members respect the job the committees do. The committee structure represents the specialization of labor that enables the Congress to function as well as it does.

Although their membership is distributed on a partisan basis, the committees have not always functioned as an arm of the leadership. Nor have they been controlled by the rank and file meeting in party caucus. As we have noted, the party caucuses lost their power to control the legislative process after Woodrow Wilson's first administration. The caucuses still met at the start of each new Congress, but they had little power over the committee system. They were presented with a roster of committee members and chairmen that they could accept or reject with a single vote, but they were powerless to discipline individual committees or their chairmen.

A partisan committee on committees recommended committee slates to its caucus in each house, but the pervasive effects of seniority limited its flexibility. The position of chairman went to the majority party member with the longest service on a committee. Once in power, he could dominate his committee because he appointed all the subcommittee chairmen, selected the committee staff, and managed the bills his committee sent to the floor. The committee chairman was subservient neither to the party leadership nor to the party caucus.

HOUSE PROCEDURES

The virtual autonomy of committee chairmen, and the sometimes arbitrary fashion in which they exercised their power, instigated the reform effort of the 1970s. The movement began among House Democrats, with the DSG playing a key role. Insofar as the committee system was concerned, the goal of reformers was to regain a voice in the selection of committee chairmen and to open subcommittee chairmanships to a wider group of congressional Democrats. In both objectives, they were successful.

Before the reforms, House Democrats used the Democratic members of the Ways and Means Committee as their Committee on Committees. These members already wielded enormous power in writing tax legislation; control over committee assignments gave them extraordinary power. In a series of steps, Ways and Means was ultimately stripped of its power to act as a Committee on Committees and in its place the party put the Democratic Steering and Policy Committee. Composed of the speaker, the majority leader, the chairman of the caucus, the chief whip and his four deputies, four additional members appointed by the speaker, and twelve members elected by regions, the new committee is more accountable to both the leadership and the rank and file.

Changes were also made in the selection of committee and subcommittee chairmen. The Steering and Policy Committee recommends committee chairmen to the caucus, but the caucus now has the power to vote individually on any nomination. If the original nominations are rejected, competitive nominations can be made from the floor. Through the new procedures, three chairmen were deprived of their chairmanships in 1975. Now chairmen are not only subject to the approval of the Democratic membership but have also lost their power to appoint subcommittee chairmen. Under current practices, committee members bid for subcommittee chairmanships on the basis of seniority. The decision rests with a caucus of Democratic members on the committee. Because other rules limit Democrats to one subcommittee chair, the effect has been to diffuse power among individual Democratic members.

House Republicans use a specially constituted Committee on Committees to allocate their committee assignments. Composed of one member from each Republican state delegation, the committee uses a system of weighted voting in its deliberations: each member is allowed to cast as many votes as there are Republicans in his delegation. The reality, however, is that most decisions are made in an executive committee composed mainly of the states (such as California, Illinois, Michigan, New York, Ohio, and Pennsylvania) that have the largest number of Republican representatives.

House Republicans have been less active than their Democratic counterparts in undertaking reform. Because they have so seldom organized the House in recent history, their leaders do not possess the authority over the legislative process that Democratic leaders have. As a consequence, their members have complained less about the distribution of power within their ranks and have focused their attention on the Democratic opposition. In 1971, however, House Republicans enacted their own reform of the seniority system. Now the ranking minority member of each committee is nominated by the Committee on Committees and voted on in secret ballot at the Republican conference. Other candidates are permitted to run against the committee's choice.

SENATE REFORMS

Committee assignments in the Senate have not produced the kind of dissatisfaction that occasioned the revolt among Democratic House members. A smaller and more informal body than the House, the Senate has always permitted individual senators a greater role in its affairs. Democratic senators get their assignments from the Steering Committee, whose members are appointed by the majority leader. Since 1953, Democrats have followed the so-called Johnson rule, a practice inaugurated by Lyndon Johnson when he was majority leader. Before any senior Democrat gets a second committee assignment, every Democratic senator must receive his first committee position. The effect of the Johnson rule has been to place even freshman senators on choice committees.

The chairman of the Republican conference appoints its Committee on Committees in the Senate. Republicans followed the rigid dictates of seniority in making their assignments until 1965, when they adopted a modified version of the Johnson rule. No Republican senator can sit on more than one of the four most desired committees (Appropriations, Armed Services, Finance, or Foreign Relations) until every Republican has had the opportunity to refuse a seat.

Both Senate parties have made modifications in the way they select their chairmen or ranking members. Because of a turnabout in electoral fortunes in 1980, Republicans use the new procedures to select chairmen, and the Democrats to designate ranking members. Republican senators on a committee vote their choice as chairman, who then must be approved by their conference. Democrats use their Steering Committee to nominate ranking members, but they have provided a way to challenge any nominee. At the start of a new Congress, the proposed list of ranking members is distributed to Democratic senators. If 20 percent check any name, a secret ballot will be held on that nominee. If he is rejected by a majority, the Steering Committee must submit a second name. Although no exceptions to the seniority principle have been made by either Senate Democrats or Republicans, the senior members know that arbitrary action can bring reprisals.

Particularly in the House, the power of the leadership in dealing with committee chairs has been strengthened. In both the House and the Senate, however, the leaders are confronted by an increasingly diffused system of power. Rules changes in both chambers have resulted in the growth of subcommittees that have considerable legislative power and have spread the subcommittee chairs among a larger number of members. Committee chairmen have lost some of their influence but their loss has not been the leaders' gain. Fragmentation of congressional power has merely magnified the tasks of the party leadership.

Party Voting in Congress

The past decade has seen changes in the composition and structure of both chambers of Congress. The power of committee chairmen has been curtailed and the power of individual members has increased. At the same time, the turnover of membership in both bodies has been immense. At the start of the Ninety-sixth Congress in 1976, for example, a third of all House members were serving either their first or their second terms. The change in Senate membership has been equally dramatic: over three fifths of that body has been elected in the past ten years. Many of these new members got to Congress by forming their own electoral organizations, raising their own money, and hiring professional experts to run their campaigns. Thus they do not owe their jobs to their party. These independent-minded newcomers fit comfortably into the new setting in which the Congress operates.

The fragmentation of power within Congress has created an atmosphere in which individual members may choose the role they wish to play. The limited resources the party leaders have in marshaling their forces are scarcely sufficient to overcome the diffusion of legislative power. Yet partisan attachment does influence how members of Congress cast their votes, and an understanding of the place of partisanship in legislative divisions extends beyond the formal agencies the parties maintain to manage the legislative process.

HOW CONGRESSMEN DECIDE

Obviously individual members cannot inform themselves on all the subjects the Congress considers in a typical session because the number and substantive variety of bills are too great for any one person to master. Therefore congressmen need to simplify their decision-making responsibilities by seeking guidance from others. From whom do they seek their cues?

According to one study, the most important guidance comes from fellow congressmen and constituency interests, followed by special interest groups and the administration, in that order. Party leadership and the congressman's staff were not perceived as particularly important, nor was the information the congressman received from the mass media very influential. Most congressmen rely on multiple cues for their voting, although the sources they call upon probably vary with the substantive content of a bill.[12]

Colleagues. Fellow legislators are a natural source of voting cues for congressmen both because they are readily available and because they possess the kind of explicit information needed to cast an intelligent vote. The colleagues a congressman calls upon for aid will vary from issue to issue, but two general criteria are important in selecting whom to consult. Congressmen turn to those who share their own fundamental political values; they seek information from those who are experts in the matter under consideration, meaning that they will ask advice from a member of the committee that handled the bill in question.[13]

Constituency Interests. That congressmen are attentive to constituency interests is natural since they are ultimately accountable to the voters who placed them in office. But it is not

DOONESBURY   by Garry Trudeau

always the mass public within their district to whom congressmen cater. In fact, mass opinion alone is not rated highly as a source of voting cues.[14] Of more significance are the interest group leaders, newspaper editors, or party activists within the constituency. These elite figures are important to a congressman's popular support and their endorsements and financial contributions enhance the incumbent's reelection chances.

Interest Groups. The pervasive effects of constituency are seen in the relatively high ranking of interest groups as voting cues. Interest groups appear to have little influence on congressmen unless they are connected to their constituency in some fashion. A Washington-based lobby can apply few sanctions against an unsympathetic or uninterested congressman.[15] For this reason, interest organizations call on their local chapters or enlist others in a congressman's district to plead their cause.

Partisan Cues. The party leadership was not ranked high as a source of guidance, which is not surprising since the leaders have few sanctions to compel discipline. The sources of party voting, then, must be looked for elsewhere.

Partisanship can be explained in part because congressmen are respectful of their constituencies. Since the coalitions that support the two parties are different, by voting the interests of those who placed them in office, Democrats will generally differ from Republicans. The strengths and limitations of the constituency explanation of partisan voting can be illustrated in a crude way by examining the urban/rural dimension of congressional districts. Northern Democrats commonly represent the most urban constituencies, while Republicans are more likely elected from rural or small-town districts. Most southern Democrats also come from the less urbanized districts. Constituency differences often reinforce the party votes cast by Republicans and northern Democrats, but not southern Democrats. As a consequence, southerners often break ranks to vote with the Republicans in the so-called conservative coalition.[16]

A second explanation of party voting is found in the partisan affiliation of congressmen who are turned to for advice by other members. One of the criteria a member uses in selecting those he seeks information from is compatibility of political values. Since the party label does sort out congressmen by their political views, it is only natural for a member to turn to a fellow partisan. Table 11-1 shows the party connection between those seeking and giving advice in the U.S. House.

Partisanship in congressional roll calls is thus a complex phenomenon. The multiple cues members of Congress receive in deciding how to vote often reinforce, rather than contradict, their partisan inclinations. A congressman's partisan ties may have begun with childhood socialization[17] and dictated which party label he ran under. His success at winning office may have depended on whether a constituency normally votes Democratic or Republican. Once in office, a congressman may have little difficulty in coming to a voting decision. On the same roll call, he may vote his convictions, his constituency, and his party.

But personal convictions and constituency ties do not always mesh with the party's stand on issues. If they did, party voting in the Congress would be greater than it is. The dissonance stems in part from a lack of clarity about the party stand. Is the official party position enunciated in the platforms formulated by the national conventions? Or is the stand taken by a majority of the legislative party the measure to be used? Does the president's program constitute the party line for members of his party? Or do state organizations determine party positions for congressmen from their state? The weakness of American party structures inevitably creates ambiguity over the meaning of partisan loyalty. Nevertheless, the collec-

Table 11-1
PARTISAN PATTERNS OF CUE GIVING IN THE U.S. HOUSE OF REPRESENTATIVES

| Informant's Party | Recipient's Party | | |
	Northern Democrat	Southern Democrat	Republican
Northern Democrat	85%	14%	3%
Southern Democrat	4	51	1
Republican	0	6	71
Mixed*	11	29	25
Total %	100	100	100
Total No.	54	35	75

*When it was not possible to classify a set of named informants, even in terms of a general tendency to belong to one party grouping or another, the responses were coded as "mixed" party.

SOURCE: John W. Kingdon, *Congressmen's Voting Decisions*, 2nd ed. (New York: Harper and Row, 1981), p. 81.

tive effect of diffuse partisan influences does show up in the divisions that emerge in congressional roll calls.

PARTY COHESION IN CONGRESSIONAL VOTING

Party government in the United States was at its height from the closing decade of the nineteenth century through the first Wilson administration. During that time, either powerful leaders or the party caucuses acted to unite the legislative parties.[18] As committee chairmen emerged as important figures in the congressional process, power became less centralized and party lines were more frequently crossed. Still, partisan forces grouped around Franklin Roosevelt's New Deal proposals with some regularity during the 1930s. Then partisanship declined in the post–World War II years. Even so, voting in Congress does not take place in a random fashion.

The Prevalence of Party Voting. That partisan affiliation remains the best guide to congressmen's voting behavior is a tiresome but important truism. Table 11-2 presents a gross pic-

Table 11-2
ROLL CALL VOTES WITH OPPOSING PARTY MAJORITIES

Year	House	Senate	Both Chambers
1960	53%	37%	42%
1961	50	62	58
1962	46	41	43
1963	49	47	48
1964	55	36	41
1965	52	42	46
1966	41	50	46
1967	36	35	35
1968	35	32	33
1969	31	36	34
1970	27	35	32
1971	38	42	40
1972	27	36	33
1973	42	40	41
1974	29	44	37
1975	48	48	48
1976	36	37	37
1977	42	42	42
1978	33	45	38
1979	47	47	47
1980	38	46	41

SOURCE: *Congressional Quarterly Almanac* for each year.

ture of party voting in Congress by showing the number of times that party majorities have been on opposing sides of roll call votes. Over the past two decades, these so-called party votes have constituted between one third and almost three fifths of the roll calls taken in each session of Congress. Because American society is not divided by deep-seated ideological cleavages, more frequent party voting is neither expected nor necessary.

A more critical test of partisanship is the cohesion the parties manage when they are on the opposite sides of an issue (see Table 11-3). On the whole, discipline within the House has been marginally better than in the Senate, in keeping with the more independent spirit of the latter chamber. In neither house have the parties succeeded in uniting to face the opposition, but members have not freely crossed party lines. Nor do all members who fail to rally behind their party vote against a ma-

Table 11-3
CONGRESSIONAL PARTY UNITY*

Year	Democrats		Republicans	
	House	*Senate*	*House*	*Senate*
1960	65	60	70	64
1961	77	74	73	68
1962	70	65	70	64
1963	73	66	74	67
1964	69	61	71	65
1965	70	63	71	68
1966	62	57	68	63
1967	67	61	74	60
1968	59	51	64	60
1969	61	63	62	63
1970	58	55	60	56
1971	61	64	67	63
1972	58	66	66	61
1973	68	69	68	64
1974	62	63	63	59
1975	69	68	72	64
1976	66	62	67	61
1977	68	63	71	66
1978	63	66	69	59
1979	69	68	73	66
1980	69	64	71	65

*The percentage of times the average Democrat and Republican voted with the party majority in roll call votes with opposing party majorities. Failure to vote lowers party unity scores.

SOURCE: *Congressional Quarterly Almanac* for each year.

jority of their partisan colleagues. Many abstain. In recent Congresses, fewer than one out of four members of either House or Senate has voted against the stand taken by a majority in his or her party.

Partisan Policy Dimensions. Aggregate figures on party voting do not reveal the type of issues on which the parties are best able to unify their respective followings. To isolate the policy dimensions in which those issues fall is to know the meaning of partisanship within the Congress.

In a study covering both houses of Congress from 1953 through 1964, Aage R. Clausen was able to place 75 percent of all roll calls in one of five policy dimensions:

1. Government management of the economy.
2. Agricultural assistance.
3. Social welfare.
4. International involvement.
5. Civil liberties.

Their votes on roll calls were used to score congressmen on how supportive they were of each policy concept. Once each congressman was given a support score, its association with the member's party affiliation was ascertained.[19]

The clearest partisan split in Congress emerged over government management of the economy (see Figure 11-1). Democrats differed from Republicans regarding the regulation of business, tax and fiscal policies, and the care and use of natural resources. Agricultural assistance was another area that produced a high level of partisanship, with Democrats more favorable to farm subsidies than Republicans. To a somewhat lesser degree, social welfare policies divided Democrats and Republicans; there were partisan differences in voting for government programs to aid the jobless, the low-income, and other needy groups in society. By contrast, international involvement and civil rights issues produced far less partisan voting.

Clausen presented further evidence of an independent partisan effect in congressional decisions by examining how a constituency was represented over time under three conditions:

1. The same person held a seat over two Congresses.
2. A constituency was represented successively by different persons from the same party (personal turnover).

Figure 11-1
**PARTY AS A PREDICTOR OF VOTING ON FIVE POLICY
DIMENSIONS**

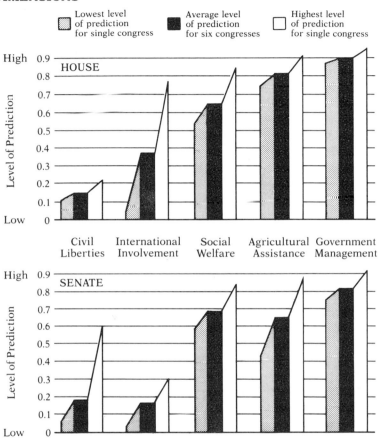

SOURCE: Aage R. Clausen, *How Congressmen Decide* (New York: St. Martin's, 1973), p. 93.

3. A congressman was succeeded by a person from a different party (partisan turnover).

If constituency interests are paramount in congressional voting, one would expect little change in how a congressional district was represented over time under any of the three conditions. If personal convictions are the key to congressional voting (and are unrelated to the party label a congressman wears), one would expect as much policy change from a personal turnover as a party turnover. If the party label is an indicator of a congressman's voting intentions, the most important changes would occur with a partisan turnover.[20]

Predictably, in both the House and the Senate, policy representation of a district was most stable under the first condition. Several factors could account for the relative stability of the policy positions taken by congressmen serving in two or more Congresses, namely, personal convictions, constituency influences, and party ties. A comparison of the changes that occurred in the two turnover conditions, however, should reveal the relative impact of partisan influences. That is, if a partisan turnover of a seat produces more change than a personal turnover, then a member's partisan ties can be said to be influential in congressional decision making.

In the areas of civil rights and international involvement, a partisan turnover produced no greater policy shifts than a personal turnover. And the shifts that did occur with a partisan exchange of seats did not follow predictable party lines. New congressmen from both parties tended to be more supportive of civil rights than the members they had replaced, whether or not a partisan turnover had occurred. Neither Democrats nor Republicans were markedly more internationally minded than their predecessors. So partisanship in these two policy areas was weak at best.

A partisan turnover produced distinctly more change than a personal turnover in the three remaining policy dimensions. The sharpest difference occurred in the area of government management of the economy, followed by social welfare and agricultural assistance, in that order. Moreover, the changes were in the expected directions in both houses of Congress. The replacement of a Republican by a Democrat commonly meant more support for government control of the economy, expanded social welfare activities, and the continuation of agricultural assistance programs. This pattern held true in reverse when Republicans displaced Democrats, although a few farm state Republicans did provide more support for agricultural assistance than the Democrats they replaced. So with constituency interests held constant, partisan influences were clearly evident in three important policy areas acted on by Congress.

Clausen's findings for the 1953–1964 period held true for Congresses of the ensuing decade.[21] Government management of the economy remained a partisan issue, although party lines were drawn somewhat less sharply than before. Social welfare and agricultural assistance also continued to produce partisan battles. As before, other voting dimensions were less inspired by partisan lines. On foreign aid, Republicans were more willing to support a Republican president, and Democrats more skeptical when it was not their man in the White House. Republicans became less supportive of civil rights as measures concerning school busing, equal job opportunities, and women's rights gained the agenda.

Two new dimensions appeared in the Ninety-first and Ninety-second Congresses. One, a minor dimension pertaining to the amounts of agricultural subsidies paid to individual farmers (not general price support levels), divided members more on urban-rural than on party lines. The other, a major dimension concerning national security commitments, arose out of the conduct of foreign policy during the Vietnam war period. It was a complex issue area involving the size of the defense budget, the appropriateness of U.S. commitments abroad, and the relative responsibilities of president and Congress in the making of foreign policy. The principal opposition to a worldwide defense capability under presidential direction came from Senate Democrats.

Government management of the economy and social welfare issues are at the core of the enduring ideological differences between the major parties. Despite the heavy turnover in Congress in recent years, the partisan debate over government's role in society continues, although the partisan divisions are not so predictable as they once were because a worrisome inflation has engendered a budget-cutting mood that even northern Democrats find hard to resist.

In the first test of strength for his administration, Ronald Reagan won handily when he proposed budget targets for fiscal 1982 that increased defense spending and cut social programs. In the Republican-dominated Senate, Minority Leader Robert Byrd made little effort to mount a Democratic opposition and the budget resolution carried easily with sizable Democratic support. Although he stated he had doubts about the Reagan priorities, Byrd voted for the resolution because "the people want to give Reagan a chance."[22] In the House, where they still had a majority, the Democrats attempted to substitute their own budget resolution for the Reagan proposal and were embarrassed when it failed to carry. Northern Democratic ranks held reasonably firm, but a majority of southern Democrats (forty-six out of seventy-eight) crossed over to join the united Republicans in rejecting the Democratic substitute. Although the northern and southern wings of the Democratic party were at odds over the Reagan program, the attitude of Democratic leaders appeared to be one of going along with the general outlines of the Reagan economic recovery program on the theory that the people would hold the Republicans accountable at a later date for what happened to jobs, prices, interest rates, housing starts, and other indicators of economic health. Party lines may have frayed somewhat, but the legislative output of the Congress under Reagan will likely be judged in partisan terms.

The Continuing Value of the Party Label. One additional fact must be kept in mind in considering the role of partisanship in Congress. Even though party ranks are broken on many roll call votes, the party label still serves as a useful guide to the voter in selecting a candidate. When the House elections of 1966 were studied with a view to comparing the political attitudes of candidates running in the same constituency, the researchers found that Democrats were more liberal (or less conservative) on domestic and foreign policy issues than the Republicans they opposed.[23] The differences were credible, even on issues where party cohesion is weak. For example, southern Democrats or northeastern Republicans may cross over to vote with the opposition more frequently than their colleagues, yet the representation of their districts would have been noticeably different if the voters had placed southern Republicans and northeastern Democrats in office. The voters in some districts may not be offered the choices they desire, but the candidates they pick will affect the aggregate balance of power within the House.

Party Influence in State Legislatures

Except in nonpartisan Nebraska, political parties play some role in the organizational and policy decisions state legislatures make. In the traditional one-party states, that role is minimal. When a party has little to fear from an organized opposition, conflict is often turned inward among contending factions, cliques, and leaders. In the South, for example, factions within the Democratic party battle for leadership positions. The Democratic party "organizes" the state legislatures only in the sense of limiting who may aspire to positions of power.

Partisan influences in the reasonably competitive states are not uniform. Party members commonly meet in caucus at the start of a new legislative session to select their leaders. In some states, however, party lines have not always held firm on the decisions reached in caucus. In two-party Illinois, for example, a bipartisan coalition once elected a member of the minority party as speaker of the house. Republicans in New York cast the decisive votes for leaders of both the Assembly and the Senate in 1965, when the majority Democrats could not agree on a single set of candidates. Nevertheless, these illustrations are the exceptions. In most two-party states, party caucuses are effective instruments for organizing the legislatures.

Party agencies in state legislatures are sometimes stronger than their counterparts in the Congress. In about a dozen states, according to one study, party caucuses meet regularly to discuss legislative issues and develop policy positions.[24] State legislative leaders often possess important formal powers that can be used for partisan purposes. The typical house speaker, for example, makes appointments to standing and select committees and controls the legislative agenda. Moreover, committees generally (there are exceptions) are not so important as competing centers of legislative power as they are in the Congress because heavy turnover reduces the number of experienced legislators and seniority is less important in the selection of committee chairmen.[25]

Even where party agencies are not strong, legislative divisions tend to follow partisan lines. The explanations are similar to those that account for party votes in the Congress. State legislators looking for cues on voting turn to their fellow partisans for guidance.[26] In many states also, the constituencies represented by Democrats and Republicans differ, so that in order to reflect their constituency interests, the two party groups vote on the opposite sides of legislative roll calls. Thus party voting is high in states where Democratic legislators represent urban, low-income, ethnic, and racially mixed constituencies, and Republicans represent middle-class, suburban, small-town, and rural districts. Inevitably, party cohesion is weaker in states where party alignments do not coincide with the socioeconomic divisions of constituencies.[27]

Partisanship is keenest where the parties represent dissimilar constituencies *and* state party organizations are strong. These conditions are often found in the urbanized and industrialized states of the Northeast, where the constituency base of party voting is strengthened by a rewards-and-punishment system available to the governor, state party officials, or the legislative leaders themselves. In states like Connecticut, Pennsylvania, New Jersey, and Rhode Island, party voting and discipline are more impressive than in the Congress.

All this being said, it would be a mistake to assume that party lines—even in the most partisan states—are regularly maintained. The degree of partisanship varies according to the issues under consideration. Predictably, matters of obvious self-interest to the parties, such as legislative organization, reapportionment, and election administration, arouse partisan loyalties. Tax bills and appropriation measures, often central to a governor's program, also frequently produce partisan voting in the competitive states. In the industrial states, labor and health and welfare issues tend to be fought out on partisan lines. The less partisan legislatures tend to divide on the same sort of issues, though the scope and intensity of the conflict are not so great. That is, more bills provoke heated party battles in the partisan legislatures and party lines are more tightly drawn.[28]

The Contemporary Parties: Congress, Congressmen, and Electoral Accountability

A paradox exists in the way the public views Congress and congressmen. Recent surveys show that citizens rate the job performance of Congress more negatively than positively. At the same time, surveys reveal that people evaluate individual congressmen, particularly House members, rather favorably. As Richard Fenno has asked, "If our congressmen are so good, how can our Congress be so bad?"[29]

The most likely explanation for the disparate survey findings is that people use different criteria for judging the work of Congress as an institution than for rating the performance of individual House members. Congress is more often evaluated on how well it solves pressing national problems, while individual representatives are judged on the basis of their personal characteristics and how well they serve constituency interests. The result is that while the American people feel

Congress is ineffectual, they seldom blame their own representatives for this ineffectuality.[30]

The available evidence suggests that senators are less esteemed than House members,[31] partly because they cannot as easily trade on their casework and constituency services to avoid accountability for their voting records. Voters are more tolerant of the issue stands of representatives than senators probably because the former have greater control over the information the public receives about them. Senators, who are more visible and whose activities are more fully covered by the media, often find themselves drawn into controversial national issues. Representatives stress their district service and build a personal base of support that is, in important respects, unrelated to their voting record. Constituency services might be improved as a result, but less time and attention are devoted to lawmaking.[32]

The voters' habit of rewarding members of the House for their district attentiveness and seldom punishing them for their voting records affects the prevailing system of legislative accountability. Only representatives from marginal districts (those that have been closely contested) may feel the effects of national political forces. Yet the turnover that occurs in those marginal districts can have important consequences for the balance of legislative power. The freshman representatives who won election with Lyndon Johnson in 1964 gave important support to his Great Society programs. In reaction to the Watergate scandals, voters replaced many Republican congressmen with liberal-leaning Democrats, and this Class of 1974 supported important reforms within Congress. And Ronald Reagan's successful attack upon the policies of Jimmy Carter in 1980 aided Republican challengers in gaining ground in the Democratic-controlled House.

The forces that produce change in the Congress are given direction by the partisan labels that individual congressmen wear. Scandals, unpopular wars, runaway inflation, and widespread unemployment are the kinds of conditions that produce electoral turnovers. Congressmen of the party occupying the White House bear the brunt of popular dissatisfactions, particularly if they are from marginal districts. These turnovers are a reflection of changes in national sentiment, so whether fair or not, the vulnerability of these congressmen from closely contested districts makes the political system more responsive.[33]

SUMMARY

Political parties bring a degree of coherence to the voting divisions that take place in Congress and most state legislatures. Only in the traditional one-party states is the party role insignificant.

At the start of a new Congress, party members in each chamber meet in caucus or conference to select their leaders and to ratify committee rosters. The caucuses are important in organizing the work of the Congress, but since the first Wilson administration, they have not been effective in establishing party policy positions. By World War I, legislative power had become decentralized. In particular, the seniority principle insulated committee chairmen from the influence of party agencies.

The caucus remained dormant until the late 1960s, when reform-minded House Democrats revitalized it to increase the power of the speaker and to make committee chairmen more responsive to the rank and file. They used the caucus in a more limited way for legislative purposes by passing nonbinding resolutions that expressed the sense of the caucus and directing Democratic members of committees to take specific actions.

Congressional Republicans charged that the Democrats were undermining the legislative process by using a party agency for policy purposes. Even Democratic committee chairmen complained that caucus resolutions were being passed before they had had a chance to hold hearings on a bill, and the Democratic leadership felt that caucus action reduced their flexibility in seeking compromises on legislation. In the face of all these complaints, and satisfied with the major procedural reforms that had been achieved, Democrats allowed the caucus to recede into the background once again. Today regular caucus meetings are sparsely attended.

Each chamber of Congress has party policy committees, but they have never served the purpose their name implies. They do meet to discuss legislative matters, but they make no pretense of establishing an overall legislative program for their respective parties. The reasons for their ineffectuality are much the same as those that have limited the role of the caucus; committee chairmen are jealous of their power, and individual members guard their independence.

The speaker of the House and the majority leader of the Senate are the chief leadership figures of the majority party. A majority leader and a chief whip aid the speaker, while the principal aide of the Senate majority leader is his whip. The leaders are responsible for scheduling legislation, devising floor strategies, and rounding up votes. When their party occupies the White House, they are expected to work closely with the president and his staff. Minority leaders in the House and Senate perform similar functions for their party.

Neither the speaker nor the majority leader possesses the sanctions to compel discipline within party ranks. Although leadership styles vary with the person occupying the office, most leaders acquire their power by providing services to individual members. They aid congressmen in obtaining committee assignments and in advancing legislation of interest to them, and, in return, expect members to support them on critical votes.

In both chambers, a whip organization assists the leaders in rounding up votes. Because it must contact more members, the House whip system is more highly developed. Assistant whips poll the membership to determine how they stand on pending legislation and to try to uncover the trouble spots of a bill. The intelligence they gather is often used by the leadership to change objectionable features of a bill or to delay its consideration until additional votes can be lined up, as well as to discover where best to apply pressure to get the bill passed.

Party leaders are hampered by the dispersal of power within the Congress. The major work of Congress is conducted through committees and subcommittees, and although committee chairmen are chosen on a partisan basis, they have often proved reluctant to ally themselves with the floor leadership. In both chambers, committee operations have been made more democratic and committee chairmen more responsive to the party membership, but the net effect of these reforms has been to increase the importance of individual members and thus further diffuse power.

Fragmentation of power has created a situation in which individual members of Congress may choose the role they wish to play, yet their party affiliation does influence how they vote more often than not. The reasons extend beyond the mechanisms the parties maintain to build party unity.

Since members cannot acquire detailed knowledge of all the legislation that comes before Congress, they seek guidance in their decision making, usually from sources that reinforce rather than contradict their partisan inclinations. One of the most important sources is fellow congressmen. Members generally turn for advice to colleagues whose political views are most compatible with their own, and this may partly explain party voting because Democrats differ noticeably from Republicans in their political attitudes. Another important source of cues on voting is the member's constituency. Because different coalitions support each party, party voting often results when congressmen vote their constituencies.

The cues received from fellow partisans and constituents, however, do not regularly produce party votes. Over the past two decades, party majorities have been on the opposite side of roll call votes on from one third to almost three fifths of the votes taken in any session of Congress, but in neither house have the parties consistently been able to unite their members in facing the opposition. Some members abstain from voting, and nearly one in four will cross over to vote with the opposition party.

On some issues, however, party ranks are fairly well maintained. The sharpest divisions have occurred over government management of the economy; Democrats disagree with Republicans about the regulation of business, tax and fiscal policies, and the care and use of natural resources. Social welfare issues have also divided the parties, with Democrats favoring aid to the jobless, the low-income, and other needy groups in society and Republicans opposing it. And Democrats have been more favorable to farm subsidies than Republicans. By contrast, civil rights and foreign policy issues have produced fewer partisan controversies.

Party agencies in some state legislatures are stronger than in the Congress. In about a dozen states, caucuses meet regularly to discuss legislative issues and to define party positions. State legislative leaders often have more power than their congressional counterparts in making committee assignments and scheduling legislation, and committees are generally not so important as competing power centers. Heavy turnover reduces the number of experienced legislators, and seniority is less important in the selection of committee chairmen.

Even where party agencies are not strong, the diffuse effects of partisanship are felt in state legislatures. The collegiality of party membership and the constituency base of voting, as in the Congress, produce party votes. Only in the one-party legislatures is the party role minimal. In the industrialized states of the Northeast, dissimilar constituencies and strong party organizations combine to produce a high level of legislative partisanship.

The available evidence suggests that voters evaluate the Congress as an institution and individual congressmen by different criteria: Congress is judged by how well national issues are met, while congressmen are judged on their personal attributes and how well they serve constituency interests. Nevertheless, the party label gives direction to the national forces that produce congressional turnovers in that congressmen of the party occupying the White House receive the brunt of popular dissatisfactions. Thus the political system is made more responsive to national sentiments.

Notes

[1]For an excellent discussion of a congressman's constituency ties, see David R. Mayhew, *Congress: The Electoral Connection* (New Haven, Conn.: Yale University Press, 1974).

[2]Randall B. Ripley, *Party Leaders in the House of Representatives* (Washington, D.C.: The Brookings Institution, 1967), p. 141.

[3]Daniel M. Berman, *In Congress Assembled* (New York: Macmillan, 1964), p. 226.

[4]For a description of the reform movement, see Norman J. Ornstein and David W. Rohde, "Political Parties and Congressional Reform," in *Parties and Elections in an Anti-Party Age*, ed. Jeff Fishel (Bloomington: Indiana University Press, 1978), pp. 280–294.

[5]Until they abolished the rule in 1977, Democrats could also bind their members on a floor vote if a caucus resolution passed by a two-thirds majority. This technique was used in 1971 to amend House rules on minority staffing.

[6]For a discussion of the problem, see Christopher J. Deering and Steven S. Smith, "Majority Party Leadership and the New House Subcommittee System" (Paper presented at The Dirksen Center's Conference on Understanding Congressional Leadership, Washington, D.C., June 10–11, 1980).

[7]On the changing structure of power in the Senate, see Norman J. Ornstein, Robert L. Peabody, and David W. Rohde, "The Changing Senate: From the 1950s to the 1970s," in *Congress Reconsidered*, ed. Lawrence C. Dodd and Bruce I. Oppenheimer (New York: Praeger, 1977), pp. 3–20.

[8]See Randall B. Ripley, "The Party Whip Organizations in the United States House of Representatives," *American Political Science Review* 58 (September 1964), especially pp. 570–574.

[9]The following discussion is taken from Barbara Sinclair, "The Speaker's Task Force as a Leadership Strategy for Coping with the Post-Reform House"

(Paper delivered at the annual meeting of the American Political Science Association, Washington, D.C., August 28–31, 1980).

[10]For an account of the DSG, see Arthur G. Stevens, Jr., Arthur H. Miller, and Thomas E. Mann, "Mobilization of Liberal Strength in the House, 1955–1970: The Democratic Study Group," *American Political Science Review* 68 (June 1974), pp. 667–681. The discussion that follows is based heavily on this article.

[11]On the cohesion of state party delegations in the House, see Barbara Deckard, "State Party Delegations in the U.S. House of Representatives—A Comparative Study of Group Cohesion," *Journal of Politics* 34 (February 1972), pp. 199–222.

[12]John W. Kingdon, *Congressmen's Voting Decisions*, 2nd ed. (New York: Harper and Row, 1981), pp. 17–23.

[13]Ibid., pp. 77.

[14]Ibid., p. 33.

[15]Ibid., pp. 150–153.

[16]Ibid., pp. 120–121. See also Lewis A. Froman, Jr., *Congressmen and Their Constituencies* (Chicago: Rand McNally, 1963), esp. chap. 7.

[17]Aage R. Clausen, *How Congressmen Decide* (New York: St. Martin's Press, 1973), p. 123.

[18]For evidence that constituency differences also accounted for the high level of party voting, see David W. Brady and Phillip Althoff, "Party Voting in the U.S. House of Representatives 1890–1910: Elements of a Responsible Party System," *Journal of Politics* 36 (August 1974), pp. 753–775.

[19]Clausen, *How Congressmen Decide*, esp. chaps. 2, 3, and 5.

[20]Ibid., chap. 6.

[21]See Aage R. Clausen and Carl E. Van Horn, "The Congressional Response to a Decade of Change: 1963–1972," *Journal of Politics* 39 (August 1977), pp. 624–666.

[22]Quoted in David S. Broder, "The Senate's Poker-Faced Democrats," *The Washington Post*, May 17, 1981, p. D7.

[23]John L. Sullivan and Robert E. O'Connor, "Electoral Choice and Popular Control of Public Policy: The Case of the 1966 House Elections," *American Political Science Review* 66 (December 1972), pp. 1256–1268.

[24]Belle Zeller, ed., *American State Legislatures* (New York: Crowell, 1954), p. 194.

[25]William J. Keefe and Morris S. Ogull, *The American Legislative Process: Congress and the States* (Englewood Cliffs, N.J.: Prentice-Hall, 1977), pp. 191–193.

[26]Samuel C. Patterson, "American State Legislatures and Public Policy," in *Politics in the American States*, 3rd ed., ed. Herbert Jacob and Kenneth N. Vines (Boston: Little, Brown, 1976), p. 183.

[27]See Hugh L. LeBlanc, "Voting in State Senates: Party and Constituency Influences," *Midwest Journal of Political Science* 13 (February 1969), pp. 33–57.

[28]Ibid., pp. 40–42.

[29]Richard F. Fenno, Jr., "If, as Ralph Nader Says, Congress Is 'The Broken Branch,' How Come We Love Our Congressmen So Much?", in *Congress in Change: Evolution and Reform*, ed. Norman J. Ornstein (New York: Praeger, 1975), p. 278.

[30]Roger H. Davidson, "Why Do Americans Love Their Congressmen So Much More Than Their Congress?", *Legislative Studies Quarterly* 4 (February 1979), pp. 54–58.

[31]Alan I. Abramowitz, "A Comparison of Voting for U.S. Senator and Representative in 1978," *American Political Science Review* 74 (September 1980), p. 639.

[32]Morris P. Fiorina, *Congress: Keystone of the Washington Establishment* (New Haven: Yale University Press, 1977), pp. 61–62.

[33]Ibid., p. 31.

12

Parties in the Executive Branch

It is common to characterize American political parties as basically decentralized institutions. Insofar as the formal party organizations are concerned, this view is not far wide of the mark, for the national committees and their headquarters staffs have but a limited impact upon party politics. Yet it is misleading to think of parties in such a restricted sense because electoral politics in the United States are more nationally than locally inspired.

The forces that are most important in developing and changing long-term partisan loyalties are primarily national in character.[1] The Democrats were led to power by Franklin Roosevelt in 1932, and many of the elements of the coalition that he put together remain intact today because the party images developed during the 1930s still color partisan perceptions. The resulting national alignments have more affected the divisions within state politics than the reverse. Rather than extending upward from the local level, political alignments extend downward from the national level.

The presidency is the focal point of American national politics. Only the president and vice president are elected by a national constituency, and only the president can hope to coordinate the diverse elements that rally to a party's banner. The congressional parties lack the centralized leadership necessary to constitute a powerful force in the party affairs of the nation. Because they are inclined to respond to the personal character and district visibility of individual congressmen, voters do not have a well-developed sense of a party's congressional role. They look to the president to solve the nation's problems; they expect him to fight inflation, reduce unemployment, maintain a flourishing world trade, promote world peace, and protect the quality of American life. Insofar as voters react to national events in partisan terms, the president is the chief object of their attention. In this sense, the president's program is the party's program. His successes and failures are the party's successes and failures. In both the long term and the short term, what presidents do when they hold office affects the electoral value of the party label for all who share it.

The President and the Party Connection

The national party came into existence as a mechanism to nominate presidential candidates, and national party organizations remain largely an arena of presidential politics. The primary purpose of a national convention is to choose (or ratify the choice of) a presidential candidate. Although national conventions also adopt party platforms, they have only the

significance a presidential candidate accords them. The winning candidate can write the planks he wants and ignore those that are imposed on him. He may make concessions to unify the convention, but if he wins the office, he will have a free hand in selecting his policy initiatives.

Events have diminished the president's ties to formally constituted party organizations. The changes in presidential nominating practices discussed in Chapter 7 have subordinated the role of political professionals and the party's officeholders in the selection of a presidential candidate. The bargaining that once took place as a prelude to picking a nominee built coalitions that helped a president not only to win office but, after he gained power, to deliver on the commitments made in the bargaining process as well.

Winning the nomination today involves direct appeals to voters in presidential primaries and open caucuses. Candidates still seek the endorsement of long-time party leaders, but their backing is less critical because they no longer have the power to confer the nomination. With the decision resting in a mass electorate, the process is more fluid. Candidates' appeals to the public lack the specificity and *quid pro quo* aspect of arrangements made in the privacy of the smoke-filled rooms.

Presidential candidates now form their own organizations to win the nomination, and the same teams direct the general election campaigns. After having relied on a personal organization throughout the electoral season, the president leans on his key political advisers to organize his administration. He tends to neglect the party organizations in place at the time of his rise to power, except insofar as they may be helpful to him. He picks the national party chairman, but his choice is not predicated on reestablishing ties with the organizational leaders he bypassed on his way to the White House. A national chairman thus chosen sees his task as one of strengthening the president's personal power rather than overseeing the work of party building. Much of the estrangement of recent presidents from their party can be explained by how they have won and maintained control of their office.

At the same time, the president cannot escape the fact that he is a partisan figure. After all, he was nominated by a political party. He needs his party, and his party needs him. So he meets regularly with his party's congressional leaders to plan his legislative strategies and relies on the popular support the party's traditional following gives him. For their part, party leaders and followers recognize the president's vast power in setting national priorities, managing crises, and making hundreds of executive and judicial appointments. As their man in the White House, the president is in a position to do them favors and to help out with any problems that arise in their states and cities.

The president does not lead a well-disciplined army as he strives to achieve the policy goals he has set for his administration. Rather he must fashion his power out of the resources at his command. How he finds support for his legislative programs and directs the immense executive establishment will be discussed in the following pages. What must be stressed here is that the president is the leading figure of his party and what he says and does in office goes a long way in defining partisan issues in the nation. Though state and local party figures may not like the turn of events that has diminished their influence, they have little choice but to adapt to the changed set of circumstances.

The President as Legislative Leader

The basic constitutional arrangement of separated powers poses obstacles to the president in securing passage of his legislative program. In contrast to the parliamentary system in which the prime minister is selected by a legislative majority, the American system provides for the independent election of chief executives and legislatures. Although candidates of both branches share party labels, they cannot always successfully bridge the gap created by the separation of powers.

When legislative caucuses made executive nominations, the effects of the constitutionally mandated separation of branches were far less severe.[2] From 1800 through 1824, all presidential successions were affected in some way by Congress. Either the choice of the Republican caucus succeeded to the presidency or, in the elections of 1800 and 1824, the House chose the president. Through the leadership of Alexander Hamilton in Washington's Cabinet and then Thomas Jefferson as president, the relations between the two national branches was one of executive dominance. After Jefferson, power shifted to the Congress and its Republican caucus. In both situations, however, there was a fusion rather than a separation of powers. Had the congressional caucus retained its power over presidential nominations, the separation of the two branches envisaged by the framers of the Constitution would have been seriously eroded.

The failure of Andrew Jackson to gain approval of congressional insiders in the 1824 election (see Chapter 7) brought an end to caucus nominations. After being nominated by the Tennessee legislature in 1828, Jackson gained the presidency through the efforts of a well-organized popular movement. From that point onward, Congress no longer had an institutional role in presidential nominations. The delegate conventions that replaced the legislative caucuses became the new focus of those seeking a presidential nomination. Presidents had an independent base of political power, and the principle of separation was finally achieved.

During most of the nineteenth century, Congress jealously guarded its constitutional prerogative to legislate for the nation.[3] With the exception of Jefferson, Jackson, and Abraham Lincoln, presidents only occasionally took the initiative in sponsoring legislative proposals and working for their passage. A more active legislative role for the president is largely a twentieth-century phenomenon. Both Theodore Roosevelt and Woodrow Wilson sought to guide the Congress in enacting their legislative programs and, aided by strong congressional leaders and disciplined legislative parties, each scored notable successes.

Republican presidents of the 1920s were less inclined to intervene in congressional deliberations. Although Calvin Coolidge and Herbert Hoover each sent legislation to the Congress, neither was temperamentally or philosophically inclined to assume an active leadership role. Franklin Roosevelt stood in marked contrast to his immediate predecessors, partly because the troubled times demanded strong leadership, and partly because Roosevelt reveled in the exercise of political power. Under his leadership, the White House became actively involved in drafting major legislative proposals and pushing them through the Congress.

Beginning with Roosevelt, all presidents have recognized the need to exert legislative leadership to secure the goals they set for their administrations. Congress now expects a president and his staff to set the priorities that will determine their deliberations. But to say that the president gives Congress its agenda is not the same as saying that the president can easily accomplish his legislative objectives. Power in Congress is dispersed and decentralized, and presidents have to fight for their legislation. Like the leaders of the legislative parties, the president has no power to command discipline from his partisan colleagues in House and Senate. He must skillfully exploit the resources he possesses to construct legislative majorities.

THE PARTISAN BRIDGE

A system of separated powers introduces divisive factors into the party system, but the party system also acts to modify the formal separation of the branches of government. Most members of Congress have a loyalty to the chamber they serve and are protective of its role in the constitutional system. Even the members of the president's party are unwilling to surrender their legislative prerogatives in cooperating with the president on goals jointly held. The long-standing rivalry between the two branches is evident in the post-Watergate suspicion that Congress holds of the presidency. Congressmen do not necessarily fear a strong president; they merely want to ensure that they exercise an independent legislative role.

At the same time, the most important source of legislative influence the president has is the label he shares with the congressional members of his party. When a president comes to

CONGRESSIONAL STROKIN' TIME

power, a substantial number of his fellow partisans in Congress already stand committed to his basic political orientation. They may differ on details, but they will be responsive to his call for cooperation in enacting his legislative program. Others in his party will be more skeptical of his legislative initiatives and may be hard to win over. On critical votes, the White House staff will use the full resources of the presidency in trying to bring them into line.

The dual loyalty of congressmen is reflected in the attitudes of congressional party leaders. When his party controlled the White House, former Senate Majority Leader Robert C. Byrd declared that "I'm the president's friend, I'm not the president's man. . . . I certainly intend to give my utmost cooperation to the president. . . . I must also keep in mind that I am a Senate man and I am the Senate leader. . . ."[4] House Speaker Thomas P. O'Neill echoed this attitude in discussing his relations with President Carter. After declaring that he was a "partisan Democrat" and that Carter was the leader of his party, O'Neill went on to say that he also was "a strong man for the prerogatives of the House."[5] The prerogatives he referred to involved consultation with the president on the legislative agenda.

CONGRESSIONAL LIAISON

At the start of each new session of Congress, the president travels up Pennsylvania Avenue to Capitol Hill to deliver his State of the Union message. A presidential budget message and economic report to Congress shortly follow. As the session gets under way, additional messages flow from the White House to Capitol Hill, most accompanied by detailed legislative proposals drafted by the president's staff or agency personnel. In this way, the president sets down his legislative priorities.

The process of selling the president's legislative proposals to Congress is now institutionalized.[6] Although key White House aides in the Roosevelt and Truman administrations maintained congressional contacts, a specific White House unit devoted to congressional liaison was a product of the Eisenhower administration. Confronted by a Democratically controlled Congress for most of his two terms in office, Eisenhower needed to establish friendly relations on the Hill. Partly as a consequence of the divided party control of executive and legislative branches, Eisenhower's liaison staff followed a soft-sell approach.

Liaison activities under John Kennedy and Lyndon Johnson were more assertive. Each of these presidents sent legislation to the Congress that embodied far-reaching social reforms. To get their programs through the Congress required more active lobbying efforts by the White House. Allowing for differences in presidential style and temperament, the Kennedy-Johnson expansion of the liaison role has been followed by later presidents. The liaison role has become more formalized and certain practices and activities have become accepted.

Lobbying activities to build congressional support begin at the top and take a variety of forms. A president commonly schedules weekly or biweekly breakfast meetings with his congressional party leaders when Congress is in session. Important administration personnel hold briefings for large groups of congressmen. Social events to which congressmen and their wives are invited afford opportunities for informal conversation with the president. Personal meetings with committee chairmen or other key legislative figures are arranged. And when critical votes are scheduled, the president telephones wavering congressmen to ask for their support. Often working in concert with the congressional party whips, the White House liaison office advises the president on how and when to bring his influence to bear.

The White House is in the position to perform a variety of services for members of Congress on matters both large and small. Congressmen want federal projects and defense contracts in their districts, turn to the president when natural disasters strike their states, and ask for presidential assistance to aid troubled industries. Timely White House intervention has forestalled the closing of military installations important to a state or district. Patronage appointments are a traditional source of partisan favoritism. When a government contract is let, the announcement is made by a member of the president's party whose state or district stands to benefit. Tickets for the early-morning tours of the White House are set aside to accommodate visitors from a congressman's district. In these and other ways, the White House displays its goodwill toward members of Congress.

These examples are not meant to create the impression that the president and his aides crudely swap favors for votes. The president might extend himself for his most loyal supporters, but he seldom employs negative sanctions. With the aid of his liaison office, he tries to be helpful to as many congressmen as he can reasonably accommodate, hoping in this way to create an atmosphere of mutual respect. Once he has succeeded in establishing amicable relations, the president can work with his party's legislative leaders in lining up the votes he needs. Given the electoral independence of congressmen, more heavy-handed tactics would likely have unfortunate consequences. Friendly persuasion, not threats, is the key to effective liaison work.

THE RECORD OF PRESIDENTIAL SUPPORT

Determining the support a president receives for his legislative program on a quantifiable basis is fraught with difficulties. Some bills are more important to the president than others. If he is successful with bills of a minor character but consistently loses battles over those that are essential to his program, he scarcely can be satisfied with the results. Yet his record may show more victories than defeats. At the same time, it must be noted that some presidents are more aggressive in making demands on the Congress. If a president submits legislation guaranteed to produce controversy, and then gets only part of what he asked for, his box score may compare unfavorably with that of presidents who shied away from bold new legislative ventures. Nevertheless, if caution is used in the interpretation of the data, some basic patterns emerge that are useful in understanding the president's legislative role.

How successful a president is in winning floor fights in the Congress is related to partisanship. Presidents whose own party controls the Congress have an easier time than those who face opposition party majorities (see Figure 12-1). The best record of any president in recent years belongs to Lyndon Johnson in 1965. With their ranks swelled as a result of the 1964 election, Democrats helped Johnson in winning 93 percent of the votes in which he had a personal stake. Richard Nixon in 1973 owns the worst record. Confronted by a Congress with comfortable Democratic majorities and troubled by the growing Watergate scandal, Nixon received congressional approval for his position only slightly more than half the time.

The presidencies of Gerald Ford and Jimmy Carter offer an interesting contrast that supports the partisan character of congressional decisions. Ford came from a congressional background—he had been the minority leader of his party in the House and was personally liked by members on both sides of the aisle. Carter was a Washington outsider whose mercurial

Figure 12-1
PRESIDENTIAL SUCCESS ON VOTES 1953–1980*

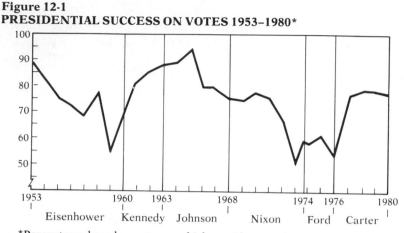

*Percentages based on votes on which presidents took a position.
SOURCE: *Congressional Quarterly Weekly Report*, January 3, 1981, p. 38.

rise to become his party's candidate surprised many experienced political observers. Despite his initial ineptitude in handling congressional relations, however, Carter won three out of four congressional votes on issues on which he took a clear stand during his four years in office. With an average success rate of 58 percent, Ford's record was less impressive. The explanation is straightforward. Carter worked with a Democratic Congress, but Ford's party was in the minority in both the House and the Senate.

Although a president enjoys greater support when his party is in control of Congress, not all his party colleagues in the House and the Senate will be willing to back his legislative

Table 12-1
AVERAGE PARTISAN SUPPORT OF DEMOCRATIC PRESIDENTS

	Kennedy (1961–1963)	Johnson (1964–1968)	Carter (1977–1980)
Democrats			
House	63%	69%	62%
Senate	64	59	66
Republicans			
House	37	43	38
Senate	40	47	46

SOURCE: Derived from George C. Edwards III, *Presidential Influence in Congress* (San Francisco: Freeman, 1980), pp. 192–193. 1980 data from *Congressional Quarterly Weekly Report*, January 3, 1981, p. 39.

Table 12-2
AVERAGE PARTISAN SUPPORT OF REPUBLICAN PRESIDENTS*

	Eisenhower (1953–1960)	Nixon (1969–1973)	Ford (1975–1976)
Democrats			
House	49%	46%	35%
Senate	45	43	43
Republicans			
House	65	64	63
Senate	69	64	66

*Because of the change of administration in 1974, the figures for that year are excluded.

SOURCE: Derived from George C. Edwards III, *Presidential Influence in Congress* (San Francisco: Freeman, 1980), pp. 201–202.

endeavors. Tables 12-1 and 12-2 show the partisan patterns in congressional support of presidents since 1953. Clearly, Democratic presidents can normally count on the support of a majority of their congressional partisans, just as Republican presidents can expect to be supported by a majority of their party's congressional members. It is just as clear, however, that party ranks are not perfectly mobilized for or against a president, so even a president whose party holds a congressional majority must enlist support from the opposition. But the same looseness of party ties eases his task of building legislative majorities. President Carter, for example, often received the support of the more liberal members of the Republican party to add to his Democratic party base.[7]

The extent to which a president wins votes by his parliamentary skills and mastery of the legislative process is disputed. For example, Lyndon Johnson's legislative successes in the Eighty-ninth Congress have been widely attributed to his leadership skills. His immediate Democratic predecessor, John Kennedy, enjoyed less success in getting the legislation he wanted. It was said that while Kennedy was an inattentive senator, Johnson had honed his legislative skills while majority leader and was therefore better equipped to deal with Congress.

A closer examination of Johnson's record does not provide clear evidence of his superiority as a legislative tactician.[8] The Eighty-ninth Congress with which Johnson was so successful had more Democrats than Kennedy's Eighty-seventh Congress. But this was not the whole story. Johnson's Democratic contingent was composed of more northern and fewer southern

Democrats than Kennedy's. Because northern Democrats consistently give their president more support than their southern colleagues, Johnson started with an advantage. He got no greater cohesion from either group than Kennedy, but he had more Democratic votes behind him. Had his fabled "arm-twisting" tactics and bargaining skills been critical to his legislative successes, they should have produced greater unity among *either* the northern *or* southern members of his party.

Additional evidence points up the limited influence that presidents have in selling their legislative programs. Surveys made of congressmen show that they rate administration spokesmen low as voting cues.[9] Moreover, congressmen show considerable stability in their voting behavior across Congresses. One study followed congressional voting over two partisan turnovers of the presidency, from Eisenhower to Kennedy-Johnson to Nixon. In domestic policy areas (management of the economy, agricultural assistance, social welfare, and civil rights), a partisan change in administration had little influence on the positions taken by congressmen who served under two or more presidents. The same was not true of international issues, but the changes that occurred in this area were more partisan in character than a result of a president's leadership skills. When their own party controlled the presidency, members of both the House and the Senate either retained or moved toward a position of support for international involvement.[10]

Still, one cannot conclude that presidential leadership has no effect on the policy positions taken by congressmen. A president may concentrate his efforts on a few critical votes that involve the most important legislation he has submitted. He may save a high-priority bill by turning around the votes of ten to fifteen congressmen. In 1967, for example, 17 percent of Johnson's House victories were decided by a margin of twenty-five votes or less.[11] When the margins are close, both the president and his congressional party leaders, if they have the skill, can turn the balance of forces into a partisan victory. Nevertheless, the president does not have unlimited flexibility in picking the bills whose passage he can affect, for how closely a chamber divides on any issue is determined by other factors.

Presidential Influence in Perspective. Presidential influence on congressional voting behavior must be placed in perspective. Although aggregate voting statistics may understate the influence a president exerts on individual legislation, these summary data cannot be dismissed out of hand for two reasons. In the first place, most analysts argue that a president strives to build goodwill toward his administration in the Congress and does not swap "dams for votes" on an ad hoc basis.[12] If this is the case, the goodwill generated should show up in support across the board for administration programs, particularly from the president's own party. In the second place, the overall pattern of support received by a president will determine how effectively he can use his legislative skills. He can only hope to turn defeats into victories if the votes are reasonably close to begin with.

Recent Republican presidents have had difficulty in enacting their programs because, except for the Eighty-third Congress of Dwight Eisenhower, they have faced opposition party control of the Congress.[13] The exception is Ronald Reagan, who obtained the massive tax and spending cuts he wanted for fiscal 1982 despite Democratic control of the House. It is important to keep Reagan's early victories in perspective, however. He was aided by southern Democrats who historically have been more conservative than their northern colleagues. And Democratic congressmen are unlikely to forego their role as the opposition party completely. Confronted by a choice of a larger-than-predicted budget deficit and a second round of spending cuts, Reagan's leadership will be put to the test in the remainder of his administration.

In this same vein, the relative successes of Democratic presidents stem from the fact that they have had to contend with a Republican organized Congress only once since 1933. But at the same time, Democratic presidents have been experiencing increasing problems even when their party enjoys a majority in both houses. Not only has the southern wing of the Democratic party often been unreceptive to presidential leadership, but the support of northern Democrats in the House has declined steadily from Kennedy to Johnson to Carter.

Several factors explain this erosion of support. The turnover of members of Congress has been unusually heavy in recent years, and the new members have not served the years of apprenticeship common to their predecessors. Also, reforms in the House have given junior members a more active role and they no longer easily fall into line at the bidding of the president or of their own legislative leaders. "It is not that the president is lacking in leadership," Majority Leader Jim Wright said of Jimmy Carter, "it is that this group does not want to be led.

They are lacking in followship."[14] Despite all these changes, one central fact remains: the partisan setting in Congress will either facilitate or restrain a president's legislative leadership.

The President as Leader of the Executive Establishment

Fulfilling partisan commitments by gaining control of the executive branch and giving direction to its policy decisions may be as difficult for the president as securing passage of his legislative proposals. The president presides over an administrative establishment that has swelled to three million civilian employees and two million uniformed servicemen. The sheer size of the work force he directs prevents him from intervening in administrative matters on a continuing basis. When he does, he may find that the arts of compromise and negotiation are as valuable in dealing with his administration as with his legislature.

Although theoretically he commands his subordinates, the president does not have an easy time convincing executive departments and agencies to follow his lead. They are staffed with career employees, civilian and military, who have developed a tradition and policy outlook of their own that is not easily shed. Often an administrative agency will be protective of its responsibilities and resist all presidential efforts to impose unwanted policies. And these administrative agencies have their congressional allies, for the committee structure of Congress parallels the organization of the executive branch and committee members and their staffs develop agency relationships that bypass presidential control.

Executive agencies have wide discretion under the laws they administer. They also are the source of new ideas concerning the programs that have been given to them. The concept of a neutrally competent civil service ready to implement policies determined from above was refuted long ago. Administrative agencies are important participants in the policymaking process and their decisions must be supervised by the president if he wishes to control the government he heads.

It is through his power of appointment that the president attempts to establish control over the executive establishment. Because there is no pool of talented partisans within the executive branch who can be placed in positions of power at every partisan turnover of administrations, incoming presidents usually appoint special personnel selection teams to prepare lists of possible appointees. Choices for the highest positions are made during the hectic postelection months before the president takes office, when time does not permit careful consideration of all appointments. Many positions are left to be filled by the Cabinet secretaries. Far from the orderly procedures of the Congress, the partisan organization of the executive branch is accomplished in a haphazard fashion that leaves a president vulnerable to hasty and unwise appointments.

THE CABINET

The manner in which appointments are made to high-level government offices illustrates the relationship of the president to his party. While there is no regularized party machinery to help the president in choosing departmental secretaries and agency heads, partisan considerations are important in two ways. First, appointments normally go only to members of the president's party. Second, the president's choices will reflect regional and factional interests traditionally associated with his party. Otherwise, the president is constrained only by the availability of candidates and the special claims that certain groups are recognized to have on Cabinet-level appointments. Cabinet secretaries, for example, must generally be acceptable to the clientele groups their departments serve.

From the standpoint of the president's personal power, two additional considerations guide his choices. He needs people with political and administrative skills who will bring credit to his administration or, at a minimum, who will not embarrass him. And he would like his appointees to be personally loyal to him and his policies.

Within the time constraints confronting a newly elected president, it is difficult to satisfy all the criteria for making presidential selections. For this reason, few modern presidents have used their Cabinet to frame the major outlines of their policies.

A president usually gives careful consideration to certain Cabinet-level appointments. Because of his constitutional responsibilities in foreign affairs and national defense, a president takes special pains over his appointments to the Defense and State departments. Treasury and Justice are other departments that claim careful attention. Together with key White House staff counselors, the heads of these four departments have been called the "Inner" Cabinet. The "Outer" Cabinet consists of domestic departments and agencies such as Labor, Commerce, Agriculture, Interior, Health and Human Services (HHS), Housing and Urban Development (HUD), Education, and Transportation. Because the Outer Cabinet departments are viewed by the White House as representative or advocacy agencies, the president has less leeway in choosing their heads and seldom includes them among his intimate circle of advisers.[15]

Clearly the circumstances surrounding the appointment of department heads do not create a team of partisan advisers to run the country. The idea of Cabinet government is foreign to American practice anyway (the Constitution makes no mention of a Cabinet as such). Nevertheless, presidents have followed the practice of meeting with their department heads and, more recently, certain White House counselors, and this group has been labeled the Cabinet. Although some presidents have held more frequent meetings than others, no recent presidents have used their Cabinet to make major policy decisions. Even the Eisenhower Cabinet, though it held almost weekly meetings and had a secretariat to prepare its agenda, neither formulated nor decided policy.[16]

The idea of the Cabinet as a representative group of fellow partisans who assist the president in shaping broad policy outlines has a certain appeal. It also has certain practical difficulties. For one, many department heads have not been active in party politics and are politically naïve. For another, the separatist tendencies and disparate programs of the agencies they lead precludes Cabinet collegiality.

It was for the latter reason that Ronald Reagan devised a system of five Cabinet councils to involve his Cabinet officers in major policy deliberations. Each council is chaired by the president, but sessions can also be convened by the leading Cabinet members. To provide coordination with other presidential advisers, a senior White House staffer serves as executive secretary of each panel. At this writing, it is too early to judge the feasibility of the Reagan plan.

Modern presidents have relied increasingly on their White House staff as their administrations have unfolded. The programs presidents have backed have been thought of as party programs, but the policies they have advanced have been largely their own choices made in consultation with a handful of loyal advisers.

THE EXECUTIVE OFFICE OF THE PRESIDENT

The growth in the size and responsibilities of the national government has necessitated an increase in the president's personal staff. At the turn of the century, a president got by with a few stenographers and clerks and a handful of personal assistants. Even the members of Franklin Roosevelt's celebrated "brain trust" were technically employed by executive agencies and not paid as presidential assistants. Upon the recommendation of a blue ribbon committee on administrative management, however, the Congress created the Executive Office of the President (EOP) in 1939 to aid the president. Today the EOP is a miniature bureaucracy with over five thousand employees.

Besides the White House Office, the EOP includes the Office of Management and Budget, the National Security Council, the Council of Economic Advisers, the Office of Policy Development, and several other staff units. Each of these groups performs important tasks for the president. The Office of Management and Budget, for example, coordinates the preparation of the budget and also acts as a clearing house for legislation originating in executive agencies. The director of the budget became a key figure early in the Reagan administration and was even given Cabinet status. Over the years, however, the president's principal advisers have worked in the White House Office.

The people on the White House staff are chosen for their personal loyalty to the president and not to placate party factions or interest groups. Often drawn from the president's campaign organization, key White House aides have both political and policy functions to perform. They oversee relations with the Congress, the press, and important party and interest group leaders. They advise the president on domestic and foreign policies, and several of them serve dual functions by heading another unit of the EOP. The White House staff has become institutionalized and comprises approximately five hundred employees, who cannot all have the ear of the president. Nevertheless, they come as close to a partisan team of advisers as the president has.

Tensions often develop between the president's personal aides and Cabinet officers. From the White House point of view, the agencies represent a particularistic conception of public policies. Influenced by the career civil servants under their command, agency heads soon become advocates of the programs they are called upon to administer. The president must consider the competing claims of several departments in fashioning his policy stands, and he turns to his loyal aides for advice on settling conflicts that arise within his administration. Because he does, some of his Cabinet officers feel isolated from the president in managing their departments.

THE BUREAUCRACY

The problems the president confronts in managing the executive departments do not arise solely from conflicts between departments and agencies over the allocation of resources or jurisdictional disputes. The president must also be concerned with how receptive career civil servants are to his policy initiatives. According to orthodox administrative theory, the career bureaucracy should follow the policies established by elected political leaders or their appointees. More than one president, however, has found the bureaucracy an impediment to his programs. Republican presidents particularly suspect the civil service of hostility because they feel it is infiltrated by Democratic partisans.

Systematic studies of the attitudes of top-level civil servants (grades GS 16–18) lend credence to the Republican suspicion. Interviews with a sample of career civil servants from eighteen federal agencies conducted in 1970 during the administration of Richard Nixon revealed that 47 percent were Democrats, 36 percent Independents, and only 17 percent Republicans. The partisan affiliations of career bureaucrats were reflected in their political attitudes. Democratic civil servants were more likely than their Republican counterparts to support an expanded role for government in providing social service programs. Moreover, Independents were closer to the Democrats in their views than to the Republicans.[17]

Frustrated by the refusal of Congress to pass either his major domestic policy proposals or his plan for the massive reorganization of the executive branch, Nixon moved to gain control of the bureaucracy and isolate it from the Congress. To do this, he appointed political executives who were loyal to him and philosophically committed to his program. He also engaged in a calculated attempt to influence the appointment of career civil servants. In the latter endeavor, Nixon was partially successful: more Republicans than Democrats were appointed to career supergrade positions during his administration. Nevertheless, even if he had managed to fill every appointment with a Nixon loyalist, he could have affected no more than 15 percent of all top-level career officials.[18]

After six years of Republican control of the White House, the attitudes of career officials had changed considerably. A second study of top-level civil servants revealed that most of them approved of Nixon's domestic policies—at least, a majority had been won over to his "New Federalism" approach (designed to consolidate existing grants and return decision making to the states).[19] Although Democrats still outnumbered Republicans, many Independents interviewed in the second study leaned toward the Republican party. Since Independents then accounted for 46 percent of the career officials, they were considered a key factor in the responsiveness of the bureaucracy to the president.[20]

This turnaround of career officials seems to support orthodox administrative theories, that is, that the career bureaucracy will support the president's program. However, it may be that the attitudes of career officials were affected by the growing acceptance of the New Federalism by the Congress and state and local officials.[21] If this is so, then the president must sell his program to the nation before he can expect loyal support from civil servants. Career officials would be another element in the American system of checks and balances the president has to pull together.

The President and Judicial Appointments

Courts occupy a unique status in the politics of the nation in that they were not designed as representative institutions, but instead were created to interpret and apply constitutional and statutory law impartially. Therefore judges must not appear to base their decisions on partisan political considerations. The bargaining and compromising that takes place openly in the executive and legislative branches would be unseemly if practiced by judicial officers. It is the appearance of objectivity, free of the popular passions of the moment, that gives the courts a measure of prestige not enjoyed by other political institutions.

To a large extent, the courts are free of the normal political pressures brought to bear on the other branches of government. Yet they are often the subject of heated political debates even if the judges themselves are not active participants in the controversy. Judges cannot escape the fact that they make public policy in resolving judicial conflicts. In recent years, the federal courts have defined the rights of individuals accused of a crime, struck down state antiabortion statutes, and moved to eliminate racial discrimination in public life. Each set of decisions—in "law and order," abortion, and race relations—divided significant segments of the American public.

Presidents are in a position to influence judicial policies because they appoint federal court judges. Franklin Roosevelt brazenly but unsuccessfully attempted to enlarge the Supreme Court so that he could appoint justices more sympathetic to his New Deal programs.[22] Richard Nixon promised to place more "strict constructionists" on the Supreme Court, and although two of his nominees were rejected by the Senate in acrimonious fights, he was finally able to appoint less activist jurists than the ones he found on the Court when he took office. During the 1980 campaign, Jimmy Carter told a black audience in Atlanta that he must be reelected to office to prevent Ronald Reagan from appointing federal judges who would negate the civil rights gains blacks had made. And the 1980 Republican platform pledged its party to "work for the appointment of judges at all levels of the judiciary who respect traditional family values and the sanctity of innocent human life," a catchphrase for the antiabortion position.

Partisanship also appears in the creation of judicial posts. The need for additional federal judgeships might appear unrelated to party politics, but congressional action is geared to the partisan control of the presidency. Although President Dwight Eisenhower promised that half of all new judgeships the Congress created would go to Democrats, the Democratic leaders in Congress waited until after the election of John Kennedy to create more judicial positions. A Democratic Congress did authorize Richard Nixon to appoint sixty new federal judges, but requests from Gerald Ford for more judges went unheeded. Upon the election of Jimmy Carter, one hundred additional judgeships were created.

If for no other reason than that judicial posts are the most sought after patronage plums, the overwhelming proportion of judicial appointments are given to members of the president's party. The president's nominees, of course, must stand the scrutiny of the Senate Judiciary Committee and the comments offered by the American Bar Association and other interest groups who evaluate judicial candidates. Although nominees are rejected from time to time, a president seldom has difficulty in giving a partisan cast to the federal judiciary.

The partisan character of appointments does have an effect on how cases are decided. In a study of federal courts of appeal, Sheldon Goldman found that the party affiliation of judges was associated with their judicial decisions, particularly in cases involving "economic liberalism."[23] Examining the full-court decisions of federal and state supreme court justices, Stuart Nagel also concluded that Republican judges differed from Democratic judges. Democratic judges, for example, were more prone to side with the defense in criminal cases, the claimant in unemployment compensation cases, the government in tax cases, the tenant in landlord-tenant cases, and the employee in employee injury cases.[24] Although both researchers found a definite association between party affiliation and judicial behavior, neither claimed that judges were directly influenced by partisan connections in their court role. Rather, judges of the same party often voted together because they had a similar philosophical outlook. The same set of values that led them to identify with a particular political party also shaped their judicial attitudes.

It should not be inferred that decision making in the courts follows the same partisan lines it does in legislative bodies. Obviously legal doctrines constrain judges in the rulings they make. Moreover, appointment to the federal courts is for life, and this insulates judges from any obligations toward the president who appoints them. Earl Warren, an Eisenhower appointee, was chief justice of the most activist Supreme Court in recent history. The Burger Court, with four Nixon appointees, has not decided cases according to any Republican battle plan. By a seven-to-two majority, for example, the Burger Court struck down state antiabortion statutes that Nixon supported. Nevertheless, appointments to the courts often shift judicial policies in the directions intended by the president. That the power of the president extends even to the courts once again points to the central place of the presidency in the nation's politics. That most judicial appointments go to members of the president's party suggests the pervasiveness of partisanship throughout government.

The Governor as Party Leader

The governor is the most prominent figure in state politics and the reasons for gubernatorial ascendancy are much the same as those accounting for the president's leadership role. There is no effective competitor to challenge the centrality of the governor's office to state politics. State legislators' local ties make them an unlikely focus of the state's electorate. Although other state executives run from a statewide constituency, none has the governor's visibility or political resources. Citizens expect their governor to solve the problems confronting their state just as they look to the president for leadership in the national political arena.

Like the president, the governor is a partisan political figure. The more successful he is as party leader, the more successful he will be in managing the affairs of his state. The typical governor must rely more heavily on his political skills than the president because he does not possess the latter's formal authority. Often governors share executive power with elected subordinates, and some do not have full control over the preparation of the budget. In several states, a governor cannot succeed himself in office or serve more than two terms. Although he lacks the full-blown executive power of the president, the governor still can exploit his position as the acknowledged leader of his state.

SETTING THE POLITICAL AGENDA

It is the governor who determines the political agenda of a state. Few major policy initiatives are undertaken without his backing and most are originated by him. But merely framing the issues is no guarantee that the legislature will act upon them. Again the comparison with the president is clear. The governor needs the cooperation of a legislative majority to put his policies into effect. In the competitive party states, he starts with the support that his partisan colleagues in the legislature normally give him in securing the backing he needs.

The party system most beneficial to the governor is one in which the same party controls both executive and legislative branches. The size of the governor's legislative majority is also important. A comfortable but not excessive majority is most likely to produce support for the governor's program because the threat of a sizable minority often unifies the majority party behind their governor out of a concern for the mutual benefits that accrue when he is successful. With nothing to fear from the opposition, a too large legislative majority may encourage factional rivalries that the governor is unable to control. The most difficult situation faced by a governor is when the opposition party organizes one or both houses of the legislature.[25] Partisan ties are strong enough in the competitive states to frustrate a governor's bid for legislative leadership when his partisan forces are in a minority.

RUNNING THE STATE PARTY

The party leadership a governor exercises is similar in many ways to that of the president. In most states, the primary election has opened the nominating process to contenders who may not have the backing of party professionals. The gubernatorial candidate establishes his credentials for office by appealing to rank-and-file party supporters, and if he is successful, he becomes his party's nominee and leader. If elected governor, he often picks the state party chairman. Even when the chairman is not his personal selection, the governor can expect cooperation from the person occupying the post. So-called independent chairmen may not act as personal agents of the governor, but they know that the future prospects of their party are tied to gubernatorial successes.

BUILDING LEGISLATIVE MAJORITIES

Partisanship within the states, as in the nation, has multiple sources. In part, the legislative support that a governor receives for his programs has a constituency explanation. Governors and legislators who share a party label are often supported by the same groups and organizational leaders. Because of the similarity of their constituency support, the governor and his legislative partisans more often than not agree on what is needed for their state. Even when their electoral support is dissimilar, a governor may be backed by his party's legislative members either because they both have the same ideological orientation or because the governor is personally popular. In some states, the size of a governor's electoral margin within a legislative district is strongly associated with the member's voting record.[26]

The governor is not without resources in building legislative majorities. As the principal political figure in his state, his public pronouncements are newsworthy and can be used to create public sympathy for his legislative policies. Although the practice is increasingly circumscribed by state law, the governor still can use jobs and contracts for patronage purposes. Advancement within the governor's party and aid in the passage of legislation useful to a member are other inducements the governor employs to obtain legislative backing.

The less reliable his partisan support, the more dependent the governor is upon his bargaining skills. Those skills become critical when factional rivalries destroy party unity, or when the opposition party holds a legislative majority. And those circumstances, as we have observed, are the least conducive to gubernatorial successes.

The Contemporary Parties: The Emergence of Chief Executives

The emergence of chief executives as the popular leaders of nation and state has altered the character of American political parties. So too has the manner in which they obtain their offices. The system of primary elections has opened the competition for gubernatorial and presidential nominations to a wider circle of contenders. Because they commonly develop their own campaign organizations, governors and presidents are less dependent on the backing of party professionals in general election contests. To this extent, leadership within the nation has become more personalized.

At the same time, the degree to which an individualized leadership has rendered useless the concept of the corporate party should not be exaggerated. Because governors and presidents run under partisan labels, the programs and legislative initiatives they back contribute to the public's understanding of partisanship. As the nation's most important leader, the president has the greatest impact on the electoral value of the party label he wears. No single president can define his party in policy terms, although his actions may temporarily affect its popular support. Over the long term, however, a party becomes known by what its officeholders, particularly its presidents, have been able to achieve during their time in power.

Chief executives are the beneficiaries of the corporate role of the party in at least two ways. First, because of the electorate's partisan attachments, they know in advance that some voters will support them merely on the basis of their party label. Second, once in power, a chief executive can expect a certain amount of cooperation from the legislative members of his own party. Though neither the electoral nor the legislative strength of their parties alone may be adequate for their purposes, few chief executives disregard their partisan connections.

The losers in the development of executive-centered parties have been the party professionals at state and local levels.[27] They are no longer able to confer the nomination, and hence are not called upon to do the bargaining and coalition building once considered so essential to the national nominating process. Today the responsibility for organizing coalitions falls to the president and his entourage. The transition to executive-centered parties may make a president's governing task more difficult, but it has not destroyed the psychological commitment of either voters or officeholders to their party. So long as partisan identification persists within the electorate, the parties will survive in some form.

SUMMARY

Voters look to the president to solve the nation's problems. Since he is elected by a national constituency, he is the focal point of American national politics.

The president is also a partisan figure, and his successes and failures are judged as his party's successes and failures. He is more responsible than his partisan colleagues in Congress for determining the policy content of the label he wears. Thus his performance in office adds to or detracts from the long-term partisan loyalties of the electorate. Durable alignments within the nation do not extend from the local level upward, but rather from the national level downward.

The national party came into existence to nominate presidential candidates, and national party organizations remain largely an arena of presidential politics. However, the president's ties to the formal party structure have been weakened in recent years by changes in nominating practices. Instead of seeking the support of political professionals and officeholders, presidential aspirants now appeal to a mass electorate to realize their political ambitions. Still, the president needs his party and his party needs him, and out of this mutual dependence, the president strives to build the political support he requires to achieve his goals.

The most important source of legislative influence the president has is the label he shares with his congressional colleagues. A president whose own party controls the Congress has more legislative successes than one who faces an opposition party majority. Party ranks in congressional voting are not strictly maintained, however, so even when his party is in the majority, a president must seek support from the opposition.

Congressional turnover has been unusually heavy in recent years. This fact, together with certain reforms that have encouraged junior members to take a more active role, has resulted in a more independent-minded Congress that does not fall into line at the bidding of the president. The changes have complicated the president's leadership tasks under all circumstances, but most especially when his party does not hold a majority in Congress.

Two pieces of evidence suggest that a president's leadership has only a limited effect on congressional voting. One is that members show considerable stability in their voting positions across Congresses. The other is that, according to surveys, congressmen rate administration spokesmen low as voting cues. Nevertheless, on close divisions, a president may turn around enough votes to save legislation he believes critical to the success of his administration.

To fulfill the partisan commitments of his administration, the president must direct and coordinate the policy decisions of the executive establishment. Often the arts of negotiation and bargaining are as important in dealing with administrative agencies and departments as they are in dealing with the Congress.

The principal means the president uses to establish control over executive agencies is his power of appointment. Incoming presidents ask special personnel selection teams to prepare lists of possible appointees. Although presidents-elect pay special attention to key Cabinet posts, the short time span between election and inauguration does not permit a careful consideration of all appointments.

Few presidents use their Cabinet as a partisan team to formulate broad policies because the separatist tendencies and disparate programs of the executive departments make a collegial Cabinet impossible. For this reason, presidents rely heavily on their White House aides for political and programmatic counsel.

Although the sheer size of the executive establishment precludes the president from intervening in administrative matters on a continuing basis, he must take care to secure the cooperation of the career bureaucracy. According to orthodox administrative theory, career civil servants are neutrally competent and capable of serving either Democratic or Republican presidents. In practice, however, presidents often encounter a recalcitrant bureaucracy when they want to institute new programs or demolish old ones. Republican presidents especially have found the bureaucracy unsympathetic, if not openly hostile, to their programs.

Recent surveys of career civil servants have revealed that more identify with the Democratic party than with the Republican party. During Richard Nixon's first term in office, the bureaucracy opposed his social policies. Before he left office, however, a majority of career officials agreed with his New Federalism approach. This turnaround may have reflected the career officials' professional commitment to neutral competence, or it may have reflected the growing acceptance by Congress and state and local officials of the New Federalism. If the latter was true, it means that the president must first sell his programs to the Congress and the public before he can hope to secure the full cooperation of the executive agencies.

Presidents can influence court policies because they have the power to appoint federal judges. Judicial appointments overwhelmingly go to members of the president's party. Although judges sever any formal party connections upon joining the bench, those of the same political faith often vote together because they have similar philosophical outlooks. A president with the opportunity to make appointments to the Supreme Court can leave his imprint on the Court for many years.

Governors are the dominant figures in state politics. They set the priorities and political agenda of the state, use their public visibility to encourage popular support for their programs, and employ the resources at their command to enhance gubernatorial leadership. In states with a semblance of party competition, governors trade heavily on their partisan connections in running their states. Even though they may have gained office more through a personal than a party effort, they cannot escape the fact that they are partisan figures. Indeed, the successful gubernatorial candidate becomes his party's leader.

The development of executive-centered parties in nation and state has not destroyed their corporate character, for executives depend on the partisan electoral support their labels give them. Once in office, they find that their fellow partisans in the legislature are their most dependable sources of support. So long as the party label has meaning for voters and officeholders, the parties will survive.

Notes

[1]Angus Campbell, Philip E. Converse, Warren E. Miller, and Donald E. Stokes, *The American Voter* (New York: Wiley, 1960), p. 557.

[2]See the discussion of Theodore J. Lowi, "Party, Policy, and Constitution in America" in *The American Party Systems*, 2nd ed., ed. William Nisbet Chambers and Walter Dean Burnham (New York: Oxford University Press, 1975), pp. 245–248.

[3]For a good brief summary of the evolution of the president's legislative functions, see Stephen J. Wayne, *The Legislative Presidency* (New York: Harper and Row, 1978), pp. 8–22.

[4]Quoted in Richard E. Cohen, "Byrd of West Virginia—A New Job, A New Image," *National Journal*, August 20, 1977, p. 1295.

[5]Quoted in Michael J. Malbin, "House Democrats Are Playing with a Strong Leadership Lineup," *National Journal*, June 18, 1977, p. 942.

[6]The following paragraphs are derived from Wayne, *The Legislative Presidency*, chap. 5.

[7]*Congressional Quarterly Weekly Report*, January 12, 1980, p. 93.

[8]See Joseph Cooper and Gary Bombardier, "Presidential Leadership and Party Success," *Journal of Politics* 30 (November 1968), pp. 1012–1027; and George C. Edwards III, *Presidential Influence in Congress* (San Francisco: Freeman, 1980), p. 200.

[9]John W. Kingdon, *Congressional Voting Decisions* (New York: Harper and Row, 1978), chap. 6.

[10]Aage Clausen, *How Congressmen Decide* (New York: St. Martin's, 1973), chap. 8.

[11]Edwards, *Presidential Influence in Congress*, p. 199. Edwards comments, however, that Johnson's marginal victories "were generally not on crucial or controversial issues."

[12]For example, see ibid., p. 190.

[13]The Republican Eighty-third Congress supported Dwight Eisenhower on 88 percent of his roll call fights, the best record of any post–World War II Republican president. Neither Eisenhower nor his Republican successors were as successful when confronted by Democratic Congresses.

[14]Quoted in Steven V. Roberts, "Eroding Loyalty Weakens House Leaders," *The New York Times*, June 4, 1979, p. D10.

[15]See the discussion in Thomas E. Cronin, *The State of the Presidency* (Boston: Little, Brown, 1975), chap. 7.

[16]Ibid., p. 182.

[17]Joel D. Aberbach and Bert A. Rockman, "Clashing Beliefs within the Executive Branch: The Nixon Administration Bureaucracy," *American Political Science Review* 70 (June 1976), pp. 456–468.

[18]Richard L. Cole and David A. Caputo, "Presidential Control of the Senior Civil Service: Assessing the Strategies of the Nixon Years," *American Political Science Review* 73 (June 1979), p. 411.

[19]Ibid., p. 409.

[20]Ibid., p. 404.

[21]Ibid., pp. 411–412.

[22]Roosevelt's "court-packing" attempt may have had an effect on the Court's decisions. At least, Justice Owen Roberts began to vote with the liberal bloc more frequently than he had in the past.

[23]Sheldon Goldman, "Voting Behavior on the United States Courts of Appeal, 1961–1964," *American Political Science Review* 60 (June 1966), pp. 374–383.

[24]Stuart S. Nagel, "Political Affiliation and Judges' Decisions," *American Political Science Review* 55 (December 1961), pp. 843–850.

[25]Wayne L. Francis, *Legislative Issues in the Fifty States* (Chicago: Rand McNally, 1967), pp. 54–58.

[26]Hugh L. LeBlanc, "Voting in State Senates: Party and Constituency Influences," *Midwest Journal of Political Science* 13 (February 1969), p. 48. See also Sarah P. McCally, "The Governor and His Legislative Party," *American Political Science Review* 60 (December 1966), pp. 923–942.

[27]The term "executive-centered parties" is that of Judson James. See his excellent discussion in *American Political Parties in Transition* (New York: Harper and Row, 1974), chap. 11.

13

The Future of the Parties

Most political analysts agree that American political parties are in a weakened state today, but disagree about just how feeble they are. Have they deteriorated to the extent that they perform no useful functions? Are they merely searching for a new political alignment that will restore order to political competition? Is there realistic hope that party organizations will ever recover the power they once wielded? These are the questions that must be addressed to understand the role parties will play in the future of American politics.

It is easy enough to find evidence of an impaired party system: partisan identification within the electorate has weakened, split-ticket voting is more common, voter turnout has declined, and Americans have become more cynical and distrustful of government. Political professionals no longer act as brokers for the diverse interests that make up their party because their role in nominating politics has been sharply curtailed. Freed from a dependence on party professionals, candidates and officeholders can adopt whatever policy positions serve their electoral aims or satisfy their consciences.

All the same, it is too early to sound the death knell of the parties, for they continue to provide the label under which most candidates run; a majority of voters still identify with a political party and support that party's candidates. The independent candidacy of John B. Anderson in 1980 was frustrated at every turn because he did not have major party backing. Denied public funds to start his campaign, he was unable to secure enough private donations to make a serious bid for the presidency. Few major political figures endorsed his effort, and his support among the voters steadily eroded as the election approached.

That the major American parties still control access to elective offices is no assurance that they perform anything more than a "gatekeeper" role. If the party label is meaningless to officeholders and voters alike, then the parties have indeed become obsolete. On the other hand, if the labels still serve to distinguish two groups seeking political power, then the parties are not useless appendages in election contests.

The State of the Parties Today

To assess the contemporary status of American parties, we must pull together the several threads of our analysis in the preceding chapters. We will then be in a position to determine how enfeebled the parties have become and what, if anything, can be done to restore their vitality.

THE ELECTORAL PARTY

A number of trends point to the weakening of partisan ties within the electorate. The proportion of identifiers who are strongly attached to a political party has diminished over the past two decades, and self-declared Independents are more numerous than in the past. Reflecting the weakened sense of partisanship, voters are defecting from their parties at greater rates in presidential and congressional elections. The results are seen in the increased proportion of voters who split their ballots between Democratic and Republican candidates in federal elections.

The weakening of partisan ties does not tell the whole story, however. Some evidence points to growing voter sophistication in responding to issue controversies, although differing conceptions of issue voting and its measurement leave the trend line murky. Voter cynicism and distrust of government and politicians have been more clearly documented. Reinforcing this picture of malaise in the electorate is the recent decline in the rate of voting participation.

If these several trends are substantially interrelated, one cannot be sanguine about the future of the party system. If it is the more sophisticated voters who are becoming less partisan, more distrustful, and increasingly reluctant to participate in electoral politics, then the major parties confront a challenge serious enough to make us question their capacity for survival. The evidence, however, does not support such a dire analysis. Quite to the contrary, it is those who are only marginally involved in politics who are the least informed, the least likely to go to the polls, and the least likely to identify with a political party and to vote their party identification consistently. The alienated citizen does not vote with the regularity of the trusting citizen, yet alienation is unrelated to political independence. Lower voter turnout and widespread disaffection and cynicism can scarcely be viewed with equanimity, yet they are less threatening to our political society than a finding that the nation's most involved and knowledgeable citizens are rejecting their political leaders.[1]

But the weakening of the electoral parties must be placed in perspective. The growth of Independents has been partially offset by the inclination of most of them to favor one party or the other. An Independent leaner exhibits most of the characteristics of the weakly identified partisan. Neither shows the loyalty of the strong identifier, but the partisan feelings both express are not meaningless.[2] Obviously, then, campaigners have a sizable partisan base upon which to build their electoral coalitions.

Not all partisans will vote for their party's candidates. Although party identification may encapsulate a voter's partisan feelings, short-term electoral forces can cause a voter to defect. In presidential elections, the candidates are well known to the public, and an election outcome turns on their popularity and the tide of national events. But the electoral dynamics of House races are different. House incumbents are better known and better liked than challengers, and House elections are relatively (but not completely) immune to the national forces that elect a president. Senate elections fall somewhere in between. Senate incumbents are less universally admired than their House counterparts, and their challengers are better known. Also, issue controversies are more important to the outcome of Senate elections. For each office, some voters will disregard their party ties to vote for the candidate they perceive as the most attractive or most capable of serving their interests.[3]

Partisan defections do not pose a serious threat to an effective party system, unless members of both parties freely cross over to vote for opposition party candidates—a pattern that is uncommon in federal elections. Substantial defections usually damage one party disproportionately, as in the one-sided 1964, 1972, and 1980 presidential contests when the winning party maintained a hold on its following while attracting votes from the losing party. Crossover voting allows an alternation of political power that would be impossible with a more rigid partisan loyalty. As long as the vote reflects a judgment on how well the nation has been run by its leaders, large-scale defections from one party are a healthy sign of electoral accountability.

Defections in congressional elections display a similar pattern, but for different reasons. Particularly in House contests, partisan crossovers are associated with the perceived attractiveness of incumbents. The loyalty of the members of the incumbent's party is usually high; it is the following of the challenger's party that is likely to break ranks.[4] Freewheeling crossovers from each party are rare, yet the partisan defections in congressional elections are imperfectly synchronized with those in presidential elections. Because the forces acting on voters in presidential elections are not the same as those determining the aggregate outcome of congressional elections, popular mandates are mixed. Electoral mandates are unclear under any circumstances, but they are even cloudier when control of government is divided between the two parties.

The insulation of congressional elections from national politics, however, can be overstated. In 1974, in the aftermath of the Watergate scandals, the voters turned out of office thirty-six House Republicans, a third of whom had won their preceding election by landslide proportions.[5] The 1980 elections were equally dramatic. Unlike 1968 and 1972, the national tide that elected a Republican president also swept in a Republican Senate and made substantial inroads into the Democratic House majority. The movement of the electorate was in a partisan direction that, while incomplete, gave Republicans a chance to run the nation.

THE PARTY PROFESSIONALS

Party organizations do not wield the influence they once did. The erosion of their authority is evident in two areas: the professionals who hold formal positions of power within party organizations cannot confer the party label on the candidates of their choice as easily as they once did; and the organizations are no longer capable of delivering a vote with any certainty. The result is that the professionals find themselves increasingly bypassed as middlemen between candidates and voters.

The Ascendancy of the Primary. The direct primary, now employed in some form in all fifty states, has undercut the power of political professionals. Introduced in the first decade of the twentieth century for the purpose of wresting political power from corrupt state and local party leaders, the primary failed at first to do much damage to the professionals because they presided over strong patronage organizations and were therefore able to use their resources in behalf of favored candidates. Slowly, however, organizational leaders found their patronage base dwindling. At the same time, candidates began to make broadcast appeals for voter support through the mass media. These developments made possible the achievement of the Progressives' goal: nomination for political office has been opened to a wider range of political contenders, and the ultimate choice of a nominee is in the hands of rank-and-file party supporters.

"Too bad this wasn't a primary — you'd be a winner."

Presidential primaries took hold more slowly. They were established in some states at the same time the direct primary was introduced, but for a long time they had little impact on the ultimate choice of nominees, which was reserved for the national conventions, then dominated by party professionals. John F. Kennedy in 1960 was the first candidate to exploit the primaries as a successful strategy in winning his party's nomination. Still, eight years later, Hubert Humphrey received the Democratic party nomination without entering one of his party's primaries. It was the reforms begun by Democrats after their 1968 convention that dramatically changed the way nominations are won. Presidential primaries have proliferated, caucuses have been opened, and the party following now plays the key role in selecting the nominee.

Voting the Candidate Rather Than the Party. Once the primary gained the ascendancy in the nominating process, the same forces that had curtailed the organization's influence over nominations weakened its power in the general election. For major political offices, old-style organizational support was superseded by the politics of the electronic media. Candidates raised their own money and built their own organizations to gain political office, and as they did, the professionals found their role further circumscribed. The upshot was that party outsiders could not only gain the nomination but even win the general election without much organizational support.

Because they no longer provide services or offer resources considered essential by office seekers, the professionals are less able to assemble stable coalitions and to mediate factional disputes. Their diminished role in the life of the party is most keenly felt in the reforms that have reduced the deliberative functions of the national conventions. The national parties are executive centered, and the selection of a presidential nominee is crucial in determining how united the party's traditional following will be on election day.

American party organizations were never so strong that they could dictate the policy views of those who ran under the party's standard, but they once were effective in building bridges to the political groups and interests that constitute the party's normal following. Because each party's support is diverse, accommodation and compromise are essential to unity. Under today's nominating practices, however, candidates compete in a way that tends to splinter rather than unite a party. The responsibility for healing party wounds opened in nominating battles rests with the candidate's organization more than with the party itself. The effects are to weaken the party further as a collectivity of leaders.

Signs of Resurgence. Despite the effects of the reforms and the new campaign style, party organizations have not become moribund. State organizations have displayed some resurgence over the past twenty years and, within budgetary limitations, are endeavoring to offer the kinds of services needed in contemporary campaigning. Republican party organizations at the national level are professionally staffed and well financed. The Democrats long neglected the organizational needs of their national party, but the 1980 election debacle brought demands for an examination of existing party resources. Having lost the presidency, the Democrats are not encumbered by a presidential staff in rebuilding their party.

Strengthening the campaign-related activities of the political parties will not restore to party professionals their power over nominations and elections. That they will probably never regain. But a greater organizational presence should aid party committees in recruiting candidates to seek political office, in making more races competitive, and in gaining credit for electoral assistance. When candidates incur a debt to their party in winning office, they may become more cooperative in seeking party goals. Cohesive parties will not be constructed in this fashion, but the trend to a more individualistic politics may be checked.

THE OFFICEHOLDERS

The inevitable consequence of declining partisanship in the electorate and the circumvention of party professionals in electoral politics is the growing independence of party officeholders. Successful office seekers feel an obligation to the constituency that elected them, but they are less beholden to the party under whose banner they ran. They may cooperate with their partisan colleagues, but they are not compelled to do so.

There is no systematic evidence demonstrating a decline in party cohesion in the state legislatures, though some studies show a striking variation across states, with the urban two-party states of the Northeast exhibiting rather impressive solidarity. The condition of the congressional parties has received closer scrutiny. Party voting has displayed an irregular but downward trend over the past twenty years, though the decline has not been precipitous. Of course, aggregate figures on roll call votes do not measure the full spirit of cooperation within the congressional parties. The ultimate test of party government is how well the president's program is supported by the congressional members of his party. If he wins legislative roll calls on bills that have been gutted by compromises, he can hardly be called successful. Many analysts believe that presidents are finding it increasingly difficult to secure the type of legislation they desire from the Congress.

Strict discipline has rarely characterized the congressional parties, though from 1890 to 1910, the parties in the House did display a high level of partisan cohesion. Two conditions produced this party discipline: power had become centralized in the hands of the speaker, and the constituency base of the legislative parties had become polarized along sectional and agricultural-industrial lines.[6] Today neither party's leaders in the House or the Senate possess the parliamentary power to compel loyalty from the rank and file. The constituency base of party voting remains important, but the electoral parties are not as polarized as they were around the turn of the century.

Collective Accountability. Even though the conditions that favor party regularity have diminished, individual officeholders cannot always escape the collective judgment rendered on the incumbent party. Frustrations over rising inflation, high interest rates, unacceptable rates of unemployment, and a perceived loss of prestige abroad were widespread enough to handicap all Democrats running for national office in 1980. Individual Democrats were punished by the voters for what their party did or did not do.

The unanticipated size of the Democratic defeat cannot honestly be laid entirely to President Carter. Because of the comfortable majorities they held in both houses during his administration, congressional Democrats must accept some of the blame for the large-scale defeat their party suffered. The 1980 elections contain a lesson the Republicans would do well to heed. Their victory could easily prove short-lived if the problems left unsolved by the administration they replaced prove intractable to their ministrations.

The system of party accountability is imperfect. Although 1980 was a Republican party triumph, the Democrats retained control of the House despite the Republican net gain of thirty-three House seats. Thus President Ronald Reagan began his term of office confronted by divided party control. As in the past, voters will assess the Republican administration by how successful it is in running the nation. That Reagan must negotiate with House Democratic leaders and committee chairmen is, in one sense, almost irrelevant. Insofar as the electorate is concerned, he and his party were empowered to govern.

Prospects for Change

The continued deterioration of the American party system is not foreordained. Some analysts believe the parties would gain a new lease on life if they could once again reflect basic issue divisions within the electorate. This would be possible if new political controversies polarized the electorate, or if traditional political debates took on new relevance. Alternatively, the parties could be renewed if their coalition-building function was restored. To strengthen the parties in this fashion, party organizations would need to improve their campaign services, and party professionals would have to regain some of their influence over party nominations. Underlying either route to revitalized parties is the assumption that the present party system is not fulfilling its responsibility to provide meaningful choices to the electorate.

Political alignments and party structures are related phenomena. Structural reforms have left the American parties porous enough to allow any group to gain entry to seek its goals; at the same time, they have weakened the parties' capacity to strike the compromises necessary to unite a following. Under these conditions, party choices will remain unsatisfactory unless the electorate polarizes around a few salient issues that are exploited by one party's leadership. It must be remembered, though, that the reforms that opened the party system were undertaken because the parties were felt to be unresponsive to political change. Party leaders often avoided taking a forthright stand on emerging issues for fear of alienating some segment of the party coalition. The dilemma confronting the contemporary parties is how to remain responsive to the electorate's diverse interests while at the same time achieving a degree of organizational and intellectual cohesion in performing its tasks.

REALIGNMENT, DEALIGNMENT, OR REVITALIZATION?

Periodically in the past, the electorate was presented with clear choices that produced new party majorities and the potential for important policy changes. In response to a new set of issues, significant numbers of older voters switched their partisan allegiance or new voters entered the election fray disproportionately on one side. Political historians have categorized the elections that lifted Thomas Jefferson to power in 1800, Andrew Jackson in 1828, Abraham Lincoln in 1860, William McKinley in 1896, and Franklin D. Roosevelt in 1932 as realigning elections because of the new and durable majorities they created. In each instance, the party system responded to the social and political needs of the nation.

Political realignments occur when political controversies develop that cut across older political alignments.[7] By definition, cross-cutting issues divide both political parties, but if one party is able to establish itself on the popular side of the new controversy, a political realignment results. The out party has a greater incentive to exploit new issues as a means of winning political power. The interest of the in party is to suppress divisive questions that threaten its majority status.

James L. Sundquist has identified four post–World War II issues that were potentially capable of producing partisan realignment:[8]

1. Communism.
2. Vietnam.
3. Race.
4. Law and order.

Communism and race appeared as divisive issues in the late 1940s, while Vietnam and law and order inflamed the electorate in the 1960s. The realigning potential of communism was over by the first administration of Dwight Eisenhower, but the race issue lingered and converged with the Vietnam and law-and-order issues to contribute to a state of national anxiety and unrest.

Communism and McCarthyism. Communism as a political issue began as early as Franklin Roosevelt's recognition of the Soviet Union in 1933, but it took on new meaning in the postwar years. During the Roosevelt administration, the threat to world peace came from fascist powers, and the Soviet Union was our wartime ally. After the war, the threat of Soviet imperialism became more real. A little known Republican senator from Wisconsin, Joseph R. McCarthy, seized upon the issue and charged there was a communist conspiracy to subvert the government internally. Attracting a substantial following that included many traditional Democratic adherents, particularly

Irish and East European Catholics, McCarthy became a political figure of national consequence. Failure to understand the menace of communism and to weed out communist infiltrators in the State Department, he charged, had led to Soviet hegemony over China and eastern Europe. Emboldened by their successes against Democratic administrations, his argument continued, communist aggressors had invaded South Korea and forced the United States into war.

In the elections of 1952, the communism issue figured prominently in a campaign in which Republicans captured both Congress and the presidency. Democrats were unwilling to concede that their liberal political philosophy made them communist "dupes," so they supported the Internal Security Act of 1950 and the Communist Control Act of 1954. After the Republicans gained power, Senator McCarthy continued to exploit the issue that had brought him national prominence until he became an embarrassment to Eisenhower and the Republican party. McCarthy's reckless charges and abuse of congressional witnesses ultimately got him censured by the Senate. With "McCarthyism" a dead issue, the differences between the parties over communism became relatively minor.

The War in Vietnam. The Vietnam war was another issue that might have realigned the electorate. During its early years, the war had popular support and bipartisan backing. As the American commitment of troops escalated, so did the antiwar protests led by the nation's youth. The electorate wearied of the war's growing cost in lives and the internal dissension it sowed. The unexpected strength shown by Eugene J. McCarthy in the New Hampshire primary of 1968 was an indication of the electorate's mood. Although clearly a peace candidate, McCarthy was astonishingly supported by hawks and doves alike.[9] Stunned by his near defeat, Lyndon Johnson stopped the bombing of North Vietnam and entered into peace negotiations.

Delegates at the stormy Democratic convention of 1968 rebuffed the move by peace forces to take over the party and gave the nomination to Johnson's vice president, Hubert H. Humphrey. Though he became increasingly conciliatory toward the peace wing of his party during the campaign, Humphrey continued to reject a policy of unilateral withdrawal of American troops. George Wallace was clearly the most hawkish of the three principal contenders in 1968, but the electorate perceived only slight differences between Nixon's and Humphrey's Vietnam policies. Once in office, Nixon pursued a policy of "Vietnamization" of the war and had removed all American ground combat troops by 1972. His Democratic opponent in that year, George McGovern, was left little ground on which to stake out a claim for an immediate end to American involvement. A tragic chapter in American history was brought to a close with neither party gaining lasting advantage from the turbulence it created.

Race and Law and Order. Since the Dixiecrat walkout over the 1948 Democratic convention's civil rights plank, racial issues have divided the northern and southern wings of the Democratic party. But the controversy became more than a sectional battle within Democratic party ranks when it became entangled with a developing concern over law and order. By the mid-1960s, violent crimes had risen dramatically and citizens were afraid to walk city streets at night. The lawlessness was not just that of ordinary criminals; whole sections of a city vented their anger and frustrations in civil riots. In both cases, the racial implications were clear: blacks contributed disproportionately to street crime, and the black ghettos in the cities were the scenes of burning, looting, and pilfering.

The breakdown of public order, however, was more than a racial issue. Antiwar protestors disrupted college campuses, tied up city traffic, and taunted police and national guardsmen trying to contain their demonstrations. A counterculture that challenged traditional values and moral concepts arose. The America that many knew and believed in was changing.

In the set of issues that developed, a realignment could have occurred only if the parties had taken distinct and opposing sides—that is, if the Democrats had emphasized an attack upon the social ills and public neglect that bred lawlessness and a contempt for traditional values, while the Republicans countered with measures to suppress their outbreak. Democratic officeholders, however, were no more willing to concede they were "soft on crime" than they had earlier been willing to accept the label of "soft on communism."

The Blunting of Crosscutting Issues. In sum, none of the four crosscutting issues Sundquist identified produced a partisan realignment because the parties did not take stands that presented the electorate with a clear choice. With the passage of time, the issues have been blunted. The Vietnam war is a fading memory in the minds of voters. The communist issue has largely spent its force, at least in the virulent form it took in the late 1940s and early 1950s. Debate continues over the size of the defense budget, the preparedness of our military forces, and the perceived threat of the Soviet Union, but foreign policy and defense issues alone are unlikely to produce a political realignment. They are even less likely to do so when neither party is willing to accept the onus for weakening our military capabilities. Support for the military is currently popular on both sides of the political aisle.

Race continues to be a thorny problem, but its potential as a realigning issue depends upon heightened racial tensions. Although such a development is still possible, opinion surveys suggest that the nation is becoming more rather than less tolerant. A majority of blacks also believe that the quality of their life has improved over the past decade.[10] The Ku Klux Klan and other hate groups have not been eradicated, but neither have they acquired respectability. The forces of moderation are strong enough in both parties to prevent blatant racial appeals. If racial antagonisms should intensify, the number of citizens directly affected would be in the minority and those less directly involved could mediate the conflict. A solution short of the reordering of the party system seems more likely than not.[11]

Social issues that center on crime, lawlessness, and the breakdown of traditional moral values no longer have the urgency they had in the 1960s. The crusade against the perceived weakening of society's moral fabric has been taken up by conservative Christian evangelical groups. Organizations such as the Moral Majority, Religious Roundtable, Christian Voice, and the National Christian Action Coalition have entered the political arena to advance what they see as moral or "family" issues. Taking stands in favor of school prayer and against abortion, the Equal Rights Amendment, homosexual rights, and sex education in the schools, these Christian groups work through local churches and spread their message by radio and television. Their effect on the 1980 campaign is uncertain. Although their message may have been well received in fundamentalist regions, there is no reason to believe that they constitute a national political force of consequence.

Other Prospects in Today's Political Climate. A regrouping of partisan forces around issues that cut across existing political alignments is not the only prospect for the American party system. Two other possibilities have been discussed by political analysts. The present party system could be revitalized if political debate centered on the appropriate role of government in society—the political controversy that, in its pristine stage, gave rise to the New Deal party system. Alternatively, if neither party makes progress in solving pressing national problems, further dissolution of the parties would be expected. Rather than shifting allegiance to a successful party, voters would dissociate themselves from party battles. Dealignment rather than revitalization would be the order of the day.

Whether forecasting dealignment or rebirth, most analysts agree on three important characteristics of today's political climate:

1. Economic issues were the dominant (but not exclusive) concern of voters in the 1976 and 1980 elections.
2. The Republican victory of 1980 did not constitute a mandate to repeal welfare state policies indiscriminately
3. The nation has become more tolerant of changing moral standards and values, despite the activity of the Christian right.

What they disagree on is the capacity of either party to translate popular dissatisfactions into a conflict that would cause a durable shift in the balance of partisan forces.[12]

In both 1976 and 1980, the depressed state of the economy, inflation, and high unemployment contributed to the challenger's success in defeating the incumbent. There were additional similarities in the two elections, however, that were masked by the partisan outcomes. Jimmy Carter campaigned in 1976 as a Washington outsider, a tactic designed to exploit public reaction to the Watergate scandals. But his promise of restoring confidence in government stretched beyond issues of public morality. He also pointed to his success in reorganizing the Georgia state government and pledged a similar overhaul of the federal bureaucracy. Although of indeterminate importance in 1976, the belief that a large, unwieldy, interventionist government created more problems than it solved was widespread by 1980. Capitalizing on the issue, Ronald Reagan told voters he would "get government off our backs."

The Reagan prescription of freeing industry from excessive government controls was standard Republican doctrine. The antigovernment mood of the electorate, moreover, was strong enough to deliver a decisive defeat to the Democratic party. Yet few analysts are willing to conclude that a new majority has been created out of the old debate because the problems confronting the Republicans in establishing a durable majority are formidable.

In the first place, more voters still identify with the Democratic party than with the Republican party. Democratic party identification is not simply a continuance of a habit acquired during early stages of socialization. The Democratic party has sizable voter support for its record in such fields as health, welfare, labor relations, urban redevelopment, environmental protection, industrial safety, and minority rights. Reagan's 1980 popular vote in a three-way race was more impressive than Republican gains in congressional elections. Although they captured the Senate, Republican candidates received only 46.9 percent of all votes caste in Senate elections. In House elections, Republicans held a razor-thin edge in popular votes (49.48 percent to the Democrats 49.15 percent), but still fell short of electing a Republican House majority.[13] Certainly congressmen are sensitive to election totals, but they confront an interesting paradox: while many Americans have become distressed over a government grown too large, they have also become dependent on the specific services or protections it provides. The Congress has proved willing to make sizable cuts in social spending, but it remains to be seen whether the consequent reduction of government services will alienate significant segments of the population.

A second problem the Republicans must confront is the lingering effect of social and cultural issues. Though clearly secondary to the public's concern over the state of the economy, such issues as abortion and ERA are militantly pursued by groups on polar sides of the controversies. Joining the fray alongside the single-issue forces, the Christian right has expressed a moral concern over drug use, premarital living arrangements, the rising rate of illegitimate births, and other developments they see as endangering traditional American values. The same types of issues failed to create a Republican majority in the 1960s; they are even less likely to secure the Republican gains of 1980.[14] As before, the sides taken on the questions cut across traditional alignments. The college educated, who give disproportionate support to the Republican party, are the most tolerant of social and cultural change. To interpret popular dissatisfaction over economic matters as a more general drift to the right that includes resistance to the pace of social change is a risky supposition.

The lasting effects of the Republican resurgence will depend upon how well the Reagan administration leads the nation. Replacing one set of leaders with another is meaningless unless the new leaders are capable of responding to troublesome issues more effectively than their predecessors. It is at this juncture that analysts differ over the capacity of the parties for revitalization. Some believe that the electorate's partisan ties are so loose that there is no stable base upon which to build a new majority. They further argue that the electorate is not polarized into opposing camps, and that party resources are inadequate for organizing a majority following. Other analysts believe that the electorate's malaise could be checked if Republican-inspired programs solve some of the economic problems that now attract the nation's attention. The electorate moved in a partisan direction in 1980, but the full implications of this shift will not be known until we see the results of future elections.

REFORMING THE PARTIES

The future of the parties does not rest solely on the development of issues that polarize the electorate and serve up a majority following waiting to be claimed. Each party's leadership is responsible for selecting the issues on which it chooses to run and for offering solutions that have some chance of success. A party's capacity to address national issues without acceding to the maximum demands of each group within its normal coalition depends upon its organizational strength. Whether the parties can be strengthened organizationally rests, in turn, upon the nature of reforms adopted and their popular appeal.

Three Reform Movements. On three occasions in the present century, reformers advocated fundamental change of the existing party system.[15] Progressives attacked the stranglehold that boss-ridden state and local organizations had on the politics of the nation at the turn of the century. Some of the measures they backed were designed to purify politics by returning control of government to the people. The initiative, the referendum, the recall, and the system of primary elections all had this aim. Other proposals, such as the merit system for filling government posts, were designed to limit the influence of professional politicians. Drawing their principal support from the white middle class, Progressive reformers hoped to replace a politics of self-interest with a politics guided by their vision of the common good. Political parties were more hindrance than help in the Progressives' search for honest, efficient, and economically run government.

The institutional reforms of the Progressives ultimately took their toll on the parties. Primary elections restricted the influence of party professionals, and merit systems for selecting civil servants cut into the patronage that sustained party organizations. Other forces as disparate as restrictive immigration laws and new government social service policies further weakened the parties. Shortly after the close of World War II, the parties had fallen into such disrepair that a new wave of reformers set out to strengthen them.

The new reformers wanted to create truly national parties that offered voters a choice of alternative programs. The responsible political parties they envisioned would possess the internal cohesion to enact their programs into law when in power. Strengthened parties would be the vehicle to overcome the constitutionally mandated system of dispersed government power and to achieve majority rule.

Confined mainly to academic circles, the argument for responsible political parties attracted little popular attention. Soon wearied of the debate over its merits, political scientists turned their attention to other matters. Later developments weakened the parties further, but the responsible party argument, at least in its earlier form, has not been revived.

The final major reform movement centered on opening the presidential selection process. Though the proposals were less sweeping, their effect on the party system nevertheless was profound. The tumultuous Democratic convention of 1968 resolved to give all Democratic voters "a full, meaningful and timely opportunity to participate" in the selection of delegates. A commission headed first by George McGovern and later by Donald Fraser specified the procedures required of state parties in selecting convention delegates. Whether they were intended to or not, the reforms encouraged a proliferation of primaries that affected Republican and Democratic candidates alike.[16] They constrained the deliberative functions of the convention and greatly reduced the influence of party professionals.

Enduring Reform Themes. Although the goals differed, common themes ran through the arguments of each of the reform groups. Each was critical of the power exercised by state and local party leaders. In varying forms, each sought a greater involvement of the rank-and-file following in party affairs. And each group hoped that the reforms would lead to a greater capacity of the political system to respond to society's needs.

The Progressive reformers fought the corruption of boss-led machines and were the most openly antiparty. They trusted an enlightened citizenry to select their leaders wisely without the intermediary of party institutions. Advocates of responsible political parties also decried the influence of state and local leaders, but from a different perspective. They wished to create national parties by bringing state and local organizations under centralized direction. Unlike the Progressives, however, responsible party advocates did not presume that a national citizenry would be guided by the same conceptions of the public good. They wanted strong and internally cohesive parties to offer alternative programs to the electorate.

Proponents of more open delegate selection procedures were not consciously antiparty, although their recommendations did have that effect. Their proposals for a more active role for the rank-and-file party member were not unlike those of responsible party advocates, but they included no additional recommendations to build an effective party organization. By ensuring popular control over presidential nominations, they hoped to force politicians to address the difficult issues of the day. Implicit in their thinking was the idea that a politics built on patronage organizations was an anachronism in an age of activist-minded citizens eager for a greater participatory role.

The Results of Reform. The effect of all the reforms has been to democratize the parties, yet the electorate's faith in the party system has steadily diminished. At the same time, office-holders and party officials are complaining of the weakened state of the parties. Dissatisfaction is so widespread that the debate over the decline of party power will surely continue. Two areas of party operations are particularly likely targets for future reform efforts: the presidential selection process and the national party's role in party building and campaign-related assistance.

A Gallup poll of January 1980 reported that only 24 percent of respondents favored the existing presidential nominating system. Unsurprisingly, a majority of respondents supported a one-day national primary. Clearly, popular participation in presidential nominations has acquired a legitimacy that cannot realistically be ignored. Yet few political leaders

favor a national primary as the route toward additional reform. The 1978 Democratic Commission on Presidential Nomination and Party Structure declared that it "would probably
spell the end of the national party system as we know it."[17]
However, if rank-and-file participation is preserved, changes in
the presidential selection process are still possible.

The proposal which appears to be making headway among
Democratic members of Congress and state party chairmen is
to make the national conventions representative of each of the
component units of the political party.[18] Under such a plan,
party officials and elected officeholders would be given *ex officio* credentials as voting delegates to the conventions. They
would take their seats alongside delegates elected by the rank
and file in primary contests. Political scientist Everett Carl
Ladd, for example, has proposed that two thirds of convention
delegates be selected in state primaries held on the same day
throughout the nation. The remaining delegates would include
each party's governors; its U.S. senators and representatives;
the chairmen, co-chairmen, and all members of its national
committee; and the chairmen and vice chairmen of each state
party. The elected delegates would be pledged to contending
candidates, but the *ex officio* delegate would not be bound.[19]

The Ladd proposal retains substantial rank-and-file participation, while ensuring a role for party professionals and of-

ficeholders. A candidate who ran particularly strong in the primaries would almost certainly pick up the additional delegate votes needed for a nomination. On the other hand, if primary votes were scattered among the contenders, a nomination would be secured only through bargaining and negotiations. The nominating prize would not necessarily go to the candidate who held an edge in popular votes, because his fitness for office would be subject to the peer review of his party's leaders. National conventions would once again serve as serious deliberative and decision-making bodies.

Since American parties are executive centered, restoring the power of the national conventions would renew the vitality of the party system. Party officials and officeholders, who share the main burden of maintaining the corporate party, would have a strong voice in saying who would head their party's ticket. A presidential contender would be forced to seek the support of the same leaders he would later rely on if he gained the presidency. Thus the selection process would be more closely tied to the governing process and the alliances formed would lend a greater organizational integrity to the parties.

Recent Activity within the Democratic Party. The likelihood of reform in the direction of the Ladd proposals is uncertain. Because of their 1980 successes, Republicans have little cause to tamper with their selection procedures. Democrats, however, are under pressure to take a second look at the reforms they have enacted.

The Winograd Commission took the first tentative step to enhance the role of party officials and elected officeholders by allocating 10 percent of the 1980 delegate seats to them. The Democratic National Committee took the second step when it overturned a resolution passed by the 1980 national convention that called for electing two thirds of the delegates to the 1982 midterm convention through local caucuses. The plan, which was overwhelmingly approved, gave delegate seats to all members of the national committee, to an equal number who would be appointed by state committees, and to one hundred who would be appointed by the national chairman with the approval of the executive committee of the national body. In addition, all Democratic governors, twenty-four House members, and eight senators were extended credentials.

Midterm conventions were first authorized by the 1972 Democratic convention as part of the reforms designed to open up the party to popular participation. Critics have charged that the "miniconventions" expose the internal divisions of the party and undermine party unity. In 1978, liberal delegates, many of them supporters of Edward Kennedy, attacked the budget-cutting efforts of the Carter administration. Only through an extensive lobbying effort by his Cabinet and senior White House staffers was Carter able to avoid a repudiation of his policies. Party officials feared the 1982 convention would become a battleground between Kennedy and former Vice President Walter F. Mondale for control of the party and would detract attention from congressional races.

Although the new delegate selection plan was justified as a cost-saving device (estimated at $1 million), committee members were well aware that their action constituted a reversal of the participatory practices of the 1970s. Many analysts see the national committee's action as the opening gun in a battle over delegate selection procedures for the 1984 nominating convention, but few believe the method of nominating a president will be changed as easily as the format of the midterm convention. Although most of those who led the reform movement within the Democratic party decry the weakened state of their party, not all are in favor of giving the professionals and office-holders a free ride to the convention.[20] The outcome of the debate that will certainly ensue is important to the future of the parties, for at the nub of the controversy are the relative responsibilities to be accorded party leaders and popular following. If the proliferation of primaries has weakened the organizational integrity of the parties, as most commentators agree, restricting their influence should have a reverse effect.

Dissatisfaction with the presidential selection process is not the only complaint of Democratic party leaders. Democratic senators and representatives believe they have been neglected by their national committee. Richard Conlon, staff director of the House Democratic Study Group, has charged that the Democratic National Committee (DNC) has not offered congressional candidates useful services since the 1960s.[21] Burdened by a sizable debt during the 1970s, the DNC lacked the resources to provide its candidates with financial backing, research, polling, and other campaign-related assistance. When the national party geared up for the election of 1980, it directed most of its efforts at the presidential race. Unable to match Republican party resources, congressional Democrats argue that they have become the victims of Republican money and campaign technology.

Under the farsighted leadership of William Brock, the national Republican party aided in the rebuilding of its state parties. Aggressive recruiting, cash contributions, and professional campaign services laid the groundwork for 1980. Capstoned by a $9 million advertising campaign, Republican commercials tied the nation's ills to twenty-five years of Democratic party control of Congress and urged the electorate to "Vote Republican—For a Change." Brock's success led Democratic leaders to call for a similar effort to rebuild their party. When the House Democratic Caucus interviewed candidates seeking the chairmanship of the DNC after the 1980 elections, its members voiced urgent concern over the future of their party. Out of similar concern, the Association of State Democratic Chairs passed a resolution calling upon the new DNC chairman to work with the state parties in fund-raising and party-rebuilding efforts.

The Contemporary Parties: A Final Assessment

A major problem confronting the parties in the final decades of the twentieth century is intellectual. Many Americans have little appreciation of the role that party organizations play in American political life. Steeped in the tradition of bosses and machines that once were widespread, citizens are wary of the middlemen of American politics. The anomaly is that, although critical of parties as institutions, voters often rely on the party label in making their candidate choices. If the parties are to be strengthened, their leaders must capitalize on the still evident tendency of voters to be cued by party labels.

National moods are not easily expressed when there are no collective sets of leaders on whom to place praise or blame. Some would say that voters are capable of evaluating candidates on the basis of their issue positions and of delivering an election mandate, but a careful review of the literature on voting behavior destroys this illusion. Although some voters take distinct sides on specific issue controversies, most Americans are not committed to particular solutions of complex governmental problems. On economic matters, for example, they want inflation held in check, interest rates lowered, and employment opportunities opened, but they do not concern themselves with the means by which these goals are to be reached—they leave that to the people they elect. Popular dissatisfaction with government policies needs a focus, and the party label provides it.

Issue voting is hardly incompatible with party voting, for surveys show aggregate differences in the political attitudes held by Democratic and Republican leaders. These differences also appear at the congressional district level.[22] While the choices may not satisfy all citizens, it is highly unlikely that both candidates will be able to ignore the views of sizable segments of their constituency.

Even though officeholders have great leeway in backing whatever policies they think will be effective or enhance their reelection opportunities, they do not altogether ignore their party ties. As we have seen, members who share the same party label often vote together in congressional roll calls because they have similar political attitudes. But it is undeniable that the party mechanisms for achieving organizational and intellectual discipline within party ranks have been weakened.

A demand for strengthened parties is unlikely to come from the general electorate. Leadership must be provided by party officials and elected officeholders. Already there are straws in the wind to suggest that they are ready to undertake that job.

The proposed changes would work no miracles, for political diversity in the United States is too great to be neatly subsumed under the two major parties. Nevertheless, a reinvigorated party system could well bring some needed order to American politics. Active party organizations might restore competitiveness to election contests that are now one-sided, officeholders who are the beneficiaries of party aid might be more willing to cooperate with their partisan colleagues, and congressmen might be more willing to work with a president of their own party if they have a greater voice in selecting him. If these changes were to take place, the electorate would have a choice between two sets of leaders with distinct, if highly general, viewpoints. The ultimate goal of parties in America—providing linkage between leaders and led—would be enhanced in the process.

SUMMARY

A variety of circumstances has weakened the American political parties, yet they have survived and continue to perform useful functions in the nation's political system. An examination of their current status reveals their strengths and weaknesses and suggests what their future role might be.

Partisan ties within the electorate have loosened: fewer voters are strongly attached to a political party, and many now describe themselves as Independents, although leaning in a partisan direction. Consequently, partisan defections and split-ticket voting are on the increase.

Americans have also become more cynical and distrustful of their leaders and fewer people are turning out to vote. There is some evidence that voters are becoming more sophisticated in evaluating presidential candidates, which might suggest that a better educated electorate is rejecting the political parties and their candidates. However, examination reveals that it is the marginally involved and poorly informed citizens who are least likely to vote or identify with a political party. Cynicism and distrust are related neither to political independence nor to a quality electorate.

Substantial voter defections ordinarily damage one party more than the other. Nevertheless, the same electoral dynamics do not influence the outcomes of presidential and congressional elections. Presidential elections flow with the tides of national events, while House elections, particularly those involving incumbents, are more insulated from national political forces. Senate elections fall in between. The different political forces acting on the several elections can produce split-ticket voting and divided party government.

Political professionals are no longer very influential in their party's nominating process, nor do they command the resources to aid candidates in their election campaigns. Because of their diminished power, the professionals are less effective in building stable coalitions to support their party's candidates in electoral campaigns. Lacking a dependable base of support, the governing party's problems in attempting to enact a legislative program are increased.

Although weakened, party organizations are not moribund. State party organizations have shown some resurgence over the past twenty years, as has the national Republican party. And the Democratic National Committee has recently committed itself to rebuilding the party. Strengthening the party organizations will not produce disciplined or programmatic parties, but it could make more races competitive and it might check or even reverse the trend toward individualistic politics.

Officeholders today are more independent. They may choose to cooperate with their partisan colleagues, but they do not feel compelled to do so. Party voting in congressional roll calls, for example, has displayed an irregular but downward trend over the past two decades.

Although a party's officeholders do not act in concert, they cannot always escape the voters' collective judgment of their party. In 1980, Democratic candidates for federal offices were handicapped by worsening inflation, high interest rates, widespread unemployment, and a perceived loss of prestige abroad. The electorate did not direct its frustrations at incumbents in general, but specifically at Democrats. Party accountability was nevertheless imperfect, because Democrats retained control of the House.

A further weakening of the party system is not foreordained. The parties could be revitalized if the electorate polarized along new or existing issue controversies and the parties presented the voters with clear choices. Alternatively, the parties could be strengthened organizationally so that their leaders would be able to build more stable coalitions and achieve a greater measure of intellectual discipline.

In the post-World War II era, controversies that cut across traditional political alignments failed to realign the electorate. Communism, race, Vietnam, and law and order were potentially realigning issues, but the parties failed to take clearly opposing sides. Democrats had the most to lose from a political realignment, and they managed to convince the electorate that they were soft on neither communism nor crime (with its racial overtones). Each party moved at a similar pace to end the Vietnam hostilities.

The 1980 elections suggest the potential for the creation of a new party majority, but over issue controversies that run along the same lines as those that have divided the parties since the New Deal. If the Reagan administration is successful in stimulating economic growth and controlling the size of the federal budget, the Republican party might gain control over the political agenda for the foreseeable future. However, the obstacles confronting the Republicans in converting their 1980 successes into a new and durable majority are formidable. Budget cutting may be popular in the abstract, but it also can alienate the interests affected. If Republican solutions to the nation's ills meet with no better success than those of the Democrats, the public is unlikely to shift in its partisan affiliations.

Waiting for the electorate to polarize around salient issues is not the only hope for stronger parties. The parties might be strengthened organizationally. The Republican National Committee has augmented its campaign services to all Republican candidates, and Democratic leaders have called for a similar effort by their national organizations. Democratic congressmen and party officials have also demanded a greater voice in the presidential selection process. Although modest proposals, these steps could give a greater institutional presence to the parties.

No one should expect the American parties to become highly programmatic and cohesive—the American electorate is too varied to support only two parties of sharply differentiated programs—but it is not unreasonable to expect the leaders of the two parties to disagree on distinct, if highly general, viewpoints. Voters could then determine how well an incumbent party had managed the nation's affairs. The ultimate goal of parties, to link leaders and led, would be enhanced in the process.

Notes

[1]For the relationships discussed, see David B. Hill and Norman R. Luttbeg, *Trends in American Electoral Behavior* (Itasca, Ill.: Peacock, 1980), esp. chap. 5.

[2]Hugh L. LeBlanc and Mary Beth Merrin, "Independents, Issue Partisanship, and the Decline of Party," *American Politics Quarterly* 7 (April 1979), pp. 240–258; and Bruce E. Keith et al., "The Myth of the Independent Voter" (paper delivered at the annual meeting of the American Political Science Association, Washington, D.C., September 1–4, 1977).

[3]For a discussion of voting in congressional elections, see Thomas E. Mann and Raymond E. Wolfinger, "Candidates and Parties in Congressional Elections," and Alan I. Abramowitz, "A Comparison of Voting for U.S. Senators and Representative in 1978," *American Political Science Review* 74 (September 1980), pp. 617–650.

[4]Mann and Wolfinger, "Candidates and Parties in Congressional Elections," pp. 620–621.

[5]Thomas E. Mann and Norman J. Ornstein, "1980: A Republican Revival in Congress?," *Public Opinion*, October/November 1980, p. 18.

[6]David W. Brady and Philip Althoff, "Party Voting in the U.S. House of Representatives, 1890–1910: Elements of a Responsible Party System," *Journal of Politics* 36 (August 1974), pp. 753–775.

[7]See the discussion in James L. Sundquist, *Dynamics of the Party System* (Washington, D.C.: The Brookings Institution, 1973), chap. 13.

[8]Ibid., chap. 15. The discussion here of cross-cutting issues relies heavily on the Sundquist analysis.

[9]Philip E. Converse, Warren E. Miller, Jerrold E. Rusk, and Arthur C. Wolfe, "Continuity and Change in American Politics: Parties and Issues in the 1968 Election," *American Political Science Review* 53 (December 1969), p. 1092.

[10]*The Washington Post*, February 1, 1981, p. A3.

[11]See the discussion in Sunquist, *Dynamics of the Party System*, pp. 355–369.

[12]For example, see the exchange between Richard M. Scammon and Ben J. Wattenberg, "Is It the End of an Era?," and Everett C. Ladd, "A Rebuttal: Realignment? No. Dealignment? Yes," in *Public Opinion*, October/November 1980, pp. 2–15, 54–56.

[13]*First Monday*, December/January 1981, p. 14.

[14]Ladd, "A Rebuttal," p. 15.

[15]See the useful discussion in James W. Ceasar, "Political Change and Party Reform," in *Political Parties in the Eighties*, ed. Robert A. Goldwin (Washington, D.C.: American Enterprise Institute; and Gambier, Ohio: Kenyon College, 1980), pp. 97–99.

[16]Ibid., pp. 111–112. See also Paul David and James Ceasar, *Proportional Representation in Presidential Nominating Politics* (Charlottesville: University of Virginia Press, 1980), esp. chaps. 1–3.

[17]Commission on Presidential Nomination and Party Structure, *Openness, Participation and Party Building: Reforms for a Stronger Democratic Party* (Washington, D.C.: Democratic National Committee, 1978), p. 32.

[18]*Congressional Quarterly Weekly Report*, January 17, 1981, p. 32.

[19]Everett Carl Ladd, "A Better Way to Pick Our Presidents," *Fortune*, May 5, 1980, p. 141. Ladd credits Austin Ranney and Thomas Mann of the American Enterprise Institute for helping him to develop the overall design of his proposals.

[20]Donald M. Fraser, who succeeded George McGovern as chairman of the first Democratic reform commission, for example, called for strengthened national parties and a greater role for party leaders and officeholders. However, he also believed that an enhanced leadership "need not be diminished by the new rules, although the leader may have to make a greater effort to achieve the desired influence." See Donald M. Fraser, "Democratizing the Democratic Party," in *Political Parties in the Eighties*, ed. Goldwin, p. 130.

[21]*Congressional Quarterly Weekly Report*, January 17, 1981, p. 139.

[22]John L. Sullivan and Robert E. O'Connor, "Electoral Choice and Popular Control of Public Policy: The Case of the 1966 House Elections," *American Political Science Review* 66 (December 1972), p. 1258.

Acknowledgments (continued)

Table 5-3. Table 2-1 (p. 31) from *Participation in America: Political Democracy and Social Equality* by Sidney Verba and Norman H. Nie. Copyright © 1972 by Sidney Verba and Norman H. Nie. Reprinted with permission.

Tables 6-1 and 6.2. From Robert A. Bernstein, "Divisive Primaries Do Hurt: U.S. Senate Races, 1956–1976," *American Political Science Review* 71 (June 1977). Reprinted with permission of the American Political Science Association.

Table 6-2. Reprinted from *Party Leadership in the States* by Robert J. Huckshorn (Amherst: University of Massachusetts Press, 1976), copyright © 1976 by University of Massachusetts Press. With permission.

Table 7-1. From James I. Lengle and Byron Shafer, "Primary Rules, Political Power, and Social Change," *American Political Science Review* 70 (March 1976). Reprinted with permission of the American Political Science Association.

Tables 7-2 and 7-5. Data are derived from Warren J. Mitofsky and Martin Plissner, "The Making of the Delegates, 1968–1980," *Public Opinion*, October/November 1980. Reprinted with permission.

Tables 7-3 and 7-4. From Austin Ranney, *Participation in American Presidential Nominations, 1976.* Copyright © 1977 by the American Enterprise Institute for Public Policy Research. Reprinted with permission.

Table 7-6. Adapted from Joseph H. Boyett, "Background Characteristics of Delegates to the 1972 Conventions: A Summary Report of Findings from a National Sample," *Western Political Quarterly* 27 (September 1974). Reprinted by permission of the University of Utah, copyright holder.

Table 8-1. From Herbert E. Alexander, *Financing Politics.* Reprinted with permission of the Congressional Quarterly Inc.

Table 8-2. Reprinted by permission of the publisher, from *Financing the 1972 Election* by Herbert E. Alexander (Lexington, Mass.: Lexington Books, D. C. Heath and Company, Copyright 1978, D. C. Heath and Company).

Table 9-1. From William H. Flannigan and Nancy H. Zingale, *Political Behavior of the American Electorate*, 4th ed. (Boston: Allyn and Bacon, 1979). Reprinted with permission.

Table 9-2. From the book, *The Political Persuaders: The Techniques of Modern Election Campaigns* by Dan Nimmo, © 1970 by Prentice-Hall, Inc. Published by Prentice-Hall, Inc. Englewood Cliffs, N.J. 07632. Reprinted with permission.

Table 10-2. From Richard A. Brody, "The Puzzle of Political Participation in America," in *The New American Political System*, ed. Anthony King. Copyright © 1978 by the American Enterprise Institute. Reprinted with permission.

Table 11-1. Table 3-1 (p. 81) from *Congressmen's Voting Decisions*, 2nd Edition by John W. Kingdon. Copyright © 1981 by Harper & Row, Publishers, Inc. Reprinted with permission.

Acknowledgments *(continued)*

Figure 11-1. From *How Congressmen Decide* by Aage R. Clausen. © 1973 by St. Martin's Press, Inc. and reprinted by permission of Congressional Quarterly Inc.

Figure 12-1. From *Congressional Quarterly Weekly Report*, January 3, 1981. Reprinted with permission of Congressional Quarterly, Inc.

Tables 12-1 and 12-2. From *Presidential Influence in Congress* by George C. Edwards III. W. H. Freeman and Company. Copyright © 1980. Reprinted with permission.

Index